Reconstructing Europe
after the Great War

Reconstructing Europe
after the Great War

Dan P. Silverman

Harvard University Press

*Cambridge, Massachusetts, and
London, England*
1982

Library of Congress Cataloging in Publication Data

Silverman, Dan P.
Reconstructing Europe after the Great War.

Bibliography: p.
Includes index.
1. International finance—History. 2. Reconstruction
(1914–1939) 3. World War, 1914–1918—Reparations.
1. Title.
HG3881.S528   332′.042   81–6836
ISBN 0–674–75025–X   AACR2

Preface

As THE First World War drew to a close, Europe's national and international financial systems lay in ruins. Extraordinary price inflation accompanied inflation of the money supply to unheard-of levels. Service of the public debt became the largest item in some national budgets, and the budgets themselves could not be balanced by legitimate revenues. International indebtedness of unprecedented proportions portended the international transfer of wealth on a massive scale. Traditional patterns of international trade had broken down, and currencies set free from the gold standard fluctuated wildly on the exchange markets.

This book furnishes an account of attempts by the victors, Britain and France—with or without American assistance—to reconstruct national and international financial and monetary systems during the immediate postwar years, 1918–1923. Surprisingly little has been written about British and French attempts to resolve the financial crisis during these critical first years of peace. It is generally assumed that the reparations issue was most critical, that French intransigence blocked a reasonable reparations settlement, and that French ignorance of sound financial and monetary principles and practices simply compounded the catastrophe left by the war.

In both methodology and conclusions, this inquiry is a profound reinterpretation of Anglo-French-American financial and diplomatic history in the immediate postwar era. Previous work on postwar European financial reconstruction is seriously biased by its narrow Anglo-American perspective. The French have been described as intransigent, aggressive, ignorant, and incompetent. It is time to place the reparations issue in proper perspective as only one of many complex financial and monetary problems facing postwar Europe. This new perspective sheds more light and less heat on the theoretical and technical aspects of the financial and monetary crisis. By examining financial and monetary theory as it was generally understood at the time, one discovers that the war produced a universal crisis and confusion in theory as well as a crisis in fact. Traditional theory proved incapable of dealing with the awesome task of stabilizing foreign exchanges, halting inflation, balancing budgets, and liquidating massive debts.

Our concern with financial and monetary theory and practice, combined with an explicitly comparative framework, produces a new view of postwar financial and diplomatic history. As the wartime financial entente quickly disintegrated, Britain sought a new financial relationship with the United States alone. Together, the Atlantic nations would try to impose their superior Anglo-Saxon economic orthodoxy on less fortunate Continental friends and former enemies. France's response was completely rational. It pursued its own national self-interest, resisting all attempts to establish a system of Anglo-American financial and diplomatic hegemony. The French rejected British and American notions of theoretical orthodoxy and laissez-faire not out of ignorance, but in accordance with a well-founded belief that Anglo-American financial theories and institutions did not operate in France's best national interest.

The core of this work describes how the British and French governments and central banks sought to stabilize their currencies, balance their budgets, manage their national debts, and restore international trade. Problems created by the existence of budget deficits and massive internal debts were intertwined with inter-Allied debts and German reparations. All of this is described through the words and actions of Treasury officials, central bankers, and financiers. We learn, for the first time, precisely how the economists, bankers, and policymaking officials in Britain, France, and the United States approached the financial crisis immediately following the First World War. In the process, the image of France is transformed from one of stubborn ignorance to one of unbending dedication to national interest.

I wish to thank The Pennsylvania State University Institute for the Arts and Humanistic Studies and the Liberal Arts College Fund for Research for grants that facilitated the research and final preparation of the manuscript. Harvard College Library, the Baker Library of the Harvard Graduate School of Business Administration, Amherst College Library, the Federal Reserve Bank of New York, the Public Record Office and the House of Lords Record Office (London), and the Service des Archives Économiques et Financières, Ministère de l'Économie et Ministère du Budget (Paris) generously made available their collections.

Acknowledgment of permission to quote from unpublished material is made to the following: the House of Lords Record Office and the Beaverbrook Foundation (A. J. P. Taylor, Honorary Director) for citations from the Lloyd George and Bonar Law papers; the University of Birmingham for citations from the Austen Chamberlain papers; the Federal Reserve Bank of New York for citations from the Benjamin Strong papers; and Baker Library, Harvard University Graduate School of Business Administration, for citations from the Thomas W. Lamont papers. Citations of Crown-copyright records in the Public Record Office appear by permission of the Controller of H. M. Stationery Office. Quotations from the Dwight W. Morrow papers are by permission of the Trustees of Amherst College.

My colleague the late Kent Forster provided enthusiastic support from the inception of the project. Donna F. Williams typed the manuscript expertly, efficiently, and cheerfully. As always, my parents have listened and offered their encouragement.

University Park, Pennsylvania

Contents

Introduction: Toward a Theoretical Framework   1

1   Financial Entente, 1914–1919   13

2   Crisis in Economic Theory   40

3   Balancing the Budget   62

4   Managing the National Debt   113

5   Inter-Allied Debt and German Reparations   145

6   J. P. Morgan & Co. and the French Finance Ministry   199

7   Reconstructing International Trade   229

8   An International Solution?   271

Notes   301

Bibliography   339

Index   341

Reconstructing Europe
after the Great War

Introduction:
Toward a Theoretical Framework

CONSCIOUSLY OR UNCONSCIOUSLY, historians relegate certain years to oblivion. Until recently, the interval between the Armistice of 11 November 1918 and the crisis of 1923–1925 that ultimately led to the "stabilization" of Europe was neglected by historians concerned with how the First World War ended and how the Second World War began. If historians examined the period 1918–1923, it was usually with reference to the important events dominated by the great statesmen. Attention focused on the major conferences (Paris Peace conference, Washington Naval Armaments conference, Genoa conference), the outstanding treaties and agreements (Rapallo, Locarno, Dawes Plan), and the shattering events or pseudoevents (Kapp putsch, March on Rome, Ruhr occupation).

Slowly, this picture has changed as historians have utilized new archival sources for the scientific examination of Europe's crisis during the early postwar years, 1918–1923. Reflecting the complex pattern of interdependent national and international questions following the Great War, many of the newer works are multinational in scope. Most accounts of the early postwar years, however, concentrated on political developments. When the social and economic revolution brought by the war was treated, it was often viewed as a clash of ideology or political personality rather than a phenomenon to be treated from a technical point of view. Capitalism versus Bolshevism, Wilson versus Lenin, Clemenceau and Poincaré versus Wilson and Lloyd George—these are the contests most often described in the literature dealing with the postwar settlement. Most notable of this genre are Arno J. Mayer's two monumental works from the 1960s.[1] Because the peace settlement hammered out by the Big Four at Paris concentrated on political-territorial issues and failed to deal with postwar economic and social reconstruction, this approach to the postwar era was valid as far as it went.

1

The decade of the 1970s brought a growing interest in the social and economic aftermath of the Great War. Often revisionist in tone, treatments of the postwar crisis began to place interwar diplomacy in the context of national and international economic and social conflict. In many respects the most satisfactory synthesis is Charles S. Maier's massive examination of the gradual development of corporatism as the European bourgeoisie's answer to the problem of stabilization against reformist and revolutionary threats.[2] Maier obtained fruitful results by examining the postwar European crisis through the quieter and more prosaic, but more decisive, questions— arguments over factory councils, taxation, coal prices, inflation, deflation, and revaluation. His work lays bare the complexity of the economic and social issues which neither domestic conciliation nor international diplomacy could resolve completely.

Some of the pieces, however, were still missing. The objects of Maier's work, France, Germany, and Italy, shared one common characteristic. They were all debtor nations. In the absence of active assistance from the creditors, Britain and the United States, no permanent solution to Europe's postwar social and economic crisis was possible. But the collapse of the entente between the Allied and Associated Powers, coupled with Germany's refusal to make reparation payments and Bolshevik Russia's refusal to honor prerevolution debts and guarantee private property rights, rendered unlikely any all-around economic reconstruction of Europe. Lacking a definitive settlement of both German reparations and inter-Allied debts, Europe could not stabilize under either a bourgeois or socialist order.

A growing body of recent literature has examined reparations, inter-Allied debts, and the role of Britain, France, Germany, and the United States in reaching or obstructing a settlement of these issues. Once again, however, the most obvious point of controversy, French policy in the Rhineland and the Franco-Belgian occupation of the Ruhr in 1923, received most attention. This focus highlighted the reparation problem at the expense of the inter-Allied debt impasse to which it was indissolubly linked (a connection never formally admitted by the United States government). Keith L. Nelson has traced the disintegration of the wartime entente between America and the Allies during the Rhineland occupation, 1919–1923.[3] Nelson's portrait of the Rhineland Ruhr imbroglio rests heavily on the political and military relations of the occupying powers, and thus represents a fairly traditional approach to the question. With Denise Artaud's 1970 article, historians began to concentrate on French and German domestic factors that pushed both sides toward confrontation in the Ruhr. Domestic social, political, and economic forces have received increasing attention in recent works by Walter A. McDougall and Hermann J. Rupieper.[4]

Historians have also begun to examine postwar economic ties between the United States and Europe. Denise Artaud has again made an important contribution,[5] but as one might expect, American scholars have produced most of the studies of American economic policy toward Europe. Early articles by Paul Abrahams and Benjamin Rhodes led the way to more substantial works by Paul Costigliola, Michael J. Hogan, and Melvyn P. Leffler.[6] Hogan and Costigliola have examined, with different results, Anglo-American conflict and cooperation in reconstructing the international economy. Hogan has added to the evidence that corporatist ideas sought to displace traditional liberal, laissez-faire attitudes in postwar America as well as Europe. The question of inter-Allied debts, moreover, has finally received its due, at least from the Anglo-Saxon perspective.

The Anglo-Saxon point of view alone, however, does not suffice for a reasonable discussion of inter-Allied debts. There were three major actors in the drama: the United States (creditor), Great Britain (both creditor and debtor), and France (debtor to both the United States and Britain). No recent scholarly work has treated inter-Allied debts from the French position. Studies based on American officials talking to other American officials, British officials talking to other British officials, and American officials talking to British officials arrive at the conclusion one might expect. Neither the Americans nor the British pursued unreasonable policies on the debt question.

Existing works support the widely held notion that the same French governments that held to an "intransigent" position on reparations proved equally intransigent in the matter of inter-Allied debts. Artaud, a French historian utilizing American source material, noted in America's debt policy "a blindness which is today astounding," and tried to determine why Woodrow Wilson and the successive secretaries of the Treasury adopted an "intransigent attitude" toward European debtors. Her conclusions were surprisingly mild. The United States government refused to cancel Europe's debts because it feared a backlash from Congress and public opinion. American Treasury officials failed to comprehend the facts of Europe's economic devastation, operated under "theoretical" deficiencies, and pursued a policy of economic imperialism. There was, however, no malevolence or lack of good will toward America's friends, and the government was not even conscious of its own imperialistic program.[7]

Most American historians have treated their Anglo-Saxon brethren with charity. Rhodes conceded that while America's "improvised" debt policy might have been somewhat more flexible, France must nevertheless carry "a major share" of the responsibility for the postwar crisis. Overall, thought Rhodes, United States debt policy "can hardly be characterized as grasping."[8] Abrahams discovered an enlightened American banking community. But the bankers failed to convince the United States Treasury Department of the need for a massive American financial and industrial reconstruction effort in Europe, coordinated by the government. The bankers "pressed the government to recognize new international financial responsibilities" throughout 1919, but "Treasury policy prevented the implementation of any of these measures." Only after the Second World War did the United States accept the "government responsibility now deemed appropriate to the position of the United States as a world creditor."[9]

Whereas Abrahams attributed to the Treasury Department the concept of "normalcy" and the tactics of obstructing organized assistance to Europe, Leffler found the Wilson administration "initially sympathetic" and the Harding administration "not unsympathetic" to France's postwar financial requirements. But America's conflicting desires to insure French security, promote European reconstruction through the revival of Germany's economy, and protect the interests of American industry and agriculture produced an impasse. Ultimately, an intransigent Congress thwarted the desire of the Treasury to extend a helping hand.[10]

Costigliola emphasized Anglo-American rivalry during the 1920s. Conflicting national interests reflecting America's rising financial power and Britain's weakened financial authority produced divergent policies. Britain sought to build an international monetary system based on monetary regulation (dominated by Britain) and conservation of gold, while the United States favored a market-regulated gold standard dominated by massive American gold reserves. The United

States defeated Britain's financial program, forced Britain and the rest of Europe to play by American rules, and thereby "aggravated British economic problems in the 1920's."[11] If one enlarges Costigliola's scope to include France, it becomes clear that American financial pressure on Britain contributed to British financial pressure on France, which in turn added to French pressure for German reparation payments.

Where Costigliola saw Anglo-American financial rivalry, Hogan found an "informal entente." A "private structure of cooperation" developed in Anglo-American economic diplomacy between 1918 and 1928. Largely patterned after Commerce Secretary Herbert Hoover's corporatist conception of the postwar economy, the informal entente rested on a private foundation in which the government's only role was to lay down the rules of fair play. Any American assistance for European reconstruction had to come through traditional private banking channels. Hogan saw no fundamental conflict between American and British banking interests. By the mid-1920s, they had forged an "Anglo-American creditor entente." Britain would fund her war debt to the United States, and together the two creditors would then face their European debtors. By eliminating one source of friction between the two strongest financial powers, the British funding agreement "provided new incentive for efforts, already underway, to devise the kind of European stabilization scheme that could insure reparation and debt transfers now needed by the British to liquidate their newly-funded debt and to guarantee cooperative action by American banks in financing European recovery."[12]

There was indeed an Anglo-American financial entente of sorts, but the "informal alliance" did not, as Hogan suggests, promote a peaceful settlement of the intergovernmental debt quagmire. Anglo-American pressure on France simply exacerbated the situation and eventually forced the Franco-Belgian occupation of the Ruhr. That shock wave finally forced the United States to make some concessions on the inter-Allied debt. It was only *after* the Ruhr occupation had begun that Britain concluded a funding agreement with the World War Debt Funding Commission in Washington.

For over sixty years, the history of interwar financial diplomacy has been Anglo-Saxon history. It has tended to be self-serving and remarkably oblivious to French financial requirements. The Anglo-Saxon powers always regarded the financial reconstruction of

Germany and Russia as the highest priorities, and it was French "intransigence" which prevented any "reasonable" resolution of Europe's postwar financial and monetary crisis. France is often left out of the postwar financial and monetary equation, and where it does enter the picture, it is usually portrayed as attempting to resist economic domination from others, be it Germany, Britain, or the United States. As a recent commentary has noted, "from the Anglo-Saxon point of view, this puts the French in the role of irresponsible wreckers."[13]

At last, the corrective seemed to have arrived with Stephen A. Schuker's study of the French financial crisis of 1924 and the adoption of the Dawes Plan.[14] The promise, however, is not quite achieved. Behind the impressive apparatus and years of meticulous research lie some unfortunate conceptual defects. The critical years 1918–1923 are treated as background to the real crisis of 1924. This emphasis may be argued as a matter of preference—each historian is entitled to write the book he or she wishes to write. But Schuker perpetuates the mythology of the superiority of Anglo-Saxon principles of sound fiscal, financial, and monetary policy. France's financial problems as the war ended were "troublesome, yet not impossible to solve." German reparations were "highly desirable, but not an absolute prerequisite to modest economic recovery from the ravages of war."[15] France's catastrophic financial and monetary situation at the close of the war was worse than "troublesome," and why should the French have been satisfied with "modest" economic recovery while the United States and Britain sought to restore Germany to its predominant economic position on the continent?

If the French could not blame their 1924 financial crisis on Germany's failure to make reparation payments, argued Schuker, neither could they place the blame on America's refusal to cancel debts and offer massive assistance. The Wall Street bankers, particularly J. P. Morgan & Co., "stand out as a remarkably able and farsighted group." On the issue of war debts, "the executive branch of the American government took a far more enlightened view than that for which it is usually given credit." If America was not more generous, it was because "Congress refused to allow the Treasury Department to handle the situation on its own."[16]

Schuker thus maintained that France emerged from the war burdened by financial problems of quite manageable proportions, problems which it could have overcome with the minimal assistance America was willing to give, and with no assistance at all from Germany. At the same time, France could have repaid war debts to both Britain and the United States under the "relatively generous arrangements" it was offered. But the French "compounded the difficulties as a result of their own inadequate responses." France's postwar difficulties resulted less from the actual burdens of reconstruction than from fiscal mismanagement and an inability to reform an outmoded taxation system. Such mismanagement was to be expected, however, because "most of the French elite at the time were abysmally ignorant even of the rudimentary principles of economics." The little economics they knew was "irrelevant to monetary problems in the postwar world." It could hardly have been otherwise, because French universities boasted few if any world-class economists.[17]

There is another side to this story, a side which has not yet been recounted. Some have already hinted at it. In his examination of France's postwar Rhineland policy, McDougall characterized French policy as one "designed to make Europe safe from Germany," but the United States and Britain "only contributed to the syndrome of appeasement, thereby negating the one possible achievement of the war, the elimination of the German threat." McDougall criticized "the Anglo-Americans' resistance to France's European policy, as well as the vacuity of their own world policies," and sympathized with "the much maligned policy of permanent restrictions on the sovereignty of the German national state—the French solution." The French solution, of course, has remained "anathema" to historians writing in the "Wilsonian tradition."[18]

The interwar years, argued McDougall, witnessed the demise of the liberal state and the growing pains of the modern directed economy. Financially dominant Britain and America rejected new forms of international financial and political organization and left it largely to private interests to reconstruct the international economy. One could not expect the financial and political leadership of the 1920s to have had the wisdom to invoke the program of 1945, "but the fact remains that the Anglo-Americans spent the interwar years looking for excuses to do nothing."[19]

Actions either taken or advocated by the Anglo-Americans were no more intelligent, effective, or realistic than those proposed or taken by the French. Anglo-Saxon policy, moreover, generally reflected an anti-French attitude. In financial matters, the advice of the "experts" (invariably Anglo-American, Dutch, or Swedish—never French) "always seemed to dictate advantage for Germany and sacrifice for the bloodied victors."[20] The United States somehow expected the Europeans to reconstruct their economies with minimal private assistance, restore international trade, earn enough dollars to pay their war debts, and continue to purchase American exports.[21]

The Dawes Plan and the gold exchange standard represented the triumph of America over Europe. Maier understood the gold exchange standard as "America's price for remitting capital back to Europe." It required Europeans to maintain a deflationary policy at home, produced a "downward pressure on employment," subjected small producers to large ones in the process of rationalization and cartelization, and generally reinforced a bourgeois and corporatist social settlement.[22] American policy as reflected in the Dawes Plan consisted of "financing Germany's return to industrial dominance, lending her far more than she would pay in reparations, while simultaneously squeezing France to pay her war debts, disarm, and hasten the dismantling of Versailles!"[23]

British policy toward France was substantially the same as that of the United States. But Britain was clearly the junior partner in the anti-French, Anglo-American financial entente. The "new order," Costigliola observed, "stacked benefits, such as trade surpluses, stable prices, and debt receipts heavily in favor of the United States and assigned adjustment burdens such as trade deficits, deflation, and debt payments primarily to Europe and the rest of the world."[24]

The present work represents a new methodology and produces some nontraditional conclusions about Europe's postwar financial and monetary crisis. It is not an attempt to write an account favorable to American, British, or French policy. It is rather an attempt to bring additional balance to the subject by escaping the narrow Anglo-American perspective. As a first step toward an adequate history of Europe's interwar financial and monetary crisis, this study rests on a methodological foundation lacking in the extant literature. First, it represents a synthesis of French, British, and American sources and viewpoints, and it begins at the beginning—the critical early postwar years, 1918–1923. French and British policies are emphasized because heretofore French sources have been most neglected and British sources have not been exploited adequately for this particular purpose.

Second, reparations disputes must not be permitted to overwhelm other basic financial and monetary problems facing postwar Europe. The financial and monetary crisis must be taken for what it was—a financial and monetary crisis—and not merely another political problem that poisoned interwar diplomacy. Financial and monetary problems did become politicized during the 1920s, and politicians and foreign ministers (Lloyd George, Wilson, Hughes, Briand, Poincaré, and Stresemann) attempted to settle these matters on their own terms. But it is a mistake to study financial and monetary history primarily through the speeches of the politicians and the records of the foreign ministries. Ultimately the dreams of the politicians and foreign ministers had to be tailored to the more realistic dimensions laid down by the central bankers, finance ministers, and the banking community in general.

Inflation and the fall of the gold standard deprived central banks of control over domestic and international money markets. As the war ended, the struggle for control began. The contest involved much more than a nationalistic competition between the United States, Britain, and France. Within each of these nations, the fight for financial control pitted central bankers against politicians, central bankers against private bankers, and finance ministries against foreign ministries. In the ultimate determination of national policy, it was often the bankers and finance ministers who triumphed over the politicians and foreign ministers. Historical analysis of postwar European money and finance must first examine the domestic national phenomena before venturing into international conflicts, and that analysis must rest heavily upon the previously underutilized records of Europe's financial and monetary authorities, insofar as they are available to public scrutiny.

The third and perhaps most critical requisite for an examination of Europe's postwar financial and monetary crisis is a proper concern for financial and monetary theory as it was understood during the early 1920s. Keynes, for example, was not yet a "Keynesian" in those days. Remarkably naive and uninformed in matters of financial and monetary theory and practice, most historians treating Europe's postwar crisis more or less ignore the theoretical and technical impediments to the "obvious" solutions. Schuker's work, which emphasizes

French "ignorance" of "modern" financial and monetary practice, possibly adds confusion to this aspect of the historical problem.

To comprehend the role of theory and technique, one need only survey historical references to the Paris Peace conference. These almost invariably lament the failure of Wilson, Clemenceau, and Lloyd George to clean up the reparation and inter-Allied debt questions and establish an enlightened program for the reconstruction of the international economy. Implied is the assumption that men of good will and ordinary intelligence could have gathered at the conference table and hammered out an all-encompassing program for economic rehabilitation in a matter of weeks. If the politicians had other pressing domestic matters to manage, then they could have and should have left the financial tangle for a speedy solution by the "experts."

It is dangerous to assume that the experts understood postwar financial and monetary issues better than did the politicians. They, too, were baffled by the enormous theoretical and technical obstacles to the solution of massive debt transfer problems, astronomical inflation of the money supply, unprecedented budget deficits, trade deficits, credit crises, and the general breakdown of the international financial and monetary system. In light of the early 1980s situation, it is at best disingenuous to imply that modern financial and monetary theory has the answers to such serious dislocations of the "normal" pattern of economic activity. Insofar as economic theory purports to describe normal economic situations, there was, and is, no adequate theory to explain post-1914 developments.

The dominant theory of the early 1920s was in fact a less sophisticated variant of modern monetarist theory. Reputable French economists who adhered to that theory did not stand alone. Artaud pointed out serious deficiencies and gaps in American economic theory during the 1920s, but added that the "ignorance" of America's financial and political leadership was not exceptional. It was "shared by a large number of statesmen of all continents," she observed. Maier noted that French deflation programs were not unique. "It was the conventional wisdom of the 1920's," he wrote, "that such wage and price cuts should be easy to make."[25]

It is not coincidental that the latest major examination of the reparation question by Marc Trachtenberg challenges the old idea of a vengeful France trying to impose an impossible settlement, and argues the relative moderation of French reparation policy.[26] In a brief but suggestive essay, David P. Calleo noted the tendency of British and American economists to give the French position "short shrift" after both world wars. He concluded that France's reputation as the "dog in the manger" and "irresponsible wrecker" is undeserved—France merely sought to resist domination from others.[27]

The Great War caused a crisis in financial and monetary theory equal in proportion to the actual financial and monetary catastrophe. Because historians generally fail either to note or comprehend the theoretical disputes of the early 1920s, they unrealistically expect solutions to the crisis itself. Economic crises cannot be managed in the absence of a viable economic theory. The crisis of modern capitalism is in fact a crisis in theory. Capitalism may well be an economic system without a theory. What generally passes for capitalist theory is more often than not "conventional wisdom"—almost invariably Anglo-Saxon conventional wisdom—often lacking empirical support.

Postwar Europe faced two alternatives. Europe's financial leadership could either develop a new theory to fit the new economic "facts," or they could try to force the economic facts back into the prewar conventional mold, primarily through the technique of deflation. To have achieved one or the other of these goals might have produced a stable international financial system, but to have achieved neither virtually assured the calamity of the 1930s. The French did not disrupt postwar financial reconstruction through their ignorance of correct financial and monetary theory. They merely refused to accept Anglo-Saxon conventional wisdom that clearly violated France's national interests. Underlying these national conflicts runs an unfortunate racial tone. British, American, German, Dutch, and Swedish financial authorities displayed a natural affinity for one another. They ostracized the French not only because they disagreed with French financial and monetary policy, but also because they regarded Latin finance as inherently inferior to Anglo-Saxon finance.

The historian who undertakes a detailed analysis of Europe's postwar financial and monetary crisis in the context of then-current theory and technical practice risks offending both historians who may find the study too technical and economists who may find the work not technical enough. Owing to the immediacy of the subject matter in the 1980s, I have attempted to satisfy both the narrower academic community and the wider financial community. The story told herein is based on what finance ministers, central bankers, private bankers, and politicians actually thought, said, and did during the immediate postwar years.

The complexity and breadth of the questions addressed in this work seemed to require a dual chronological-thematic approach. The narrative begins with a description of the manner in which Britain and France financed the war and joined in an Anglo-American-French financial entente. This triple entente, never firm to begin with, began to crumble as the end of the war came in sight. During the Paris Peace Conference the wartime configuration began the transformation into an incipient Anglo-American, anti-French financial entente.

Peace brought decontrol, boom, and recession between 1919 and 1923. The British and French individually developed domestic financial and monetary programs to deal with this succession of events. Regulation of the money supply, taxation, balancing the budget, and managing the national debt (both internal and external) became focal points of national debate. Ultimately, these national policies had to be reconciled with the requirements of reconstructing the international economy. Domestic financial and monetary policies had somehow to be connected in a rational way to national attitudes toward stabilization, devaluation, and the return to a gold standard.

If they were to place their own national finances in order, Britain and France had to reach a settlement on inter-Allied debts and German reparation payments. National economic recovery also depended upon the reconstruction of international trade, which in turn required a solution to the near-total stoppage of international credit. Western Europe, it seemed, required the markets and natural resources of Soviet Russia and the assistance of American capital to lift it from the deep recession of 1921–1922 and repair the damage of four years of total war. Underlying every approach to postwar financial and monetary reconstruction lay a fundamental question: could the ravages of war be rectified by action conforming to traditional financial institutions and prewar conceptions of economic freedom and the sanctity of private property? How would the costs of war be apportioned between the vanquished and the victors, and among the victors themselves?

1

Financial Entente, 1914-1919

Under the inexorable pressure of war we have . . . been swept from our old financial moorings . . . and have embarked on an uncharted sea.
—*The Round Table*, 1919

There has been nothing approaching this destruction of life and wealth in the history of the world . . . this stupendous conflict has produced the greatest economic revolution of which we have any record.
—Edgar Crammond, *The Quarterly Review*, 1919

As THE ARMISTICE was signed on 11 November 1918, the old international financial and monetary system lay in ruins after four years of total war. This was true as much for the victors as for the vanquished. To win the war the Allied and Associated powers had spent two-and-one-half times as much as the Central Powers had spent to lose it. The total war expenditure by all belligerents of about $210 billion, a fraction of the annual trillion-dollar GNP of the United States in the 1970s, represented an enormous and devastating sum in terms of the 1914 world economy, notwithstanding Derek Aldcroft's recent assertion that "the crux of the problem was not so much the magnitude of the outlay as the way in which it was financed."[1] No matter how the war had been financed, the result must have been catastrophic either for the generation which fought the war or for those which followed. Analysts who stress the reluctance of the belligerents to tax their populations more heavily during the war seem oblivious to the impact on national and international monetary and financial systems, and on the capitalist system itself, that would have resulted from the removal of a sum of $210 billion from the hands of the public over a four-year period.

By 1919, the prewar monetary and financial system had largely disappeared. Economic "facts," upon which traditional theory had been anchored, no longer bore any relationship to "normal" reality. The world had been cast adrift from its traditional moorings, and the signing of the Armistice brought no immediate relief. Indeed, most of the financial and monetary indices deteriorated rapidly as the international economy experienced a postwar boom, accompanied by widespread speculation in currency, commodities, and commercial enterprises, followed by a serious and persistent depression by the middle of 1920. Britain and France, the victors, found themselves in the midst of a financial and monetary crisis as the war ended, and watched the crisis grow as uncontrolled postwar activity finally gave way to a collapse of economic activity.

The economic revolution produced by the First World War touched all sectors of financial and monetary activity. The requirements of war finance produced a fundamental transformation in the size and term structure of government debt, and reversed the normal relationship and relative importance of public and private bills. The national wealth and income of most of the belligerents had been mortgaged to service of the national debt. For the next seven years the fortunes of the French franc would be tied up with public perception of the desirability of holding *Bons de la défense nationale*. In Britain, the war had been responsible for the rise of the Treasury bill. Before 1914 the annual issue of Treasury bills had rarely exceeded £30 million, whereas it fluctuated for most of the 1920s in the range of £600 million annually. Britain's internal public debt grew by £5.5 billion during the war, while deposits at joint stock banks increased by only £1 billion. Compared with other forms of property, the magnitude of Britain's internal public debt shifted drastically during the war. Prewar estimates placed total private property at between £11 billion and £12.8 billion, while the nominal value of the public debt stood at approximately £650 million. In 1925, the value of total private property ran to an estimate in the range of £20 billion, while internal public debt stood at £6.5 billion. The value of private property had barely doubled, as the value of the internal public debt increased tenfold.[2] The existence of this massive public debt severely complicated the conduct of postwar financial policy and threatened the stability of interwar financial markets. Public debt, which redistributes income from one sector to another, often serves some socially useful purpose. But the size and structure of the British and French public debt in 1919 militated against social utility and endangered the security of the national financial systems of both countries.

About one-fourth of the funds borrowed by the French government during the 1914–1918 period came from abroad (it owed the United States and Britain a total of $7 billion), and another 42 percent took the form of short- and medium-term securities. The heavy foreign debt constituted a real and potential menace to foreign exchange stability, while the massive floating debt posed a constant threat to national solvency. In March 1919, Britain owed the United States $4.7 billion, and 23 percent of its internal debt was short term. Service on these debts would consume 30 percent of early postwar British budgets, and nearly 50 percent of the French "ordinary" budget of 1922. Under these circumstances, there would be no "land fit for heroes."

Inflationary economic policy, deficit financing, had financed the greater part of the war effort. All states, including the neutrals, had created money in the form of notes and bank deposits. This wholly unprecedented wartime growth of the world's money supply rendered the normal functioning of fiscal and monetary policy ineffective. Monetary inflation in turn produced enormous price inflation. Such internal price movements, in view of the suspension of normal gold payments, eventually disturbed prewar currency parities. The entente powers minimized this disturbance by "pegging" the pound sterling and the French franc at near-parity with the dollar. But once the supports were removed in March 1919, these currencies, weakened by the war effort, quickly found their "true" values.

British and French techniques for financing the war barely differed. The story of insufficient taxation, short-term Treasury bills, *Bons de la défense nationale*, Bank notes (France), currency notes (Britain), and foreign borrowing has been told before. In most postwar comparisons of British and French wartime fiscal policies, the British inevitably won. Analysts of the day generally agreed that the British had based war finance on principles of "sound finance," while the French "spent without counting."[3] A more evenhanded analysis, however, indicates that in both cases, the question of how the costs of war were to be paid was deferred until the conclusion of the war. This tactic, which may seem irresponsible in retrospect, resulted from the general belief in 1914 that the war would be short, and later from the assumption that the Germans would pay their share and that the Allied and Associated Powers would cooperate in bearing the burden of war costs. In any event, French leaders equated "sound finance" with defeat. France had to survive, no matter what the price.

Britain's tax structure in 1914 was better suited to the strains of total war than that of France. The income tax, well-established and accepted by the public, served as a broad base on which the British government could expand existing taxes and add new ones to finance up to one-quarter of war costs through revenues. In the course of the war, the standard rate of income tax rose, and a super-tax was imposed on incomes above £3,000. In combination with the income tax and super tax, a new levy, the corporate excess profits duty (EPD) became the backbone of the British revenue system. Although the EPD was a temporary tax, postwar governments could find no substitute for the large revenues it produced; it was not dropped until 1922. The general thrust of British taxation policy was to shift the emphasis toward direct taxation, which was considered more socially just than indirect taxation.[4]

Owing to vested interests highly resistant to tax reform, France entered the war with a taxation system dating back to the National Assembly of 1789, a system based on real estate taxes on land and buildings, taxes on doors and windows, personal property taxes, and professional licensing taxes. In July 1914, the French parliament approved a modest income tax, but it did not take effect until 1916. Between 1916 and the end of 1918, it yielded less than one billion francs. French wartime taxation thus continued to rely on existing taxes for which collection machinery already existed. The government did introduce a war profits tax in 1916, but it yielded only 0.8 billion francs during the next two years. The only effective increase in revenue came from sharply increased general consumption and luxury taxes, which prompted complaints of added injustice in the taxation system.

National defense bonds (*Bons de la défense nationale*) maturing in three months, six months, or one year formed the backbone of French wartime finance. These bonds might have performed a useful function in the French financial and monetary system had the total amount issued been held to a reasonable level. In June 1922, the amount of outstanding bonds reached a high of 63.8 billion francs. The government did not halt the sale of three- and six-month bonds until June 1927. The Finance Ministry did not have a completely free hand in the matter. Major French financial institutions found these securities a source of liquidity which in other national banking systems might normally be found in regular treasury bills or commercial paper. They were reluctant to give them up, and their resistance complicated attempts by the government to fund the floating debt during the early postwar years.[5]

Without some sort of economic and financial cooperation among the Allies, their individual efforts could not have provided the financial resources to win the war. Yet, so circumscribed was the wartime economic entente that it was only after the war was over, at the Paris Peace conference in January 1919, that the Allies created a Supreme Economic Council. Anglo-French economic and financial cooperation began in February 1915, when the Allied foreign ministers agreed in principle to collaborate in the granting of credits, the floating of joint foreign loans, and closer liaison between central banks. In April, Britain granted a substantial credit to France, the first of many loans by Britain to its allies prior to American entry into the war. The central banks of France, Russia, and Italy "loaned" gold to the Bank of England, intended as collateral for British credits. A conference including delegations from Britain, France, Italy, Belgium, Portugal, Russia, Serbia, and Japan convened in Paris during the summer of 1916 to lay the foundation for further wartime economic cooperation and to plan a program of postwar economic collaboration. Largely at the urging of French Minister of Commerce Etienne Clémentel, the conference adopted plans for a postwar Allied economic entente. Russia and Italy remained cool to Clémentel's proposals, and the United States, which as a neutral did not attend, ultimately rejected international control over American resources.[6]

With American intervention in the war, the Allied financial burden fell increasingly upon the United States Treasury, which advanced the Allies $7.1 billion between April 1917 and the Armistice. The pace of inter-Allied economic cooperation quickened with the creation of the War Purchase and Finance Council and the Allied Maritime Transport Council. These councils, however, had evolved out of America's desire to limit and coordinate Europe's requests for assistance and thereby relieve the demands being made on the United States Treasury.[7]

Prior to American intervention in the war, private firms in the United States, most notably J. P. Morgan & Co., assisted in the co-ordination of the Allied economic effort. Morgan's expedited the purchase of war material in the United States, facilitated loans in the New York market, and advanced funds from the firm's own resources. Early in 1915, Morgan's became the British government's purchasing agent in America, on the assumption that Morgan's connections and knowledge of American markets would facilitate the acquisition of scarce goods for which many nations were competing. Soon, French Finance Minister Alexandre Ribot arrived in London to sign an agreement in which Morgan's assumed the role of purchasing agent for both the British and French governments, thereby centralizing purchases and avoiding Allied competition for American goods.

French official missions in the United States now became little more than technical advisers to J. P. Morgan & Co., thus inverting the normal relationship between governments and private firms. The Allies believed Morgan's assistance in obtaining war supplies and foodstuffs was essential, and willingly paid a high price to obtain it. On the French contract, for example, Morgan's received a 2 percent commission on the first $50 million worth of purchases, after which the commission fell to 1 percent. To further sweeten the deal for Morgan's, the contract stipulated a commission of one-eighth percent on the value of any goods purchased in America by the French government without Morgan's assistance. This system remained in effect until May 1917, when the French government sent André Tardieu to Washington as French high commissioner, and French missions resumed responsibility for purchases in the United States. But Morgan's continued to help the missions find vendors and prepare contracts, for which services the firm received a one-half percent commission.[8]

During the final months of the war, Anglo-French financial cooperation reached its zenith when, in January 1918, the two Allies jointly negotiated a $200 million credit ($100 million each) with the Argentine government to cover purchases of wheat.[9] But this type of unified financial action barely survived the signing of the Armistice, and by the time the Paris Peace Conference convened on 18 January 1919, the wartime financial entente was beginning to fall apart. In fact, relations between the members of the entente had never been smooth. During the war, French financial representatives in America complained that the British were getting more than their fair share of the credits granted by the United States Treasury, and the United States Treasury raised all sorts of issues with the French concerning unjustified expenditures, the use of American dollar advances to pay off British and neutral creditors (the funds were supposed to be used only for purchase of American goods and services), and failure to keep the franc exchange at agreed rates. French officials further alleged that during a speaking tour of America in 1917, the governor of the Bank of England, Lord Cunliffe, had spread anti-French propaganda implying that French bank notes would not be convertible into gold after the war.[10]

As the war ended, the financial triple entente quickly began to transform itself into a new dual alliance between the Anglo-Saxon powers. Benjamin Strong, governor of the Federal Reserve Bank of New York, warned Montagu Norman, deputy governor of the Bank of England, that the world would be plunged into a period of "economic barbarism" if England and the United States could not agree on a program to limit international economic competition. Britain and America, Strong believed, must take the lead in establishing "some sort of economic partnership in which every self-respecting and deserving nation may participate." On the English side, Norman agreed that "in any case and whatever happens, let us stand together and hope for the best."[11]

Out of such nebulous attitudes there gradually emerged a wavering but nonetheless clear Anglo-American financial entente in which the French found themselves the chief victim. While this new political-economic constellation owed something to specific French financial policies, it seems to have developed mainly from a widely held belief in the superiority of the Anglo-Saxon race and a preference for the Germanic economic system. British Treasury officials drew unfavorable comparisons between Anglo-Saxon and Latin taxation systems, French leadership was faulted for not being sufficiently international, French politics was portrayed as reactionary, the French central bank was viewed as both incompetent and subject to undue political pressure, and, as the director of French financial services in

New York put it, the French had gained the reputation of being "a nation of swindlers, cowards, and slackers."[12] Such unflattering views of the French apparently prevailed in other European capitals. In conversations with Gerard Vissèring, president of the Netherlands Bank, Strong gathered that Dutch financial leaders viewed France as a nation without leadership (Clemenceau was premier), a nation in the hands of professional politicians incapable of any carefully planned financial policy, playing for political gain rather than the nation's welfare. The French peasants and workingmen, Vissering believed, had been "spoiled by too high wages and life in the army." "Throughout the conversation," Strong wrote in his diary, "Mr. Kent and I both detected at times a rather German leaning, not so much sympathy as possibly greater confidence in German ability and capacity to make plans and adopt a consistent national policy."[13]

At the Bank of England, Montagu Norman joined the list of central bankers who lined up with Germany and Austria against the French government. Norman advocated prompt settlement of Britain's war debt to the United States, after which the two nations, "on terms of equality as it were," would call a general meeting of their debtors and face them in a united front.[14] The financial rehabilitation of France was not high on Norman's agenda, as he believed Central Europe held the key to European stability and peace. After a workable (meaning scaled-down) reparation settlement with Germany, "the next step should be an attempt to rehabilitate Austria as a step towards the rehabilitation of distressed Europe."[15] The French government agreed that Austria's plight was serious, but insisted that Austria's financial system be placed under the control of an Allied supervisory body. Norman refused to place the Austrian economy under French control, and assured Strong that he was "going to fight so far as possible for what is economically best for Austria as against what is politically best for the Entente," meaning France. He later told Strong that any scheme for Austria would have to be "palatable to Vissering, to yourself, and to this Country."[16] French requirements did not matter.

As the peace conference approached, discussions on arrangements for repaying U.S. Treasury advances split the French from the remainder of the financial entente. As early as August 1917, French officials believed funding arrangements to replace the unsecured sight obligations were essentially complete, with nothing more than a few formal details to be cleared up. But snags quickly developed, as American Treasury officials now insisted on a repayment conversion rate of 5.18 francs to the dollar, the prewar gold parity. In June 1918, French financial officers in New York believed the United States was prepared to consider all inter-Allied debts as a single question "in a manner so as not to create, as far as possible, privileges in favor of or to the detriment of one country as against another."[17] But that agreement also soon came apart.

Either the French had misunderstood the Treasury's position, or the American position failed to hold in the face of British maneuvers in both Washington and London. By the end of 1918, British Treasury officials had decided it was time to begin dismantling the financial entente. Britain's desire to break the financial entente quickly and dismantle wartime controls, both domestic and international, closely paralleled American thinking. The British Treasury desired to cut off credits to France by 3 January 1919, but efforts by Finance Minister Louis L. Klotz convinced London to continue existing arrangements for the moment.[18] But the British were already at work on a separate agreement with Washington that would leave the French out in the cold.

In December 1918, French financial officials in the United States again approached the Treasury on the possibility of funding the sight obligations. Finding the Treasury receptive, the French contacted British financial representatives in America to try to establish a common front in dealing with the United States Treasury. The British rebuffed this French initiative. London had already ordered the British financial representative in Washington, Sir Hardman Lever, to treat immediately and separately on the matter of funding Britain's debt to the U.S. Treasury. In response, Paris cabled the deputy French high commissioner in Washington, Edouard de Billy, that the official French position favored "a complete entente between the English and French governments and a common effort" for an arrangement with the U.S. Treasury. All such debts should be taken up at an inter-Allied conference in Paris (not Washington), and only after the conditions of peace (German reparation payments) had been fixed.[19] The U.S. Treasury, however, had already adopted the position it would maintain throughout the 1920s, that there was no connection between inter-Allied debts and German reparation payments. The Allies would have to settle up regardless of what the Germans would or could pay.

Being on the tail end of the American-British-French financial chain, the French government found itself under constant pressure from both partners. Both the American and British Treasuries claimed that severe political and financial problems ruled out any further assistance to Paris. Treasury officials in Washington were not very helpful when they told French representatives that the United States "partially" recognized the validity of France's contention that all inter-Allied debts should be treated in common at the Paris peace conference. If Britain wished to take the initiative and fund its debt, Washington could not refuse. In London, Controller of Finance Basil Blackett was telling Joseph Simon, representing the French Finance Ministry, that Britain merely wished to begin "conversations" with the U.S. Treasury to sound out America's position. Blackett assured Simon that Britain did not intend to sign a definitive agreement with the United States.[20] In this case, Blackett was telling Simon the truth, for the British Treasury and the Bank of England did not agree on the wisdom of early funding of the debt to America. At the Bank, Norman viewed funding as an indispensable step toward restoration of the pound sterling to prewar parity with the dollar. But the Treasury was not yet prepared to commit Britain to a long-term repayment scheme so long as there remained the possibility that a better arrangement might be worked out in a general inter-Allied settlement. As Austen Chamberlain told Benjamin Strong in July 1919, it would be a relief to have the debt terms settled once and for all, "but in that matter he felt that the creditor should make the first move, and it would be rather unbecoming of the debtor to make any suggestion."[21]

In January 1919 the French Finance Ministry notified its financial agents in New York that because the U.S. Treasury had ended its assistance to London, the British could no longer help France with additional credits. This news produced a visit by French officials to the office of Assistant Secretary of the Treasury Albert Rathbone. After assurances from Washington, French financial agents telegraphed Paris that British reports of deteriorating Anglo-American financial relations were greatly exaggerated and ill-founded. The message concluded that "whatever may be the verbal understandings [between the British and American treasuries], the American Treasury will not abandon the English abruptly if they truly have an imperative need for new advances and cannot procure the funds on honorable terms in the New York market." French financial agents assured the Finance Ministry that the U.S. Treasury had undertaken to conclude no debt arrangements with Britain without informing France; in any negotiations the American Treasury would protect the interest of France vis-à-vis Britain and the United States. The French agents in New York remarked optimistically that "the history of two years of collaboration in Washington is a guarantee for us that neither the Americans nor the British wish to do us a bad turn."[22] Officials at the United States Treasury were not so naive.

From conversations with de Billy and other French representatives in Washington and New York, the U.S. Treasury concluded that the British were playing a hard game with the French, at the ultimate expense of the American Treasury. The specific problem involved French dollar transfers to Britain under terms of a 29 May 1917 agreement between the French finance minister and the British chancellor of the exchequer. With American entry into the war in April, the United States Treasury had assumed most of the financial burden for financing the Allies formerly carried by the British Treasury. Counting on American assistance, France renounced British financing of French purchases outside the British Empire, and promised to reimburse Britain in dollars for any expenditures incurred by the British government for the French account outside the British Empire and Canada. Under an additional convention of 28 June 1917, France agreed to deposit weekly in a British Treasury account in New York a payment of between $8 million and $10 million. The British Treasury actually opened two transfer accounts in New York, one for direct payment in dollars by the French Treasury for goods purchased in the United States by Britain for the French account, and one for repayment in dollars for goods originally purchased in pounds sterling in neutral countries for the French account. The United States Treasury agreed in principle to dollar transfers for goods purchased in America, but from the beginning expressed reservations on dollar transfers for goods purchased in pounds sterling in neutral countries. When the war ended, the total amount involved was in dispute, ranging from a low estimate of $94 million to a high of $119 million, with at least $79 million owed to countries other than the United States.[23]

On 10 February 1919 Rathbone informed de Billy that he was asking Sir Hardman Lever for a precise statement of the account on which France was making dollar transfer payments to Britain. Noting that France had asked for more dollars from the U.S. Treasury to finance reconstruction, Rathbone wondered why the French government continued to use its precious dollar resources for these payments to Britain, without first consulting the U.S. Treasury. Rathbone told de Billy that the Treasury had to conserve its own dollar resources, and could not indefinitely furnish France with transfer payment funds. Two days later, Joseph Simon was in Rathbone's office, warning him that to "avert catastrophe" France would have to increase its February transfer payment to Britain by $10 million. Simon advised Rathbone that the time had come to lay down the law to the British. He was "convinced that English policy was to bluff us, with a view to pulling from us every dollar possible," and that the only way to check the British was to "solidify the [U.S.] Treasury to our cause."[24]

According to the French report sent to Paris, "the results of the Simon-Rathbone meeting were immediate; in the very presence of M. Simon, M. Rathbone jumped on his telephone and did not put it down until he had been put through to Sir Hardman Lever in New York." Rathbone asked Sir Hardman to obtain from his government an immediate explanation of its claim that sterling support for France was conditional upon transfer of equivalent sums in dollars either from France's own resources or from advances from the U.S. Treasury. He also demanded detailed and complete accounts of the transfer payments. Rathbone then telegraphed Assistant Secretary Norman Davis in Paris, asking him to address the most serious representations to the British financial delegates at the peace conference, and to call a meeting including Klotz and the British financial delegates to study France's financial situation. The Treasury would approve no further advances for transfer payments until Davis's report on the results of the meetings was received in Washington.[25]

Secretary of the Treasury Carter Glass soon intervened personally in the transfer payment case. In separate letters to de Billy and to the British ambassador, Lord Reading, on 4 March 1919, Glass asserted his authority to both the French and British governments. He informed de Billy that the U.S. Treasury must retain control over the use of dollars advanced to the French government, and that no funds from the American Treasury were to be used to pay French debts owed to other Allied governments. Glass cited recent operations on the New York exchange market by which the Bank of France had transferred considerable amounts of sterling to Britain, "in effect from loans to your government from the U.S. Treasury [which] furnish a striking example of the transactions which most emphatically I am unwilling to have continued."[26]

To Lord Reading, Glass wrote a scathing letter denouncing Britain's refusal to cooperate in sustaining French financial solvency. French dollar payments to Britain were to be halted temporarily, as the U.S. Treasury was not willing to advance funds to France for payment of debts in Britain. The United States, Glass assured Lord Reading, was willing to continue legitimate financial assistance to France, but the American government believed that,

> unless the British Treasury is prepared to cooperate in providing funds to meet the necessary expenditures of France in the British Empire, the financial credit of France cannot be successfully maintained ... The present critical situation of French credit has, I understand, been brought about by the refusal of the British Treasury to make sterling advances to France except to meet the interest falling due on the French obligations held by the British Government.

Glass claimed Sir Hardman Lever's figures demonstrated that over $1 billion of the French current account with Britain had been paid with American loans to the French Treasury. During the three months prior to March 1919, the Bank of France had used $72 million to purchase sterling for transfer to Britain. This practice appeared to violate an agreement signed on 26 March 1918 by André Tardieu and Russell C. Leffingwell, in which the French government agreed that all advances to the Bank of France would be used for dollar payments on accounts in the United States.[27]

At the instigation of the U.S. Treasury, Chancellor of the Exchequer Austen Chamberlain met with representatives of the French and American Treasuries in Paris on 7 March 1919. After discussing France's financial and foreign exchange crisis, Chamberlain made what might be termed a "final offer" of British support for the French Treasury. He agreed to discount in sterling a further sum of £25 million in French Treasury bills. Additionally, during the two months beginning 12 March, £21,500,000 was to be placed at the disposition of the French Treasury agency in London, "by the Bank of England agreeing to release for outright sale to the British Treasury the gold now deposited with them by the Bank of France as collateral for the outstanding loans from the Bank of England to the Bank of France." Upon the expiration of the two-month period, "the British treasury will not be expected to accord further financial assistance by the discount of further French sterling Treasury bills." Chamberlain regretted that he could not furnish funds to maintain the franc exchange in London, but doubted that any level of support could maintain the franc at its overvalued level. The chancellor terminated his propositions to the French with a clear statement that additional assistance would not be forthcoming. "I make this proposition in the hope that it will be completely understood that these sums constitute the final installment of the financial aid which the British Treasury is furnishing the French Treasury by reason of the war."[28] Following Chamberlain's offer, which Klotz accepted, the United States Treasury opened in April 1919 a $50 million credit for settlement of the French transfer account with Britain, but use of the account required the approval of the secretary of the treasury. French Finance Ministry records indicate the secretary consistently refused to give his authorization as late as August 1920.[29]

Chamberlain's "final offer" of 7 March 1919 had been conditional upon French agreement to permit the Bank of England to sell to the British Treasury gold deposited in London as collateral for wartime Treasury advances to France. It later developed that the French questioned whether such a stipulation was consistent with the agreements under which they had deposited the gold in London (the Calais agreement of 24 August 1916, as modified by the Avenol-Blackett agreement of 13 December 1919), since the agreements provided that Britain would return the gold when France repaid the advances. Furthermore, some French officials later disputed Chamberlain's claim that the French government had accepted his stipulations for further assistance. Finally, since the French gold deposited in the Bank of England actually belonged to the Bank of France, it was questionable whether the French government had acted legally and properly in promising to sell the gold to the British Treasury.

The Bank of France refused to sell the gold in question, and the French finance minister, Klotz, may not have been entirely candid with either the Bank of France or Chamberlain when he agreed to the sale at the 7 March meeting. Since this incident contributed heavily toward British refusal to conduct any further joint financial operations with the French Finance Ministry, it is worth describing in some detail. The British version emerges clearly in exchanges between Chamberlain, Klotz, Joseph Avenol, French financial delegate in London, and Edwin S. Montagu, secretary of state for India and a member of the British delegation at the Paris Peace Conference.

In the 7 March meeting between Chamberlain and Klotz in Paris, Chamberlain agreed to additional advances up to £21 million during the next two months, and instructed London to place £2 million at the disposal of French authorities at once. It seems that no more than this initial £2 million was advanced to France, as the French backed down on the agreement to sell gold to the British Treasury. As the agreement began to unravel, Chamberlain wrote Klotz on 13 March that "M. Avenol gave me the assurance that I might regard it as certain that the gold of the Bank of France deposited with the Bank of England would be placed at the disposition of the French Government. In the circumstances, I at once telephoned to London to place £2,000,000 sterling at the disposal of the French authorities."[30]

Responding to Chamberlain the following day, Avenol acknowledged that Chamberlain had specifically asked whether the French Finance Ministry supported the sale of the Bank of France's gold. Avenol had given Chamberlain his "moral assurance" that the sale would be effected, and told Chamberlain that this assurance "rested on a decision taken by Clemenceau in my presence. The French Government is determined to use all its influence to obtain this sale." Avenol conceded, however, that the ultimate decision on the sale of gold to the British Treasury rested with the general council of the Bank of France. If the Bank refused to approve the sale, said Avenol, Britain, of course, would not advance additional funds to the French government, an eventuality the French government was willing to accept if necessary.[31] Chamberlain, of course, had already approved an advance of £2 million. The chancellor informed Avenol that Klotz now wished to keep the 7 March agreement secret, "and particularly as to the use of the gold of the Bank of France." The need for secrecy, he told Avenol, had never been mentioned during the negotiations, and Chamberlain warned that if questioned in the House of Commons on the matter, he would have to furnish all information requested.[32]

The correspondence between the chancellor of the exchequer and Edwin S. Montagu reveals the depth of the chasm between Chamberlain and Klotz. On 28 March, Montagu described a visit from Edouard Rothschild, an officer of the Bank of France. Lord Cunliffe, governor of the Bank of England, had referred Rothschild to Montagu after Klotz had advised Rothschild to negotiate directly with the Bank of England on the sale of the French gold. Rothschild told Montagu that Klotz had never communicated to the Bank of France or to the French financial agency in America the notice of termination of wartime financial agreements between England and France given by Bonar Law in November 1918, although Finance Ministry records show Klotz did notify the New York agency. Rothschild also told Montagu that the Bank of France "do not want to part with their gold, which they always expected to receive back at the end of the war." Reminding Chamberlain that Klotz had been told at the 7 March meeting that the offer of £21 million was the final installment, "he then not dare come to you again, but sends the Bank of France to make pathetic appeals for more or for alternative plans," wrote Montagu. "Rothschild," according to Montagu, "suggests that we should lend her small sums of money to pay for absolute essentials, so that England at least would be represented as helping France to avoid starvation and ruin." Montagu advised the chancellor that "this plan does not seem to me to be very practicable, and after all, where are we going to get money to pay for essentials? The key of the situation is in the hands of our philanthropic cousins, the Americans, but unless they do something, and something quickly, Europe will have gone to perdition."[33]

In a dictated telephone message for Montagu on 31 March, Chamberlain reiterated that the French could not expect the assistance mentioned in the 7 March agreement if they now refused to sell the gold as agreed. Later the same day, in a long letter to Montagu, the chancellor declared that "it is difficult to deal with a government which acts as the French Government have done in this matter." Chamberlain stressed his understanding that Klotz had accepted his 7 March offer of assistance after consultation with the president of the Council, Clemenceau, and that Klotz had given assurances that the French government would use all of its influence with the Bank of France to effect the sale of the gold. "I cannot believe," wrote Chamberlain, "that their influence is not sufficient for the purpose if they choose to exert it. In any case it seems to me impossible that I should admit in the midst of our own difficulties that the resources of the British Treasury are more available to the French Government than the resources of French institutions [such as the Bank of France]." Concerning the plight of the franc, Chamberlain pointed out that, having abandoned support of sterling, the British Treasury could hardly support the French franc "in its highly artificial and insecure position."[34]

By the end of March 1919, Chamberlain had become disgusted with Klotz and the French Finance Ministry, and was prepared to break all financial ties with France. After a year-end dinner party at the Spanish embassy in Paris, Lord Derby, the British ambassador in Paris, reported a conversation with André Tardieu, in which the former French high commissioner in Washington attributed financial difficulties between France and England to "Austen Chamberlain and Klotz not talking matters over. Apparently they had had trouble in the Spring and there had been no communication between them since, and that if this thing went on it was going to be very bad for the financial position of both countries and would have a very bad result on the political aspect."[35]

After the crisis of March 1919, the Anglo-French financial entente disintegrated precipitously on several fronts. Cooperative efforts involving Argentine credits, shipment of British coal to France, and the Anglo-French dollar loan of 1915 all collapsed less than a year after the signing of the Armistice. As the January 1918 Argentine joint credit operation with Britain and France approached maturity, the Argentine government proposed in April 1919 an extension of additional credits in a new joint operation involving Britain, France, and Italy. France needed both the additional foodstuffs and the additional credits, but the British Treasury refused to become involved in another operation with the French. The new French finance minister, Frédéric François-Marsal, regarded Britain's position on this issue as part of Austen Chamberlain's "policy of isolation." In point of fact, the French Treasury owed Britain Argentine pesos for foodstuffs purchased by Britain for the French account. While Chamberlain did not wish to join France in obtaining additional Argentine credits, the British Treasury would not object if France could obtain the credits on its own. Whereas earlier in 1919 the British Treasury had pressured France to repay its advances out of proceeds from loans from the U.S. Treasury, now it was pressuring the French Finance Ministry to repay Argentine peso credits out of proceeds of additional credits from the Argentine government. The tactic failed, as both the American and Argentine governments recognized what the British were doing, and refused to grant the French government additional credits to pay off British loans.[36]

Disputes over British coal shipments to France further contributed to the breakdown of the economic entente during the spring and summer of 1919. In June 1916, Britain had agreed to sell coal to France and her other Allies at controlled prices below world market levels. On 9 May 1919, the cabinet voted to end forthwith the controlled coal prices charged to France, Italy, Belgium, Portugal, and the United States as a wartime favor. The cabinet's decision followed an earlier request from the French government in December 1918 asking for continuing arrangements to insure that Allied controls over essential commodities including fuel be removed gradually by coordinated action of the several interested governments, and that raw materials be made available to all Allied nations at uniform prices. According to the British coal controller, "We agreed in principle, but with the reservation that its application to different commodities would depend on special circumstances."[37]

During the ensuing exchange of verbal assaults, the newly appointed president of the Board of Trade (Sir Auckland Geddes), the British coal controller, and the director of the Coal Mines Department argued that the French had in fact received more than their share of British coal, that British taxpayers had in effect subsidized a £40 million gift to the French, and that the French government had failed to pass on these savings to French consumers. The French in turn claimed that a British embargo on coke exports in the spring of 1920 led to the default on delivery of 3.5 million tons of contracted coal, forcing the French to purchase inferior, high-priced coal on the spot market.[38]

Negotiations for the repayment of the joint Anglo-French dollar loan of 1915 produced a further split in the financial entente during 1919–1920. The five-year loan matured in August 1920. In talks with the British Treasury in December 1919, the French Finance Ministry indicated its desire to try to obtain an extension. Basil Blackett, controller of finance, told Joseph Avenol, the French financial delegate, that repayment of the loan would "clear" the financial markets for further borrowing. The Finance Ministry agreed with Blackett in principle, but simply lacked the dollar resources required to make the repayment. Blackett apparently suggested that the French Finance Ministry sell additional dollar-denominated French Treasury bills in New York, but the Finance Ministry correctly pointed out that the market for such bills had practically dried up. Blackett then asserted that Americans were no longer willing to subscribe to joint Anglo-French loans (presumably owing to lack of confidence in the French), a claim the French hotly disputed. The Finance Ministry believed "the 'hesitation' to which Blackett refers seems to reside only in the mind of the British Treasury, which seems not to want to continue with us the operation effected in common in 1915." If Anglo-French solidarity collapsed, warned the Finance Ministry, the two governments would have to compete in the financial markets for funds with which to repay the loan, and France would inevitably lose such a competition.[39]

François-Marsal, the finance minister, took over negotiations on the Anglo-French repayment personally, and on 11 February 1920 he traveled to London to conclude an agreement. In conversations with Chamberlain, the finance minister learned that there was no chance for renewal of the loan; the chancellor of the exchequer favored an immediate declaration by both parties of their intention to repay the loan, coupled with a shipment of gold to New York as a sign of good faith. François-Marsal thought a gold shipment "premature," but, at Chamberlain's insistence, he agreed to issue a press release indicating their intent to repay the loan and to take measures to secure the resources required for repayemnt. The finance minister was disappointed with the results of his discussions with Chamberlain, and left London with the impression of "the very firm and in my view definitive determination of the Chancellor of the Exchequer to henceforth never engage in any joint operation with us."[40] The Anglo-French entente was definitely broken.

While financial relations between London and Paris deteriorated on the questions of Argentine credits, British coal shipments, and the Anglo-French loan, the entire economic alliance between Britain, France, and the United States was coming apart at the Paris Peace conference. Two successive secretaries of the treasury, McAdoo and Glass, issued specific instructions to U.S. Treasury delegates that inter-Allied debts were not to be discussed at the peace conference.

The Treasury, however, was unable to block discussion of Italian, French, and British proposals for the redistribution of inter-Allied debt and the connection of that debt with Germany's reparation obligation. Each of these proposals would have required the American Treasury to underwrite a heavier portion of the total war debt, and their outright rejection by the Wilson administration caused much bad feeling among the Allies. Ultimately, however, divisions began to surface in the American financial delegation, some of whom came to believe that the United States must at least discuss inter-Allied debt at the peace conference and play a greater role in the financial rehabilitation of Europe.

In early March 1919, Italian delegates attempted to place on the agenda of the Finance Commission a plan to redistribute the costs of war among all of the Allies. Klotz supported the Italian proposition, but Britain and the United States registered strong objections. Albert Rathbone, representing the United States Treasury, addressed a letter to Edouard de Billy, deputy French high commissioner in Washington, indicating an American veto on any discussion of plans to cancel, consolidate, or redistribute the debt obligations signed during the war by the French government. Rathbone added that further advances would be denied to any government that supported such a proposition. Joseph Simon, representing the French Finance Ministry in Washington, lodged a protest with Rathbone, citing what he termed the "aggressive attitude taken *ab iratio* by the Treasury." But de Billy went even further, sending Rathbone two letters denying French involvement in any proposals regarding discussion of the debt, and a telegram passed on to the U.S. Treasury contained the same assurance from Clemenceau himself.[41]

Unfortunately, de Billy's representations were untrue, or, as French financial agents in New York explained the situation, the attitude of the French government in Paris "changed." Klotz did present to the Financial Commission debt redistribution schemes which involved the "internationalization of taxes," which were to be pooled and used for the amortization of inter-Allied war debts.[42] Rathbone, meanwhile, had placed de Billy's letters denying French participation in such schemes in the record before the House Ways and Means Committee, and the "shift" in the French position greatly embarrassed both Rathbone and the French financial representatives in Washington. French credibility was not improved by this incident.[43]

Nevertheless, de Billy's use of the term "aggressive" to describe the U.S. Treasury's response to French proposals on inter-Allied debt seems accurate in view of the evidence. America's rejoinder to similar British proposals, while equally disapproving, carried a much friendlier tone and was carried on at the highest level in an exchange between President Wilson and Lloyd George.

On 23 April 1919, Lloyd George sent to Wilson a detailed proposal, drawn up by John Maynard Keynes, for the "Rehabilitation of European Credit and for Financing Relief and Reconstruction." Behind the innocuous title lay a plan to mobilize the reparation payments of the Central Powers, and tie them to the payment of inter-Allied debts. Keynes's scheme called for Germany, Austria, Hungary, Bulgaria, Roumania, Poland, Czechoslovakia, Yugoslavia, and the Balkan States to issue bonds of a determined value, carrying 4 percent annual interest. Those bonds would take priority over all other obligations of the issuing states, including any additional claims for reparations not covered by the bonds. Interest payments would be guaranteed jointly by the issuing states; in the event of failure to pay, the Principal Allied and Associated Powers, joined by the three Scandinavian governments, Holland, and Switzerland, were to guarantee interest payments up to a total of £1,500,000,000. The United States, Britain, and France would assume the largest share of the guarantee, 20 percent each, with Italy and Japan assuming 10 percent each, Belgium, 5 percent, and the rest together 15 percent. Germany would turn over to the Allied and Associated governments bonds of present value of £1,000,000,000 on its reparation account. These bonds were to be accepted in payment of all inter-Allied indebtedness, and as first-class collateral for loans at the central banks of all issuing or guaranteeing states.[44]

Accompanying the Keynes plan, Lloyd George sent to Wilson, Clemenceau, and Orlando a letter in which he stressed the danger of a Bolshevik conquest of Europe if "some bolder solution" for financial rehabilitation were not adopted. Through either an American or an international initiative, Europe must be enabled to "trade on their prospects of Reparation from the Enemy States or to capitalize their future prospects of production." The British plan, concluded Lloyd George, would satisfy the highest principles of international order as well as the material interests of every nation on earth.[45]

President Wilson sought comment on the Keynes proposal from

Thomas W. Lamont, a J. P. Morgan & Co. partner and member of the U.S. Treasury delegation at the peace conference. Lamont prepared a memorandum which Wilson used practically verbatim in his 3 May 1919 response to Lloyd George. Wilson rejected the British proposals to share the burden, but in a tone much more accommodating than that employed by Rathbone in rejecting similar French proposals. Wilson made no threat to cut off financial assistance, as Rathbone had in his note to de Billy. Rather, Wilson politely observed that Britain's suggestions were economically unsound and politically impossible. How could the Allies strip Germany of her capital through reparation payments, and then expect the United States to replenish it through loans? In any event, it was time for both the British and American Treasuries to "retire at the earliest possible moment from 'the banking business.' "[46]

If Wilson's logic was unassailable, his argument failed to comprehend the new economic facts of life, as they were understood by Lloyd George. Responding to Wilson on 26 June, the prime minister asserted that if Britain was pressing Germany for reparation payments while simultaneously putting forward a plan for European financial rehabilitation, "it does so because it has already bled itself white for the sake of the Allies." Britain "asks for nothing which is impossible, but it does claim that it has the right to ask its colleagues of the peace conference both to compel Germany to pay whatever she is capable of paying and to place their own credit unreservedly at the disposal of the nations for the regeneration of the world as Great Britain placed hers unreservedly at the service of the Allies in order to save the freedom of the world." America could not escape its postwar responsibility as a great power. "The responsibility for the reconstruction of the world," the prime minister told Wilson, "depends in an exceptional measure upon the United States, for the United States is the only country in the world which is exceedingly prosperous and is not overburdened, in proportion to her resources and population, by external or internal debts."[47]

In Washington, U.S. Treasury officials reacted sharply to Keynes's plan. Albert Rathbone cabled to Norman Davis in Paris that the British proposal was "financially indefensible and politically impossible." "It would be far better," he added, "to cancel some part of Europe's debt to us than to assume additional liability imposed upon United States by plan. As you know, Treasury is opposed to cancelling any part of such debt and has so stated to Congress and to public generally." Rathbone warned that "acceptance of plan would have most calamitous consequences and that its discussion with British would be grave mistake." Albert Strauss pointed out that new loans floated on American markets under Keynes's plan would depreciate the value of U.S. Liberty Bonds and choke up America's banking system with foreign issues, to the detriment of American firms seeking credit. Russell C. Leffingwell echoed Strauss's fears, adding that opening the American market to tax-free enemy bonds would produce "further stupendous inflation." Calling the plan "preposterous," Leffingwell told Davis that "I am bitterly disappointed that the British Government should have presented such a plan and that Keynes, whom I had come to regard very highly, should have associated himself with it." Secretary of the Treasury Carter Glass indicated that the observations of Rathbone, Strauss, and Leffingwell "substantially represent my view." Glass was "not a little amazed that such a proposition should have come from Great Britain," though he "would not have been astonished at such a suggestion from any other of the Allies." The Treasury secretary repeated his dictum that "matters of this kind should not form part of the discussions at the Peace table but should be discussed and settled at Washington."[48]

By April 1919, several American financial representatives at the peace conference had concluded that the European Allies were determined to evade their own financial responsibility in the postwar era. In a memorandum for Norman Davis, George W. Whitney warned that "so long as the countries in Europe fool themselves with the belief that the United States is in a position to render unlimited assistance, just so long are they going to hesitate in taking some steps on their own shoulders to help themselves." The French proposition for redistributing the war debt burden was in Whitney's view "nothing more than an attempt to turn over the whole serious financial situation in France onto the back of the United States, in the hope that France will not, therefore, have to face it, as the politicians have refused to do during the last four years."[49] But some members of the American delegation, notably Thomas W. Lamont, began to question the Treasury's intransigent insistence that inter-Allied debt could not even be discussed at the peace conference.

In a letter to Leffingwell, Lamont suggested that the United States take the initiative in proposing a debt funding program to the British and French delegations. Lamont admitted that on his arrival in Paris he had shared the Treasury's belief that such discussions should not be held at the peace conference, "but my views have changed radically" after observing first-hand the financial condition of Europe. Lamont assured Leffingwell that his injunctions against any such discussions "have been followed to the letter," but cautioned that there could be no real peace in Europe unless trade were resurrected. "All the countries are in a state of suspended animation," wrote Lamont, "and the signing of the peace will not restore that animation." Reflecting the tone of Lloyd George's response to Wilson's rejection of the Keynes plan, Lamont argued that "America holds the key to the door which is locked . . . In the hands of the Secretary of the Treasury today I believe is the power to conclude a real and lasting peace; if he fails to exercise that power, no one can foresee the consequences—consequences with almost as terrible results for America as for the rest of the world."[50]

For some reason, Lamont did not send this plea for action to Leffingwell; some years later, when Lamont found the letter in his peace conference files, he sent it to Leffingwell as an item of historical interest. Leffingwell returned a note to Lamont with the inscription, "Darn good letter. I wish you had signed it and sent it."[51] Lamont and Benjamin Strong, governor of the Federal Reserve Bank of New York, were among a small group of New York bankers who understood Europe's need for generous American assistance. Strong advised Leffingwell that "in the case of France our help is undoubtedly needed and deserved and must be given freely to avert a period of great depression and poverty among the poorer people." Noting that France lacked a sound system of direct taxation, Strong did not join those Americans who criticized the French government for its timidity in raising taxes; a substantial increase in indirect taxation would only deal another crushing blow to the poor.[52]

If America wished to assist the French through the postwar financial and monetary crisis, it would have to do it alone, for Britain was developing its own plans for restoring free markets and limiting any losses it might incur in behalf of the French. In a memorandum on postwar trade policy, Sir Auckland Geddes told the prime minister that "so far as the rehabilitation of business activity is concerned, it is of high importance to secure the maximum freedom with the minimum delay."[53] As chancellor of the exchequer, Andrew Bonar

Law had urged that any postwar controls on raw materials and shipping must be as short-lived as possible, "for no one, I think, can fail to believe that the sooner the free play of individual effort is permitted the better."[54] The "free play of individual effort" applied to the international economy as well as to Britain's domestic markets. British assistance to France would be limited by both philosophical reservations and the material limitations of Britain's resources.

As Chamberlain understood the situation, the basic problem was France's inability to pay for imports. Britain imported on credit the raw materials required to manufacture the exports sent to France, "and if we export for credit instead of cash we can only obtain these foreign credits by ourselves getting into still deeper debt to foreign countries." Britain could not go further into debt in order to supply the French after the war. "This does not mean," continued Chamberlain, "that we should decline to create credits for our European allies altogether. Such a course even if economically desirable (which I do not think it would be) would be politically impossible, but it does mean that we cannot create such credits to an unlimited amount." Chamberlain warned that Britain could not afford to "stimulate trade with customers who cannot pay at the expense of the trade with customers who can . . . if we once embark on such a policy competing claims will come in from all sides and there will be no halting place."[55]

In the absence of support from the British Treasury, French importers of British goods attempted to raise credits in London's private financial markets. Concerned by reports of French attempts to raise large sums in London, Lloyd George brought the matter before the Cabinet Finance Committee in July 1919. Treasury adviser Sir John Bradbury confirmed that the City was arranging a considerable amount of short-term credits for French importers. Chamberlain observed that had private sources been unwilling to extend these credits, the French would have had to come to the British Treasury, "which was very undesirable." It was preferable to send the French into the private market. But Bradbury warned that such short-term credits constituted a "very dangerous form of borrowing," and that one day the British Treasury might be confronted by the City asking for assistance. Swayed by Bradbury's argument, Lloyd George expressed doubts about the expediency of permitting large credits to France in the private market, but concluded it might be permitted if the funds were to be spent in Britain. Bradbury doubted the wisdom of granting the credits even with the prime minister's stipulation, since goods the French might purchase in Britain were manufactured from raw materials purchased in the United States at high prices and at unfavorable exchange rates.[56] There was no way, it seemed, that Britain could provide financial assistance to the French, either through public or private sources, without sacrificing Britain's own financial integrity.

During the first months of 1919, the Allied financial entente broke apart, or, more precisely, reshaped itself into an Anglo-American bloc facing a prostrate Europe. Leading British and American financial and political authorities, ranging from Lloyd George to Austen Chamberlain, Montagu Norman, Benjamin Strong, and Thomas W. Lamont, called for and envisioned an Anglo-American financial entente as the guiding force in the postwar international financial system. Strong suggested to Norman that the key to solving Britain's postwar financial problems lay in "such understanding as may be arrived at between our two countries by which the Federal Reserve Bank's banking resources can be made of service to yourselves . . . I believe the greatest difficulty comes from a fear on the part of your London bankers of the Holden type that we are going to encroach upon the English banking preserves."[57] Lamont, too, suggested "some sort of working partnership in business betwixt Great Britain and America." Citing America's "ample credit resources" and Britain's "wonderful credit machinery all over the world," Lamont proposed a merger "by our buying a half interest, no more, in a lot of your banks, and thus make a combination of your machinery and our credit resources." Lamont tried out his idea on Keynes, who indicated that British bankers "wanted to run their own business and didn't want any interference from outside."[58]

If British financial leaders rejected what they considered American attempts to encroach upon Britain's traditional banking preserves, they nevertheless were most anxious to establish a common front with the United States against France on the questions of inter-Allied debts and German reparations. Norman and Strong agreed that it would be entirely proper for Britain to make a funding arrangement with the United States Treasury, and then have the United States and Britain, "on terms of equality as it were," call a general meeting of their debtors, including Germany.[59] Britain's insistence on being treated separately from France, on a preferred basis, comes through clearly in a cabinet Finance Committee memorandum of 23 September 1919.

> While it is desirable that at least the French Treasury should be generally aware of the British Treasury's negotiations with the United States Treasury in these matters, it is important that the British Treasury should insist on its position as a fellow creditor with the United States Treasury rather than as a fellow debtor with the French Treasury.[60]

Lloyd George himself provided the clearest statement of the developing Anglo-American financial entente, directed against the French, during the early months of 1919. Writing to Bonar Law of his difficulties with President Wilson over the question of including damage to combatants in the cost of reparations demanded of Germany, the prime minister indicated that "I told him that unless this were included I might as well go home as I had no authority to sign unless this were admitted." But, he added, "you must not assume from this that relations are strained. Quite the reverse. Wilson has been working very well with the British delegation, and the Americans have done their best to be helpful. They are becoming more and more anti-French, and I think I may say that in proportion to their increasing suspicion of the French is their trust of the British." If Britain and America were finding an ever-increasing common ground for a financial entente it was, in Lloyd George's view, because "the French have been extraordinarily greedy."[61] From New York, the French financial agency reported that "without saying it too loudly," the United States Treasury believed France's financial and monetary mess was due in part to "a lack of banking organization and to the ignorance and egoism of our people."[62] It was this conception of a greedy, incompetent, and ignorant French financial and political leadership that fostered the postwar Anglo-American financial entente and the isolation of France.

2

Crisis in Economic Theory

The destruction is now caused by three scourges of mankind which should be written everywhere in letters of fire as a fearful warning: ignorance–hesitation–selfishness.
—Gerard Vissering, Netherlands Bank, 1920

JUST BEFORE THE GREAT CRASH, the noted economist Gustav Cassel prophesied in 1929 that "in all future times people will go back to the monetary revolution of our age, be astonished at all the amazing mistakes of monetary policy in this period, and take the highest interest in the consequences of these mistakes and in the means by which it at last proved possible to return to normal conditions."[1] Some economists would argue later that the attempt to return to "normal conditions" was itself the most amazing mistake of all.

Economists and historians have sought for sixty years an explanation for the interwar financial and monetary crisis. Missing from these analyses have been a discussion of the most serious legacy of wartime finance, a general crisis and confusion in monetary and financial theory. The impact of this crisis in theory has been neglected universally by writers seeking to place the blame for the postwar financial crisis on inappropriate policies pursued by the British, American, and French central banks and Treasuries, speculators in the money markets, irresponsible borrowers who refused to spend less and save more, workers who demanded more social programs and shorter hours, Americans who refused to cancel debts, Germans who refused to pay debts, and above all, ignorant, incompetent, and intransigent French politicians and financial officials.

Each of these factors may have contributed somewhat to Europe's postwar financial crisis, but the fact remains that the experts could not agree on how to deal with that crisis. Disarray among the economists extended beyond the policy level and ran directly to the theory itself. Two distinct problems confronted postwar monetary

40

and financial theory. First, the prewar international economy based on the gold standard had been shattered and fragmented into rival national economic systems. No longer was there a single international economic theory valid for the entire system. Each state would now utilize the theory most useful in protecting its national economic interests. The Anglo-Saxon nations attempted to impose their notions of economic orthodoxy on less fortunate Continental friends and former enemies. The French response was completely rational. They resisted all attempts to establish a system of Anglo-American financial and diplomatic hegemony. France rejected British and American notions of theoretical orthodoxy and laissez-faire not out of ignorance, but in accordance with a well-founded skepticism that Anglo-American financial and monetary theories and institutions operated in France's best national interests.

Second, traditional monetary and financial theory did not appear to fit the new facts. The debate during the early postwar years produced a fundamental schism between those who advocated new theories to fit the new facts, and those who were determined to turn the clock back to "normalcy" and force the economic facts back into traditional theoretical molds. In this perspective, French economic theory and policy was in some respects more progressive than that of Britain and the United States.

Several questions urgently demanded answers. How should Europe deal with the mass of new paper currency now in circulation? How could Europe return to the gold standard? How could foreign exchanges be stabilized and international trade revived? To what extent would wartime financial and monetary controls be required in the postwar era? With fundamental theory in a state of turmoil, responsible Treasury and central bank officials could hardly act decisively.

Much of the theoretical debate and confusion during the postwar era stemmed from disagreements over cause and effect relationships in which the quantity theory of money ultimately came into question. The conflict between monetarists and antimonetarists was beginning to take shape. Because the leading French economists were either theoretical antimonetarists or practical inflationists, they have been either severely castigated or relegated to oblivion in British and American studies of the financial and monetary history of the 1920s.

Table 1. British and French paper currency circulation, 1913, 1918–1923 (£ million, fr. billion).

	1913	1918	1919	1920	1921	1922	1923
U.K.	29.60	302.00	423.00	458.00	436.00	400.00	389.00
France	5.71	30.24	37.27	37.55	36.41	35.95	37.76

Source: E. V. Morgan, *Studies in British Financial Policy, 1914–1925* (London: Macmillan, 1952), p. 222; France, Institut national de la statistique, Service d'études économiques et financières, Statistique et études financières, Supplément no. 175, *Supplément rétrospectif 1900 à 1930* (Paris: Imprimerie Nationale, July 1963), p. 1003. French figures are for December, U.K. figures are for June of each year.

The quantity theory of money is an early version of monetarist theory, which attempts to define conditions under which changes in the supply of money lead to proportional changes in the nominal value of such variables as income, prices, wages, and exchange rates, while leaving real magnitudes unchanged. Swedish economist Gustav Cassel emerged in the 1920s as one of the most vocal proponents of the quantity theory, on which he based his exchange theory of purchasing power parity. Cassel drew a causal connection which began with a change in money supply that produced a change in price levels, and ultimately affected exchange rates. He believed the fundamental cause of postwar price increases and exchange depreciation was the drastic increase in the money supply. Treasury and central bank authorities evaded their responsibility by attributing rising prices and declining purchasing power to profiteering middlemen and speculators rather than to their own policies.[2]

During the early 1920s, prominent economists such as Keynes and Yale University's Irving Fisher accepted the basic notion of the quantity theory and most of the implications for prices and exchange that Cassel derived from it. In his *Monetary Reform* (1923), Keynes endorsed the quantity theory in his cash balances approach to the determination of the value of money. "This theory," asserted Keynes, "is fundamental. Its correspondence with fact is not open to question." The problem, argued Keynes, lay with those he termed the "careless adherents" of the quantity theory, who assumed that an arbitrary doubling of cash in circulation must raise the price of consumption units to double what it would have been otherwise. They assumed an overly simplistic relationship between money supply and price levels. In the long run, admitted Keynes, such a relationship is probably correct, but the long run is a misleading guide to current affairs. "In the long run," observed Keynes, "we are all dead." The "old fashioned advocates of sound money," he thought, placed too much emphasis on holding the money supply and bank reserves steady in order to maintain price stability. More critical than the total money supply, he believed, was the amount of cash and bank deposits actually held by the public.[3]

American and French critics of the British-backed quantity theory of money and its offshoot theory of purchasing power parity pointed out the difficulty in distinguishing between causal relationships and merely chronological relationships, and argued that causes and effects were often reciprocal and intricately related. Empirical studies, moreover, often demonstrated causal relationships quite different from those claimed by proponents of the quantity theory.

Of the members of the wartime financial entente, the French took the heaviest criticism for their inflationary monetary policies. It is thus significant that French economists were among the staunchest critics of the quantity theory of money. The sharpest French opponent of the quantity theory, an economist of some stature, was Bertrand Nogaro. Nogaro was a professor at the University of Paris, a member of the Chamber of Deputies, and former minister of public edu-

Table 2. British and French wholesale prices, 1919–1923 (average of 1913 = 100).

	U.K.	France
January 1919	227	—
June 1919	234	—
January 1920	305	447
June 1920	339	535
January 1921	244	414
June 1921	197	333
January 1922	170	306
June 1922	169	325
January 1923	167	346
June 1923	171	394

Source: E. V. Morgan, *Studies in British Financial Policy, 1914–1925* (London: Macmillan, 1952), pp. 362–363. Morgan uses Federal Reserve Board indices.

cation. His work, nevertheless, "has quite failed to attract general attention of any sort in France, favorable or unfavorable," and still less abroad. This despite the fact that one American analyst believed Nogaro had produced "the most convincing and far-reaching attack on the English position of which I know."[4]

This was probably Nogaro's problem—he had dared to attack the entire English classical doctrine of money and international trade. The classical theory, he maintained, was inadequate in normal times no less than during the postwar crisis; the quantity theory had never provided a plausible explanation of cause-effect relationships. Credit expansion, usually considered an inflationary move, could produce a decline in prices if the credit was utilized to increase productivity. Efforts by Cassel and others to establish a causal sequence of monetary inflation, price increases, and the movement of exchanges failed. They were simply caught up in a tautology, Nogaro argued. A rise in the price level and monetary depreciation are synonymous—one does not "cause" the other.[5]

Acceptance or rejection of the quantity theory of money implied significant policy decisions. Keynes believed a correct understanding of the quantity theory demonstrated the need for central bank control over *all* factors in his cash balances equation—currency and bank deposits held by the public, cash reserves kept by the banks, and the amount of cash in circulation. Benjamin Strong, governor of the Federal Reserve Bank of New York, rejected the quantity theory held by the head of his own bank's statistical department, Carl Snyder. The governor suggested that Snyder's statistical charts presented an empirical rather than an analytical picture of the situation. That is to say, statistics on money supply and price fluctuations did not necessarily indicate a cause-effect relationship. As he wrote to Montagu Norman in 1921, "We have struggled for some years with the views of those who rather slavishly stick to the quantity theory of money, assuming that it explained all of our financial and economic ills, and that an increase in bank loans and currency is the inevitable cause of higher prices, but are unwilling to accept the view that sometimes bank loans and currency expand in response to advances in prices, which arise from other causes than the 'quantity' of money or credit."[6] Strong implied that it might be impossible to control prices simply through manipulation of the money supply. Deflation of the money supply might merely create a recession with relatively high price levels. The "dear money" policy pursued by British monetary authorities during 1920 produced such a situation.

Behind the controversy over the quantity theory of money lay another fundamental problem. Financiers and "experts" who hardly understood what money and credit were under the new inconvertible paper money system could not be expected to grasp the implications of expansion and contraction of the money supply. Contrary to widespread belief, this kind of ignorance was not confined to France's financial leadership. Testimony before Britain's Parliamentary Committee on Currency and Foreign Exchanges after the War, chaired by the former governor of the Bank of England, Lord Cunliffe, indicated confusion among British bankers on the nature and function of currency and credit. The Committee recommended reduction of the fiduciary issue with a view to the return to an effective gold standard. How this could be achieved was unclear. The City's understanding of modern currency and credit systems was questionable at best. Bankers appeared confused about the technical operation of the banking system, and uncertain about the relationship between credit and currency supply. Those who advocated a reduction in the supply of currency notes often advanced simplistic schemes for achieving that end.

Brien Cokayne, who had succeeded Cunliffe as governor of the Bank of England, favored a plan similar to the François-Marsal Convention later adopted in France, under which the British Treasury would hand over to the Bank of England each year a specified amount of currency to be "canceled." Cokayne was vague on the mechanism for cancellation of currency, but the chairman of the London Joint City and Midland Bank, Sir Edward Holden, supplied the Committee with a detailed account of how to withdraw "surplus" currency from circulation. The exchange between Holden and Cunliffe reveals what one might call "the state of the art" of British banking in 1918. Though he did not advocate a return to the circulation of gold coin, Holden proposed to convert the currency note into a gold note, which would require a large reservoir of gold equal to the amount of currency notes in circulation. He did not explain where the Bank of England would obtain such a mass of gold, but indicated the problem could be managed because "after the war, you will not keep out in circulation the present amount of currency notes."

HOLDEN: These currency notes will gradually begin to come back. As the shopkeeper, the merchant and the manufacturer get credit, there will not be the same necessity for the currency note, which will begin to be paid into the joint stock banks all over the country. It will then find itself in the reserves of the joint stock banks in London, and the banks will pay it into the Bank of England for payment by the Government. That is how the surplus currency notes will come in from circulation after the war.

CUNLIFFE: When you get the currency notes in from the trader, will you not in order to foster trade have to lend them to another?

HOLDEN: You do not lend the currency notes to the traders or to the manufacturers. You allow them to credit a debit balance with you.

CUNLIFFE: At bottom is not that the same thing? Does it not really amount to the same whether it is a currency note or a cheque?

HOLDEN: If you look upon the currency note as a reserve upon which you are going to loan, then of course it is a very important factor. Loans are now made on the basis of the reserve, whatever those reserves may be—gold, Bank of England notes, currency notes, or a balance at the Bank of England.

CUNLIFFE: I do not quite follow; if you are not going to restrict credit, how are you going to reduce either your currency notes, or your circulation of gold, or your cheque circulation?

HOLDEN: If you give more credit there will be less necessity for the currency note. Supposing a shopkeeper can get credit from his merchant, then he will begin to draw his cheque, and he will not use his currency note. He is compelled now to use his currency note because he could not get the credit which he has hitherto enjoyed. Has your tailor not told you that you must pay cash in the future instead of getting credit for your clothes?

CUNLIFFE: In the end you have got to pay for your clothes. You may get three months' credit, and some people get three years, but it comes to the same in the end.

HOLDEN: The shopkeeper will not give you credit. If you pay your shopkeeper cash, if you give him a cheque, he will use that cheque through his banking account. If you do not pay your bill for three months, and his merchant tells him that he will not give him credit but he must pay cash, what has he got to do? He has had his credit withdrawn from him and the currency note has had to take its place. Now give him credit again, and let the merchant give him credit again, and he will go on as before and the currency note circulation will be curtailed. I may be wrong, but that is my reasoning of it.

CUNLIFFE: Of course, I agree. The cash you pay your tailor goes in wages, and the tailor has got to get currency in some form, either gold or notes, from his banker in order to pay these wages. At the present moment of the currency notes (which you see are increasing week by week)—far the greater portion of them—go to the dockyards, the munitions workers, and those people; but where they all go to I am sure I do not know.

HOLDEN: It is a mystery to me where they all go, but there they are, and I am assured that it is a genuine circulation.[7]

It is less than reassuring to see two of England's leading bankers groping for an understanding of currency and credit, and remaining to the end mystified as to where all the currency notes went. Sir Walter Leaf, president of the London County Westminster and Parr's Bank, appeared to have a more sophisticated grasp of the subject. He told the Cunliffe Committee that to cancel and destroy currency notes as they came in was impossible, as the British had to pay their debts with something. Cancellation of notes by the Bank of England would not be an automatic process. It could only be done by calling upon debtors to pay up, and until they were in a position to do so the cancellation could not be carried out. Currency notes could be canceled, thought Leaf, only if the government ceased its borrowing, balanced its budget, and provided a sinking fund for the reduction of public debt.[8] Where Leaf attributed postwar credit expansion to a profligate government, Robert H. Benson, senior partner of Robert Benson & Co., London merchant bankers, pointed the finger at private bankers who were not performing their function of rationing credit. "It is the duty of the bankers to teach their customers to sell and repent," opined Benson.[9]

Britain's bankers opposed the Bank's attempts to raise money rates, fearing such action would put a premature end to the postwar boom. The bankers themselves refused to ration credit for fear their customers would simply take their business elsewhere. The City's great bankers agreed to a man that the demand for credit was legitimate, and that raising interest rates and placing arbitrary limits on currency circulation was either ineffective or dangerous. Leaf warned that arbitrary controls and limitations were "like trying to cure a fever by plugging your clinical thermometer at 'normal'; the only result would be that you will burst your thermometer."[10]

As Britain's postwar boom threatened to run wild, Chancellor of the Exchequer Austen Chamberlain summoned on 9 and 10 March 1920 representatives of every major bank in the City, as well as Cokayne and Norman from the Bank of England. The bankers refused either to support the chancellor's bid for higher money rates or to limit their own lending. The bankers would stop lending only if the Bank should undertake no further advances to the government. Cokayne replied that the Bank could not refuse to lend funds on approved government securities.[11] By now, everyone at the Treasury, including Chamberlain, Basil Blackett (controller of finance), Otto Niemeyer (principal assistant secretary), and R. G. Hawtrey (director of financial enquiries) agreed with the Bank that only a most stringent "dear money policy" would cool the economy. For Blackett, the critical factor in a tight money policy was consistency, for "once the community realizes that a high rate policy is being unswervingly pursued, the change from rising prices to falling prices will be a sudden one."[12]

Keynes shared these views on the necessity for a tight money policy. In a personal meeting with Chamberlain, he argued that continuing high rates of inflation posed a threat to the "whole basis of contract, of security, and of the capitalist system generally." He suggested, according to Chamberlain's notes on the meeting, "whatever rate is necessary—perhaps 10 percent—and keep it at that for three years." Such a high rate, he believed, might produce "a crisis," but since industry already had far more orders than it could fill, little if any unemployment would result.[13]

On 15 April 1920, Bank rate rose to 7 percent, where it remained for nearly a year. Virtually the entire British banking community blamed the Bank and the Treasury for the commercial stagnation and unprecedented levels of unemployment which followed. By 1922, bankers such as Reginald McKenna (wartime chancellor of the exchequer and now chairman of London Joint City and Midland Bank) argued for reduction of Bank rate, and some went so far as to favor outright inflation of the money supply. McKenna feared Britain was about to enter a treadmill of alternating inflation and deflation, "a regular alternation between the two policies, each to be adopted in turn as a remedy for the other." Both policies were bad for the nation, warned McKenna. Monetary inflation brought high prices, and deflation brought unemployment. It was no coincidence, he observed, that the highest unemployment rates were found in the two countries which had recently pursued deflationary policies, the United States and the United Kingdom.[14]

Six years later, in 1928, McKenna's staunchest supporter turned out to be J. M. Keynes, the same Keynes who had advocated 10 percent money rates in 1920 as a means of breaking the back of inflation. McKenna, explained Keynes, had made an astute distinction between two wholly different types of inflation. First, there were what McKenna termed "periods of speculative inflation," when prices have risen out of proportion to wages. In such instances, exceptionally high profits, stimulated by excessive expansion of bank loans, encourage excessive production. To deal with this type of inflation, the Bank rightfully, and successfully, may have recourse to the traditional remedies: raising the discount rate and restricting credit. But there was a second type of inflation. This was the inflation left as a legacy of the war, characterized by a parallel rise in wages and prices in such a manner that profits do not become excessive.

For this new type of inflation, argued McKenna and Keynes, the classic cure was not only ineffective but disastrous. In the nonclassic type of inflation the credit squeeze simply forced industry to give up its less profitable operations, thereby creating more unemployment. Ultimately, the credit squeeze contributed to the failure of industries facing ever-shrinking profit margins owing to foreign competition or high wages. Such industries must either produce at a loss, or try to force their workers to accept lower wages. Generally, they end up doing both.

By 1928, Keynes could announce that the Bank had succeeded in half of its task—increasing unemployment. But the other half, forcing labor (through unemployment) to accept lower wages, proved nearly impossible in a postwar world where organized labor resisted such pressure. Keynes believed that the ongoing struggle between organized labor and the official deflationary policy of the Bank and the Treasury explained why the period of economic stagnation and high unemployment had lasted so long in Britain. Many had now come to recognize, wrote Keynes, that it would have been much wiser to stabilize prices and wages at a higher level, and thus avoid the commercial losses, unemployment, and heavy surcharge on the public debt.[15]

As the financial community turned increasingly on the Treasury and the Bank as the cause of the slump, Treasury officials, particularly Niemeyer, blamed the workers for causing their own unemployment by producing less and demanding unrealistically high wages. He proposed to cut unemployment benefits to "the barest minimum needed to prevent starvation." Large payments to the unemployed, he argued, would produce "vehement hostility by the mass of those on whom the Exchequer depends for support of its present and imminent debt maturities." Britain's savers and lenders would not purchase government securities to support workers unemployed by their own greed.[16]

Ultimately the government was forced to act; the Treasury reduced bill rates, and Norman followed suit by reducing Bank rate to 6.5 percent on 28 April 1921. "Financially," he told Strong, "such a change can hardly be justified." Why, then, did he do it? Only because the Treasury had reduced bill rates, and "whether the Treasury was right or wrong in reducing their rate last month, it is essential that the Bank and the Treasury should work together. Rather than one do what is absolutely right and the other perhaps what is wrong, we had both better stand together and together do what is perhaps wrong."[17] In Norman's conception of sound monetary and financial policy, cooperation was the central notion—cooperation between the bank and the Treasury, and cooperation between central banks on both sides of the Atlantic.

Governor of the Bank Cokayne had proposed to Chancellor of the Exchequer Chamberlain in July 1919 that "power to control the market should at once be restored to the bank."[18] The easing of interest rates in 1921–22 seemed to represent a setback for the Bank, but it was in fact merely a pause in the Bank's drive to rejoin the gold standard at prewar parity. In 1925, Norman triumphed. In France, on the other hand, talk of returning to gold at prewar parity was simply irrational in the early postwar years, given the condition of the French economy and the depreciation of the franc. Yet, many French economists and politicians held views more deflationist than those of their British counterparts. The fact that implementation of French deflationary policy fell short of the results achieved in Britain should not mask the more radical intent of an important segment of France's financial leadership.

The goal in France was to reduce sharply or eliminate entirely the use of paper currency in France. The government would repay advances made by the Bank of France, and the Bank in turn would burn the notes returned by the government. Some suggested that the Bank buy back its notes with the gold held in its vaults. The Bank would be left with "a little less gold," but there would be "a lot less notes."[19] A few prominent French economists, including Charles Gide, Charles Rist, and C. J. Gignoux, and the British economist R. G. Hawtrey, dissented from the conventional wisdom on deflation. Gide pointed to the stimulative effects of monetary inflation. The resulting price inflation "acts like a tonic; it is a symptom of good economic health." A sharp decline in French prices would affect the French economy like a "cold shower."[20]

Gignoux calculated that an annual reduction of the note circulation by 2 billion francs for the next ten years would be required to reestablish the prewar ratio between the Bank's gold reserve and the fiduciary issue. Given French commercial requirements, price levels, and levels of bank deposits, such a deflationary program could produce only "catastrophe."[21] Rist considered a return to prewar parities as unrealistic for the United States, Britain, and France. If France wished to return to a gold standard, it could not hope to achieve the level of deflation required for prewar parity simply by reducing note circulation through repayment of Bank advances. France would have to accept an "irreducible residue of inflation" and return to gold at a new parity.[22] Rist's views, as we shall see, coincided with those of Keynes.

Another British economist, Hawtrey, added his voice to those arguing against a radical French deflation. During the 1920–21 recession, the purchasing power of the franc had doubled without provoking a French crisis comparable to those in Britain and the United States. Hawtrey pointed out that it was the high level of government spending on reconstruction that had prevented French business failures on the scale experienced in Britain. But some were convinced that if the franc's purchasing power had doubled once, perhaps it could do so again and permit the stabilization of the franc at prewar parity. Hawtrey dismissed such a goal as theoretically possible but politically suicidal. As prices declined, the resulting unemployment and growth of the debt burden would become intolerable.[23]

The deflationist viewpoint prevailed and resulted in the so-called François-Marsal Convention between the Bank of France and the Finance Ministry in April 1920. The agreement obligated the Finance Ministry to reimburse the Bank 2 billion francs at the end of each year. In substance, this Convention emulated the policy recommended for Britain in the Cunliffe Committee report. French intentions, on the whole, resembled those of the British, but the practical results were quite different. The Finance Ministry intended to combine the repayment of Bank advances with the creation of new taxes to cover expenditures in the "ordinary" budget. As for the "extraordinary" budget of war-connected expenditures, the government was pledged to keep such payments within limits which could be met by borrowing real savings from the French public, without further recourse to the Bank of France.[24]

These pledges were not kept, and the government finally had to claim that the budget could not be balanced without German reparation payments. Nor could the French Finance Ministry meet its obligation under the François-Marsal Convention, owing to the immensity of the public debt and the demands of reconstruction. The Treasury made an initial full payment to the Bank, but was unable to do so in subsequent years. Note circulation rose and eventually forced parliament to raise the legal limit. France avoided financial catastrophe for a time by ignoring the François-Marsal Convention.

Financial leadership in both Britain and France was virtually unanimous in recommending stabilization of the exchanges and a return to gold as the ultimate cure for Europe's economic crisis. Norman's biographer, Andrew Boyle, did not exaggerate when he commented that "anyone rash enough to have advocated a different course might well have been locked up and certified as insane."[25] Only the process through which stabilization was to be achieved (deflation or devaluation), the precise level at which each currency should be stabilized (prewar gold parity or a new parity), and the precise form the resurrected gold standard should assume were at issue. These questions involved not only monetary theory, but also the concepts of justice, honor, and national prestige. On such basic issues no one was willing to compromise. The French, as usual, appeared most intransigent on these matters.

Why Europe's financial leadership so revered the gold standard is a complex question. Both ethical and practical considerations played a role in the drive to reconstruct an international gold standard. Norman considered the gold standard as both a test of the nation's financial strength and "also a mystical symbol of all that was finest

Table 3. Pound sterling and French franc currency fluctuation, 1914, 1919–1923.

	$ per £	fr. per £	fr. per $
August 1914	4.86	25.22	5.18
January 1919	4.76	25.99	5.45
June 1919	4.61	29.78	6.38
January 1920	3.51	46.55	11.74
June 1920	3.96	48.42	12.62
January 1921	3.87	54.80	15.77
June 1921	3.75	46.75	12.40
January 1922	4.23	51.80	12.25
June 1922	4.41	52.82	11.46
January 1923	4.65	85.00	14.98
June 1923	4.58	75.30	15.88
December 1923	4.33	84.85	19.02

Source: E. V. Morgan, *Studies in British Financial Policy, 1914–1925* (London: Macmillan, 1952), pp. 349–353; Alfred Sauvy, *Histoire économique de la France entre les deux guerres*, 4 vols. (Paris: Fayard, 1965–75), I, 445; France, Institut national de la statistique, Service d'études économiques et financières, Statistiques et études financières, Supplément no. 175, *Supplément rétrospectif 1900 à 1930* (Paris: Imprimerie Nationale, July 1963), p. 1007.

in the struggle of mankind to better its lot on earth." Countries on the gold standard were bearers of a superior civilization. To the leader of Britain's Sound Money Association, D. M. Mason, the nation's moral fiber was in question; Britain could take "the easier and less courageous course" of inflation or devaluation, or the "painful and costly" choice of returning to gold. Many Frenchmen agreed that "a difficult but honest conversion at par" was "the only honorable way to escape from the régime of paper money." Finally, there were many who believed the international financial and monetary system was too delicate an instrument to be left in the hands of mere humans. They sought to restore the system to the "automatic" control of the gold standard, for "if the gold standard is abandoned, the standard of value will be turned into an absurdity, at the mercy of politicians or financiers, and society would be turned upside down."[26]

Europe's postwar exchange problem was in reality two problems. Short-term violent *fluctuations* disrupted the exchanges and long-term *depreciation* ruined European currencies. In the absence of a gold standard, economists could form no consensus on the cause and effect relationships governing foreign exchange. Some experts emphasized monetary inflation and higher price levels, others stressed Europe's unprecedented import surplus as the culprit disrupting the exchanges. There was also the ever-present burden of inter-Allied debt in the dangerous form of sight obligations, and the uncertainty of German reparation payments. Another popular villain in the exchange crisis was the speculator. Speculation presumably rested on the state of mind of the money traders—their confidence in the currencies they traded—and this notion opened the way to a psychological theory of exchange popular among French economists. Keynes and Cassel, however, argued that financial authorities (particularly the French) had attempted to use all of these extraneous factors as scapegoats for their own misguided inflationary monetary policies.[27]

In his 1944 study, *International Currency Experience: Lessons of the Inter-War Period*, Ragnar Nurkse identified the war-caused shortage of working capital in Europe as the source of currency fluctuation and depreciation. This capital shortage produced heavy import surpluses and movements of capital. Government-induced inflation was in Nurkse's opinion not the critical factor in the exchange problem. He argued that while maintenance of stable exchanges "presupposes an appropriate domestic credit policy or at any rate sets certain limits to the freedom of domestic credit policy," domestic credit policy alone is not a sufficient means of assuring exchange stability. There must be some form of direct stabilization through official purchases and sales of currency.[28]

Postwar currency depreciation ranged from moderate (Britain) to severe (France) to total collapse (Germany and Austria). No prewar theory of exchange accounted for these phenomena. The most widely discussed postwar exchange theory was Cassel's purchasing power parity theory. Starting from the quantity theory of money, Cassel derived a basic rule of exchange rates: "When two countries have undergone inflation, the normal rate of exchange will be equal to the old rate multiplied by the quotient between the degrees of inflation in both countries."[29] Cassel believed the rate calculated by this method must be regarded as the new parity between two currencies, the balance point toward which the exchange rate will always tend despite temporary fluctuations. This parity Cassel called the purchasing power parity. Criticism of Cassel's theory centered on empirical studies which proved that actual exchange rates were either higher or lower than they ought to have been under Cassel's formula. But the underlying, generally unspoken objection to the purchasing power theory probably had nothing to do with technical difficulties in matching theory and fact. "Sound money" advocates rejected Cassel's scheme because it sanctioned a system of moving exchange rates, rather than rates eternally fixed in concrete under the prewar gold standard. Stabilization under Cassel's system would not necessarily fix the pound sterling at $4.86, or at any other particular rate. However defensible Cassel's ideas may have been theoretically, they did not meet the emotional requirements of Europe's financial leadership during the 1920s.

To establish conditions for a return to the gold standard, some economists suggested either lowering the general level of prices to stretch the available supply of gold, or changing the general opinion of what constituted an adequate gold reserve for paper currencies. Cassel rejected price reduction (deflation) and its side-effects of recession and high unemployment. Europe, he believed, would have to accept inflated postwar price levels and adjust (economize) its monetary demand for gold to those high levels. The return to a gold standard might unleash competition for the world's existing stock of gold as central banks sought to shore up their reserves. To prevent such disastrous competition, central banks would have to cooperate in the "rational regulation" of the monetary demand for gold. It was, after all, the quantity of currency in circulation, not its gold backing, which determined the value of that currency. Cassel remained optimistic that "just as the public has been taught that gold cover ought to reach 50 percent, it can be taught that 25 percent is enough."[30]

Hawtrey followed Cassel in calling for international agreements to economize the use of gold. Because the United States and Britain controlled a large portion of the world gold stock, an agreement between those two countries "would be almost sufficient by itself." An Anglo-American convention on gold which extended to controls on note issue and credit, Hawtrey believed, would provide a standard more trustworthy than the prewar gold standard. He recognized, however, that strongly divergent national interests militated against an effective international gold agreement. Debtor nations had an interest in holding down the value of gold, while creditor nations might wish to enhance the value of the medium in which the debts were to be paid.[31]

The creditor nation Hawtrey, Cassel, and Keynes had in mind was the ultimate creditor, the United States. Under a gold standard, the United States could use its massive gold stocks to influence price levels and the value of the currency of every other gold standard country. Neither Keynes nor Cassel placed much confidence in the competence or sense of responsibility of the Federal Reserve Board. Keynes counseled Britain against surrendering control over its price levels and handling of the credit cycle to American monetary authorities who were "still liable to be overwhelmed by the impetuosity of a cheap money campaign." Cassel charged the Federal Reserve Board with an "arbitrary reduction of prices" in 1920–21 which disrupted Europe's attempts to stabilize. Keynes regarded the gold standard as a "barbarous relic," and believed a scientific system of "managed currency" was inevitable. But the science had yet to develop to the point at which management could be entrusted to a single authority. "The best we can do, therefore," he wrote, "is to have *two* managed currencies, sterling and dollars, with as close a collaboration as possible between the aims and methods of the managements."[32]

As Nurkse pointed out, when a de facto gold exchange standard finally emerged in the late 1920s, there were in fact two "centre countries," the United States and Britain. Nurkse considered divided responsibility "a special source of weakness" because it required a level of cooperation between central banks that did not exist during the postwar era.[33] London wished to regain its position as the world's financial center, and New York sought to preserve the advantages it had gained during the war. Jules Décamps, an economist at the Bank of France, viewed his country as the unfortunate victim caught in a crossfire involving the "rivalry of the two exchanges," sterling and the dollar.[34]

Out of the search for a way back to the gold standard under the necessity of economizing gold emerged the gold-exchange standard of the latter half of the 1920s. This was an exchange reserve system designed to stabilize exchange rates as under the gold standard, but the means of settlement and the international monetary reserves were currencies that were on the gold standard rather than gold itself. The dollar and the pound sterling became the "reserve currencies" because only the United States and Britain appeared capable of maintaining their currencies on a gold standard when the gold-exchange standard was being discussed between 1922 and 1925. Central banks would hold dollar and sterling reserves in addition to or in place of traditional gold reserves. The money supply of each country participating in the system would thus be determined in part by the policies of American and British monetary authorities. It is not surprising that British economists, notably Keynes, formed the vanguard of those advocating the gold-exchange standard during the early 1920s.[35]

Urged on by Keynes and Montagu Norman, the 1922 Genoa economic and financial conference adopted resolutions recommending establishment of a gold-exchange standard and the devaluation of weak currencies. France, Italy, and Belgium did not concur in those resolutions. Keynes, Cassel, and Hawtrey agreed that all currencies should become exchangeable against gold as soon as possible. The main roadblock was argument over the value at which each currency ought to be stabilized. These three economists shared the belief that monetary authorities had confused the problem of *fixing* the relative value of monies with the problem of *raising* the absolute value of certain national currencies. The aim of improving an exchange destroyed any hope for stabilization, since it amounted to a deliberate policy of altering the exchanges. Keynes, Cassel, and Hawtrey argued that "it is more important to fix the exchanges than to improve them."[36]

The international commerce on which Britain's economy so heavily depended could not be revived if stabilization were delayed by nations hoping that fluctuations would tend to move upward. Keynes and Cassel believed only Britain, Holland, Sweden, Switzerland, and possibly Spain could reasonably hope to restore prewar parity anytime soon. Other nations were advised to fix the gold value of their currencies at a lower level which could be maintained comfortably. For countries such as France, this meant devaluation. "It would," claimed Keynes, "make small difference to the financial prestige of France whether the franc was stabilized at 40 or 50 to the gold sovereign." For Germany, Keynes observed that "it is of no consequence to [international merchants] whether the dollar is worth five marks or fifty marks, provided the figure is always the same and is known beforehand."[37] From a strictly international (meaning British) point of view, Keynes may have been technically correct, but to the French and Germans it *did* matter whether a franc or a mark was worth more or less.

It is difficult to avoid the conclusion that the gold-exchange standard was at least in part a scheme devised to restore Anglo-American hegemony over the international financial system. For Britain, devaluation was unthinkable, but for the French it was a reasonable step which would in no way affect national prestige. The fate of the franc would be tied to British and American monetary policies, but that, too, should not bother the French. The French, however, refused to place themselves in the same league with the Netherlands Indies, Argentina, and Brazil, countries which had adopted schemes similar to that suggested by the British at Genoa. Through Anglo-Saxon eyes, the French now appeared aggressive and intransigent.

Anglo-Saxon critics attributed France's exchange problems as much to political deficiencies as to misguided monetary policies. France was viewed as politically reactionary and warlike in its foreign policy. In speaking of France, Keynes referred to "the finances of Humpty Dumpty" and "the home of absolutism of all kinds, and hence, sooner or later, of *boulversement*."[38] Lord Hardinge, Britain's ambassador in Paris, hoped the fall of the franc would have a salutary effect on French foreign policy. The exchange dislocation might impress upon the French the fact that "unless confidence in the soundness of French foreign policy is restored in the world, the phenomenon of the 'flight from the mark' will be repeated in the case of the franc."[39] A plummeting franc might force the French to adopt a more "reasonable" foreign policy.

From Auckland Geddes, the British ambassador in Washington, the message was identical. Morgan partner Thomas W. Lamont told Geddes that in response to a query from French Finance Minister Charles de Lasteyrie concerning the sharp decline of the franc in New York, he had placed the cause bluntly on "the present trend of the foreign and fiscal policy of France." France, according to Lamont, could expect no improvement in the franc exchange "until her foreign policy became less aggressive in character and until some more serious attempt was made to balance the French budget."[40]

Peace and disarmament stood out as critical prerequisites for monetary rehabilitation, and in the Anglo-Saxon view, it was the French rather than the Germans who stood in the way. Germany's half-hearted attempts to pay reparations raised havoc with all European exchanges. As the Germans converted any foreign exchange they held (sterling and francs) into dollars, those currencies fluctuated wildly. This latest disruption of the European monetary system provoked from Cassel a violent outcry against "the victors," "the countries claiming reparations"—in other words, France. Germany's forced currency sales had "degenerated into an absolute swindle" made necessary by the victors' "unreasonable demands." "It is time," he proclaimed, "that the world learnt to see through all this business, and no longer allowed itself in this way to be sucked dry for the benefit of the countries claiming reparations."[41]

French resistance to the gold-exchange standard was not rooted in aggressive intransigence, nor was it founded upon ignorance of the theoretical and technical operation of such a system. In fact, two important French economists, Nogaro and Décamps, accepted in principle the gold-exchange standard. Décamps termed it a "rational and simple" system, France's only hope for returning to a gold standard. With the exception of the absence of an internal gold circulation, the new system would function in the same manner as the prewar gold standard. Nogaro believed the gold-exchange standard was a simpler, more logical alternative to the less desirable alternatives of either devaluation or waiting for the franc to improve to prewar parity. Only the public's ignorance of how it would work, he thought, prevented its acceptance in France.[42]

Most French opponents could point to strong technical grounds for their reservations concerning the gold-exchange standard. The system was recommended for countries with weak currencies, but it was difficult to see how it could work for any but the strongest economies. François-Marsal observed that countries with a steadily adverse balance of international payments might lose both their gold and their reserve currencies quite rapidly. And if devaluation of the franc were involved, the French public would never believe that the first devaluation would be the last. Financial panic would ensue. Ironically, François-Marsal's argument for the franc was precisely Hawtrey's argument against devaluation of the British pound. "If its gold value were changed once," warned Hawtrey, "it might be changed again. A return despite difficulties to the former parity [$4.86] is a pledge of stability."[43]

François-Marsal and Germain Martin ruled out any franc stabilization scheme that did not include as prerequisites a balanced budget, reduction of fiduciary circulation, increase in the gold reserve, repayment of Bank advances to the state, and the funding of 64 billion francs in National Defense Bonds for which the public could demand notes at any time. All of these measures were consistent with the best Anglo-Saxon sound money theory of the day, and all were clearly beyond the reach of France prior to 1925.[44]

French financiers believed as firmly in sound money as did their English counterparts. But they also believed in honor and justice. Former Finance Minister Joseph Caillaux prophesied that "the peoples will never agree to a formula of devaluation of their currency. They will prefer bankruptcy to the acknowledgement of their insolvency." This may be bad economics, Caillaux admitted, but "no economic solution is valid when it is not on the same plane with public opinion."[45] Most French economists agreed that conversion at a rate below prewar parity amounted to "partial bankruptcy" and represented an "abnormal way" to convert. Devaluation represented a "grave attack on the principle of fixity and inviolability of the monetary unit, the basis of any sound money."[46] All borrowers, including the state, were obligated to repay the full value of the money borrowed. Devaluation, as François-Marsal observed, presented a moral question, "the execution of obligations freely consented to."[47]

The few French economists who recognized the desirability of devaluation always found such a measure premature. These moderates were attacked by inflexible defenders of the franc who labeled devaluation "criminal" rather than premature. Radical opponents of devaluation were not confined to France. Gerard Vissering, president of the Netherlands Bank, described devalued money as "a wild growth, a weed which has spread with alarming rapidity." Because devaluation was such a humiliating experience, "any state of any importance with a sense of honor will only accept such a solution in case of extreme emergency."[48] No major European state admitted to being in such a state of emergency. The French maintained that "the depreciation of the franc is recent and imputable to an accidental cause."[49] This was merely another way of saying that a permanent devaluation was an inappropriate cure for a temporary, accidental disease—the Germans had caused the problem and it was they who ought to straighten it out.

Anglo-Saxon economists shared the French concern for monetary justice and honor, but they held different notions as to how these ideals could be achieved. Yale economist Irving Fisher, for example, pointed out in 1922 that most old contracts were no longer in force; they had already been executed. "The injustice in their execution," he wrote, "has been done and can never be undone." Europe must rest content with "securing justice only where justice can still be secured." Using such an approach would convince most countries that devaluation is both practical and just. Countries with depreciated currencies would simply have to recognize that "bygones must be bygones."[50] Fisher's political acumen clearly did not match his expertise as an economist.

Preoccupation with prewar parities postponed Europe's financial and monetary reconstruction and perpetuated a very dangerous situation. From his vantage point of 1970 Lord Robbins conjectured, "How much difficulty would have been avoided, how much unemployment and loss of product might have been spared, if those who advised us had banished from their minds the nonsense about making the pound look the dollar in the face and stabilized at a lower level. The whole history of the world would have been different."[51]

Perhaps early stabilization at a realistic level would not have changed the history of the world. But as Keynes warned, those who resisted stabilization, because it might mean devaluation, were playing a very dangerous game. Europe's bankers shrank from the risks of every proposed stabilization scheme; but the real risk lay in the ongoing failure to place Europe's monetary system under some control. Keynes warned that any "profound modification" of Europe's social and economic structure would most likely emanate not from the doctrines of Marx or the intrigues of labor, but from "the timid and shortsighted ways and stupid heads of its own conservative leaders."[52] In the matter of exchange stabilization, both Britain and France adopted a policy of waiting *(politique d'attente)* in hopes that their respective exchanges would improve. To do nothing, as Keynes argued, might have been the most dangerous policy of all. The waiting game dealt a near-fatal blow to capitalism.

3

Balancing the Budget

Knowing that for direct taxation the ruling principle of this
country is taxation by reference to ability to pay, those who
had command of wealth undertook to lay themselves under
tribute year by year to bear the burden of interest. It amounts
to some £350,000,000 every year.
                                            —Sir Robert Horne,
                              chancellor of the exchequer, 1922

FOUR YEARS OF TOTAL WAR left its legacy in the form of the deficit.
Enormous deficits could be found everywhere—in the production/
consumption ratio, in the external balances of trade and payments,
and in national budgets. Europe's first task was to eliminate these
deficits, and the national budget appeared to be the logical place to
begin. Governments, which had become the largest consumers, could
exercise direct control over expenditures and taxation. Balancing the
budget thus became a major issue in Britain and France as soon as
the Armistice was signed.

In an age of tax revolts and demands for constitutional amendments requiring balanced budgets, one must discard the notion of
fiscal and taxation policy as mere technical matters best left to the
experts. Budget-balancing and tax reform imply some fundamental
questions of social philosophy, political expediency, and national
security. In 1918, these questions stood out clearly. Who should pay
for the war? The Germans who had caused it, the Americans who
had grown wealthy on it, or the Allies who had suffered most from
it? Should the costs be borne by the present generation which had
fought and suffered (taxation), or by the future generations which
would benefit from a world made safe for democracy (borrowing)?
Did social justice require that the burden be shifted from the poor
(indirect taxation) to the rich (direct taxation)? Should the capitalists pay for the war through a levy on capital, or should the working

class pay by working harder, producing more, and foregoing the "land fit for heroes"?

Should countries that had handled wartime finance wisely and responsibly (Britain and the United States) be asked to assume additional fiscal burdens for countries that had not (France)? In an era when the French could see nothing but Germans threatening on the Rhine and the British saw peace through appeasement, how far could military expenditures be reduced? If the British and French governments were slow to develop a coherent postwar taxation and budget policy, it was not owing to ignorance of modern fiscal and monetary principles. Fiscal and taxation policy had to satisfy a very complex set of political, social, and national security demands that emerged after the war.

The Armistice ushered in a period of stock-taking and reflection on wartime finance. Regardless of the methods used to finance the war, the task of balancing the peacetime budget posed an enormous challenge to both Britain and France. Britain's budget deficit for the year ending 31 March 1919 came to over £1.6 billion ($7.7 billion at par), and the French deficit for 1918 exceeded 34.2 billion francs ($6.6 billion at par). Anticipated reduction of direct military expenditures was insufficient to close the gap between national revenues and expenditures in the foreseeable future. Even if new taxes could be passed, which remained doubtful, efficient machinery to collect them did not exist. The war severely disrupted French financial services and budgetary procedures. Complicated budgets rendered it impossible to tell precisely how the nation stood. The system dated back to arrangements established by Napoleon III in 1862, which "seem to have been conceived by the Second Empire with the object of concealing the results of the government's financial management from the public and parliament."[1]

During and after the war, French accounts were confused, disorderly, and full of unexplained gaps. The Finance Ministry was never certain exactly how much the government was spending. Accounts might run several years before being closed "definitively"; in such cases, the government made no attempt to determine the amount spent during each fiscal year. Parliament habitually passed budgets long after the fiscal year had begun. To allow government services to continue, the Chamber and Senate violated the principle of the unitary budget and passed monthly *douzièmes provisoires*. By the end of a fiscal year, no one had any idea of the actual amount appropriated and spent. Between 1919 and 1925, only the French budget of 1922 was voted before the beginning of the budget year. In 1963, the French Finance Ministry published supposedly "definitive" retrospective accounts, but according to Alfred Sauvy even these "merely copied the errors and obscurities of the time."[2]

Some of the disorder in the accounts resulted from negligence, and some represented conscious efforts by both British and French finance officials to make a bad situation look somewhat better. Normally, a chancellor of the exchequer or finance minister must present a balanced budget to parliament. The balance is based on estimated revenues and expenditures, and it is always possible that the expected balance may not materialize. In normal times, however, it should be possible to predict revenues and expenditures relatively precisely.

Because the period 1914–1923 was highly abnormal, budget predictions had little value. The end of the war brought scant relief in this respect. Demobilization took either more time or less time than expected. Prices continued to rise sharply during 1919 and then fell drastically during the second half of 1920. The boom of 1919–20 produced more revenue than expected, and then the sharp recession of 1920–21 produced less revenue than expected. British chancellors of the exchequer produced budget estimates hardly more reliable than those of their French counterparts. It has been suggested that to assuage public opinion at home and abroad (particularly in America), French finance ministers deliberately overestimated revenues in order to produce a balanced budget.[3] British chancellors of the exchequer have been treated more charitably; their estimates were bound to miss the mark given the chaotic financial situation of the early 1920s. Receipts on particular items might differ from estimates by millions in either direction. "In these circumstances," concluded a British analyst, "normal budgeting was impossible, and financial administration cannot be criticized very closely." Moreover, the turnover of chancellors of the exchequer militated against the development of a coherent policy—a point even more appropriate to the French situation.[4]

Wartime distortions and subterfuges drastically altered the traditional form of British and French budgets. Traditional distinctions between current accounts and capital accounts fell into disuse, and new distinctions between "ordinary" expenditures and "extraordinary" expenditures began to appear. While such distinctions did not affect the total amount spent by the government, they had a vital impact on how the government proposed to raise the money. Under sound budgetary procedures, ordinary current expenditures are covered by regular taxes upon which the government can count each year, while extraordinary capital expenditures are met either by borrowing or through special taxation for a specified period of time. As the war progressed, the French Finance Ministry developed the notion of an ordinary budget composed of purely civil expenditures, and an extraordinary budget for all activities related to national defense. Included in the extraordinary budget were funds for the production of war material, and the purchase and subsidization of foodstuffs for the general public. On the assumption that *all* military expenditure was "abnormal," all of it was placed in the extraordinary budget, notwithstanding the fact that all modern governments run up substantial peacetime military outlays. Within these two budgets, the Finance Ministry created any number of "special accounts," thereby creating further disorder. One gets the impression that this manipulation of the budget was in fact an awkward attempt to conceal a massive deficit.

After the war, the French Finance Ministry added to the extraordinary budget's military expenditures certain capital outlays for reconstruction of the devastated regions. In 1920, the Finance Ministry created a third budget category, "expenditures recoverable from Germany in execution of the peace treaties." In this new category were placed the funds required to reconstruct the liberated territories, and certain classes of war pensions and war indemnities due French citizens. These funds represented a French "loan" to Germany. Until Germany paid, the government covered the extraordinary and recoverable budgets by resorting to additional borrowing, special taxes, monetary inflation, the sale of surplus war stocks, and other temporary measures. The British Treasury also resorted to these expedients to cover the costs of war, but they had far lower expenditures to cover because reconstruction of devastated areas was not for them an issue.

In gradual stages, the French Finance Ministry brought the budget back to a more businesslike basis, although the deficit was not eliminated until 1926. In 1920, nonexceptional military expenses were reintegrated into the ordinary budget. Beginning in 1921, special accounts for railway and food subsidies were phased out, and at the end of 1921 the extraordinary budget was absorbed in the general budget, where it was now posted as "exceptional expenditures." By 1923 the Finance Ministry had more or less reestablished the integrity of the ordinary budget, although the special recoverable expenses budget remained until 1925, when the Dawes Plan made it clear that such expenditures were for the most part not recoverable at all.

Wartime shifts in spending patterns tended to limit flexibility in financial matters and added to the difficulty of balancing the budget. After the war the largest items in the budget were the least susceptible to reduction. As a percentage of the total, debt service, defense, and military pensions stood out as the largest items in postwar British and French budgets; in the French budget, reconstruction costs topped the list. As a percentage of the ordinary French budget, debt service consumed a frightful 48 percent. Discouraging as they are, these debt service statistics take no account of repayment of inter-Allied debt, because refunding agreements had as yet not been signed. The problem of servicing the debt clarifies the French connection between repayment of inter-Allied debt and German reparation payments. In the absence of German payments, the French believed they faced two choices: either a permanent budget deficit, or a balanced budget in which exhorbitant debt service charges caused by German aggression precluded spending on basic social services such as education.[5]

Parliaments lost their traditional control over expenditures during the war. To turn down any request for funds would have seemed unpatriotic. In the postwar era, parliaments would have to learn once again how to reject funding bills. But appetites once developed are difficult to curb. In France, jurisdictional disputes and philosophical differences between the Chamber of Deputies and the Senate delayed and diluted the government's attempts at fiscal reform. The French Finance Ministry itself experienced a severe crisis marked by an increasing backlog of business, sinking morale, and numerous resignations. The finance minister termed it "a situation which seriously threatens the national interest," and proposed to remedy the situation by increasing by over 2 million francs the salaries of himself, the under-secretaries, and the personnel of the Finance Ministry's central administration. The Chamber of Deputies' budget commission, however, concluded that the Finance Ministry was overstaffed, "particularly with respect to the female employees, whose number seemed to us far too high." In the opinion of the commission, the Finance Ministry's morale problems resulted from irregular pay scales under which certain supervisory officials received less than the employees they supervised.[6]

In his first peacetime budget of 30 April 1919, Austen Chamberlain placed his country on the road to fiscal and financial integrity. Stanley Baldwin had set the expected tone in remarks before the House of Commons on 5 March. His call for sacrifice, later borrowed and immortalized by President John F. Kennedy, was quickly forgotten by the British.

> Until the time comes when the ordinary man, instead of asking himself, "what can I get out of the State?" will ask himself, "what can I do for the State?" we shall never be able to put that drag on Governments which is absolutely essential in the interests of sound finance.[7]

Chamberlain, however, recognized that he was faced with a parliament and a people whose wartime spirit of sacrifice was fast evaporating. The chancellor proposed nothing heroic. His postwar program came straight out of the prewar tradition of conservative, prudent, sound policies endorsed by the Bank of England. He proposed to reduce government spending, meet expenditures from revenues, borrow only "real" savings, repay the Ways and Means advances, and fund short-dated Treasury bills.[8]

The chancellor obviously meant to inform the country that more hard sacrifice lay ahead even though the shooting had ceased, but his remarks seem to have created a rather different impression among some of the public. The Round Table complacently reported that after listening to Chamberlain's budget message "the whole country was pleasantly surprised that our financial situation was so comparatively satisfactory" and that the nation was "still keeping its head above water." It was reassuring to know that the nation's financial position "is so reasonably secure and comparatively so much better than that of our Allies on the Continent, to say nothing of our enemies." But Britain could never be satisfied with "comparative" financial well-being. Its goal was international financial supremacy and a pound sterling restored to gold at $4.86. "Everything," cautioned *The Round Table*, "depends on whether this spirit of effort and sacrifice can be quickly recovered. For the moment it has been lost."[9] The British people had sacrificed their money and their lives in what the government had portrayed as a struggle for civilization. Could the government now convince those same people to sacrifice their money and their jobs in a war to bring the pound back to $4.86?

Chamberlain's budget proposal for 1919–20 represented a series of compromises between principle and expediency. In a budget designed to ease the transition from war to peace, such compromises may have been most appropriate. The chancellor rejected advice from some of his subordinates to end the system of war finance by one swift stroke and replace it with a system of new, permanent taxes. Sir Otto Niemeyer, then an assistant secretary at the Treasury, advised the government to drop immediately the special wartime excess profits duty (EPD), because the war was over. He considered it unwise to alter rates on the income tax and super-tax until the royal commission studying those taxes had submitted its report, and he conceded Britain could not count on repayment of inter-Allied debts or German reparation payments "for present purposes." Instead, Niemeyer proposed a new "business profits tax" with an estimated yield of £50 million, higher death duties (£10 million additional), and sharp increases in beer and spirit duties (£56 million additional).[10]

Chamberlain accepted Niemeyer's proposals to increase death duties and taxes on beer and spirits, but out of both practical and philosophical considerations he did not substitute any new business profits tax for the temporary EPD. The chancellor admitted to the king's private secretary, Lord Stamfordham, that "as regards the EPD, my original intention had been to abolish the existing tax and to impose a new tax of a permanent character on what I call the excess profits of business . . . but the time at my disposal was not sufficient to enable me to devise a new form of taxation which would operate fairly as between one business and another." The problem was to find a taxation plan which would "operate fairly." His reference to "what I call the excess profits of business" indicated the source of the problem. Businessmen did not consider their war profits "excessive." For the budget year 1919–20, it seemed that "the best policy would be to continue as a temporary measure the existing EPD for one year, but at the same time to reduce the rate from 80 percent to 40 percent."[11]

Philosophically, Chamberlain's concern for sound fiscal policy predisposed him to drop the EPD. The war was over, and war taxes ought to have been wound up, too. But as the chancellor noted in his budget message, "neither this year, nor next year, nor perhaps the year after will be entirely normal," because the costs of war did not cease the day the Armistice was signed. Chamberlain foresaw expenditures in fiscal 1919–20 for £301.5 million in special subsidies alone. Bread subsidies, railway subsidies, pensions, costs of demobilization and resettlement, and loans to the Dominions and Allies inflated the budget and produced a deficit of £233.8 million which would have to be covered by fresh borrowing. If a peace treaty could be signed, reductions in military spending might enable the government to balance the 1920–21 budget. "We are beginning to see daylight through the trees," Chamberlain assured the House of Commons, but for the moment "we have, in short, another year of war expenditure."[12] Another year of war expenditure justified retention of the EPD at a reduced rate.

Another year of war expenditure also justified inclusion in the budget as "revenue" several extraordinary sums derived from the sale of assets held by the government. In this category were surplus assets controlled by the Ministry of Munitions (£140 million), the Ministry of Shipping (£50 million), the War Office (£50 million), and the Admiralty (£14 million). Had Chamberlain felt it politic to close out food subsidies at that time, he might also have sold the vast stocks of foodstuffs held by the Ministry of Food. Inclusion of the one-time sale of such assets in the budget under the head of "revenue" was unorthodox and "undoubtedly obscured the true character of the balance sheet."[13] The actual deficit was considerably larger than it appeared, and to make matters worse, the government was accused of disposing of the stocks at "break-up prices." Moreover, because only about one-quarter of the cost of the war had been met by taxation, one could assume that about 75 percent of the cost of the stocks now being liquidated had been covered out of wartime loans contracted by the government. But the proceeds of the sales were not earmarked for repayment of public debt—they were to be counted as current revenue.[14]

In his budget message of 30 April 1919 Chamberlain attempted to project expenditures for a typical "normal" year, compared these projected expenditures with existing "normal" taxes, and then proposed increased taxation in his 1919–20 budget to cover what he estimated as the "normal" deficit of £114 million. This procedure explains how he left a deficit of £233.8 million in his 1919–20 budget, to be covered by new borrowing. The £233 million represented the excess over the normal deficit of £114 million. In a normal budget of £766 million, Chamberlain estimated £110 million for the military (40 percent above the prewar figure), £190 million for the civil services, and a stupendous £400 million for debt service (£40 million above his allowance in the 1919–20 budget).[15]

Early attempts to estimate France's postwar fiscal requirements produced little agreement. One economist calculated the postwar budget at three times the size of prewar budgets, and another estimated the budget deficit in a "normal" year at about 15 billion francs. There were no reliable figures on which to base even short-term estimates, and projections of the first "normal" French budget prepared by "equally competent persons" varied by as much as 5 billion francs. Several factors contributed to this uncertainty. No one knew how much Germany would pay in reparations, and no one knew what course inflation would take. Certain "fixed" costs were not fixed at all. War pensions would decline as the pensioners eventually died. One of the more optimistic estimates for France predicted five or six years of "the most severe financial problems any country has ever experienced" before the return to normal budgets.[16]

Against this backdrop of gloomy estimates, Finance Minister Klotz astonished the world with his proposals for the 1919 budget. He was asking for only 9 billion francs in the ordinary budget, for which no new taxes would be required. With some increases in existing consumer taxes on wine, coffee, mineral water, gas, electricity, tobacco, matches, as well as higher tariffs, Klotz calculated that his budget would cover service of the war debt for the coming year. As his critics pointed out, the finance minister was making no provision for repayment of the principle on the public debt, repayments of advances to the government from the Bank of France, reparation of war damage, and pensions for disabled veterans, widows, and orphans. Nor did the budget acknowledge that the government would have to continue borrowing, adding still more to future debt service charges.[17]

Klotz assured the Deputies' budget commission that the Finance Ministry was considering means to achieve a definitive solution to the French financial crisis. In hearings held 10 February 1919, Klotz intimated his endorsement of German reparation payments and a 20 percent tax on capital as the favored method of balancing the budget. In a letter to the commission dated 17 April, the finance minister conceded that regardless of the amount Germany might pay, the Finance Ministry would have to reform completely its fiscal administration and the French people would have to make new sacrifices. But he reiterated his previously stated position that "we refuse to address this appeal to the French taxpayers so long as the amount of the enemy's debt has not been established."[18]

In principle, Klotz's position appeared unassailable: the government would not ask the French people to tax themselves for expenditures which might be paid eventually by the Germans. Yet, Klotz would have accepted the judgment of the distinguished economist Germain Martin that "the peace treaty leaves to France a heavy portion of the charges of the war."[19] What, then, did the finance minister have in mind when he proposed his 1919 budget? In his formal budget message of 27 May 1919, Klotz described the requested 1.28 billion franc tax increase as "a partial, but important effort" which would lead ultimately to a "definitive restoration of the finances of our country." Limited as they were, the tax increases would "show our allies that France still knows how to make the sacrifices the situation demands, and thus deserves . . . the maintenance of the agreements in the military, economic, and financial sphere which have produced the victory of right over might."[20]

Klotz had finally exposed his hand. France must tax itself just severely enough to persuade the United States to lend more money. If his budget turned out to be inadequate, the Americans, he insisted, would furnish the credits required to enable France to meet her obligations during the coming year. When his budget still had not been passed in mid-June, Klotz asked the Chamber of Deputies to act on it without further debate, assuring the deputies again that the Finance Ministry would cover any deficit with credits from the United States. The Americans would be impressed by the "firmness and wisdom" with which the French conducted their affairs. With the budget safely passed, there would be plenty of time to tell the nation the truth about France's financial plight.[21]

Of course, it might be necessary to deceive the Americans if they were expected to grant new credits. André Tardieu, former French high commissioner in the United States and now Commissaire

Général aux Affaires de Guerre Franco-Americaines, informed his chief agent in New York, Maurice Casenave, of his desire to "give the Americans an exact picture of our budgetary situation." He then proceeded to paint an optimistic picture quite at variance with the facts as understood by Klotz. Liquidation of the extraordinary charges in the budget depended upon prompt payments from Germany—an implied plea for American support in enforcing the peace treaties. But the ordinary budget presented no problems. Rising revenues from the reconstructed regions and a reintegrated Alsace-Lorraine, liquidation of surplus war stocks, and repayment of French loans by some of the minor allies would balance the ordinary budget. In fact, claimed Tardieu, the budget could be balanced without these extraordinary resources if necessary.[22]

During the course of 1919, financial leaders in Britain and France gradually came to doubt that any combination of traditional taxes—including the income tax—could pay off the cost of the war. Many technically feasible taxes seemed politically impossible, and some alternatives appeared to threaten certain social classes. Reversing a trend established during the war, Chamberlain's 1919–20 budget placed increased reliance on indirect taxes for a greater share of new revenue. Higher taxes on beer and spirits were to produce an additional £50 million, while death duties would produce only an additional £10 million, and the rate on the EPD was halved. This was a prescription for social confrontation, as Britain's bourgeois leadership sought at the same time to increase the nation's productivity as the only way to pay off the war debt. The working classes were asked to work harder and give up their increased earnings in the form of higher taxes. Would the capitalists be asked to make a corresponding sacrifice? Against the backdrop of the Bolshevik takeover in Russia, serious economists, financiers, and politicians in both Britain and France could not escape the possibility of a levy on capital.

In the long run, a combination of high taxation, high productivity, and moderate inflation might have reduced the war debt to a point where ordinary peacetime budgets would again become feasible. But such a program would have required generations of fiscal discipline and social cooperation, rare attributes in postwar Europe. It was tempting to search for a "quick fix," a single, simple solution that would make the war debt and budget deficits disappear overnight—not necessarily a painless process, but at least a scheme which would make the pain as short-lived as possible. Labor had been conscripted during the war. Why not capital?

Proponents of the capital levy saw it as the shortest route to national solvency. The benefits of social justice would more than compensate for any temporary damage to the economic system. A levy on capital would adjust fortunes unduly inflated by war profits or by the ordinary injustices of the capitalist system. Defeated nations could use such a levy as a means to pay off indemnities and emancipate themselves from heavy financial obligations imposed by the peace treaties. In victor and vanquished nations alike, all of which were experiencing postwar labor unrest, a capital levy might serve as a sort of insurance premium for the capitalist classes against revolutionaries advocating a more drastic confiscation of wealth.

Although the levy on capital was rejected ultimately in both Britain and France, both the chancellor of the exchequer and the finance minister at one time considered the capital levy as a realistic means of paying for the war. Klotz raised the idea of a 20 percent capital levy in March 1919. Mere mention of the scheme sent shudders through French financial markets and set off political repercussions that eventually ended Klotz's career as finance minister. Shortly after Klotz dropped his bombshell, Lord Derby, the British ambassador in Paris, observed to Lloyd George after talks with other members of Clemenceau's cabinet that "it would appear as if the tax on capital would have to be dropped." "I have no doubt in my own mind," continued Derby, "that Klotz will fall," an eventuality which the ambassador did not view with alarm. "Klotz," he wrote, "of course is not a financier. He is by profession a lawyer and I do not think his going will really weaken Clemenceau's Government."[23] The budget Klotz proposed to the Chamber of Deputies on 27 May 1919 contained no provision for a levy on capital. Clemenceau's cabinet fell on 18 January 1920. The new finance minister, François-Marsal, violently opposed any levy on capital. For a time, he considered withholding French representation at the 1920 international financial conference at Brussels because the capital levy appeared on the preliminary agenda. François-Marsal was a banker.

Britain's flirtation with the levy on capital seems to have been more serious and long-lived. Andrew Bonar Law, the chancellor of the exchequer, raised the possibility of such a postwar tax in November, 1917. Public reaction caused Law to issue an "explanation" of his remarks in the press. Here, he gave the impression that a capital levy would be an optional arrangement under which those with sufficient means might compound a portion of their ongoing tax payments in a single capital sum. But subsequent statements by Law conveyed to some the impression that he favored "a general levy on capital after the war in order to reduce the volume of debt, and that this must necessarily involve a partial conscription of the War Loan." Law's alleged opinion that "a portion of these patriotic investments should be confiscated after the war" was thought by some to have affected the sale of government war bonds and jeopardized investment in vital war industries and agriculture.[24]

Law later defended his advocacy of a levy on capital as a reasonable position while the war still raged and no one could foresee how Britain could pay for it without resort to "some desperate remedy." In May 1919 he opposed the levy he had earlier supported, but only because Britain did not appear to need such a tax and because the majority of the nation appeared to oppose it. He still refused to concede that the concept of a capital levy was inherently evil. "For all that," he wrote, "there is, in my opinion, more in it than probably you would be ready to acknowledge, if it could be looked upon simply as a fiscal measure without the prejudice involved in it by the fact that the Labour Party are putting it forward for the express purpose if not of confiscating capital at least of making it pay to finance every kind of social reform." In short, the capital levy might have had a chance had the Labour party not advocated it! Law considered the levy on capital a fiscally sound technique for raising large sums, but he recognized that in financial matters human psychology often counts for more than does "correct" policy. He understood that "a shock to confidence in all matters financial is probably the greatest possible evil," and nothing would shake the confidence of the British capitalists more than a levy on capital.[25]

Law's reluctance to give up the notion of a levy on capital was not without significance. As Lord Privy Seal and leader of the Coalition government in the House of Commons in 1919, his opinion carried a good deal of weight. In May 1920 segments of the electorate continued to believe that the government was still considering a levy on capital. Law was warned that "the anxiety is universal," and that the capital levy was "the one topic of conversation." The government, cautioned one high-ranking Scottish official, would be turned out if it passed such a tax. Law assured him that the government had decided not to go with the war tax levy, as it was now called. A Cabinet committee had studied the matter, and "from the time the Committee sent their report I was strongly against it, and Chamberlain has taken the same view."[26]

The issue was not quite so cut-and-dried as Law implied, for on 21 May 1920 another influential Conservative Scottish politician, Sir George Younger, had indicated to Law that there might be some political capital in a properly constructed capital levy. Younger noted that "an idea has got abroad that some members of the Cabinet think it would be a great electoral asset to do something in the way of taxing war wealth, and if this could be restricted to windfalls of an exceptional kind, they possibly might be right." But an unrestricted levy on capital would produce a financial crisis and topple the government. Younger recounted a conversation with a banker who threatened to call in his loans and restrict further credit in response to a capital levy. The banker "had no intention whatever of allowing the government to take the cream out of these concerns and leave him with the dregs."[27]

By the spring of 1920, most British businessmen and politicians viewed the levy on capital as the worst of all possible alternatives for raising money. The choice, it seemed, lay between continuing the excess profits duty (EPD) at a higher rate or a levy on capital. As the ambassador for Scotland told Law, "people hate EPD as the devil hates holy water, but its strongest opponent would vote for it to a man I believe as against a capital levy." Younger, too, told Law that "much as I object to the EPD being dealt with as Austen proposes, it is at all events a much safer tax [than a capital levy] in the present position of our finance . . . [and] as it has been pretty clearly shown to be impossible to restrict a levy to those who ought to pay, of the two evils, the EPD is decidedly the least."[28] In his 1919–20 budget, Chamberlain had reduced the rate on EPD from 80 percent to 40 percent, and implied it would be phased out completely the following year. But in his budget for 1920–21, he asked that the rate be raised back to 60 percent. As opponents of the capital levy predicted, the House of Commons accepted an increased EPD as the lesser of two evils, but not, as we shall see, without complaint.

Participants in the drama surrounding the capital levy perceived the real issue to be nothing less than the survival of western civilization. In 1918, the British historian J. A. R. Marriott admonished his countrymen that "civilization is not the product of capitalism; but the security of capital is essential to civilization." Another British writer cautioned that "civilization may not depend upon capitalists—probably it does not; but it does most certainly depend upon capital in the sense of a stock of commodities, held somewhere, sufficient to go round, and capable of employment for the creation of fresh wealth." Lacking these conditions, he warned, "all the arts, conveniences, and amenities of civilization must perish." The author of these words, Francis Gribble, offered an ominous prophecy for later generations. "The world," he wrote, "is living on its capital . . . the stock of capital approaches exhaustion and the day of the scramble draws nearer. And that is the end of civilization."[29]

The final report of the 1920 international financial conference in Brussels pointed to the massive destruction of capital during the war as the ultimate cause of the world's financial predicament. The conference produced no proposals for creating new capital, but rather suggested means of allocating efficiently the existing pool of resources. R. H. Brand, a partner in the London firm of Lazard Brothers, posed the central question when he told the conference that "the inadequacy of capital and consequently of productive power is fundamental . . . since there is not enough capital to go around, which is to have it—government or private industry . . . which is likely to use capital more productively—governments or private industry?"[30] The consensus at Brussels, and among bourgeois financial experts everywhere, favored the private sector as the most efficient employer of capital. This conclusion alone ruled out a levy on capital that would transfer substantial savings from the private to the public sector.

The extent of the alleged shortage of capital in postwar Britain and France is by no means clear. Through taxation and domestic borrowing, the French people found the capital to rebuild their country without substantial reparation payments from Germany. At the Bank of England, Montagu Norman frequently complained that London's interest rates were lower than those prevailing in New York, at a time when capital was supposed to be scarce in Britain and plentiful in America. Logic tells us that western Europe's capital must have been depleted by the Great War, but only twenty years later the world was plunged into another holocaust of even greater proportions. The civilized world's ritual of capital destruction continued at an ever-increasing tempo between 1939 and 1945, only to be followed by the cold war arms race, the Korean war, and the war in southeast Asia. Nevertheless, the people of Western Europe enjoy today a higher standard of living than ever before. Nations devastated during the Second World War have emerged as the world's leading economic powers. Where is the shortage of capital? Is there a basic flaw in the capital shortage theory, or is the world simply living on borrowed time and borrowed capital? Did the decade of the 1930s provide a much-needed rest during which the world's capital stock was reconstituted? Will the decades-long waste and destruction of capital finally catch up with the industrial nations during the 1980s?

Having rejected, rightly or wrongly, the levy on capital, the British and French Treasuries continued the search for alternatives that might raise the revenue required to balance the budget.[31] British and French budgets of 1920, 1921, and 1922 were patchwork affairs employing a variety of old and new taxes. The British Treasury and French Finance Ministry both employed devious methods to achieve a nominal balance, and in some years there was no balance at all, nominal or real.[32] The two Treasuries considered every conceivable tax on every conceivable item and transaction. Some were found to be unjust, others were found to be unproductive, some were considered to be politically dangerous, and some were rejected simply because the British Treasury considered them inconsistent with Anglo-Saxon notions of sound taxation policy.

Of the methods employed by the British Treasury to balance the budget during the first postwar years, none was more controversial than the sale of surplus war assets. This practice was criticized in Britain as being unsound, and in France as unjust. The French government, purchaser of much of the surplus left behind in France after the war, objected to the terms of sale. In certain defined territories, the French government was to purchase all British stores and physical facilities deemed surplus by the British government, at a price fixed by the British government. When the French Ministry of Industrial Reconstruction refused to carry out the agreement signed by the French government, the British Ministry of Munitions asked the Cabinet Finance Committee for economic sanctions (restrictions on wool and coal shipments to France) against the French government—sanctions of the type no British government ever suggested when the Germans defaulted on reparation payments. Rejecting explicit sanctions against the French, the Cabinet Finance Committee, at the request of the chancellor of the exchequer, instructed the foreign secretary to "exercise the strongest possible pressure" to force the French government to honor the agreement of sale.[33]

Domestic complaints relating to the sale of war surplus centered on the Treasury's decision to use the proceeds to balance the 1920–21 budget rather than applying them toward the redemption of war debt. The Treasury defended the practice with the argument that 1920–21 expenditures were by no means ordinary. The budget included £300million in charges arising directly from closing down the war. In any event, the taxpayers needed a break, and should not be deprived of the benefit from the sale of war surplus by earmarking the £31 million proceeds to debt retirement. The Treasury was not being entirely candid, because retirement of £31 million in public debt would have reduced the annual interest charge in the budget— although admittedly not by £31 million.[34]

Another scheme designed to assist in balancing the British budget was the proposal to "spread pensions." Under such a plan, the government's pension liability would be entered in the annual budgets over a thirty- to fifty-year period at a fixed amount actuarially calculated. The charge during the earlier years would be met by borrowing, to be repaid out of an expected surplus during the final years. Controller of Finance Sir Basil Blackett opposed any scheme which might add to the national debt, observing that "instructed opinion everywhere condemns the present French Budget which hides away the War Pension Charge under the 'Budget of Recoverable Expenses,' where it is supposed to be balanced out of Reparations Receipts from Germany which are partly problematical and partly nonexistent as far as the year covered by the particular Budget is concerned." Blackett could see no advantage in a "plan which will suggest to the world that Britain is beginning to camouflage her Budget position." Deputy Controller of Finance Sir Otto Niemeyer reiterated Blackett's derogatory remarks concerning French financial practices and characterized pension-spreading as "merely a more pleasing form of saying that the annual charges of the state are not met out of its revenue and that the state is prepared to budget for a deficit." In 1922, Niemeyer suggested that the best way to save money on war pensions was to reduce them from levels fixed during the boom of 1919 as the cost of living fell during the subsequent recession.[35]

Heavier taxation on beer and spirits furnished the British Treasury with revenues increasing from £60 million in 1913 to £260 million in 1920. But these revenues eventually reached a point of diminishing returns; in 1923, the beer duty stood at a rate thirteen times higher than the prewar level, but revenue from the tax was only seven times higher. Many Britons were switching to imported wines, which were relatively cheap owing to low import duties. To protect its threatened beer and spirits revenues, the Treasury proposed to increase wine duties in 1920, a move opposed by the Board of Customs and Excise on the ground it would jeopardize friendly relations with Portugal and France.[36]

Another tax considered and rejected by the British Treasury on several occasions was the so-called turnover tax—a type of sales tax—on business transactions. Important in the Treasury's deliberation on this levy was the question of whether Britain should adopt a tax which was being employed in France, Belgium, Italy, Germany, Czechoslovakia, Hungary, Roumania, the Serb-Croat-Slovene State, and Luxembourg. As the Board of Inland Revenue noted, "general sales taxes have always sprung from urgent financial necessity." Britain certainly would not wish to convey the impression of near-bankruptcy, and with more than a hint of racism the Board pointed out that "the only Anglo-Saxon community which has adopted such a tax is Canada." The yield on the French turnover tax fell far below estimates, although the French Finance Ministry attributed disappointing revenues to slack trade and falling prices.[37]

The turnover tax was arguably not a particularly productive tax during a recession, but the tax was first considered by the British Treasury during 1918 and 1919, when the economy was experiencing the postwar inflationary boom. The Board of Inland Revenue rejected the turnover tax at that time because of its direct inflationary impact on consumer prices. The turnover tax was thus inappropriate in any case, whether the problem was inflation or recession. The revenue boards consistently argued that Britain did not face the dire financial situation that had forced other European countries to adopt such a tax of last resort.[38]

While a turnover tax may have been financially unnecessary in

Britain, it might have been adopted owing to its social utility in shifting the burden from direct to indirect taxation. Before the war, Britain's Treasury relied on direct taxes for 57.5 percent of its revenue. The income tax and the super-tax on incomes exceeding £5,000 formed the cornerstone of the nation's revenue system. Owing to increases in the rates on direct taxes during the war, they furnished 68 percent (79.5 percent if the EPD is included) of all revenue by 1918. But after the war, the Treasury shifted back toward greater reliance on indirect taxes, although by 1923 the prewar ratio had not been restored.[39]

Neither the Board of Inland Revenue nor the Board of Customs and Excise desired to take a clear position on the relative merits of direct and indirect taxation. They preferred to leave to the politicians the responsibility for increasing the tax burden on the poorer classes. But the revenue boards did point out that any shift toward indirect taxation would meet stiff trade union resistance. The Treasury might take in a little more revenue, at the cost of a major struggle between capital and labor. Given the new-found power of the unions, capital would probably lose. The working class would simply demand and obtain higher wages, ultimately shifting the cost of a turnover tax to the industrial classes and middle-class consumers. This alone seemed a convincing argument against a turnover tax, but the Board of Inland Revenue could not resist the clinching argument—the difference (meaning superiority) between the "tax psychology" of the Anglo-Saxons and the Latins.

> What may be called the "tax psychology" of Anglo-Saxon countries, particularly in Great Britain, differs markedly from that of Latin countries, especially as regards the public attitude towards direct and indirect taxation. The Anglo-Saxon wants, as a general rule, to know what taxes he is paying. The Latin does not; he prefers to have them served as powder in the jam. French opinion—and France has a very comprehensive turnover tax—remains doubtful of the merits of direct taxation.[40]

Austen Chamberlain's promise to end the excess profits duty set in motion at the Treasury a frantic search for possible replacement taxes on bicycles, betting, carriage license duties, duties on imported motor vehicles, virtually any goods and services that might be taxed. At the 40 percent rate imposed under the 1919–20 budget, the EPD was expected to generate £175 million at then-current profit rates. It finally became apparent that no combination of "nuisance" taxes could replace the considerable revenue derived from the EPD. Nothing less than a major new tax would enable the Treasury to balance the budget. The question was, who should bear the burden of the new tax? As the postwar boom dissipated into the postwar recession, it was questioned whether anyone could pay such a tax. Many believed the nation's taxable capacity had been reached.

Just before the postwar boom collapsed, Chamberlain shocked Britain's business community as he delivered his 10 April 1920 budget message introducing his 1920–21 budget. Far from dropping the EPD, he proposed to raise the rate back to 60 percent and add to it a new "corporations profits duty" of 1 percent on *all* corporate profits. The resulting uproar failed to move the chancellor from his position. Chamberlain's resistance to massive pressure from the business community must go down as one of the most heroic examples of a public official's determination to place the national interest above what he considered the greed and irresponsible demands of the bankers and industrialists.

Chamberlain justified continuation of the EPD—a special war tax —by pointing to over £600 million in war-related expenditures in the 1920–21 budget. This was still a war budget. Moreover, the postwar boom and exceptional profit levels resulted largely from government expenditure and government monetary policy. Chamberlain's 1920–21 budget thus represented an attempt to pay for the war and tax the postwar boom. This budget marked the high tide of war finance, and as Ursala Hicks has written, "in the financial sphere the war ended not in 1918 but in 1920." Chamberlain was determined to put an end to wartime deficit spending and balance the 1920–21 budget.[41] Opponents of Chamberlain's budget wondered why he had chosen to balance the budget by increasing taxation rather than by reducing expenditures. Prime targets of the economizers were armaments expenditures, and subsidies for bread, coal, housing, and transportation.[42]

Had Chamberlain succeeded in finding a satisfactory substitute, he probably would have abolished the EPD in his 1920–21 budget. The tax appeared to favor some businesses over others, and would prove unsatisfactory from the Treasury's point of view in the event of a recession. Businesses were liable to the EPD based on their average profits in two of the best three years prior to the war. The law considered a 7 percent return on investment as reasonable. This figure reflected the prewar belief that businesses had to show a 6 percent return in order to attract new capital. By 1920, these rates no longer bore any relation to reality. Based as it was on each firm's best prewar performance rather than current profits, the EPD came to "represent a permanent endowment of pre-tax businesses with a prosperous past at the expense of less successful or newer rivals."[43]

On 29 March 1920 the Board of Inland Revenue warned that during a recession, there would be no excess profits to tax. The Board advocated a general tax on all corporate profits as a replacement for the EPD. Still another feature of the EPD foreshadowed trouble for the Exchequer. Under the law, firms that had paid heavy taxes on large profits during good years could later demand partial reimbursement from the Treasury during years of lower profits or losses. During a severe recession, the Treasury might find itself paying out as much as it was taking in. This is precisely what happened in the 1920–21 recession, and the calamity prompted the suggestion that the Treasury make the reimbursements in government securities rather than in cash. The Board of Inland Revenue, of course, lacked authority to issue government securities to meet its obligations—it would have to purchase such stocks on the open market. Furthermore, those entitled to reimbursement were legally entitled to cash, not securities. In any event, securities so issued would be traded for cash by the firms receiving them.[44]

Most damaging from the Treasury viewpoint was the provision that firms could pay the EPD in government securities rather than in cash. The same provision held for payment of death duties by private individuals. The mechanics of the process proved costly to the Treasury. Firms paid in to the Exchequer securities that then had to be converted to cash for payment to Inland Revenue and the National Debt Commission. The Treasury obtained the cash by selling Treasury bills and obtaining Ways and Means advances from the Bank of England. These procedures added to the floating debt, and the amounts involved were significant. In 1919–20, the Treasury had to pay out £7,717,000 for bonds surrendered in payment of death duties, and £61,144,000 for securities paid in on EPD. For 1920–21, these figures rose to £18,813,000 and £65,427,000 respectively. In a two-year period, the Treasury was forced to borrow the staggering sum of £153,101,000 in order to cover death duty and EPD payments.[45]

Delegations representing the National Union of Manufacturers (smaller trades) and the Federation of British Industries (large industry) discussed the future of the EPD with Chamberlain during February 1919. They left the distinct impression that business desired to convert the EPD into a welfare program for distressed firms. When a Mr. Marston of the N.U.M. threatened that "we shall have to take our factories, our ability, our industries, abroad" if businesses did not receive immediate tax relief, the unperturbed chancellor replied, "Have you picked your country yet, Mr. Marston?" The business delegations suggested that the rate on EPD be reduced, that firms be permitted to retain a portion of the tax owed as a government loan to be used as working capital, that the government lend money to distressed firms to enable them to meet their tax payments, and that the EPD be continued so that distressed firms could collect rebates on taxes paid in during the wartime boom years.[46]

Chamberlain proved unsympathetic to the demands of the industrialists. He told the N.U.M. that "what you are asking is that the tax should be kept on in order that A, who makes a profit, may pay B, who makes a loss." To the F.B.I. he responded that "it has become perfectly obvious that you want the tax continued in order to continue the right of recovery . . . you ask that it should be continued in order to get a continued and recurring right to claim back money already paid." Chamberlain warned that "I cannot give up this tax and put nothing in its place. If the EPD goes, industry must contribute in some other way," adding that a new tax would contain no right of recovery. Marston had urged the chancellor to "relieve the burden on the producers and place it on the shoulders of the people who are consuming in a manner which is not for the benefit of the nation." Chamberlain was determined that the capitalist class would not escape its responsibility to pay its share of the costs of war.[47]

From within the government, both Chamberlain and his predecessor, Bonar Law, encountered pressure for repeal of the EPD as soon as the Armistice was signed. On 15 November 1918 two officials of the Board of Inland Revenue, N. F. Warren Fisher and H. P. Hamilton, forwarded to Law a note on "Repeal of the Excess Profits Duty." They predicted a postwar recession and advocated repeal "at the earliest possible moment." The EPD was distorting normal business decisions. The mining industries in particular were restricting output in expectation of repeal of the tax. Meanwhile, certain other firms engaged in "a certain extravagance in expenditure" as they paid out higher wages, advertised more, and hired additional consultants rather than pay out their "excess" profits as EPD.[48]

By March 1920 the Federation of British Industries had modified its position and now asked Chamberlain to end the EPD at once.[49] But Chamberlain could not ignore what he considered "abnormal and often extravagant profits" and recommended an increase in the rate on EPD back to 60 percent in his 19 April budget message. This brought vigorous objections from the minister of shipping, Sir Joseph Maclay, who reminded Chamberlain of his earlier promise to close out the EPD. "However unwittingly," he scolded the chancellor, "industry has been misled in this matter and . . . it should be put right."[50] During the spring of 1920 delegations representing Britain's commerce and industry arrived at Chamberlain's office practically every day. W. P. Rylands, president of the Federation of British Industries, suggested to the chancellor that if the government was determined to raise a large sum from industry, "there does not appear to us to be any valid reason why we should not write our own prescription for the medicine we have got to take." In other words, the government should permit British industry to write its own tax legislation. Still not intimidated by the industrialists, Chamberlain complained that "you really set me an insoluble problem when you say reduce the debt, and at the same time say to every tax I propose, that I should do something else."[51]

Coupled with the increase in Treasury bill and Bank rates to 7 percent, the government's request for an increase of the EPD to 60 percent threatened to halt all investment activity. Sir Harry Foster, representing the National Union of Manufacturers, told Chamberlain that if the government could find no better way to raise its revenue, "then one is bound to say that it appears like the bankruptcy of financial ability—I had almost said the bankruptcy of statesmanship." Chamberlain responded that he could reduce the rate on EPD to 40 percent only if the nation were willing to accept a levy on capital. He attributed the business slowdown to overpriced stocks. "When you are able to sell your boots at prices we can afford," he commented, "you will find no difficulty in getting rid of your stocks." The chancellor once again attempted to convince his listeners that the government was not going to allow the business community to escape its obligation to pay its share of the cost of the war. "I can always get suggestions from delegations to tax somebody else," he observed. "I have not asked for that . . . Assuming that the same classes are to produce an equal amount of money, is there any other way in which they would prefer to produce it."[52]

By July 1920, Britain's postwar boom was over. The slump produced cries from business and finance pointing to the government's fiscal and monetary policies as the cause of the recession. Sir Herbert Dixon expressed to Chamberlain the view of the Federation of British Industries that his latest budget had produced the trade depression. "We were going distinctly badly before the budget come out," he complained, "but since it came out, we have gone a great deal worse." Chamberlain replied that recession or no recession, it was too late to change the entire budget in July. In any event, he suggested, "I think the budget is made to bear a good deal more than it is responsible for."[53]

The Treasury, it seems, wished to take the credit when the economy was sound without accepting the blame when it turned sour. Before the extent and depth of the recession had become evident, Blackett had noted a "small but real deflation of credit" accompanied by a decline in wholesale prices during the period April–June 1920. Sterling exchange had recovered from $3.18 in early February to nearly $4.00 by July. Blackett asserted that these favorable developments "can be claimed without hesitation to be due to the combined effects of" payment of public debt out of current revenue, stiff money rates which forced banks to cut back on credit expansion and enabled the Treasury to raise funds without resorting to "manufactured" credit, and "the shadow of heavy taxation to come produced by the Budget proposals." The government's wise fiscal and monetary policy was cooling off an overheated economy in a judicious manner, and the opposition "even where honest is very shortsighted."

Opposition there was, as Blackett noted attacks on the government's policy from all directions: those sincerely disturbed by the size of the budget, "people who have to pay the EPD," elements in the financial and business community who thought the trade boom would last forever, and "the bankers who shouted for deflation until it came." The government's program, acknowledged Blackett, would never win a popularity contest, "but it will surely stand the verdict of history." If Britain was not yet the world's strongest financial power, she had at least assumed the role of moral leader of the international financial community. As commentators on the international economy have asserted recently, the leader must be prepared to sacrifice its immediate interests for the long-term common good—and this, argued Blackett, was precisely what Britain had done. "The United Kingdom has given the lead to the world and largely owing to the action of the United Kingdom the movement towards lower prices has become world wide. This fact adds to the gloom of the immediate outlook here, but gives promise of an earlier restoration of sound conditions than would otherwise be possible."[54]

While Chamberlain shared Blackett's desire that the government receive credit for any improvement in the overall economic climate brought by the readjustment of price levels, he emphasized the government's lack of responsibility for any distress occasioned by the slackening of trade during the summer of 1920. The chancellor felt there was "really too great a disposition to attribute all evil consequences to the Government, and none to the inevitable process of events, and none to any indiscretions on the part of any of those engaged except the Government." Chamberlain did not want all of the credit for the recession—he wished to share it with the "inevitable process of events" and the "indiscretions" of the businessmen themselves.[55]

As the recession set in during the summer of 1920, the debate over the EPD shifted to the question of whether or not the country had reached its "taxable capacity." The notion of how much taxation a national economy can support at any given moment was no less nebulous than was the question of Germany's "capacity to pay." The Board of Inland Revenue admitted in December 1920 that no one knew how great was the "taxable capacity of the nation."[56] The controversy produced an interesting confrontation between an important British banker, Reginald McKenna, and a prominent British theorist and Treasury official, R. G. Hawtrey. McKenna argued in June 1920, and continued to believe through 1922, that Britain had reached its taxable capacity, which he estimated at no more than £1,000 million annually. Hawtrey considered McKenna's notions of the effects of taxation "utterly untenable." McKenna implied that the whole of any increase in taxation is met from savings. He thus wrongly assumed, argued Hawtrey, that the aggregate sum available for savings and taxation is fixed, and that no one changes his life-style when taxation is increased by diminishing current spending in order to continue to save. In any event, contended Hawtrey, the government returned to the economy much of the money it taxed away—in the form of interest on the public debt paid to people like McKenna and his shareholders. Hawtrey conservatively calculated the nation's taxable capacity at £1,800 million.[57]

Chamberlain held his own views on Britain's capacity for taxation. In a cabinet memorandum of 7 June 1920 he observed that "it was argued the other day in Cabinet that the limit of taxation had been reached. I believe this to be substantially true." Chamberlain appears to refer here not to any technical limit imposed by the economic facts of life, but rather to psychological factors governing the public's willingness to pay additional taxes. He cautioned that "the public—at least our public—will not support us in imposing further burdens and will be bitterly and angrily disappointed if the reduction of debt to secure which they have submitted to these heavy taxes is not obtained."[58] Chamberlain disagreed with Lord Robert Cecil, who had argued that the nation's taxable capacity had been reached. Relying on a memorandum drawn up by Sir Otto Niemeyer, the chancellor echoed Hawtrey's points that the national economy was not static, and that a significant portion of taxation "returns direct to the taxpayers and through them to investment."[59]

As the slackening of trade developed into a full-scale depression by December 1920, the Treasury decided to terminate EPD in February 1921, although the government would continue to collect arrears. The move drew applause from the business community, but on 10 February the Federation of British Industries informed Chamberlain that payment of arrears, estimated at £300 million, would cause grave problems, "especially at a time when their competitors on the Continent are enjoying the advantages of a ridiculously low scale of taxation."[60] British industries were losing their competitive advantage owing to high taxation, because none of the continental powers were pursuing a responsible fiscal and monetary policy.

Officials at the Treasury, Hawtrey in particular, ascribed the growing problem with EPD arrears not to the recession, but to the "imprudence" of firms that had paid out large dividends during the 1919–20 boom without worrying about how they would pay their taxes later on. The EPD law allowed firms to pay taxes averaged over a three-year period instead of paying the total amount due each tax year. In 1921, many firms were still paying EPD taxes on profits made during the 1919–20 boom, but as the recession deepened they had no funds with which to pay.[61]

During the summer of 1921, officials at the Board of Inland Revenue warned the Treasury of a possibly massive default in tax payments. H. P. Hamilton observed to Blackett that "it would, of course, be unwise to advertise a serious deficiency as being due to a prospective inability of taxpayers to meet their obligations when they fall due. Any such announcement would be seized upon by taxpayers as an excuse to defer payment and the difficulties of collection would be multiplied." But by December 1921 the situation had become desperate to the point where the Cabinet Finance Committee authorized the new chancellor of the exchequer, Sir Robert Horne, to arrange with distressed firms to spread their tax payments over a five-year period. The Finance Committee voted that "the Chancellor of the Exchequer should have full discretion to make the best arrangements possible in the circumstances."[62] Under the weight of the recession, Britain's fiscal system appeared to have collapsed—to the apparent benefit of the capitalist class.

As the recession deepened, the growing weight of the public debt increasingly tied the government's hands. Horne told King George V's private secretary, Lord Stamfordham, that heavy debt maturities during 1921 and 1922 ruled out any tax reduction apart from the cessation of the EPD already announced. In fact, revenue would cover only about one-third of the £300 million in maturing debt; the government would have to borrow the remainder through a conversion loan.[63] But the industrialists continued to press for additional tax cuts, and under pressure from the Federation of British Industries, the Board of Inland Revenue and the Board of Customs and Excise submitted to Horne in January 1922 a joint memorandum on "Industry and the Weight of Taxation."

The Board's tax memorandum began with a statement that sounded remarkably similar to the British government's position on German reparation payments. The tax burden on industry was indeed heavy, particularly in view of the collection of EPD arrears estimated at a net value of £200 million. "True, industry is not at the moment paying this debt, mainly because it is unable to do so, but this fact only intensifies the burden. In only too many cases, the necessity of redeeming the debt hangs as an incubus over all business thought. In its effect upon the mind, it is like a mortgage, fixed in amount, upon assets continually shrinking in money values." The conclusion drawn in this case, however, differed from Britain's position on German reparation payments. "It must be pointed out," the report continued, "that these present disabilities, great as they are, are transient, and at root they can only be remedied by heroic measures of a transient kind." The British never demanded "heroic measures" from the Germans—only from the French.[64]

If only the British industrialists tried hard enough, argued the Boards, they could pay the EPD arrears. They *had* to pay, because "the assumption on which this note is written is broadly that the Budget must be balanced, and that it cannot be balanced during the next few years if taxation is reduced." A small adjustment of taxes would not help business, and a large adjustment would wreck the Exchequer. In recommending against a tax cut for industry, the Boards emphasized the transitory nature of the trade depression. Organized labor would oppose any move to increase indirect taxes, and the resulting strikes would be costly to both industry and the nation.[65] In special comments appended to the Boards' memorandum, A. W. Flux, a member of the Board of Trade, castigated industry for distributing boom profits without consideration for tax payments. He condemned the industrialists as "taxpayers who have had the privilege of using for their own purposes sums which are ultimately due from them as taxes," who were now attempting "to throw off on to other classes a part of the burden justly assessed upon them."[66]

During 1922, the debate on taxation swept through the Treasury and divided the Cabinet. One of the first to bring the issues into focus was E. S. Montagu, secretary of state for India. His 9 December 1921 memorandum to the Cabinet Financial Committee proposed some highly unorthodox methods for meeting the fiscal crisis brought on by the recession. Looking forward to the 1922–23 fiscal year, Montagu adopted the premise that "the Chancellor of the Exchequer should frame his Budget on the basis that the desperate financial position of the taxpayer necessitates an immediate and substantial reduction in taxation." "Microscopic" or step-by-step tax reductions would do no good for either the government or the taxpayers.[67]

Montagu calculated that economies in government could save the taxpayers £60 million, and the arms limitations proposed by the Washington Conference would pare off another £20 million, leaving an effective deficit of £85 million which Montagu proposed to cover by new borrowing. Because the crisis was temporary, the borrowing should be short term in the form of additional Treasury bill sales or short-dated loans. So massive was the public debt that another £85 million would have no impact on the nation's financial standing. Borrowing to cover a budget deficit was unthinkable by British standards of sound finance, but in Montagu's opinion such "theoretical objections" ought to be met by the "obvious fact that the present financial position is not only startling but alarming, not only novel but unprecedented." "Is it conceivable," he asked, "that England should prostitute herself to the level of France and budget for a deficit," and cover that deficit by borrowed money? For Montagu the answer was clearly affirmative because Britain was "paralyzed by high taxation."[68]

The first Treasury official to respond to Montagu was Basil Blackett, in a 24 March 1922 memorandum, "Budgeting for a Deficit." Blackett considered Montagu's proposals a dangerous attack on long-standing principles of British financial policy. Blackett could recall "no instance since the Napoleonic Wars when the British government has deliberately budgeted in peace time for a deficit or provided for its ordinary expenditure out of borrowed money." It was this "stern observance of the rule" which explained why "the British financial system has for generations been held up to the admiration of the world as a model." "It would come as a terrible shock to the world to see Great Britain budgeting for a deficit," and continental governments valiantly trying to balance their budgets would lose their main source of moral support. But the devastating impact of deficit budgeting, warned Blackett, would be felt most strongly in Britain itself. "Once admit that expenditures can proceed without relative taxation," he wrote, "and the floodgates are opened . . . The ultimate end of the new system is so clearly either a confiscatory levy on capital or a repudiation of the Government's internal debt under the guise of currency depreciation that the Labour extremists could not wish for better."[69]

A second serious proposal for deficit budgeting came from Alfred M. Mond, formerly minister of works and now minister of health.

Having read Blackett's memorandum on "Budgeting for a Deficit," Mond submitted his response on 30 March. Mond attributed much of the trade depression to taxation "beyond the capacity of the country to bear," and advocated a tax reduction even if it required deficit budgeting. "I should not hesitate myself," he wrote, "to adopt the expedient [borrowing] which under ordinary circumstances might be looked upon as of doubtful financial soundness." Mond shared Montagu's disdain for the conventional wisdom of the experts. Montagu had written that "I cannot convince myself that it is necessary to be so worried as orthodox financial opinion is inclined to be at the size of the floating debt." Mond doubted the efficacy of all economic theory and the wisdom of the experts. "In this matter I feel sure we should not be guided too much either by pure theory or by the advice of financiers; both are apt to regard this question too little from the general point of view of the welfare of the nation and too much from the point of view of their own particular angle of vision."[70]

Horne could count on Hawtrey, Niemeyer, and Blackett to back him against the proponents of deficit budgeting. Hawtrey condemned the "imprudence" of businessmen who could not pay their taxes, and Niemeyer cautioned that a budget deficit covered by additional borrowing would ruin the planned Conversion Loans. Blackett argued against making "concessions to the weakness of human nature" during the crisis. The crisis passed, everyone would condemn the expedients adopted, but the expedients would leave additional financial burdens which future generations would have to pay.[71]

Horne nevertheless could not resist pressure for some form of tax reduction in his proposals for the 1922–23 budget. He agreed to reduce the standard rate on the income tax from 6s. to 5s. in the pound, grant some relief to agriculture and industry on EPD arrears, and reduce tea duties. Some termed this a "rich man's budget" because the lower classes got only a 4d. reduction on tea duties while the bulk of the benefits went to the farmers, landlords, and industrialists. Horne achieved these tax reductions by suspending all sinking funds —that is, by suspending repayment of public debt. This gave the chancellor about £30 million for tax reductions and an estimated budget surplus of £706,000. In fact, the actual surplus at the end of the fiscal year came to £101,516,000, part of which was applied to debt reduction.[72]

In the preparation of the budget, the Cabinet had discussed and rejected the possibility of raiding the pension funds by "spreading pensions." Horne vigorously opposed such an expedient, reporting to Lloyd George, who was in Geneva during these Cabinet budget talks, that "while the financiers may gird at our departure from 'pure finance' in suspending sinking funds in peacetime, they would be *violent* [his italics] if we at the same time 'spread pensions'; and our prospects of a conversion loan on cheap terms might have been appreciably affected."[73]

Even as he prepared to give them some relief in his 1922–23 budget, Horne prepared an all-out attack on the industrialists and financiers who complained so loudly about the burden of direct taxation. In his "Notes for Speech on the Budget, 1922–23," the chancellor condemned the leaders of industry and trade who "have conducted and are still conducting an organized campaign throughout the whole country against its burden." These leaders saw only two facts —the trade depression and the high rates of taxation—and drew the conclusion that the two were connected causally. Their view, argued Horne, was too narrow. The real problem, the basic cause of Britain's economic difficulties, he believed, was the fact that 40 percent of the budget had to be earmarked for debt service. There was no place in the budget to accommodate a large tax reduction by making a corresponding reduction in expenditure.[74]

While the high level of debt service was unfortunate, it resulted, Horne observed, not from errors of the present government, but from the manner in which Britain chose to pay for the war. "Governments," wrote Horne, "are blamed for many things—but I have never heard them blamed for unduly light taxation. Yet if present taxation is unbearable, some part of that fault must be traced back to the past distribution of the burden between taxation, loans, and inflation."[75]

When the nation decided to pay for the war largely through raising the national debt, it pledged its credit to pay the interest on those loans. In Horne's view, "the tacit bargain was that for immediate loaned (instead of taxed) wealth, the nation would year by year raise by taxation of each year's production the income necessary to pay the interest." Now, argued Horne, the wealthy classes should not be surprised to find themselves bearing that burden, for, "knowing that for direct taxation the ruling principle of this country is taxation by reference to ability to pay, those who had command of wealth undertook to lay themselves under tribute year by year to bear the burden of interest. It amounts to some £350,000,000 every year." The wealthy classes, implied the chancellor, now wished to repudiate their "tacit agreement" to pay the war's debt service charge by shifting the burden to the working classes through increased indirect taxation. If the business community insisted on that route, warned Horne, they would only wind up with direct confiscation of their capital by the Labour party.[76]

With the passage of Horne's 1922–23 budget, Britain's Exchequer had set the general lines of postwar fiscal policy. By and large, the government would follow orthodox fiscal policies, rejecting taxes that seemed incompatible with British or Anglo-Saxon tradition, and repudiating for the most part unsound or opportunistic methods of balancing the budget or drastically reducing the public debt. Britain renounced the capital levy. But though it was far from friendly toward Labour, Lloyd George's Coalition government appeared determined to enforce the "tacit bargain" under which the capitalist class would bear its share of war costs. Following these policies, British finance regained stature in the international community. The pound was restored to $4.86, and sterling became a reserve currency under the gold exchange standard established in the mid-twenties. Whether the pursuit of these orthodox fiscal and monetary policies produced a British recession which began in mid-1920 and lasted until the Second World War is still a matter of debate.

By British standards, France did not pursue a sound fiscal program during the early postwar years. As noted at the beginning of this chapter, the French Finance Ministry had managed to reestablish the "unitary" budget and eliminate most of the special accounts by the end of 1922. Despite this progress toward rationalization of the budget, French financial services continued to show significant operational weaknesses. Relatively minor officials engaged the state's resources without authorizaton, often spending funds for which the official budget made no provision. Only in January 1921 did the Council of Ministers rule that no one could obligate the state without the written approval of the Contrôleur des dépenses engagées on each purchase order. At the end of 1922, Finance Minister Charles de Lasteyrie admitted to the Cour des Comptes that "certain principles of our financial legislation must be revised; certain methods of work must be simplified; the multiplicity of superimposed controls is perhaps on balance more onerous than beneficial." He conceded that the Finance Minister still lacked a centralized procedure for controlling income and expenditure.[77]

Interministerial conflicts complicated the management of France's postwar finances. Because reconstruction costs dominated postwar budgets, it was perhaps inevitable that an unfortunate conflict arose between Minister for Liberated Regions Emile Ogier and Finance Minister François-Marsal. Ogier incessantly requested guaranteed funding of ever-larger amounts for reconstruction, while François-Marsal refused to guarantee any specific amount owing to the uncertainty of tax receipts. The finance minister told Ogier that the Ministry of Liberated Regions "has never had any limit [on expenditure] other than the capabilities of the Treasury." But the Finance Ministry had met Ogier's demands not from tax revenues, but by selling additional Treasury bills, a procedure François-Marsal regarded as a sign of his "extreme desire to reconcile as much as possible the needs of the invaded regions and the very serious situation of the Treasury." Following a three-month exchange of rather nasty letters, the finance minister finally told Ogier to stop sending requests for funds that he knew the Finance Ministry did not have.[78]

Balancing the French budget was rendered difficult by certain expenditures that the war had either created or inflated to abnormal proportions. Military expenditures continued to consume 16 percent of the French ordinary budget in 1922. There were costly special accounts for the reintegration of Alsace-Lorraine, management of the Saar, and subsidies for railways, shipping, and foodstuffs.

After forty-seven years of German rule, the return of Alsace-Lorraine to French sovereignty involved a costly reconversion process. The Finance Ministry created a special account in the budget to cover the cost of reintegration. One particular expense, the redemption of German marks circulating in Alsace-Lorraine, required another special account at the Treasury under the head "Exchange of German money held by Alsatians and Lorrainers, French prisoners of war, and inhabitants of the liberated regions." In a decree of 26 November 1918, the president of the Council, Clemenceau, had fixed the redemption of German marks circulating in the recovered territory at the prewar rate of 1.25 francs to the mark. In view of the precipitous decline of the mark after the war, Clemenceau's action might seem premature at best, and may have stemmed from the belief that "Germany will pay." By 1922, the special account for conversion of marks came to 2.25 billion francs—all of it a charge against the French taxpayers.[79]

Conversion of German marks at an unfavorable exchange rate was a costly but necessary procedure. Having complained about German policies in Alsace-Lorraine for forty-seven years, the French now had to prove that they could do better. When the Germans recovered their "long-lost Alsatian brothers" in 1871, they showed no desire to make any sacrifices for them or to facilitate the integration of the Reichsland into the German Empire.[80] But 1918 was different. No matter what redemption ratio the French government had chosen, the decline of the mark was so precipitous and disastrous that French taxpayers were destined to lose money on the transaction. Werner Wittich observed in 1922 that the nature of the situation required some sacrifice on the part of the French. France had to restore the economic connection between Alsace-Lorraine and France, and this could be achieved only with the prompt introduction of the French franc. The value of prompt economic reintegration, argued Wittich, outweighed the monetary losses sustained by the French people in the process.[81]

Another temporary fruit of victory was the Saar. Though nominally under the international control of the League of Nations until the 1935 plebiscite returned the territory to Germany, France exercised de facto control of the region. The League assigned the presidency of the international governing commission to France. In theory, the Saar was to provide France with coal to replace the lost production from French mines destroyed by the Germans. In fact, the Saar budget remained in chronic deficit, largely owing to substantial losses on railway operations. The Saar deficit was covered by a 20 percent tax on coal production, which provided nearly the entire revenue of the territory. Who ultimately paid that coal tax? French consumers of the Saar's coal paid it, and thereby contributed about 100 million francs annually to the Saar budget. When François-Marsal attempted to reorganize the Saar's finances in 1920, he cited the "intolerable burden" on French consumers as the primary complaint. But the situation equally displeased the population of the Saar, who were disenchanted with French officials who could not so much as balance the territorial budget. François-Marsal warned that the projected plebiscite would go badly for France if the Saar's financial situation were not straightened out promptly.[82]

Railway and shipping deficits plagued the French budget during and after the war. Requisitioned by the government in August 1914, the French railways had exceeded their revenues by about 5.5 billion francs when the war emergency controls ended on 24 October 1919. The government continued to cover the railway deficit in a special account in the budget. Shipping subsidies also burdened the taxpayers. Ships acquired by the state for the merchant marine during the war operated at a loss. The government had advanced funds to armament firms for the construction of merchant ships, further adding to the public debt. Not until 1921 did Finance Minister Paul Doumer conclude that the government could no longer afford the luxury of a merchant fleet supported by funds from the Treasury. He deleted from the budget funds for construction of ships, and proceeded with the disposal of the merchant fleet owned by the government without awaiting parliamentary approval of the sale.[83]

Of the special accounts in the French budget, the most costly and controversial was that for foodstuffs, the Compte spécial du ravitaillement. Scandal, mismanagement, and incompetence plagued this account. The law of 16 October 1915 establishing the foodstuffs account stipulated that it would be closed three months after the hostilities ended. With the signing of the Armistice, the under secretary of state directing the account began to liquidate his stocks in anticipation of the impending closing down of the operation. In view of the escalating cost of living, however, the government now decided to continue to offer the French public subsidized foodstuffs during the postwar transition period. Having depleted its stocks, the Services commerciaux du ravitaillement had to reconstitute them at higher prices. Some questioned the propriety of government food subsidies during peacetime, but everyone agreed that the foodstuffs services had failed to follow businesslike procedures in managing the account. In August 1919, the Finance Ministry decided to take remedial action.

On 28 June 1920, the finance minister, supported by a report prepared by the Controleur des dépenses engagées and endorsed by an inspector general at the Finance Ministry, recommended to the president of the council that the foodstuffs account be deleted from future budgets. According to François-Marsal, mismanagement had run up a deficit in the account of 3.3 billion francs on 30 June 1919. A year later, the deficit had soared to 6 billion francs. The finance minister calculated that interest on funds required to cover the deficiency, as well as capital tied up in the foodstuffs account itself, came to 300 million francs.[84]

The foodstuffs deficit, however, was only the tip of the iceberg. The Services commerciaux du ravitaillement, which sold subsidized foodstuffs to the public, had fallen about three months behind in its reimbursements to the Treasury. By 1 May 1920 these arrears amounted to about 750 million francs, on which the Treasury was losing approximately 50 million francs in interest. Worse yet, when the foodstuffs account used up its original allocation of funds from parliament, it continued to purchase and redistribute commodities without any appropriation. The foodstuffs service was spending funds which it did not possess, and, having no special budget for such funds, it spent with no limit whatsoever. The Finance Ministry eventually paid the bills.[85]

The memorandum from the controller and the inspector general suggested that before the Treasury was asked to make new sacrifices in order to feed the nation, "there ought to be a limit set to these sacrifices." At subsidized prices, grain was being used to feed pigs, chickens, and dogs. "Would it not be prudent policy," wrote the inspector general of finance, "to limit the sacrifice of the state on grain to guaranteeing the feeding of the population?" The political implications of this farce were not wasted on the inspector, who warned that "the opposition will have a fine time when you [the finance minister] go to parliament to ask for two or three millards not just to feed the people, but to provide the rich with pastries and fatten livestock." The controller's memorandum advised that the present deficit be wiped clean, and that parliament vote new funds with the proviso that they be renewed by parliament when they ran out. At least the government would then know exactly how much the food program was costing the taxpayers. The finance minister, however, concluded that the entire food subsidy program should be liquidated.[86]

Given the complexities of the French budget, deficiencies in procedure and organization at the Finance Ministry, interministerial conflicts, and massive deficits in uncontrolled special accounts, a truly balanced budget based on sound fiscal principles was out of the question. Klotz, as we have seen, did not attempt to reorganize French finances in his 1919 budget. He intended his modest tax increase only as a token of good faith to encourage the American Treasury to resume its loans. By 1920, however, something more than a token effort was required if France were to avoid financial catastrophe. But Klotz's 1920 budget, which he represented as an essay in "energetic fiscal measures," contained nothing to indicate a vigorous, innovative program to reconstruct French finances.

Expected revenue from existing sources would leave a 9 billion franc deficit in the 1920 budget. To balance the ordinary budget, Klotz proposed a complicated assortment of increases on old taxes as well as some new taxes, which he described as "a case of reconstructing the national finances." By assuring equity of burden through a wide variety of taxes, Klotz hoped to instill a sense of "fiscal patriotism" which would enable the French people to "rediscover the sense of sacrifice they demonstrated during the long years of the war." Klotz warned against adopting expedients for the upcoming fiscal year, but his package of proposed new taxes, spearheaded by a "turnover tax" (tax on the *chiffre d'affaires* or gross receipts from all sales and commissions on sales) left a gap of about 1.8 billion francs in the ordinary budget. The finance minister proposed to close this deficit with temporary taxes on war profits and a tax on increases in wealth that exceeded 1914 levels by over 20 percent.[87]

Klotz believed his budget would promote "the financial security of France." The "sacrifice" demanded of the taxpayers would be well worth the price, for "it will reinforce the credit of France and will show our allies that we know how to do our duty in the civic as well as in the military arena . . . it will enable the nation to pursue its noble destiny and it will assure us the force necessary to demand, with the complete execution of the treaties of peace, the whole of the reparations to which the enemy is committed." In short, Klotz's taxation program would return practical benefits in the form of new loans from the Allies and reparation payments from the Germans.[88] Skeptics such as the editor of *L'économiste français*, André Liesse, commented sardonically that Klotz's *compte provisionnel* for special taxes on war wealth and profits would more aptly be termed the *compte providentiel*, because it could produce the expected revenue only by a "miraculous multiplication of milliards."[89]

The ordinary budget of 17.8 billion francs came to less than half of the 47.45 billion francs represented by the combined budgets. Extraordinary expenditures caused by the war came to 7.5 billion francs, and the budget of expenditures recoverable from Germany totaled 22 billion francs. Klotz proposed to meet these expenses largely through government borrowing of 26.5 billion francs. The future generations which would benefit from projects financed by these loans, Klotz argued, should share in the costs. As to the recoverable budget, Klotz viewed it as "not only a budgetary necessity, but also a political necessity." To have inscribed such expenses, for which others were liable, in the ordinary budget would have presented a false picture of French finances. Klotz did not wish to hide Germany's obligations in the French budget; by listing them separately, the world could compare easily the effort the French were making with the effort the Germans were making—a comparison which could only be favorable to the French. Germany would be pressed by world opinion to pay its obligation.[90]

While Klotz was explaining his 1920 budget to parliament, the government of which he was a member was disintegrating. Clemenceau lost to Paul Deschanel in the French presidential election of 17 January 1920. He resigned as president of the Council on the 18th, and two days later Alexandre Millerand (former socialist, now listed as *non inscrit*) formed a new cabinet with Frédéric François-Marsal as finance minister. In the midst of this cabinet crisis, the French Finance Ministry found itself unable to float loans or sell its Treasury bills in either London or New York. Pressure for a balanced budget thus became all the more intense. At the British Treasury, Hawtrey wondered "whether the budget of Mr. Marsal will be less improvident" than the one proposed by Klotz. "In any event," he concluded, "a change of Ministers at the very moment when the budget is maturing is unfortunate."[91]

British observers characterized the Millerand cabinet as pronouncedly Anglophile and portrayed the new finance minister as "thoroughly imbued with the necessity of maintaining the Anglo-French alliance on as firm a basis as possible."[92] Francois-Marsal apparently believed the British could show their solidarity by lending France more money. Barely settled down at the Finance Ministry, he went to London the first week of February 1920 to assess prospects for French loans in the London market. The City told him precisely what J. P. Morgan & Co. was telling him from New York; under existing market conditions a major French operation was out of the question.

The finance minister's real problem, however, was the condition of the French budget rather than the condition of the markets. Upon his return to Paris, François-Marsal met with the finance commission of the Chamber of Deputies. Asked whether he planned to proceed with the budget and revenue law proposed by Klotz, the new minister replied that his first priority was a new loan for reconstruction, for which he was pursuing negotiations with the Allies. To obtain the loan, the French would have to demonstrate to investors in London and New York their determination to limit public and private spending, work harder, and produce more. The general lines of Klotz's program would be preserved, but the budget would have to be pared to the bone and taxes increased. He urged the finance commission to accept those proposals by Klotz which seemed uncontroversial, but indicated he would suggest major changes in his predecessor's plans for a super-tax on incomes and taxes on increases in wealth since 1914.[93]

Before the new finance minister had announced his own program, *The Economist* in London had portrayed François-Marsal as "animated with a desire to introduce several entirely new principles in taxation, which in their application must inevitably entirely revolutionize the French fiscal system."[94] In fact, François-Marsal, a Parisian banker, proposed nothing more revolutionary than a reduction of direct taxation and an increase in indirect taxation. He accepted the turnover tax proposed by Klotz, but would increase it from 1 percent to 1.5 percent. He proposed to raise the income tax rate on wages, salaries, pensions, and annuities from 3.75 percent to 5 percent, but proposed no increase on income derived from property and investments. He deleted Klotz's proposals to tax wartime increases in wealth. François-Marsal's drive to reduce expenditures also affected the poorer classes most directly—it was he who recommended an end to food subsidies. By cutting the ordinary budget by half—8 billion francs—and increasing revenue by an estimated 8 billion francs, François-Marsal's plan would reduce the deficit to be made up by borrowing from 26 billion francs to 10 billion.[95]

François-Marsal was looking toward the financial markets of London and New York as he proposed his revisions to Klotz's budget. Allied objections to French financial practices were becoming more biting than ever. The French ambassador in Washington, Jules Jusserand, reported derogatory remarks made by Secretary of the Treasury David F. Houston in a speech to the Chicago Chamber of Commerce. The following morning, Jusserand went to see Houston, who assured the ambassador that the press had misquoted his Chicago speech. He had never spoken of French "stupidities," nor had he represented the French as having a "beggerly" attitude. Houston admitted he had mentioned that France was less heavily taxed during the entire war than was America or England in a single year, but these, he said, were public figures taken from a work published by the Carnegie Endowment. The secretary had never tried to hide his opinion that it was always better to rely as much as possible on taxation and to limit borrowing to a minimum. To this Jusserand added his own advice. "Perhaps circumstances made it impossible for us," he observed to the foreign minister, Millerand, "but nothing would profit us more and contribute more to renewing their [America's] disposition to aid us, which was so strong in the beginning, than if we raised our taxes and ceased our borrowing."[96] This, of course, was the goal the new finance minister was aiming for.

François-Marsal's hopes were disappointed. The parliament did not pass the 1920 budget until July, when they should have been debating the 1921 budget. In its final form, the 1920 budget represented a compromise, or, as the editor of L'économiste français described it, a budget of "waiting." It is not clear what the parliament was waiting for—perhaps reparation payments from Germany—but in the end the Senate supported most of François-Marsal's propositions for tax increases and budget cuts while the Chamber by and large rejected them. Parliament approved the turnover tax, but at Klotz's rate of 1 percent rather than François-Marsal's 1.5 percent. Certain of the increments in the tax on war profits were approved— a victory for Klotz—but the tax on increments of wealth during the war was rejected—a victory for François-Marsal. The Senate shifted some expenditures from the extraordinary budget to the ordinary budget, without adding the 2 billion francs in ordinary revenue to cover the shift. By this tactic the Senate merely managed to increase the deficit in the ordinary budget. In any event, the deficit would be larger than estimated, because passage of the 1920 budget in July meant that new taxes would be collected for only half of the fiscal year.[97]

With the passage of the 1920 budget a wave of complacent self-congratulation swept France. In a November journal article, Klotz described passage of the budget as a courageous act, a "milestone" in French financial history. As he presented his 1921 budget only one day after parliament had passed the 1920 budget, François-Marsal told the parliament that "a fiscal effort without precedent in France, a sacrifice, one may say, without precedent, had just been asked of the country and courageously consented to by it." The nation's taxable capacity, he said, had been reached in the 1920 budget, and no additional sacrifice would be asked in the 1921 budget. Excessive taxation would only provoke massive evasion and possibly paralyze the nation's economic activity. France, François-Marsal believed, needed to reconstitute her capital resources and intensify production.[98]

Without additional taxes, François-Marsal's 1921 ordinary budget showed a deficiency of 1.48 billion francs. He proposed to cover it with funds derived from the sale of surplus war stocks and receipts from the tax on war profits, neither of which was a permanent source of revenue. Such procedure was not in accord with the principles of sound finance, but the finance minister asserted that such revenues "constitute nevertheless a true fiscal charge added to those which the taxpayers bear." "The balance of the ordinary budget," he concluded, "is thus assured by tax recepits."[99]

The confidence exuded by François-Marsal in his public defense of the proposed 1921 budget disappeared in his remarks to the French cabinet on the morning of 12 November 1920. He was particularly concerned with the adverse effects on the French Treasury stemming from the use of receipts from the tax on war profits and the sale of surplus war stocks to balance the ordinary budget. The tax on war profits, he pointed out, was legally payable in government securities. Far from bringing in new resources, such payments were destroying a portion of the consolidated, long-term debt and forcing the government to replace it with short-term or floating debt. As to the sale of surplus war stocks, the finance minister warned that "one cannot consider the product realized as definitive returns to the French Treasury, since the American stocks were purchased from the United States for $400 million, repayable in ten years."[100] In other words, income from the sale of surplus stocks was not income at all. The French government realized only about $220 million of the $400 million it owed the United States on the purchase of American surplus.

François-Marsal gave the cabinet an equally disquieting report on the extraordinary budget for 1921. He admitted it had been artificially inflated by the inclusion of all military costs. Consolidation of floating debt through the recent 6 percent loan had in fact added 500 million francs in interest charges to the extraordinary budget. Treasury reimbursements to the Bank of France under the François-Marsal Convention would cost 3 billion francs in 1920 and 2 billion in 1921, and foreign debt coming due in 1921 would add another 3 billion francs to the extraordinary budget. The finance minister assured the cabinet that these expenditures could be met from the very revenue sources he had just characterized as dangerous and unsound —the tax on war profits, the sale of surplus war stocks, and the sale of additional Treasury bills. He bluntly told his colleagues that "we have arrived at the extreme limit of our financial possibilities."[101]

Finally, there was the budget of expenditures recoverable from Germany. It was this item which most concerned France's allies and creditors. In his public defense of his budget, François-Marsal made no apologies for the recoverable budget. It was, he said, merely a "provisional solution, discounting the payments Germany must make to us." The French public had been more than generous in responding to the government's bond issues, but the government could not go on borrowing forever. The interest charges appeared in the budget, and the burden on the taxpayers grew more onerous each year. If the government failed to make progress toward Germany's execution of the peace treaties, the lenders would withdraw their generous support. "The execution of the Treaty," he concluded, "is thus the indispensable condition for the complete rehabilitation of our finance."[102] The implication of the finance minister's statement was unmistakable. The Allies and Associates who criticized French fiscal practices might assist in a constructive manner by supporting French efforts to enforce the Treaty of Versailles.

As the 1921 budget passed through parliament, the Chamber of Deputies cut the extraordinary budget by nearly 2 billion francs and increased the ordinary budget to 22.8 billion francs, 500 million above François-Marsal's request. To balance the revised ordinary budget, the Chamber merely exaggerated estimated revenue.[103] The balance was thus no balance at all, a fact which did not escape the attention of financial and political observers in London, New York, and Washington. The irony of the situation is that Klotz, whose policies as finance minister had drawn vicious criticism from opponents in the Chamber, had warned against such fraudulent budgeting only six months earlier. Budget figures, he had written, must be supported by "solid bases of reality." The value of a budget lies in its "sincerity," and its "balance" is "valid only if the estimates have been established without optimistic exaggeration and . . . based rigorously on the collections of preceding years, with corrections as are supported by precise justifications."[104]

When the cabinet of Georges Leygues fell on 12 January 1921, Paul Doumer (gauche démocratique) became finance minister in the government of Aristide Briand. Although Doumer's 1922 budget has been characterized as a "violent criticism" of his predecessors' policies, the new finance minister merely continued the deceptive practices of the past and contributed a few innovations of his own. There was, in truth, no honest way to balance the French budget in 1922. Doumer, however, believed the budget *had* to be balanced, and set about to end the postwar "budgets of disorder and ruin." "It is high time," he told parliament, "to return to regularity, to rigorous management, to balancing expenditures and resources." He rejected "simple palliatives where an effective remedy, a radical measure, is required." Borrowing had to be stopped, and the public debt had to be consolidated and eventually reduced. The only way to halt the growth of the public debt was to balance the budget.[105]

Doumer thus isolated the massive public debt and its annual service charge as the primary budget problem. Half of his proposed 1922 budget of 25 billion francs represented debt service, and only 7 billion remained for current expenditures. He noted the paradox that "as our budgets increase, the disposable resources to assure the functioning of public services decreases." But the debt had to be serviced and repaid—unless America agreed to cancel a portion of it and Germany met her treaty obligations. Otherwise, the French people would have to make additional sacrifices.

Doumer asked for sacrifice, but not equally from all social classes. His 1922 budget proposals placed most of the burden on the poorer classes. The special accounts which had subsidized railways, coal, and foodstuffs were to be closed out. Funds for reconstruction of the liberated regions would no longer appear in the budget. Loans and advances for that purpose would have to be arranged by individual departments, cities and towns, professional groups, and the Crédit National. The state would limit its role in financing the liberated regions to transmitting German payments to those entitled to the money.

Doumer's proposed economies left an estimated deficit of 2.5 billion francs. The finance minister asked for no new taxes because, as he explained, they would not produce revenue quickly enough to cover the 1922 fiscal year. Rates on the income tax could not be increased because that tax "needs reform." Doumer thus proposed to double the rate on the turnover tax from 1 percent to 2 percent. Because this tax was passed on to the consumers, it was essentially a tax on the poorer classes. Opponents in parliament charged that owing to the business recession this was the worst possible moment for an increase in the turnover tax. The Finance Ministry department responsible for collection of the turnover tax had in fact consistently reported returns far below expectations, and massive noncompliance. The Chamber's finance commission forced Doumer to back down to a rate of 1.5 percent, and advised him to crack down on evaders. To balance the budget, the commission simply raised its estimate of revenues.[106]

The 1922 budget was thus no more honest than its predecessors. Doumer's reforms affected the form rather than the substance of the budget. He combined the ordinary and extraordinary budgets simply by listing the extraordinary expenditures at the end of the ordinary budget. He balanced this new combination by once again resorting to extraordinary revenues from taxes on war profits and the sale of war surplus. Doumer justified this unusual package with the argument that "it is no more abnormal to include extraordinary expenditure than extraordinary recepts in an ordinary budget."[107]

As approved by the Chamber's finance commission, the budget contained a deficit of 1.6 billion francs which the commission proposed to cover by issuing more Treasury bills. After parliament had passed the 1922 budget, François-Marsal told an audience attending a monetary conference in Paris that borrowing was not the answer to the budget deficit. France, he said, must choose between four definitive methods of balancing the budget: increased taxation, reduced spending, false money created through inflation, and forcing Germany to meet its reparation obligation. The last alternative was the ex-finance minister's first choice.[108] As the year 1922 drew to a close, occupation of the Ruhr loomed ever larger as the definitive solution to France's fiscal dilemma.

The 1923 budget, introduced on 31 March 1922, represented the end of the line for France's postwar fiscal policies. The old expedients no longer sufficed. France had to develop either a totally new financial program to balance the budget, or a completely new foreign policy to force Germany to pay. When the Briand cabinet fell on 12 January 1922 and Raymond Poincaré became president of the council and minister for foreign affairs, it was clear that France had chosen the latter alternative of a new, forceful foreign policy. The new finance minister, Charles de Lasteyrie, reflected this turn of events in his 1923 budget.

Lasteyrie brazenly presented parliament an unbalanced budget showing a deficit of 3.9 billion francs. The budget, he said, could not be balanced in the absence of sweeping fiscal reforms that would come too late to help the government during the coming fiscal year. He then pointed out that the 3.9 billion franc deficit approximately equaled the interest as of 1 January 1922 on sums France had advanced to Germany on her recoverable account. Rightfully, he asserted, the Finance Ministry could have inscribed the deficit in the recoverable budget—thus presenting parliament a balanced general budget—but "desiring to be sincere, we decided it should be inscribed in the general budget."[109]

In a period of economic recession, argued Lasteyrie, additional taxation was out of the question. The government would have to balance the 1923 budget by additional borrowing. He admitted that "such an expedient would be without doubt inadmissable in a normal period." But because the deficit resulted from German noncompliance with its treaty obligations, Lasteyrie contended, "before asking the French people for new sacrifices, the Government's duty is to use all means in its power to oblige Germany to repair the ruins and devastation she has caused."[110] The finance minister was doing his part to set the stage for the occupation of the Ruhr.

Parliament amended Lasteyrie's budget to reduce the projected deficit to 364 million francs, despite an increase in projected expenditure of 222 million francs above the amount requested by the finance minister. Parliament accomplished this miraculous reduction of the projected deficit accompanied by an increase in estimated spending by raising its estimate of revenues by 3.7 billion francs.[111] With the 1923 budget completed, events now pushed France toward fateful financial and political decisions by the end of 1922.

In June 1922 a special bankers' committee headed by J. P. Morgan, Jr., advised the Reparation Commission that a widely discussed loan to Germany could not be floated in the private financial markets of the world. Most non-French experts concluded that without the loan, Germany required a moratorium on reparation payments. Poincaré rejected any moratorium which was not accompanied by specific "guarantees" or "pledges," German properties placed under French control to assure eventual payment. In December 1922 Germany presented its own proposal, which "amounted in effect to a calculated decision by Germany to force a confrontation." Within the French government, pressure for an occupation of the Ruhr continued to mount, although Poincaré apparently did not support such a move in the 13 November cabinet meeting.[112] A Paris summit meeting on 2–3 January 1923 between the British and French premieres failed to break the deadlock, and on 11 January French and Belgian troops entered the Ruhr.

As the Ruhr occupation approached, the French government took steps to strengthen its financial and moral position at home and abroad. In a letter of 8 January 1923 to the president of the Chamber of Deputies' finance commission, Lasteyrie outlined the situation as it had evolved since the government had introduced the 1923 budget in March 1922. The Finance Ministry had hoped that the deficit might be covered by higher returns on existing taxes, borrowing, and "substantial" German reparation payments. The Chamber had accepted the government's position, but by December the situation had deteriorated to the point where the Chamber had invited the government "in the name of the endangered public credit, to demand of the country the indispensable sacrifices." The Finance Ministry continued to defer action in the hope an international loan could be arranged for Germany.[113]

The loan had fallen through, and the 2–3 January Paris conference had failed, according to Lasteyrie, owing to a lack of British support for the French position. In the absence of British support, wrote

Lasteyrie, France would have to take other guarantees and find new methods to exploit German pledges (*gages*) lying at her doorstep. This was a clear reference to the approaching Ruhr occupation. "By the same token," continued the finance minister, "it [lack of British support] requires us to take internal measures which will support our external action, this twin coordinated effort manifesting the inextinguishable will of the nation to save itself and to preserve in the world that ethical position which belongs only to peoples who know how to simultaneously accomplish their tasks and have their rights respected."[114]

Lasteyrie had described a political, financial, and ethical crisis in which "the government believes, in the present circumstances, and whatever it costs, the ordinary budget must be placed immediately in real balance." To achieve this end he proposed a 20 percent increase in rates on all existing taxes, the so-called *double décime*. He acknowledged the *double décime* would work a hardship on the French taxpayers, but it was the simplest solution and the only way to get immediate results. The crisis was immediate and left no time for legislating and implementing new taxes.[115]

The finance minister chose to dramatize his request for the *double décime* by presenting it to parliament on the very day French troops began their march into the Ruhr, 11 January 1923. His tactic failed. Parliament rejected the tax increase ind instead balanced the budget, as noted above, by raising the estimated revenue for the fiscal year. This maneuver was not completed until 30 June. Stephen Schuker has suggested that "the cabinet soon made it clear that it did not intend to risk a vote of confidence on the matter," and that "Poincaré believed that the exigencies of parliamentary politics made it inadvisable for him to push too hard. The essential issue for his ministry was the occupation of the Ruhr. A conflict with the Chamber over increased taxes could only obstruct efforts to rally the population behind the Ruhr policy."[116]

Poincaré's cabinet itself was by no means united behind Lasteyrie's call for the *double décime*. If the essential issue for Poincaré's ministry was indeed the Ruhr occupation, Lasteyrie had made it clear that French financial solvency was essential for the success of that military operation—a point which Poincaré may not have understood. Poincaré also may not have comprehended the financial and monetary problems raised by the occupation of foreign territory.

These had already been demonstrated by French attempts to exploit the Saar coal mines, as agents of the Finance Ministry reported as early as 1920 that Saar coal might cost France more than it was worth. The 20 percent tax on Saar coal cost French consumers 100 million francs annually, the Saar railways planned to raise rates to compensate for heavy losses, the mines themselves required costly improvements to make them competitive, and labor disputes reduced productivity.[117] France might have given more serious consideration to its frustrating experience in the Saar before launching the Ruhr occupation.

One of the most perplexing monetary problems associated with the Ruhr occupation concerned the use of French currency in the occupied territory. On the eve of the occupation, Poincaré sought Lasteyrie's advice concerning the possibility of authorizing French occupation forces to settle commercial exchanges in francs rather than in the local currency, the German mark. Lasteyrie warned that introduction of the French franc would be disastrous. The mark might disappear from circulation, forcing a corresponding increase in the use of francs. These francs, he pointed out, could come from only one source, the French Treasury. The resulting charge to the Treasury might run as high as 200 million francs annually.[118]

Lasteyrie understood Poincaré's desire to reap the political advantages which might derive from introduction of the franc in the Ruhr, but he considered the financial risk unacceptable. If Poincaré desired monetary reform in the Ruhr, he should introduce not the French franc but rather an entirely new monetary unit based on gold. This step, Lasteyrie observed, implied the creation of a new bank of issue, and that meant conferring of sovereign power in some organ of local government in the Rhineland—in short, Rhenish separatism. "It seems," concluded Lasteyrie, "that we cannot but be favorable to a monetary reform of a nature to singularly facilitate our Rhenish policy." But Lasteyrie cautioned that introduction of a new monetary unit based on gold could be risky, since a comparison between the gold Rhenish franc and the paper French franc "could only be prejudicial to our interests." The government would also have to take precautions "that any monetary reform in the Rhineland not arouse any hopes of an annexationist tendency on the part of France, as unjustifiable as such hopes may be."[119]

In the absence of the French franc, monetary requirements of the occupation forces were met by seizure of German marks forcibly taken out of circulation and handed over to the French forces. By March 1923 this source began to dry up, forcing the French Treasury to purchase German marks in the foreign exchange markets. The Finance Ministry quickly ordered an end to this practice, which supported the mark exchange at a time when Germany's wholesale use of the printing press was pushing the mark down. The Finance Ministry suggested that if a sufficient supply of marks could not be taken from notes in circulation, the occupation forces should seize them at branches of the Reichsbank located in the Ruhr area. The Finance Ministry had earlier ruled out such seizures on the grounds they might provoke a monetary crisis in Germany. But now that the Germans were provoking their own monetary crisis, the seizures could proceed with a clear conscience.[120]

As the Ruhr occupation entered its sixth month with no apparent gain for France, Poincaré began to take a personal interest in the economic and monetary reorganization of the occupied territory. He informed Lasteyrie that France would have to demonstrate to the local populace its intention to stay in the Ruhr as long as necessary. The best way to demonstrate this intent, believed Poincaré, was to reorganize the territorial monetary system, railways, and customs. Poincaré sought Lasteyrie's advice on the possibility of introducing a new currency in the Ruhr, establishing an independent railway system in the territory, and setting up a tariff barrier between the occupied and unoccupied portions of the Ruhr.[121]

Lasteyrie sympathized with Poincaré's goals, but expressed serious reservations as to the proposed means. The question of a new monetary system for the occupied Ruhr, he noted, had already been submitted to a Franco-Belgian committee of technical experts. The committee had established a stand-by program for creating a new bank of issue, but advised that the plan not be implemented "except in the case of absolute necessity." Technical problems associated with the introduction of a new currency were legion, but most critical in Lasteyrie's view was the fact that monetary problems in the Ruhr could not be resolved until the outstanding political questions had been settled. He in effect told Poincaré that introduction of a new currency in the Ruhr implied a number of political decisions that in fact had not yet been made—and probably never would be made.[122]

Poincaré apparently did not understand the implications of issuing a new currency in the Ruhr. Lasteyrie spelled it all out for him. "We can do nothing serious from a monetary point of view," he told the premier, "without first having defined the length and methods of our occupation in the Ruhr and in the Rhineland." Introduction of a sound local currency presupposed a budget specifically adapted to the regions in question, taxes paid in the new currency, and public expenditures fixed in the new money. "That amounts to saying," Lasteyrie observed, "that we must control the administration and be quasi sovereigns of the region." Perhaps France intended to assume quasi sovereignty over the Ruhr, but that was a political decision which could not be achieved through any monetary reform.[123]

Lasteyrie admitted his approach might be criticized as excessively timid, but he warned Poincaré that problems the occupying forces were presently encountering would pale into insignificance if France made a "monetary error" in the Ruhr. In any event, the Franco-Belgian technical committee had indicated that any new issue operation in the Ruhr would require formal guarantees from the Allied governments, and such guarantees were clearly unobtainable. The finance minister suggested the seizure and shipment to France of the mined coal already above ground. If the Germans refused to replenish those supplies, France would be entitled to take the mines under the reparation clauses of the Vesrailles Treaty.[124]

So long as French forces occupied the Ruhr, there was no way to keep the French franc out of the territory. In November 1923 Lasteyrie joined the governor of the Bank of France, Georges Robineau, in expressing to Poincaré their "grave concern caused by the circulation of the franc in the occupied territories." A few days later, the finance minister told Poincaré that it was "entirely inadmissible that authorization be given for any issue of franc notes in the Rhineland or in the Ruhr."[125] The French money supply was already overinflated.

If the Ruhr occupation was undertaken as the only hope of balancing the French budget, it must be judged a failure. The 1923 deficit was 2 billion francs larger than that of 1922. With the liquidation of the occupation and recovery of the French economy, revenues increased and the deficit gradually decreased. The 1926 budget showed the first surplus since 1913.[126]

Lasteyrie recognized the Ruhr occupation as a financial disaster as early as July 1923. At that time he recommended to Poincaré that the chief of the French financial mission in Düsseldorf be recalled to his normal duties at the Finance Ministry in Paris. There was nothing more for him to do in Düsseldorf. Owing to the German resistance, none of the services established to handle the taxes on coal, the export licenses, and the tariffs had ever functioned as intended. Those services, observed the finance minister, had become pointless. The role of the French financial mission in the Ruhr was reduced to "creating cadres and programs for the day when, German resistance having ended, the system could function."[127] Germany abandoned passive resistance in the Ruhr on 25 September 1923. But as Stephen Schuker has ably documented, France would have to pass through the financial crisis of 1924 and the adoption of the Dawes Plan before it could bring its finances to order. By that time its reputation as a Great Power had suffered irreparable damage.

4

Managing the National Debt

La France victorieuse sera-t-elle accablée à jamais sous le
poids de sa victorire?
—L. Paul-Dubois,
Revue des deux mondes, 1919

Success has to be paid for in much the same currency as
failure.
—H. J. Jennings,
Fortnightly Review, 1917

To THE VICTORS as well as the vanquished the war left a crushing
legacy of debt. As the military crisis terminated in 1918, Britain and
France had to resolve the debt problem and proceed with the financial reconstruction of Europe. Would their attack on public debt
reflect their battlefield heroism, or would they search for expedients
more in keeping with the expectations of a world exhausted by war
and longing for peace?

From the outset critics complained of the belligerents' failure to
manage the public debt in a responsible manner. The politicians, it
was said, lacked an understanding of the fundamental principles of
sound economics; had not Clemenceau thanked heaven he had not
been born an economist?[1] It is understandable that in the heat of the
crisis sixty years ago shortcomings in monetary and fiscal policy and
management of the public debt were attributed to economically
ignorant politicians. It is unfortunate that the same argument con-
tinues to inform some of the most recent scholarship. Stephen A.
Schuker, for example, has claimed that "most of the French elite at
the time were abysmally ignorant even of the rudimentary principles
of economics . . . What little economics middle-aged men in positions
of responsibility remembered from their youth generally was irrelevant to monetary problems in the postwar world." Schuker noted

Keynes's complaint of a "time lag" in the general diffusion of economic knowledge, and added his own comment that "the problem was even more acute in France than in Anglo-Saxon countries."[2]

Keynes certainly heaped ridicule and scorn upon French politicians and economists, but of his own prime minister's economic expertise he wrote that "Lloyd George has proved himself the least capable of enduring and constructive statesmanship of any man who has held long power in England." Keynes thought rather little of all politicians, lamenting that "No! The economist is not king; quite true. But he ought to be!"[3]

Both the old and the new critics have done an injustice to the politicians who in the final analysis bore responsibility for finding a way out of the postwar financial tangle. When the politicians sought the advice of financial experts, they usually heard many different voices. Schuker's flat assertion that the economics politicians remembered from their youth "was irrelevant to monetary problems in the postwar world" ignores the question which divided the experts most. Responsible financial and monetary authorities in Britain, France, and the United States disputed the validity of traditional theory and practice in the postwar situation. The experts could not agree as to what constituted correct theory and practice. One thus cannot sweep away complex fiscal, financial, and monetary problems with the assertion that "there were heated political struggles over questions which should have been settled mainly by impartial technical experts."[4]

Europe's inability to achieve a definitive solution to the debt problem during the early 1920s cannot, as is often the case, be attributed to the failure of individual politicians or entire political systems. The massive public debt created by the war raised a multitude of political, ethical, technical, and theoretical questions for which there were no clear-cut answers. Enormous as the debt burden was, there were those, particularly in Britain, who envisioned a way out through a combination of monetary depreciation, increased production, and vigorous imperialism. An empire four times larger than the United States, holding riches "gigantic beyond all conception . . . and . . . absolutely unfathomable" would enable Britain to pay off her debt with ease. Compared to the empire's population, production, and wealth 100 or 200 years hence, the war debt would seem a "ridiculous trifle." The debt, in fact, would "scarcely be felt in a decade or two." The optimism of 1918 may have faded by 1922, but some Englishmen continued to believe that the productivity of the British Empire could solve the unemployment problem, relieve the burden of taxation, and provide the resources for domestic social and economic programs.[5]

It was even suggested that Italy, deprived of some of her promised territorial gains by Woodrow Wilson's insistence on the principle of national self-determination at the Paris Peace Conference, might be compensated for "her bravery, her gallantry, her sufferings" with an endowment from the superabundant resources of the British Empire. Endowed with these "rich and empty territories," the Italians could pursue "the creation of a Greater Italy . . . which may bring about another awakening of Italian genius, another Cinquecento."[6]

Such dreams of salvation through imperialism rested on the assumption that Canada, Australia, South Africa, and the rest of the empire would contribute to the rehabilitation of the United Kingdom. Britain, after all, had fought the war "for the British Empire and the British race"—not for Britain alone. This dubious proposition did not go unchallenged by those who believed Britain owed a debt for "the unrehearsed and spontaneous mobilization of the British Empire" which more than any other factor had "sealed the fate of Prussianism." These idealists—perhaps they were truly the realists—understood that after the war Britain would have to redeem her debt to the subject races for their steadfastness and good faith by working "to render life for them fuller, happier, and more prosperous than it has been in the past." "There is only one way," wrote one Briton in 1916, "in which we can vindicate our right to hold nearly one quarter of the earth's surface—we must make the most of its resources in the service of humanity."[7]

As the war ended, Britain set her sights on Germany's African colonies. Acquisition of additional territory in the African tropics would provide Britain with "a remedy for all the economic difficulties arising out of the war," and "the right use of our control of the tropics . . . would also enable us to control Germany." Britain would realize her Cape-to-Cairo dream at the expense of Germany's *Mittel-Afrika* fantasy.[8] This was Britain's version of how "Germany will pay," and unlike the French, the British managed to make their demands sound like a humanitarian gesture. The Germans would hand over their colonies to the British, who were the wisest of colonial rulers. The Englishman, it was said, "has a genius for entering into the minds of non-European stocks, savage or semi-civilized or decadent, and for gaining their confidence."[9] Britain was merely more fortunate than France. To extinguish Britain's war debts, the Germans would certainly pay. But so would the Canadians, the Australians, the South Africans, and all of the "inferior" races scattered throughout the British Empire.

Their envy aroused by such talk of empire, the French began to reassess their own colonial position. In a work published in 1922, *La mise en valeur des colonies françaises*, Albert Sarraut, minister for colonies and former governor-general of French Indo-China, stressed France's pressing need to exploit more effectively her impressive colonial resources. Including North Africa and metropolitan France, the French empire encompassed a population of 100 million. At a time when France was purchasing foreign foodstuffs and raw material for postwar reconstruction purposes, resources from the colonies might have protected the nation's foreign exchange and slowed the increase in foreign debt. But France had never systematically developed her colonies prior to the war. Before they could begin to supply the requirements of metropolitan France, the colonies would consume massive capital infusions for irrigation, railways, roads, scientific methods of agriculture, and vastly improved health care for the native labor force.[10] In view of the immediate need to reconstruct the devastated areas of France, such large-scale colonial investment seemed remote. For the French, colonialism posed a painful paradox. They desperately needed resources from the colonies, but they lacked the capital required to develop them. Germany's failure to make reparation payments may have saved France's colonies from more intense exploitation.

If accelerated colonial exploitation appeared as an unethical or impractical way out of the national debt imbroglio, other shortcuts easily come to mind. The state, for example, might declare partial bankruptcy. But if some considered colonialism immoral and others considered it impractical, nearly everyone considered national bankruptcy dishonorable. Even French politicians rejected repudiation of public debt as inconsistent with the national honor. In an article titled "Economic Metaphysics," former foreign minister Gabriel Hanotaux criticized the hard-boiled economics of such practitioners as Keynes because it "is concerned only with the material element in human affairs. The moral element escapes it." The average Frenchman, believed Hanotaux, considered sentiment stronger than material economic considerations, and "in French, this sentiment is called honor."[11]

One of the few French analysts who did favor a declaration of partial bankruptcy suggested that such a course was not nearly so disastrous as methods being used to avoid it, particularly the issue of more paper currency. If the word "bankruptcy" offended one's sensitivities, other more acceptable terms were available. One could speak of "conversion" of government bonds, "cancellation" of foreign debt, and "drastic reduction" of current expenditures. The economist who suggested the state declare partial bankruptcy assumed no technical obstacles stood in the way. Lack of will among the politicians was the only problem. Financial recovery through partial bankruptcy would be relatively painless, but "without doubt, that requires a government other than the one we have now."[12]

French demands for cancellation of war debts to Britain and the United States, discussed at length in the following chapter, might well seem inconsistent with the French concept of honor. French proponents of cancellation, however, considered the sums due not loans in the technical sense but rather nonrepayable contributions by Britain and the United States in the common struggle to save Western civilization from German barbarism. One wonders whether the advances would have been forthcoming had the French government taken this position when it borrowed the money.

Even more intriguing is the question whether millions of British and French patriots would have purchased National Defense Bonds and subscribed to war loans during the war had they fully realized what they were doing. Government war bond posters never featured H. J. Jennings's warning that "Success has to be paid for in much the same currency as failure."[13] It was only after the war, in 1920, that the president of the Netherlands Bank, Gerard Vissering, explained in terms the layman could understand precisely how governments had financed the war.

Governments, observed Vissering, floated loans and sold bonds to their citizens, giving in return only an acknowledgment of debt. The patriotic subscribers accepted and considered these claims on their governments as assets, a notion the governments encouraged. Subscribers understood that they would eventually receive their money back with interest. It therefore came as a rude shock after the war when many finally discovered that "they had . . . accepted as an asset something that eventually for each of them proved to be part of their own liabilities." The people owed themselves massive sums which could be recovered only through confiscatory levels of taxation or by making the Germans pay.[14]

During the early postwar years, up to 50 percent of the French ordinary budget would be held hostage to interest payments on the public debt. For some analysts, debt service of such a magnitude posed no real problem. Was it not simply a matter of redistribution of the national income? Someone paid higher taxes and someone received additional income, but the overall national wealth was not affected adversely. If the logic of this proposition seemed unassailable, it failed on both technical and political grounds. Technically, at a time when increased productivity was required to reconstruct war-torn Europe, many financiers regarded debt service as a totally unproductive expenditure. Retirement of the public debt, and the accompanying elimination of debt service charges, would free up real savings which could be invested in productive enterprises.[15]

The public debt was a political time bomb. Everyone agreed on the financial danger posed by such massive debt, but any attempt to deal with it threatened to destabilize Europe's political and social structure. The Great War shattered the Old World forever and ushered in an era of conflicts between generations and classes. In the public debt these conflicts found a focal issue. Unresolvable social confrontations often ruled out technically acceptable solutions to the debt problem. The most obvious technical move was to convert the floating debt and short-term loans to long-term securities which would not pose a constant threat to national solvency. But even when there was a market for such long-term securities—and often there was no sufficient market—there were some critics who believed that funding of the debt was simply a disguised form of repudiation by the present generation and a forced loan on future generations.

Future generations, however, did not vote in the elections of the 1920s. The immediate social conflict was that of the classes. In his *Recasting Bourgeois Europe*, Charles S. Maier played down the importance of class conflict in the postwar years. Issues such as public debt, inflation, and currency revaluation, he argued, cut across class lines, producing divisions between those who regarded themselves primarily as producers, consumers, and savers.[16] Nevertheless, if

Table 4. British and French public debt, 1913, 1914, 1919–1923 (£ million, fr. million).

End of fiscal year	Domestic debt						Foreign debt	
	Long-term		Floating		Total domestic			
	U.K.	France	U.K.	France	U.K.	France	U.K.	France
1913	—	31,556	—	2,081	—	33,637	—	—
1914	636.8	31,825	13	6,985	649.8	38,810	—	—
1919	4,736.0	106,144	1,406	111,704	6,142.1	217,848	1,293	62,370
1920	5,347.1	126,624	1,252	119,399	6,599.1	246,023	1,230	(70,000)[a]
1921	5,180.2	163,988	1,273	(86,000)[a]	6,453.2	249,988	1,129	75,164
1922	5,550.9	178,205	1,038	(88,000)[a]	6,588.9	266,205	1,085	117,037
1923	5,793.7	217,866	821	(87,000)[a]	6,614.7	304,866	1,156	165,500

Source: E. V. Morgan, Studies in British Financial Policy, 1914–1925 (London: Macmillan, 1952), pp. 107, 147; Alfred Sauvy, Histoire économique de la France entre les deux guerres, 4 vols. (Paris: Fayard, 1965–75) I, 520; United Nations, Department of Economic Affairs, Public Debt, 1914–1946 (Lake Success, N.Y.: United Nations, 1948), pp. 64, 147; France, Institut national de la statistique, Service d'études économiques et financières, Statistiques et études financières, Supplément no. 175, Supplément rétrospectif 1900 à 1930 (Paris: Imprimerie Nationale, July 1963), p. 1008.

a. Estimate based on above sources.

service of the public debt involved a radical redistribution of national income, then it was important to know who held the debt and who was going to pay the bill.

Precise statistics on the distribution of the public debt in post-war Britain and France are not obtainable. In France, there was no accurate accounting of the government securities placed during the war. National Defense Bonds, for example, were sold over the counter at banks and post offices, with no registration required. These bonds comprised a highly negotiable, liquid form of debt, and in some instances they may have been used as money. Irregularities in the Treasury's bookkeeping led the government to overstate the amount of National Defense Bonds in circulation by nearly 7 billion francs in December 1921. Not until 1963 did the Ministry of Finance

Table 5. British and French debt service and budget balance, 1913, 1918–1923 (£ million, fr. million).

	Debt service[a]				Current balance[b]	
	Amount		Percent of budget			
	U.K.	France	U.K.	France	U.K.	France
1913	23	1,284	14	25	−1	+25
1918	248	5,277	11	12	−1,331	−34,276
		6,832		16		
1919	310	6,357	22	58	−427	−26,688
		7,008		17		
1920	320	9,847	34	44	+54	−17,139
		10,047		25		
1921	303	10,513	31	45	+10	−9,273
		10,513		32		
1922	307	12,315	36	46	+24	−9,766
		12,315		27		
1923	315	11,744	41	46	+38	−11,806
		11,744		31		

Source: C. H. Feinstein, *National Income, Expenditure and Output of the United Kingdom, 1855–1965* (Cambridge, Eng.: Cambridge University Press, 1972), table 12, p. T31; France, Institut national de la statistique, Service d'études économiques et financière, Statistiques et études financières, Supplément no. 175, *Supplément rétrospectif 1900 à 1930* (Paris: Imprimerie Nationale, July 1963), pp. 960–961.

a. Under France, top figure represents ordinary budget, figure below is combined ordinary, extraordinary, and recoverable budgets.

b. French balance represents combined budgets.

issue a statistical "Retrospective Supplement" covering the years 1900–1930, but some of the statistics in this "definitive" account appear to be incomplete or inaccurate.[17]

The British government kept more accurate records, but a 1952 study of the structure of the public debt cautioned that "the question of where this great volume of debt was held is one which is shrouded in mystery . . . It is therefore possible to present only a very approximate picture of the ownership of the debt." E. V. Morgan calculated that between 31 March 1914 and 31 March 1925, government securities in private hands as a percentage of total private property rose from 2.5 percent to approximately 25 percent. Public debt had thus become one of the most important forms of private property.[18]

Of the total internal public debt of £6,525 million in 1924, Morgan estimated that £790 million was held in the form of "small savings," and another £1,775 million was held by "British Persons, other than Small Savings." The British banking system held another £740 million, and corporate and foreign holdings accounted for an additional £2,315 million. These 1924 figures, however, do not accurately represent the 1919 debt structure, for during the intervening years the Treasury had withdrawn a large amount of short-term Treasury bills and issued Conversion Loans which increased the proportion of debt held in long-term bonds. The proportion of the debt repayable in less than one year, over 25 percent in 1919, had been reduced to less than 12 percent by 1925.[19]

During the war it was "necessary to appeal to private property owners of all types from the small saver to the millionaire, and also to businesses with funds to invest."[20] By 1919, rich and poor, consumers as well as producers, all had a significant stake in the public debt. Did any one of these groups exercise undue influence over the government's debt policy? From the Treasury's point of view, the floating debt was most critical. In the form of Treasury bills, this portion of the public debt was held primarily by banks and professional dealers. The British banking system could spread chaos through the national financial machinery by failing to renew its three-month or six-month Treasury bills. The Bank of England had lost control of the money market. Raising the Bank rate above the Treasury bill rate would precipitate a "flight from the Treasury bill" with disastrous consequences for the government. The Bank had lost control to the Treasury, and the Treasury had lost control to the bankers. It was in the interest of both the Treasury and the Bank to withdraw Treasury bills and reduce the floating debt. But the banks preferred Treasury bills as a safe form of liquid assets—and they were reluctant to give up their leverage with the Treasury.

Before the Armistice was signed, the governor of the Bank, Brien Cokayne, advised Chancellor of the Exchequer Andrew Bonar Law that with the end of the war in sight "the Government would do well to consider at a very early date the funding of as much as possible of its internal unfunded debt." Cokayne admitted that "it may seem anomalous and unreasonable for a Government to embark on a funding operation at a time when it is still borrowing on a gigantic scale," but he believed both psychological and financial arguments supported early funding of the floating debt. The most favorable atmosphere for funding, observed the governor, might come with the anticipation of peace rather than with the realization of peace.[21]

Cokayne feared that termination of the war would expose Britain's new position as a debtor nation. High postwar money rates would be needed to protect Britain's foreign exchange, and the lifting of wartime controls on money and investment would lure British capital toward foreign investment opportunities. Under such conditions, warned the governor, the cost of Britain's floating debt would rise significantly. The government would have to offer a "handsome rate" to fund existing short-term securities, most of which had been issued with the privilege of conversion to long-term obligations yielding about 5.4 percent, well above wartime short money rates. Cokayne conceded his "fear that at no rate, within reason, would it be possible to fund a great part of the floating debt," but sooner or later the government would have to attempt it. The chance of success, he believed, was likely to be greater before peace than after the end of the war.[22]

Cokayne's argument for early funding of the floating debt rested on the assumption of a postwar capital shortage and sharp competition between the public and private sectors for the available funds. The Bank thus pressed the government for an immediate funding loan while money was still relatively cheap. Although the Treasury resisted a funding operation, it did so for political reasons, and not because it rejected the Bank's basic assumptions. Treasury officials such as Sir John Bradbury opposed borrowing for housing and other postwar reconstruction projects because such competition by the government for scarce capital would send interest rates up and thereby increase the debt service burden on the British taxpayers.[23]

Both the British and American Treasuries believed in sound, orthodox policies so long as they did not cost the government too much. British Treasury officials resisted a funding operation because it "would standardize the present high rates of interest on Government obligations for a very long period" and "the State would be saddled with a standard rate of interest on its liabilities of 5 per cent or 6 per cent (say) for 65 or 99 years."[24] The United States Treasury delayed funding for the same reason. Central bankers took a different view. In 1921, Montagu Norman expressed to Benjamin Strong his disappointment that the U.S. Treasury had decided to delay funding merely because "interest rates still seem a bit high." The Bank had finally persuaded the British Treasury to begin funding operations, and Norman suggested to Strong that "the mere fact of funding is far more important than the actual interest charge—at least that is how we have looked at things here."[25] British Conversion Loans of the early 1920s actually increased the annual debt charge in the budget, but reduction of the floating debt was thought to be worth the price. Strong concurred, and cautioned Norman that postrecession competition for credit might drive the British Treasury to the Bank for additional advances. "It is simply another indication, to my mind," observed Strong, "of the need of your Treasury now [1922] funding every shilling of floating debt that can possibly be funded at this time."[26]

As a follow-up to his 16 October letter to the chancellor, Cokayne, accompanied by Deputy Governor Norman, met with Bonar Law on 17 December 1918. Four prominent City bankers, Sir W. H. N. Goschen, Lord Inchcape, Sir Edward Holden, and Walter Leaf, joined the discussions. Cokayne and Norman urged a prompt funding operation, but Holden opposed any such operation. Goschen supported some type of action on the debt but felt the present moment inopportune, Leaf vacillated between action and inaction, and Inchcape agreed with some of the arguments on both sides of the question. Lacking a consensus among the experts, the chancellor decided to take a wait-and-see position. After Austen Chamberlain replaced Law as chancellor of the exchequer on 10 January 1919 the stalemate continued. The Bank continued to press the government for a funding operation, but the rest of the cabinet was engaged at the Paris Peace conference, and Chamberlain felt he could not act for an absentee government.[27]

After the Armistice, government borrowing from the Bank leveled off, but when the Treasury's indebtedness to the Bank rose by £11 million during the week ending 8 February 1919, Cokayne again expressed his alarm to Chamberlain. The Bank's advances to the government may have been legitimate during the war, he conceded, but the practice "should not be permitted to continue, and still less increase, now that the fighting is over." Cokayne advised the chancellor to raise his funds from the public and thus put an end to advances from the Bank, "which are already very excessive and constitute probably the most potent of all factors creating the 'inflation' from which the country is suffering." In a response based on a memorandum by Sir John Bradbury, Chamberlain said the Bank had become "unduly alarmed" at the increase in Treasury borrowing from the Bank, which he described as nothing more than a "natural reaction" to the January War Bond campaign. Once the "effect of the special causes which operated during January has exhausted itself," government borrowing from the Bank would stabilize. In any event, Chamberlain noted, the £11 million increase in Bank advances during one particular week in February was more than counterbalanced by a £95 million reduction in government indebtedness to the Bank between 31 December 1918 and 1 February 1919.[28]

By May 1919, the government was prepared to bow to pressure for a funding operation. The chancellor met with the Committee of Clearing House Bankers on 15 May to discuss terms for such a loan. Chamberlain believed extremely attractive terms would be required to insure the success of an early funding loan, but the bankers opposed excessive concessions to potential subscribers. The Labour party was certain to object strongly, and political losses would outweigh any financial advantage from increased subscription. Chamberlain then wondered if the government might not warn of compulsory measures if the fuding operation proved unsuccessful. The bankers suggested holding off any such threat until the results of the operation were known.[29]

Chamberlain's second meeting with the Bankers' Committee on 28 May, with Bradbury and Cokayne present, hardly reassured the chancellor of the bankers' support for a funding operation. Chamberlain suggested delaying the operation until fall. He cited the continuing peace negotiations, problems in Egypt and India, the possibility of a coal strike, and a threatened police strike as factors working against the success of a funding loan. The bankers argued that conditions would not be much better by autumn, and the foreign exchange situation might be worse. When Chamberlain then asked the bankers for a guarantee of £500 million in new money in return for an early funding issue, he was refused. The bankers promised only that if the loan failed to meet the government's expectations, the banks would assist the chancellor "to the utmost of their power."[30]

Chamberlain's assessment of the prospects for a funding loan proved all too accurate. On 2 June 1919 the House of Commons authorized a funding loan and the sale of Victory Bonds. The combined operation produced "the rather pitiful sum in cash of 473 millions, of which 92½ millions were subscribed by banks under official pressure." The general investor, claimed *The Economist*, shied away from this issue in the belief that proceeds would not be used to fund the floating debt. Instead, the funds would be "muddled away by official extravagance."[31]

Barely had the Treasury completed its Victory Loan operation when Chamberlain received a letter from Cokayne urging the chancellor to use at least a portion of the proceeds to pay off the government's short-term indebtedness to the Bank. Cokayne assured Chamberlain his request for the money was due "not merely to a Banker's importunity for the payment of debts due him," but also to a "desire to rid the country of a very pernicious form of inflation."[32] But the disappointing results of the Victory Loan rendered repayment of the Bank advances improbable at that time. Prominent bankers now began to voice the opinion that nothing short of a compulsory funding loan could wipe out the floating debt.

At the Bank, Deputy Governor Norman had pressed the chancellor for a compulsory loan throughout the spring and summer of 1919. He had in mind an assessment added to ordinary tax returns, with payment spread over a twelve- to eighteen-month period. Norman allegedly met Chamberlain in the House of Commons and urged the imposition of what he termed a "forced loan" on the "nouveau riches" who had done so well during the war. The compulsory funding loan would thus be made to look like a tax on war profits—to which no sincere patriot could object. Norman's diary indicates that Chamberlain was "strongly against a forced loan which he was assured would produce panic—and I could not guarantee the contrary."[33]

Norman, however, was not alone in pushing for some sort of compulsory loan or tax to fund the floating debt. In April 1920 Frederick Goodenough, chairman of Barclay's Bank, proposed to Chamberlain a variation of the capital levy scheme. To those paying the levy, the government would issue a twenty-year bond bearing 3.5 percent interest, which the recipient could either hold to maturity or sell on the open market for perhaps 65 percent of face value. Chamberlain rejected Goodenough's scheme, arguing that such a war wealth levy "would at once be converted into a forced loan at 3½ per cent interest," with no reduction in the total funded and floating debt. Moreover, if £100 twenty-year bonds were worth only £65 under existing market conditions, then the government would be receiving only £65 from people who were actually liable for £100. Goodenough countered that such a levy would reduce immediately the level of the floating debt, if not the level of total public debt, and that was in itself sufficient reason to pursue his plan.[34]

The City was in fact suggesting that a forced loan, on which the government paid interest, was preferable to a capital levy. As Controller of Finance Blackett noted, the war wealth levy proposal had "frightened the City out of its wits."[35] London's financial community considered the forced loan preferable to any form of heavy taxation, the excess profits duty in particular. One example was the proposal of G. L. Bevan, a London broker connected with Ellis and Co., suggesting a new issue that would appeal to the investor's self-interest as well as his patriotism. Bearing at least 5 percent interest, "the loan should be voluntary in appearance but compulsory in fact." Those with incomes of £500 or more would be "invited and expected" to subscribe an amount three or four times their income, and holders of Treasury bills and short-dated bonds would be "invited" to convert them. The City, of course, would have to give its prior approval to such an issue, for there was a feeling in some quarters that programs coming from the Treasury "bear the hall-mark rather of the theoretical economist than the practical financier."[36]

Blackett advised Chamberlain against Bevan's plan, which he

characterized as a forced loan made to appear voluntary by a "yield sufficiently attractive to soften the compulsion." While suffering the disadvantages of compulsion, Bevan's proposal lost the most attractive feature of a forced loan, the possibility of funding cheaply. In July 1920, Blackett cautioned against any type of funding operation, because the demand for commercial and industrial credit was soaking up funds that might be invested in long-term government securities. Only through excessively high rates could the government attract money, and even that would depreciate existing issues and dry up funds for government housing programs. A "successful" funding operation in the second half of 1920 might deflate credit sufficiently to bring on a real financial crisis. Blackett suggested that the government put off a funding operation until the summer of 1921.[37]

How long could the government put off a funding operation? In his 19 April 1920 budget address, Chamberlain admitted that during the first ten days of April the nonrenewal of Treasury bills had forced the Treasury to borrow an additional £55 million from the Bank. A temporary solution to the immediate crisis, he believed, might be found in raising simultaneously the Treasury bill rate and Bank rate. But reduction of the floating debt was the only permanent remedy for the Treasury's embarrassing situation.[38] But the bankers opposed credit controls, and the government rejected a compulsory loan—and there seemed to be no acceptable way to fund the floating debt. Searching for a way out, some politicians advocated a form of outright gambling, the lottery or premium bond. In France, such bonds had been sold successfully in peacetime, and even more successfully during the wartime crisis when "the principle of patriotism and the principle of roulette would be linked together."[39]

During 1917, a Select Committee of the House of Commons considered proposals to sell premiums bonds in Britain. For 4 percent tax-free securities, subscribers would receive 2.5 percent interest, the remaining 1.5 percent forming a common pool. In periodic drawings by lot, owners of successful bonds would receive from the pool prizes ranging from £1 to £1,000. Every subscriber would receive back the principal, but those who failed to win in the lottery (the great majority) would lose three-eighths of their interest. Bowing to stiff opposition, the Select Committee rejected the scheme. Opponents such as Herbert Samuel stressed the immorality of a gambling system which would destroy the hard-won English virtues of thrift and hard work. "Unless of exceptional strength of character," Samuel warned, lottery winners would be "demoralized by the windfall."[40]

Most damaging of the arguments against the premium bond was the concern for Britain's reputation as a great financial power. Samuel believed the sale of premium bonds "will be humiliating to the country which has prided itself for so many years on being the financial centre of the world, harmful to our credit, demoralising to the investing public, disastrous to the War Savings movement, and, lastly, ineffective in its results." Other nations (Samuel politely refrained from mentioning France by name) might resort to lottery bonds, "but the United Kingdom has not hitherto been content to accept the methods of her neighbors as the standard of her finance ... Now we are urged to lower our standard to that of others."[41]

The Select Committee on Premium Bonds concluded in its final report of 16 January 1918 that revenue from lottery bonds would be insufficient to justify "any change of a contentious character in our financial methods." Before trying anything so controversial, the Treasury was urged to render conventional issues more attractive to investors.[42] Officials at the Treasury and the Bank shared the Select Committee's disdain for premium bonds. Niemeyer feared their impact on Britain's financial reputation, and argued that they would bring in very little new money at great expense to the Treasury. Norman was surprised when discussion of premium bonds surfaced again late in 1919; he had thought the issue dead after the report of the Select Committee. Norman considered the scheme ineffective, antithetical to the "spirit of saving," and believed the country "needed a rest from further excitement or speculation of any kind."[43]

Collapse of the postwar boom after April 1920 forced the British government to take some action on the public debt. As prices declined, the burden of the debt grew. A public debt of £7,000 million expressed in terms of inflated prices represented the equivalent of £10–12,000 million at normal prewar price levels. In a belated attempt to tax the boom, Chamberlain's budget for 1920–21 called for an increase in the excess profits duty (which had just been halved in the 1919–20 budget) from 40 percent to 60 percent. But attempts to reduce the floating debt encountered resistance from the bankers, who wished to retain their Treasury bills as a convenient form of liquid assets and prevent the Bank and the Treasury from regaining control over the money market. The Treasury began a series of Conversion Loans in 1921 designed to siphon funds out of the short-term market into long-term government securities. The bankers did not encourage this move, and as E. V. Morgan commented, the first 3.5 percent Conversion Loan of April 1921 "represents the nadir of government borrowing in the period."[44]

Decisive action to curb the floating debt required precise timing. In the event, measures conceived at the height of the boom were implemented in the depths of the recession, with possibly counter-productive results. The floating debt, moreover, was not merely a technical problem for the experts. It was a pawn in the political struggle between politicians who had promised a "land fit for heroes" and required "cheap" money to finance it, and those who viewed recovery of Britain's position of financial supremacy as the first order of business after the war. In Britain as in France, considerations of sound finance often deferred to political expediency during the critical years 1918–1923.

At the center of the political maneuvering was the determination of the Bank of England to regain control over Britain's financial and monetary system. In the Bank's drive to reconquer its lost financial supremacy, management of the floating debt emerged as the principal issue. The Bank's governor after March 1920, Montagu Norman, preferred to speak of a need for the "independence" of central banks from political control, but he actually sought to establish the supremacy of the Bank in financial affairs. The key to independence or supremacy for the Bank was reduction of the floating debt, as the Norman-Strong correspondence clearly demonstrates. "So long as a Government has directly or indirectly a large floating debt," he observed to Strong, "I wonder if any system can leave the Central Bank of that country really free to manage affairs from a purely financial standpoint." Norman welcomed the first Conversion Loan as a "step toward this freedom" though it came "even at some cost of interest."[45]

Norman's willingness to purchase "freedom" for the Bank "even at some cost of interest" raised interesting questions of political expediency and technical appropriateness. The Treasury assisted in keeping down annual interest charges in the national budget by providing large amount of Treasury bills at relatively low interest rates. But the practice was clearly inflationary and produced in the opinion of some financial experts "a basic contradiction in British financial policy."[46] The British Treasury combined an inflationary method of financing public debt with a deflationary monetary policy (mandated by parliament) which placed strict limits on currency note issue. In this respect, however, British policy—in principle if not in scale—paralleled similarly conflicting strategies being pursued by the French Finance Ministry during the 1920–1922 period. As Stephen Schuker recently observed, "The Finance Ministry succeeded in following contradictory policies . . . This double policy of fiscal inflation and monetary deflation appeared feasible only because the French public expected large payments from Germany." To insist that the "blunders" of the French Finance Ministry be attributed to "illusions over the size of German payments" may be unjust, because the British Treasury, which held no such illusions, followed essentially the same course.[47]

Reference to a few political and technical considerations may explain the reluctance of the British Treasury to act promptly on the floating debt. In 1935, the economist Noel F. Hall, in line with Norman's earlier views, argued that Britain would have been better served "had a very large part of the debt been funded regardless of cost at, say, 6 percent in 1920 or 1921." The possibility of a more rapid return to the gold standard would have justified the high cost of such a funding program.[48]

A high-cost funding program in 1920 or 1921, however, would have been politically difficult. Bitter recriminations against what many considered the unnecessarily high cost of the wartime loans still reverberated in the City and in the halls of parliament. Reginald McKenna's 1915 loan contained expensive privileges, conversion rights, and tax concessions believed necessary to insure its success. Critics believed the 5 percent rate on the 1917 war loan was excessive, and because purchasers of earlier war loan issues and Exchequer Bonds at lower rates could convert them to the new 5 percent loan, the total debt structure was adversely affected. A large portion of the public debt was channeled into one security bearing a high 5 percent interest rate and maturing on a single date. The issue of loans at substantial discounts further increased the ultimate cost of the debt. In 1938, Ursala K. Hicks concluded that "it would appear that with more forethought, or better preparation, long-term financing might have been more economical."[49]

Montagu Norman and his colleagues who called for funding of the floating debt at any cost faced stiff opposition from experts and politicians who felt the cost of the debt was already too high. Moreover, testimony before the Colwyn Committee between 1925 and 1927 indicated a lack of consensus among the experts on the safe limit for the size of the floating debt. By 1926, the floating debt had been reduced from a high of £1,570 million in June 1919 to £704,296 million. A majority of the witnesses and the Colwyn Committee itself favored a further gradual reduction, if only to place the Treasury in a stronger position should another emergency arise. Only Keynes argued that there was *no* theoretical safe limit on floating debt. The public's appetite for short-term securities, he contended, should be the only limit on the floating debt. The floating debt, in Keynes's opinion, was relatively cheap at prevailing money rates during the mid-1920s. In such circumstances, the sound policy was to maintain short-term debt at a high level, provided the short interest rates remained below the average of long-term rates. The final report of the Colwyn Committee adopted an ambiguous position. Floating debt, it said, should be "strictly limited," but "the exact amount which the Floating Debt may, with safety, be permitted to reach at any time can, we think, only be decided in the light of the circumstances of the moment."[50]

The series of 3.5 percent Conversion Loans begun in April 1921 produced results which surprised experts, politicians, and the general public alike. As the Colwyn Committee completed its work in 1927, the Conversion Loans had increased the total face value of the internal public debt from £463 million to £693 million—a £230 million inflation in face value. To attract subscribers to the 3.5 percent long-term securities, the Treasury felt it had to offer a premium to those who converted higher-rate short-term obligations. What, then, was the point of funding the floating debt? The advantage, according to the Colwyn Committee, lay in the improved (from the Treasury's point of view) interest position, and the rearrangement of maturity dates to the benefit of the Treasury.

Chamberlain conceded that the Conversion Loans would increase the total nominal debt, but pointed to the floating debt as the critical immediate issue. In any event, he argued, the British taxpayer was mainly concerned with the debt's annual cost to the budget rather than its total face value. Most witnesses before the Colwyn Committee, however, doubted the soundness of Conversion Loans that added to the capital sum of the public debt. In another noncommital statement, the Committee concluded that only future developments would determine whether the Conversion Loans were justified.[51]

In British financial and political circles, the floating debt was a hotly debated issue. No consensus existed among the experts, and the experts often disagreed with the politicians. For the Bank of England, the reduction of floating debt formed the centerpiece of its drive to regain control over the money market, and London bankers regarded perpetuation of a large floating debt as the best guarantee of their independence. Parliament opposed floating debt because it was not subject to parliamentary control—thus suggesting one more power struggle—between the Treasury and parliament—in which the question of the floating debt played a critical role.

At no time between 1918 and 1923 did the Treasury, the Bank, the London bankers, and parliament develop a consistent, rational program for dealing with the floating debt. The actions taken were sometimes self-contradictory, and tended to reflect changing market conditions (boom and recession) rather than any rational plan. In some respects, the 1920–1922 recession somewhat eased the Treasury's position. In May 1922 Chancellor of the Exchequer Sir Robert Horne commented that the market price of government securities had improved substantially "owing in no small measure to the economic depression," and he expressed the hope that market conditions would continue to "improve" so as to render possible further conversion operations. Horne apparently took this idea from Blackett's memorandum of 22 March 1922, "Budgeting for a Deficit." Blackett had pointed out that if the Treasury's floating debt position seemed improved, it was owing to the fact that the business depression had encouraged investment in Treasury bills. An improvement in business conditions, he warned, might plunge the government into serious difficulties with the floating debt.[52]

The Treasury's attempt to reduce the floating debt through Conversion Loans was not universally accepted. Reduction of the floating debt increased the nominal value of the funded debt, an apparent regression which some, but not all, experts believed was counterbalanced by interest rates and maturity dates more advantageous to the Treasury. Demands of political expediency and special interest groups, as well as genuine disagreement over technical issues, obstructed an early regulation of Britain's postwar public debt. In some respects the French experience followed that of the British.

On a per capita basis, the French public debt in 1920 came to an estimated $1,099 (conversion at par), compared to $816 for the United Kingdom and $233 for the United States. As a percentage of estimated per capita income, the French debt stood at 158 percent, the British at 140 percent, and the American at 31 percent. Though estimates vary widely, one can say that Britain financed approximately 28 percent of war costs through taxation, while the corresponding French share was about 15 percent. These statistics supposedly prove the superiority of British fiscal policy.[53]

Statistical comparisons prove very little because the impact of the war on France was much more direct and brutal. German forces occupied and devastated ten French departments which accounted for approximately one-fifth of the nation's taxable capacity. Taxes from this region were unavailable to the French government during and immediately following the war. Comparisons involving national income are likewise misleading. By war's end, French production was 30 to 40 percent below the prewar level, and did not recover to that level until 1924. With much of her productive capacity destroyed, France continued to import on a massive scale after the Armistice—with no possibility of balancing these imports with exports. The foreign debt rose accordingly. Collection of taxes during the war was rendered difficult because France was the battle zone. Finally, postwar reconstruction costs added to the public debt.

By any statistical measure, the French public debt at the close of 1922 was enormous. But perhaps even more critical than the sheer size of the debt was its structure. To a far greater extent than Britain, France financed the war through heavy reliance on floating debt in the form of national defense bonds (*bons de la défense nationale*) and advances from the Bank of France to the French Treasury. For France the Armistic marked the end of the war and the true beginning of the financial crisis. The franc collapsed and the public debt skyrocketed. The government sold more national defense bonds after the war than during the period of hostilities.

Public debt placed severe strains on every segment of the French financial and monetary structure. Consuming between 44 percent and 57 percent of the ordinary budget between 1919 and 1922, debt service charges left very little for other needed services. The high proportion of national defense bonds and Bank advances in the public debt contributed directly to postwar monetary inflation and depreciation of the franc on foreign exchange markets. Foreign loan markets dried up, as potential lenders doubted France's ability to repay her existing debts. Successful handling of the public debt thus appeared to be the cornerstone of any program to rehabilitate the French financial and monetary system.

Analysts have pointed variously to deficient political leadership, unworkable political institutions, illusions over German reparation payments, and selfish policies pursued by France's one-time friends and allies in explaining France's failure to attack the debt problem vigorously after the war. While foreign and domestic political factors did play a role here, such interpretations fail to do justice to the technical problems and social conflicts involved in attempts to either fund or reduce the public debt. The debt was only one segment in a long chain of financial and monetary problems. Programs which might alleviate the debt burden quite often produced adverse effects in other areas of financial and monetary policy.

Where should one begin the war against the public debt? As in Britain, the floating debt—particularly the advances from the Bank of France to the Treasury—called for immediate attention. Jules Décamps, director of economic studies at the Bank, considered the Bank advances as "the origin and fundamental cause of our monetary disorder." The Bank was under no legal obligation to advance funds to the government. "The Bank of France," as one critic of the cozy relationship between the Bank and the Treasury observed, "was not created to respond to every demand of the State, and still less to satisfy all of its prodigalities."[54]

The history of the wartime Bank advances goes back to the Agadir crisis of 1911. Though the crisis was settled peaceably, the French cabinet decided to make financial preparations for war with Germany. On 11 November 1911 the finance minister concluded a convention with the governor of the Bank of France. In the event of mobilization, the Bank agreed to place at the disposition of the government, in the form of an advance, the sum of 2.9 billion francs. This convention remained secret until the war began; parliament ratified it on 5 August 1914, when it also established bank notes as compulsory legal currency. When the original advance quickly proved inadequate, the Finance Ministry requested on 18 September that the limit on advances be raised to 6 billion francs. The Bank agreed to furnish the funds in the convention of 21 September 1914, with a stipulation adding to the advances a 1 percent interest charge, to be increased to 3 percent after the war.[55]

The government had discovered a gold mine deep within the bowels of the Bank of France. Where else could one find money so cheap, with no immediate burden on the budget? But this was a highly dangerous and inflationary way to finance a war—even a short war—for each advance from the Bank in effect pumped more currency into circulation. Unlike other forms of government borrowing, this method of increasing the government's purchasing power did not impose a counterbalancing reduction in the public's purchasing power. By the end of 1918, the legal limit on Bank advances had been raised to 24 billion francs, and actual advances came to approximately 18 billion francs. With each increase in the legal limit on Bank advances, the legal limit on note circulation also had to be raised. At the end of 1913, 5.7 billion francs in Bank notes circulated in France; by the end of 1918, the figure had soared to 30.2 billion francs.[56] As cumulative Bank advances and note issues approached each successive limit, panic struck the financial community. What would happen when the limit was reached? During the war, the Bank dared not cause any difficulties for the government, and approved all requests to raise the limit on advances. Patriotism temporarily replaced the Bank's traditional fiscal conservatism. But with the signing of the Armistice, the bank, supported by the Chamber of Deputies, attempted to regain its control of the money supply and reestablish sound money policy in France. On 5 March 1919 the Chamber withdrew the government's power to determine the note issue limit by decree. Henceforth, the Finance Ministry would have to seek a change in the limit from parliament. This "resistance of the Chamber encouraged that of the Bank of France," which now decided to cease its advances to the Treasury.[57]

The Bank and the government were now squarely at odds. In December 1918 Finance Minister Lucien Klotz had informed the Senate, which was considering renewal of the charter of the Bank of France, that further advances would be required to pay the troops and to retire German marks in Alsace-Lorraine. On 12 April 1919 Klotz requested from the Bank a new advance of 3 billion francs. This would also require raising the legal limit on Bank advances from

24 billion francs to 27 billion, and the limit on note circulation to 39 billion francs. Three days later Klotz had his reply. The Board of Directors, noting the end of the war crisis, rejected Klotz's request. The Directors desired to protect the Bank note from further erosion. The Treasury would have to scale down its expenditures to match its resources. The Directors indicated they might relent if the government agreed to certain conditions—namely, that the government repay the latest advance as soon as expected Treasury revenue began to flow in, or, that the advance be repaid out of the proceeds of the next loan floated by the Treasury.

Klotz surrendered to the Bank, and agreed that the latest advance would be repaid out of the proceeds of the next loan. But when would the government issue the next loan? It has been suggested that the terms imposed by the Bank may have contributed to the delay in funding the floating debt. Klotz may have delayed deliberately the issue of a funding loan because the proceeds would only find their way to the Bank of France. A funding loan would only intensify the scarcity of capital desperately needed for foodstuffs, raw materials, and reconstruction.[58]

The era of cheap money appeared to be over. The Bank had put a de facto end to the advances. But the government still had to repay more than 25 billion francs in advances outstanding at the close of 1919. The solutions suggested closely resembled those proposed by British experts to overcome similar difficulties on the other side of the Channel. There was a proposal for a 12 to 13 billion franc compulsory loan payable in specie only (to prevent the trading in of other government securities) as a first step toward repayment of the Bank advances. A less realistic proposition surfaced during the 1920–21 recession, when it was proposed to pay off the Bank advances and much of the remaining public debt with a new 150 billion franc Bank note issue. The plan, nothing more than a barely disguised declaration of national bankruptcy, allegedly had the support of some influential deputies.[59]

Additional government borrowing seemed a more reasonable method of securing funds with which to repay the Bank. On 31 July 1921 parliament approved a loan issue which was to be used in part to repay Bank advances. But at the same time Finance Minister François-Marsal asked parliament to raise the limit on note issue from 40 billion to 43 billion francs. He claimed the Bank, heavily committed to aiding the government, lacked sufficient Bank notes to provide commercial establishments with rediscount services.[60]

Such action constituted a contradictory policy, but what were the alternatives? Some financial commentators saw no connection between the level of Bank advances and the amount of Bank notes in circulation, but most responsible officials and economists did recognize the connection. In principle, everyone recognized the need to repay the Bank advances, and in principle, most people in responsible positions agreed that the floating of new loans and the sale of additional national defense bonds, undesirable as that might be, was preferable to massive Bank advances and mushrooming note circulation. But when principle was tranlsated into practice, every solution was fraught with serious difficulties.

The borrowing power of the state had its limits, and at some point the lenders would (and did) refuse to lend. Increasing the amount of national defense bonds to reduce the level of Bank advances placed the Treasury in greater jeopardy from a sudden demand for reimbursement of the bonds. If borrowing was the only way to repay the Bank advances, then long-term borrowing was clearly the most advantageous way to do it. But long-term borrowing in the existing money markets was extremely difficult, and the government would have to offer abnormally high rates to attract investors. As in Britain, many financial and political leaders saw little value in debt retirement if in the process the government created new obligations on more onerous terms. Why should the state pay *any* interest on sums which Bank notes could furnish practically free of charge? Most financial experts agreed that the advances had to be repaid, but only when this could be done at reasonable cost and risk to the government. Meanwhile, balancing the budget and increasing national productivity might bring more worthwhile results.[61]

Proponents of prompt repayment of the Bank advances imposed their will in the so-called François-Marsal Convention of 29 December 1920, in which the Treasury undertook to reduce by 2 billion francs annually the total amount of the advances. An initial reduction to 25 billion francs was to be achieved by 31 December 1921, followed by reductions of 2 billion francs each year thereafter. Under this "automatic mechanism of amortization," reimbursement would be complete within thirteen years (fifteen years if advances made to foreign governments were included).

Because the budget was already in deficit and no new taxes to pay for the reimbursements were contemplated, funds to implement the Convention would have had to come from new borrowing. From the outset, then, the François-Marsal Convention lacked proper financial support. The Convention was "rigorously respected" for just one year, 1921. When the Treasury announced it could not meet its obligations under the agreement owing to a decline in tax revenue caused by the recession, parliament passed the "exceptional" laws of 31 December 1922 and 27 December 1923, reducing the required reimbursement for 1922 to 1 billion francs and for 1923 to only 800 million francs.[62]

Critics have attacked the François-Marsal Convention as both ineffective and totally unrealistic. Both charges are justified. But such attacks are usually joined to the implication that French financial authorities were unusually incompetent for their time. Stephen Schuker recently observed that "many treatments of the monetary policy of the Bank of France are tinged with passion." Schuker's own treatment of the Bank's policy unfortunately falls into this category, for he writes that,

> Leading officials of the Bank have been accused of focusing single-mindedly on two figures, the magnitude of the Bank's advances to the state and the corresponding increases in the total money supply, as the sole determinants of inflation. Did they really believe that the process of monetary inflation could be reversed without consideration of fiscal policy, balance of payments, or the volume of debt, foreign and domestic? Apparently Bank officials did entertain the rather simplistic notion that . . . progressive reduction of the permissible upper limits or *plafonds* governing the level of advances and the amount of currency in circulation would "restore" the currency . . . Modern notions of flexible currency management being developed in other countries . . . were held not to apply to the French case . . . The criticism directed against the Bank of France was undoubtedly warranted.[63]

It is not clear to what "modern notions of flexible currency management being developed in other countries" Schuker refers, but the "simplistic notion" he condemns is nothing but an early French version of the modern monetarist theory advocated by Nobel Prize winner Milton Friedman. French policy was neither simplistic nor very different from contemporary programs in supposedly reputable quarters. The British, after all, placed their own *plafonds* on Bank advances and currency note circulation.

The François-Marsal Convention quickly became a dead letter as the legal limit on Bank advances was either raised or violated by questionable indirect advances made through private banks. As in Britain the situation involved a power struggle between the Finance Ministry and the Bank, a struggle in which the issue of control possibly outweighed the urgency of repaying the Bank advances. An indication of this rivalry between Bank and Treasury may be seen in a regulation issued by the Finance Ministry just twelve days prior to the conclusion of the François-Marsal Convention. The French Treasury agreed to accept demand deposits from private banks and the general public. Funds so deposited were to earn interest carrying from 1.5 percent to 3 percent. The Treasury was to turn these deposits over to the Bank of France in repayment of advances.

For an apparently minimal benefit, the Treasury was taking a high risk. As James Harvey Rogers observed, to repay the advances the government created another form of indebtedness which was payable on demand. [64] The timing of this deposit plan suggests that the Finance Ministry, aware of the risk involved, wished to announce its own voluntary plan to repay Bank advances in an attempt to head off the more drastic compulsory François-Marsal arrangement.

Technical difficulties and political expediency, rather than ignorance of the principles and practices of modern financial and monetary policy, delayed a definitive program to repay Bank of France advances to the state. In several important respects, the French approach to the reimbursement of Bank advances resembled steps taken in Britain. Examination of French attempts to deal with the other major component of the floating debt, the national defense bonds, reveals once again the centrality of complex technical problems and social conflicts rather than ignorance of sound economic practice.

The origin and growth of the national defense bond as the backbone of French wartime finance has been traced in Chapter 1. By June 1922 the outstanding balance of such three-month, six-month, and one-year securities stood at 63.8 billion francs. At first, small holders purchased most of these bonds, but by 1918 major financial institutions began to hold them in large quantities. For banks and other financial institutions, national defense bonds provided the liquidity which other national banking systems provided by way of regular Treasury bills or commercial paper. The bonds might have played a useful function in the French financial system had the total amount been held to a reasonable level. But when Finance Minister Paul Doumer responded to critics of a new issue of national defense bonds in 1921 bearing 6 percent interest, he noted that the original laws of 1915 and 1917 authorizing such issues placed no limitation on the government's issuing powers. The sole regulation was a twenty-year limit on maturity dates. Doumer reminded parliament that former Finance Minister Ribot had thanked the Chamber of Deputies for giving him "complete freedom" in issuing the obligations.[65]

What portion of the national defense bonds was held by major commercial banks may never be known with precision, for as Rogers noted in 1929, bank statements did not distinguish such bonds and short-term Treasury paper from the regular commercial portfolio.[66] It is safe to conclude, however, that French banks held large amounts of national defense bonds between 1918 and 1927, when sale of bonds maturing in less than one year was discontinued. The banks obstructed government attempts to fund the floating debt during the early postwar years.

Had the national defense bonds constituted the only threat to French financial stability after the war, their withdrawal through a funding operation would have posed relatively few technical problems. But the success of a massive funding operation depended upon favorable money market conditions. So long as the French franc fluctuated wildly in foreign exchange markets, investors would turn away from long-term securities. People wanted easily negotiable instruments, liquid assets enabling them to adjust to sudden changes in the value of the franc and prices of commodities.

The market for long-term French government securities was drying up by 1921, especially as it became apparent that proceeds from previous loans had been used not to pay off Bank advances or to consolidate floating debt, but to balance the current budget. French financial experts understood the theoretical advantages of a funding operation. But if such an operation should fail, public confidence in the franc would collapse, bringing catastrophic results for the national financial system.[67] Who among the politicians was willing to take responsibility for such a gamble when the experts advised that chances for success were slim?

Prospects for shifting the burden to long-term debt were virtually nil. Short-term issues, the Finance Ministry admitted, tended to increase between the long-term issues. In 1922, Ribot charged that the government was issuing national defense bonds as fast as it was retiring long-term debt, thereby transferring consolidated debt to the floating debt![68] Perhaps the major consideration in the government's lack of vigor in controlling the issue of national defense bonds was the fact that a large portion of the proceeds paid for reconstruction of the devastated regions, expenses charged to the budget recoverable from Germany. The exact proportion of national defense bonds issued to cover recoverable expenditures could never be ascertained. The answer to that question depended on the assumptions one made—*which* government issues had been made to cover reconstruction costs. Given the size of the reconstruction bill, one could argue that *all* government borrowing had been used to cover recoverable expenditures.[69] In any event, it seemed both politically and financially unwise to attempt to fund debts at a permanent cost to French taxpayers when the Germans were obligated to pay.

Evaluation of France's postwar financial and monetary policy must consider the relationship between the enormous public debt and the need to attack inflation. A concerted effort to deflate the economy through tight money policies would have had a considerable impact on the public debt. French economists, politicians, and bondholders understood the implications of choosing between inflationary and deflationary policies. They generally believed that a deflationary policy would increase the burden of internal public debt and decrease the burden of the foreign debt. For the most part, however, France was not repaying her foreign debt during the early postwar years, as the government still hoped to negotiate a settlement of inter-Allied debts either linking them to German reparation payments or canceling a portion of them. France's immediate concern, then, was the internal public debt.

Massive infusions of paper bank notes into the money supply had accompanied drastic price increases ranging up to 350 percent of prewar levels. Most of the public debt had been contracted at these inflated price levels, and annual debt service charges consumed approximately 50 percent of the ordinary budget. Deflation, which in itself seemed a sensible policy, invited a business recession that would reduce the tax base, and the government would be unable to meet its fixed annual debt service obligations. Should that happen, the government would either declare bankruptcy or borrow additional funds from the Bank of France.

It was this consideration of debt service which prompted one French economist to suggest that "a moderate and permanent augmentation of monetary circulation is from now on a modern necessity." Another French economist, Germain Martin, expressed concern over the government's debt service requirements, but nevertheless supported a deflationary policy. Deflation, he suggested, would be accompanied by a lowering of interest rates, thereby reducing the government's debt service burden. To satisfy investors who had purchased government securities when interest rates and prices were high, the government would guarantee the return of equivalent purchasing power.[70] Martin, however, failed to explain how the government could make such a guarantee of purchasing power, or why anyone would believe in it.

Reimbursement of the Bank of France advances to the state and retirement or funding of the national defense bonds represented a deflationary program affecting various interests groups in different ways. However theoretically desirable this type of deflation might be, powerful interest groups would oppose the Bank and the Treasury. The power struggle between various elements of the French social and economic system dominated the purely technical aspects of the question. Businessmen, bondholders, and bankers tended to place their particular interests before the national interest in the search for ways to deal with inflation and the public debt.

Raising domestic purchasing power by means of fiduciary inflation produced the countereffect of reducing French purchasing power abroad as the franc exchange fell. Some French protectionists thus favored monetary inflation as a substitute for protective tariffs at levels they would ordinarily never dare to demand.[71] For the small bondholders, deflation seemed on the face of it beneficial, because they might receive back more purchasing power than they had given up to purchase the securities. But as Martin warned, they might not receive anything back if deflation forced the government to default. The debate on deflation opened up the entire question of the relationship between debtors and creditors. Debtors, especially those who had contracted obligations after the inflationary explosion was well underway, resisted financial or monetary reforms that would make repayment of their debts more expensive.[72] In this case it was the debtors, rather than the creditors, who insisted on the sanctity of the original contract.

For the bondholders, reduction of the floating debt raised the question of priorities. Assuming the government lacked the resources to concurrently reimburse the Bank advances and retire the national defense bonds (and this seemed to be a safe assumption), which should be the first priority? The Bank of France naturally argued that its advances constituted the most urgent claim upon the state's resources, while the public considered its portfolio of government securities as the most sacred of the state's liabilities. Both the Bank and the bondholders could support their cases with strong technical and moral arguments, which meant that the final decision depended on the political influence wielded by each party.

French bankers appeared to hold the key to reform of the floating debt. Germain Martin and other economists referred to "the menace placed on the public credit by the possibility of nonrenewal of the National Defense Bonds." Banks, insurance companies, and other large institutional holders of national defense bonds maintained a potential stranglehold over the government's financial and monetary policy. In his 1929 work on French public finance, Robert M. Haig concluded that the government had to consult these large institutional investors on every financial move.[73] The floating debt could not be reduced because the banks resisted the compulsory conversion of their most liquid assets into long-term obligations. Owing to the absence of a regular, organized money market in France, many bankers believed they could not continue normal business operations if they had to convert their national defense bonds. If the government wished to consolidate the floating debt, the bankers would have to receive some sort of compensation. This they received in the form of interest-bearing demand deposits at the Treasury described above. The Finance Ministry attempted to place a limit on the floating debt when it began to discontinue the sale of national defense bonds during the summer of 1926. But with the rapid growth of the Treasury deposits, no real reduction in the government's liabilities was achieved.[74] The bankers had apparently defeated the government.

By 1919, the *Union sacrée* of 1914 was beginning to fall apart. The war had made some wealthy and had ruined others. The war had created a deeper division between debtors and creditors, not only in France but throughout the world. French society could now be divided between those who held government securities and those who did not. To meet the interest obligation, the government had to raise immense sums from one group and give them to the other. The extent to which this redistribution of national income actually occurred depended upon who held the securities, the method of taxation chosen, and the fairness of the distribution of the tax burden.

The possibility of class conflict over the public debt was real, and the threat was not limited to France. A leading British journal warned that it would be undesirable to divide the nation between a *rentier* class living on interest from the war debt, and the remainder of the population paying tribute to that class. In France, Joseph Caillaux proclaimed that the state would have to "compel the wealthy classes to agree to indispensable sacrifices" in the form of a reduction of the interest or principal of the public debt, or a levy on capital.[75]

Was the French public debt a form of "socialism for the rich"? Could the floating debt have been funded without some sort of social revolution? Funding or retirement of the public debt appeared to require that someone make a sacrifice for the general welfare. Neither the Bank of France, nor the bankers, nor the businessmen, nor the bondholders, nor the taxpayers wished to become the sacrificial lamb. Could they be blamed for obstructing the national welfare? From an ethical point of view, the French nation could argue and did argue that it had already made the supreme sacrifice in blood and property. Perhaps the financial sacrifice should now be made by someone else. This claim leads naturally to the consideration of another type of public debt—inter-Allied debt and German reparation obligations.

5

Inter-Allied Debt
and German Reparations

There is no relationship more dangerous to friendship than
that of a creditor towards his debtor.
—Gerard Vissering, 1920

To forgive an inividual debtor is sometimes (not always) the
worst thing in the world you could do for him. It simply en-
courages slackness and extravagance.
—Thomas W. Lamont, 1921

But we are the victors. The entire world, and our allies in
particular, only await a signal to collaborate in the work of
our economic recovery.
—Raphael-Georges Lévy, 1919

DISPUTES AT THE PARIS PEACE CONFERENCE threatened to destroy
the wartime league between the Allied and Associated Powers. After
the Conference, wrangling over final settlement of inter-Allied debts
and German reparation payments eroded what remained of the wartime financial entente between Britain, France, and the United
States.

Borrowing to finance extraordinary expenditures during and immediately after the war raised inter-Allied debt to approximately
$26.5 billion. Claims held by the United States government on its
Associates came to about $11.1 billion. Britain owed the United
States $4.7 billion, but held claims on other countries amounting to
$11.1 billion, giving her a net credit status of $6.4 billion. France
held credits of $3.5 billion due from other countries, but she had
borrowed $4 billion from the United States and $3 billion from
Britain, leaving her a net deficit of $3.5 billion.

Under the London Schedule of Payments of 5 May 1921, Germany owed in reparations the sum of 132 billion gold marks ($33 billion), though the distinction between A, B, and C bonds reduced the effective reparation debt to 50 billion gold marks ($12.5 billion). Inter-Allied debts combined with German reparation payments thus required the transfer of $39 billion ($59.5 billion if the full $33 billion is used for German reparation payments). The transfer of wealth on such an unprecedented scale posed insurmountable technical problems which soon produced an international power struggle. The debtor nations determined not to pay what they considered impossible and unjust sums.

Detailed examination of the reparation disputes of the 1920s lies outside the scope of this work. Germany's "capacity to pay," French "intransigence," and the extent to which inter-Allied debt was or should have been tied to German reparation payments remain controversial questions today. The Allies carefully considered Germany's capacity to pay, but for reasons unintelligible to the French, they refused to give France the same consideration in the matter of inter-Allied debt. The precise measure of Germany's capacity to pay remains a matter of dispute. The effective obligation of 50 billion gold marks (rather than the nominal value of 132 billion generally cited) established by the London Schedule of Payments has been variously described as "reasonably consonant with German capacity to pay," "not outrageous, even in German eyes," and "an impossible amount" by three recent commentators.[1]

The Allies' capacity to pay their debts to one another remains no less questionable. Stephen Schuker recently credited American authorities with showing themselves "willing to make relatively generous arrangements with the individual European debtor nations, based in each case on a fair appraisal of capacity to pay." But "Great Britain nevertheless stoutly resisted negotiations for a reasonable scaling down of its debt until late in 1922. Unlike France or Italy, Britain could hardly plead inability to pay." The British thus hoped that by delaying a settlement they could "embarrass the United States into outright cancellation."[2] This, of course, is the same tactic generally attributed, justly, to the French.

"Capacity to pay" is, in a technical sense, not a particularly useful concept. It can be defined to suit the requirements of either the debtor or the creditor. Capacity to pay, insofar as the term has any validity at all, is essentially a state of mind. It more accurately reflects the state of the national will than the state of the national resources. Thus understood, Germany's capacity to pay was very slight, France's capacity only somewhat greater, and Britain's capacity fairly substantial.

Both legally and morally, inter-Allied debt appeared to represent an obligation more binding than German reparations. The Treaty of Versailles was not a "contract" in the normal sense of the term, and the "war guilt" clause upon which the reparation obligation rested remains to this day a matter of controversy among reputable historians. Inter-Allied debt, however, rested on generally accepted principles of contract. "The loans," a recent study concedes, "had been contracted in good faith and the United States had never at any time intimated that they would be cancelled, scaled down or adjusted in any way. The U.S.A. therefore had a perfect legal right to insist on collecting its claims, if not a moral one."[3]

British and French tactics regarding settlement of inter-Allied debt remained nearly identical throughout the period 1918 through 1922. At the Paris Peace Conference, the United States rejected British and French plans to redistribute the debt. Britain and France demanded a general consideration of the entire international debt problem and an all-around reduction in obligations. If the United States would not agree to such a scheme, then both governments would "delay" funding of their debts to the United States.

During the summer and autumn of 1919 the British government was prepared to discuss with the United States Treasury plans for payment of interest and funding of its debt. Chamberlain feared the political and diplomatic dangers that might arise from the existence of massive inter-Allied debts, and was prepared to write off British advances as part of a general international settlement of debts. In the absence of such a general settlement, Chamberlain preferred to leave inter-Allied debt in its original form, sight obligations with no definite maturity date. He would gamble that the U.S. Treasury would never demand immediate payment of such a sum. By February 1920, however, Chamberlain had given up hope for an international debt settlement, because the United States "vehemently opposed" mutual cancellation of debts. He now asked his cabinet, "should we act without them" in a unilateral cancellation of debts owed to Britain? Noting that much of the Allied debt was probably uncollectible and that America could hardly refuse to follow if

Britain acted spontaneously, Chamberlain requested the cabinet to study a memorandum prepared by Controller of Finance Basil Blackett.[4]

Blackett's memorandum of 2 February 1920 more closely resembled an emotional attack on American financial policy than a reasoned program for Britain. Britain, he observed, had attempted to persuade the United States to join in the "deflation of the world's balance sheet," to clear away "the useless obstruction of a vast mass of paper indebtedness between Governments," and to "wipe out the whole of such indebtedness by the stroke of the pen." This mass of external indebtedness "lay like a dead weight upon the credit of continental Europe and made reconstruction even slower and more painful than it needed to be." But Britain met only the intransigence and bullying of the United States Treasury, which refused to cooperate in a "common policy toward our common debtors." Blackett charged that America "abuses its position as our creditor" and forced Britain to abandon its own position and "accept the views of the United States Treasury." Worse yet, the U.S. Treasury "often goes further and demands that we shall put forward its views as if they were being pressed on it by us."

It was time, Blackett asserted, to reassess this attitude of "one-sided cooperation" and consider the possibility of unilateral cancellation of Allied debts by the British Treasury. The advantages might well outweigh the risk. Relieved of the debts, the European economy would improve, opening new markets for British exports and simultaneously closing them to American exports. If at the same time Britain paid off its debt to America, the United States would be open to British exports. "Ultimately, in self-defense," Blackett conjectured, "the United States Government might be driven to beg us to accept as a favor the wiping out of our debt to it," and "in the meanwhile we should surely have earned the gratitude of the world."[5] Blackett, it should be recalled, was considered to be an astute economist.

Enthusiasm at the Foreign Office for Blackett's plan knew no bounds. Officials there regarded unilateral cancellation of Allied debts to Britain as a diplomatic coup, but one which would have to be very carefully prepared to avoid alienating American opinion. Assistant Foreign Secretary R. A. C. Sperling tipped Britain's hand when he observed that "strictly speaking it is of no concern of the

United States if we like to write off the Allies' debts to H.M.G., but if, as I understand, we want to shame the United States into following our example and writing off our debt to them, the most careful stage-management will be required." Others at the Foreign Office believed Blackett's policy would promote Britain's foreign relations "for a generation to come" while assuring His Majesty's Government "the incontestable moral leadership of the world." And by linking remission of Allied debts to other negotiations, "there are a good many territorial questions, e.g. with Italy (in Africa) and France (in Morocco) which might be brought in with advantage."[6]

Those more conversant with financial affairs did not share the Foreign Office's fascination with Blackett's proposal. Sir Auckland Geddes, president of the Board of Trade and slated to become ambassador to the United States the following month, warned that cancellation by Britain would alienate the United States and bring on financial disaster to Britain. He believed it was mistaken to assume France would never pay her debt to Britain. France, he thought, would get more out of reparations than most people imagined. If Britain canceled France's obligations, Geddes predicted, and the United States refused to cancel Britain's obligations, then "ten years hence France might be in a stronger economic position than this country." "It is a gamble," concluded Geddes, "and the position is too serious to be settled in such a way."[7]

Whether such a gamble would pay off for Britain depended on her ability to shame the United States into following her example. It also required an accurate assessment of the ability of Britain's Allies to repay their debts. Treasury officials considered Class A debts owed by India and the Dominions as "good and immediately so"; Class B debts owed by France, Italy, Portugal, and the Congo as partly recoverable, though not at once; and Class C debts owed by Serbia, Belgium, Roumania, Montenegro, Greece, and Russia as "of very hypothetical value."[8] Reports to the Foreign Office from Washington indicated little hope that America would cancel any debts. Sperling finally concluded that "as long as the President is unable to transact business there is not the slightest chance of getting a definite answer from the U.S. Treasury to a question on such an important subject as this."[9]

Weighing the pros and cons, the cabinet eventually decided against unilateral action. On 4 March 1920 Sperling drew up a note to the British embassy in Washington informing Counselor R. C. Lindsay that "Proposed cancellation of Allies' indebtedness to H.M.G. referred to in my telegram of February 24 has been abandoned and you should therefore not mention the subject to anyone."[10] Instead, Britain again suggested to the U.S. Treasury a general cancellation of intergovernmental debts.

David P. Houston, who had just replaced Carter Glass as secretary of the treasury, denounced Britain's latest proposition in a cable to Chamberlain. "Apparently," observed Houston, "there are those who have been laboring for some time under the delusion that the inevitable consequences of war can be avoided."[11] The secretary's blunt statement temporarily ended British feelers for cancellation of inter-Allied debt. Blackett instead pursued discussions in London and Paris with U.S. Treasury representative Albert Rathbone in an effort to reach agreement on terms for funding Britain's debt to the American Treasury. By June 1920 these talks had collapsed.

The Foreign Office apparently believed "a substantial agreement was reached on the main question involved" when the talks were suddenly shifted to a higher level (Wilson and Lloyd George), Rathbone left for Paris, and France added her own stipulations to any debt agreement. British Treasury records tell a different story. According to Blackett, the United States did not wish to have the debt funded; the sight obligations constituted a powerful diplomatic weapon which the American government did not wish to relinquish. This might explain why, in Blackett's opinion, America's demands on minor points "were felt to be perfectly intolerable," and "the specific demands put forward by Mr. Rathbone . . . for dealing with the points at issue were preposterous." The United States intended to "exact payment in full as early as might be" from Britain, while asking Britain to treat France and Italy on a capacity-to-pay basis. Chamberlain added to Blackett's memorandum his own note declaring "I would sooner pay if I could, and default if I could not, then sell my country into bondage by signing any document containing language like that quoted from his draft by Mr. Blackett."[12]

The Blackett-Rathbone talks broke down because both Blackett and Chamberlain flatly rejected Rathbone's terms. The addition of French demands for adjustment of their debt had nothing to do with Britain's delay in funding its own debt to the United States. The Foreign Office probably wished to use France as a scapegoat. In any event,

President Wilson now warned Lloyd George that the long delay in funding was "already embarrassing the Treasury." In a 3 November 1920 note to the prime minister, he advised Lloyd George to send to Washington "without delay" a representative empowered to arrange a funding settlement.[13]

Since his arrival in Washington as ambassador, Sir Auckland Geddes had been warning Foreign Secretary Lord Curzon that "people here regard themselves as groaning under a load of taxes mainly incurred in the interest of foreign people and are in no temper to be generous." Geddes gained this impression in talks with the secretary of the treasury (who was speaking for the president) and the secretary of state—sources which the Foreign Office might have taken seriously.[14] It thus seems inconceivable that official Britain could still delay funding in the hope of American cancellation. But as the British cabinet met on 3 November 1920, the day Wilson sent his letter to Lloyd George, the government was apparently living in an unreal world of illusion. The cabinet was inclined to ignore Wilson's request that they send a representative empowered to negotiate a funding agreement. They believed a Republican administration under Warren G. Harding would impose terms certainly no more stringent than those demanded by the Wilson administration. The cabinet instructed Curzon to explain to Geddes Britain's policy of delay.[15]

Curzon's letter to Geddes "explained" Britain's reluctance to fund the debt to America. The foreign secretary claimed the U.S. Treasury had always demanded that it should have the right to sell Britain's funded obligations (now long-term securities) to the American public after an interval of perhaps five years. This was "most objectionable" from the British standpoint. Once Britain's obligations passed into private hands, it would be impossible for the United States Treasury, if it should desire to do so in connection with a general scheme for settlement of inter-Allied debts, to cancel any part of Britain's debt. "For all these reasons," concluded Curzon, "we think it better to let sleeping dogs lie."[16] It should not go unmentioned that while the British government resisted any funding plan under which its obligations might fall into the hands of the American public, it consistently pushed such schemes for a German "reparation loan," in which the burden of collecting would fall to American bondholders rather than the Allied governments. For a supposedly pragmatic people, consistency is not a virtue.

Wilson's 3 November letter to Lloyd George convinced at least Chamberlain that Britain could no longer afford to "let sleeping dogs lie." The chancellor reacted to Wilson's threats with uncontrolled rage. In a 30 November 1920 memorandum and supplementary note to the cabinet, Chamberlain advised that Britain pay the Americans their interest and try once more to reach a funding agreement. The United States, he was convinced, would never consent to any adjustment of inter-Allied debt. Chamberlain further asked the cabinet to reconsider its rejection of his 12 May proposal for unilateral British cancellation of Allied debts. He believed most of those obligations "as of little worth" to Britain, but they continued to haunt the budgets and fiscal arrangements of the debtor nations. "There cannot be good relations in the world," Chamberlain observed, "when the first and principal connection of those who should be most closely united is that of debtor to creditor." Unilateral British cancellation might be decisive in determining the policy of the incoming Harding administration.[17]

If Chamberlain's assessment of American public opinion was accurate, however, he could expect no more from Harding than he had received from Wilson. "The American people," wrote Chamberlain, "are living in a different continent—I might say in a different world. It is useless and worse than useless to criticize their insularity, blindness and selfishness, and it is not compatible with our dignity to appear as suitors pressing for a consideration which is not willingly given."[18] Britain might as well stop pleading and pay up.

Chamberlain received little support from the Foreign Office, which appeared to ignore Geddes's notes from Washington urging a funding mission. The Foreign Office, remarked one official, was not really involved in funding negotiations except as a channel of communication between London and Washington. The decisions were up to the Treasury. Finally, however, Chamberlain appeared to have won the battle in the cabinet, and the Foreign Office cabled Geddes on 17 December 1920 that Britain was sending Lord Chalmers as special commissioner with authority to negotiate a funding agreement.[19] Formerly chairman of the Board of Inland Revenue, Chalmers was now a permanent secretary at the Treasury.

Now that funding had become a real possibility, the Foreign Office took a more direct interest and tried to block the negotiations. Sir William George Tyrrell, assistant secretary for foreign affairs, directed R. C. Lindsay, counselor in the British embassy in Washington, to prepare a memorandum on inter-Allied debt. Lindsay, "who owing to his close personal relations with the Harding people at Washington is in a very good position to advise," did not share Geddes's enthusiasm for an immediate funding agreement—which is no doubt why he rather than Geddes was directed to prepare the memorandum. Unilateral British cancellation of French and Italian debts at the moment when Lord Chalmers was going to Washington, advised Lindsay, would be "really bad psychology." The United States would regard such a move as pressure to follow suit and cancel debts—"just what Norman Davis [at the U.S. Treasury] always told me we ought not to do."[20]

Apparently hoping to impress his superiors with his inside information, Lindsay referred to his frequent conversations with Russell C. Leffingwell, former assistant secretary of the treasury, and Norman Davis, who after serving Leffingwell had become an under secretary of state. Both had told Lindsay they were "almost inclined to think" it would be in America's interest to cancel Britain's debt. The only obstacle was American public opinion. Only a catastrophe, Lindsay believed, could change American opinion. "I do not really think anything will really bring the truth home to America," wrote Lindsay, "except repudiation. I presume this is bound to come soon from France or Italy." When Europe collapsed, Lindsay predicted, "I find it impossible to believe that America will not spontaneously give to Great Britain any facilities which circumstances will compel her to give her other Associates."[21]

If only Britain could postpone funding a little longer, Lindsay seemed to be saying, America would be forced to cancel all inter-Allied debts as Europe's financial system collapsed. In retrospect this position appears irresponsible, but at its 7 February 1921 meeting the British cabinet decided that nothing was to be gained by negotiating with the lame-duck Wilson administration when better terms might be obtained from incoming President Harding. The cabinet suspended the Chalmers mission to Washington.[22]

As the Harding administration settled in, Ambassador Geddes sounded the waters for any change in United States policy. He found none. After a meeting with the new secretaries of state and treasury, and the new assistant secretary of the treasury on 2 May 1921, Geddes informed the Foreign Office that "it is evident that neither he

[Mellon] nor the United States Government contemplates any cancellation. His views on the whole coincide with his predecessor's." Mellon based his determination to collect in full on a very optimistic assessment of Europe's economic future. Geddes reported that "for reasons not clear to me," Mellon confidently expected an early expansion of trade and the restoration of general prosperity in Europe, enabling Europe to pay her debts.[23]

Undaunted, the British ambassador continued to press London for an early funding agreement. With the cancellation of the Chalmers mission, Geddes asked the British Treasury to send someone to assist the embassy with informal funding conversations with the United States Treasury. Treasury officials who had never accepted Chamberlain's 30 November 1920 memorandum urging Britain to go ahead and pay quickly put the brakes on Geddes's request for informal talks. Blackett told Under Secretary for Foreign Affairs Sir Eyre Crowe that "the policy of His Majesty's Government may be said to watch events and avoid bringing on any premature discussion of the problem, in the expectation that as time passes conditions may be counted upon to become more favorable to its solution." Britain still held out for a "round-table discussion on the broadest possible lines of the whole problem of inter-Governmental indebtedness arising out of the War," and the Treasury "propose simply to wait until the United States Government formally suggest discussions of the matter."[24]

British and French initiatives toward the end of 1921 and early 1922 precipitated a series of moves which ultimately induced the United States Congress to establish in February 1922 the World War Debt Funding Commission (WWDFC). Congress felt compelled to act because Britain and France were discussing schemes to either cancel inter-Allied debts or to have Germany assume those debts in return for a reduction in her reparation obligation under the treaty. Such proposals threatened the position consistently taken by the United States government that there could be no connection between inter-Allied debts and German reparation obligations. Even in the United States some ranking financial authorities were beginning to question their government's official position, and Congress wished to act to prevent any cancellation or exchange of debt. Two central bankers, Montagu Norman and Benjamin Strong, rejected the logic of settling reparations and inter-Allied debts at separate conferences.

"Such a possibility," wrote Norman, "is too ridiculous! Having, let us suppose, steadied the Exchanges by some Reparations adjustment, we are immediately to see them unsteadied by Inter-Allied Debt payments." Strong agreed on the wisdom of a simultaneous settlement of all intergovernmental debts, but both bankers recognized such a solution was "not practical politics."[25]

Proposals for a reciprocal cancellation of German reparations and inter-Allied debts involving Germany's assumption of Allied debts had circulated in European capitals since early 1921. Germany's foreign minister, Dr. Walter Simons, informed the American commissioner in Berlin on 21 March 1921 that Germany was willing to assume, within the limit of her capacity, interest payments and amortization of the liabilities of individual Allied countries, if the Allies and their creditors so desired. Britain's ambassador in Berlin, Viscount D'Abernon, supported such a scheme both because he believed it was likely to work and because he felt "there are large advantages in bringing America (the ultimate creditor) and Germany (the ultimate debtor) face to face in the way which the scheme would effect."[26]

Initial reaction at the Foreign Office to the Simons plan was cool. Because there was little chance the other Allies would ever pay their debts, Britain appeared to be the largest gainer if Germany took over its payments. At best, the proposal seemed impolitic and likely to further alienate American opinion. But Sir Eyre Crowe regarded Simons's proposal as an attempt to split the Allies which had to be quashed immediately. "We cannot afford," Crowe wrote, "to toy with any scheme which would separate Great Britain from France, Italy, and Belgium, but chiefly France, in the treatment of the general question of war debts due to the United States. I believe there is some sort of understanding with the French government in this matter."[27]

At the British Treasury, however, Simons's offer received a more favorable hearing. Basil Blackett prepared his own plan in December 1921. Britain and France would agree to demand payment of debts owed by other allied governments (excluding Russia) only insofar as they themselves were called upon to repay debts owed the United States. The remaining "contingent liability" would then be assumed by Germany, whose reparation obligation would be reduced by the full amount of the original inter-Allied debt. Blackett described his plan as "at least logical and possible," though not likely to be accepted by the United States. Blackett revived the matter in a memorandum of 18 February 1922 to the chancellor on the "Relation Between Inter-Allied Indebtedness and German Reparations," in which he returned to his earlier proposal for German assumption of inter-Allied debts. At the 16 March 1922 Paris meeting of the Allied finance ministers, the Italian delegation put forth a plan based on Blackett's scheme "to the effect that the German capital debt should be divided into two parts, and that payment of one part, which would correspond to the amount of inter-allied indebtedness (viz. about 65 of the 130 milliards) would be indefinitely suspended and finally waived."[28]

Blackett understood that the United States government was in no mood to participate in any scheme involving mutual cancellation of debts. Britain's only alternative was a funding agreement with the United States in which Britain obtained terms at least as favorable as her less solvent Allies. But Britain, he conceded, was at the mercy of the United States. "Our only effective rejoinder," Blackett concluded, "is to threaten to force France and Italy to repudiate their debts both to the United States and ourselves." Britain was faced with a most critical decision: "Is the British Government to accept boldly the position however inequitable of being the only one of the Inter-Allied Debtors to begin effective payment of the interest and principal of the debt, or does the British Government intend to veil a repudiation of its own obligations under the cover of threatening to force general repudiation?"[29]

The United States could not stand aside while Europe went about canceling its debts. President Harding and Secretary of the Treasury Mellon had no intention of repudiating any portion of the inter-Allied debt, but they wanted a free hand for the Treasury to negotiate funding arrangements on a nation-by-nation basis. Congress suspected the administration would use such discretion to cancel part of the debt. On 9 February 1922 Congress passed a Debt Funding bill which severely restricted President Harding's freedom of action in negotiating foreign debt settlements. The bill permitted nation-by-nation settlements, but only within strict guidelines. Each debtor nation had to repay the principal in full. Any adjustment for capacity to pay had to be made through the interest rate, which could not be set at less than 4.25 percent per annum, or through a time extension, which could not extend beyond 15 June 1947. Once a government agreed to a specific funding plan, it could not seek changes at a later date. To remove control from the Harding administration, Congress established a Debt Funding Commission charged with negotiating the agreements. The original Commission included Andrew Mellon (chairman), Herbert Hoover, Charles Evans Hughes, Senator Reed Smoot, and Representative Theodore Burton. Three new members were appointed in 1923.[30]

With the creation of the Debt Funding Commission, the United States government issued on 25 April 1922 what Blackett referred to as a semiofficial invitation to the Allies to send representatives to Washington for discussions with the Commission. The dreaded moment had arrived. To go to Washington or not to go to Washington, that was the question. The American invitation raised suspicion among the Allied governments, and created internal dissension within the British and French governments. Which government would be the first to respond, and what should that response be? The conflict and confusion among European debtors was fueled by ambiguous statements by leading American financiers giving them false hopes that a lenient settlement might yet be obtained through further delay. Once the World War Debt Funding Commission (WWDFC) learned the facts, Americans would understand that the guidelines laid down by Congress were impossible.

Unofficial spokesmen in the United States such as Thomas W. Lamont, Benjamin Strong, Russell C. Leffingwell, and Oscar T. Crosby (a Morgan partner, governor of the Federal Reserve Bank of New York, former assistant secretary of the treasury, and former acting secretary of the treasury, respectively) ridiculed America's attempt to collect in full and even suggested that the debtors refuse to pay on such onerous terms. They indicated that the Harding administration was divided and probably would not insist on following the terms of the funding bill, that the WWDFC itself would not recommend settlements along the lines of the bill, and that enlightened opinion both within and without the government recognized the futility of the stipulations laid down in the funding bill.

Lamont was cheered by delegates at the American Banker's Association convention when he called for a just and generous view of the debt situation and rejected "ill-advised steps for the collection of that debt, every penny, principal and interest." Leffingwell found

Lamont's approach "precisely right," but supported debt concessions only if they were linked to "imposing reasonable conditions" on European finance ministries—balanced budgets, honest money, removal of trade barriers, settlement of international debts (meaning reparations), and disarmament. Crosby, on the other hand, rejected such conditions because they implied unwarranted criticism of French financial policy. "Great Britain," he noted, "has been excepted from the charge of arrogance, militarism, and imperialism, while those serious faults are strongly urged against France. Hence, French policies specially are to be put in tutelage to our omniscient righteousness." Crosby hoped to dispel "this much heralded gospel of American superiority and French inferiority in moral and political vision." Aside from the injustice done to France, America's misguided views imperiled its own material interests. "If France should be purile enough to take direction from us," warned Crosby, "we should be bound to assume grave, though ill-defined, responsibilities toward a host of unsuspected European complications."[31]

By May 1922 officials at the Foreign Office had come around to Ambassador Geddes's view that funding talks ought to proceed. They believed Treasury officials placed too much credence in statements by American bankers and financiers. American policy on such matters, they pointed out, was made not by the financiers, but by a Congress which was determined to "make them pay." Treasury officials had apparently taken too seriously statements allegedly made by Lloyd George to French Minister for Justice Louis Barthou in Genoa between 29 April and 2 May 1922. The British prime minister was trying to gain French support for British plans for European peace and reconciliation by implying that the success of the Genoa conference might bring more lenient terms from America. The Genoa conference, of course, was not successful, and the Foreign Office discounted Lloyd George's remarks to Barthou as "misleading." Sir Mauric Hankey confidentially informed the Foreign Office that the prime minister was simply "doing a bit of bluffing" and that "we should disregard what was said to M. Barthou at that point." A first secretary at the Foreign Office, Horace James Seymour, added his opinion that "the conclusion, I fear, is that the wish is father to the thought in the minds of both the Treasury and of Mr. Lloyd George."[32]

On 17 May, Geddes informed the Foreign Office of reports that

France had notified the United States government of its readiness to send a special mission to Washington. Britain could not afford to alienate American opinion by rejecting the invitation while its Allies trooped to Washington in a show of good faith. As Seymour noted, "If this report is true it furnishes an additional reason for our starting negotiations." Assistant Foreign Secretary Sperling added that "the French and Italians are both nervous lest any other Power should get ahead of them in accepting the United States proposal to send delegates. The French asked us on April 18 whether we were doing so." But the British cabinet still officially was "opposed to committing HMG to paying up in full and so losing the possibility of using such payment as a lever in inducing the United States to deal comprehensively with the Allied debt as a whole." After reading Blackett's latest memorandum of 6 June 1922, however, Sir Eyre Crowe concluded that "the Treasury now seems to be veering round in favour of funding and unconditional payment."[33]

Blackett had indeed abandoned his earlier advocacy of delay. No American government in the foreseeable future was going to remit, cancel, or exchange British debt for German or French obligations. Britain thus had nothing to lose by funding now rather than later "if we are once agreed that the debt must eventually be funded and paid." Funding in fact would hasten the day when Britain could stabilize the pound sterling at prewar parity; this was impossible so long as the debt was nominally payable on demand. Funding of the debt would also help in the government's fight against the recession. The export of British capital through debt payments, Blackett reasoned, would help foreign customers purchase British goods. He now advised that Britain "cut the gordian knot, even at the cost of giving up whatever hope there might otherwise be of escaping part of the burden of the debt to the United States Government."[34]

Blackett's position now coincided precisely with the attitude expressed by the executive secretary of the WWDFC, Eliot Wadsworth. According to Lamont, Wadsworth had commented that "they want Great Britain's courageous meeting of the situation to act as much as possible as a precedent for other governments."[35] If that was the case, it was doubly important that Britain be the first nation to accept the invitation to talk with the WWDFC. But Britain apparently was not up to the expected sacrifice, as Norman informed Strong on 19 June 1922 that "it is quite decided that no commission or Representative will at the present time be sent from this country." "This," pleaded Norman, "is far from what I should like to have done—far from what I advised."[36]

Blackett also felt compelled to explain to Lamont what had gone wrong. On 26 June he admitted that "we here have known what needs doing and could have done it if we had taken our courage in our hands and determined to settle up inter-European debts without waiting for America. But it meant our being the chief payer of a war indemnity, if not absolutely the only payer."[37] There was no question of Britain's capacity to pay. Britain simply was not going to pay its debts if no one else was going to pay theirs.

Britain's dilatory tactics were beginning to wear thin in Washington. On 5 July 1922 the American ambassador in London, Colonel George Harvey, accompanied by William Howard Taft, met with Lloyd George, Bonar Law, and Winston Churchill. Harvey bluntly told the prime minister that he should have sent representatives to Washington for funding discussions. Instead, it was the French who had shown the way by agreeing to send their number-two man at the Finance Ministry, Jean Parmentier. The fact Parmentier was only going to say that France could not pay was beside the point— at least he was going, and the British were not.

Harvey then explained that the United States government had hoped to clear up the Anglo-American debt so that the two countries could then stand together in dealing with the remainder of the European debt problem. At the crucial moment in Anglo-American relations, lamented Harvey, Britain had failed to respond. The ambassador concluded with the dubious observation that if talks with foreign debtors had indicated the present scheme was too restrictive, the lame-duck Congress might have passed more liberal legislation.[38] Comments such as this, of course, only reinforced Britain's tenacious hope that America would eventually scale down the debt.

Possibly jolted by Harvey's tongue-lashing, the British cabinet decided on 7 June that delegates should go to Washington for funding talks during the first week of September. Ostensibly because Secretary of State Hughes was to be in Rio de Janeiro at that time, the State Department asked that the visit of the British delegation be postponed until the beginning of October. Lloyd George's government fell in October, and on the twenty-third of that month Stanley

Baldwin became chancellor of the exchequer. The change of government necessitated a further postponement of the funding talks, and it was not until 27 December 1922 that a British delegation headed by Baldwin and Norman sailed for Washington. Meanwhile, the entire complexion of the debt funding issue had been changed by the French Parmentier Mission to Washington during July and August, and the notorious Balfour Note of 1 August 1922. By the end of August, prospects for any settlement of inter-Allied debts appeared virtually nil. Financial relations between the former entente powers had reached a new low.

With good reason, the French government was wary of sending a delegation to discuss funding with the WWDFC. Previous attempts to settle with the United States government relatively small inter-government accounts and to arrange for repayment of the 1915 Anglo-French loan had proved very unpleasant for the French Finance Ministry. Jean Parmentier, now director of the Mouvement général des fonds, had been sent in August 1920 to straighten out matters with the United States Treasury. In all financial negotiations between the two governments since the Armistice, American representatives had assumed an intransigent, sometimes rude position. American financial representatives practiced sharp bargaining tactics which invariably cost the French Treasury money it did not have.

To understand France's reluctance to undertake funding talks with the WWDFC, one need only examine previous negotiations for settlement of the so-called "Franco-American balance"—special accounts hastily established during the war to provide French and American troops in France with necessary food and supplies. Neither government knew how much the other actually owed on these accounts, which were entirely separate from the advances furnished by the United States Treasury. The Franco-American balance thus became a matter for negotiation after the Armistice. The record of these negotiations does nothing to enhance America's reputation for common decency toward its wartime friends.

Settlement of the Franco-American account encompassed five separate agreements: The Bayne-Voisin accord of 1 October 1919, the Delano-LeHenaff agreement of 1 October 1919, the Parker-Morel accord of 25 November 1919, the Ignace-Parker agreement of 1 December 1919, and the Mellon-Casenave agreement of 28 June 1921.

In a related matter, the United States and France agreed on the sale of American surplus war stocks on terms which greatly displeased the French Finance Ministry.

Prior to any of these agreements, Finance Minister Klotz and U.S. Treasury representative Albert Rathbone agreed that settlement of any claims against the United States government would not result in money payments to the French Treasury. Any sums due France would be credited toward reduction of French debt owing to the United States Treasury. Klotz later regretted this agreement. Dollar payments from the United States during 1919–1921 would have provided the French government with funds to finance a portion of its current account deficit with America. Lacking these dollar resources, the Finance Ministry was forced to sell dollar-denominated French Treasury bills in New York.

Prompt settlement of the Franco-American balance was vital to the French Finance Ministry. Lacking an overall settlement at a fixed rate of exchange, each French ministry owing money to the United States had to pay the bills as they came in. The burden increased as the franc depreciated against the dollar. The French expected to obtain a better-than-current exchange rate in a general settlement. The debts, after all, had been incurred when the franc had been pegged close to prewar parity. The exchange rate chosen was important. On 7 October 1919 the French Office of Liquidation estimated the French debt to America under the Franco-American account at $200 million (it was eventually settled at $223 million), and the American debt to France at 2 billion francs (later settled at 1.9 billion). Precisely how these franc and dollar sums added up depended on the chosen exchange rate. Rathbone calculated the United States debt to France at $19,303,887.06, while French financial representative Frédéric Bloc claimed a French credit of $145,905,127.46. The discrepancy, said Rathbone, resulted largely from the use of different exchange rates in the calculations—Rathbone figured 10.30 francs to the dollar (current rate), while Bloc took the rate at the time the franc was unpegged in March 1919, 5.75 francs to the dollar.[39]

Within the French government itself, there was great confusion as to the amounts involved in the Franco-American balance. Officials at the Office of Liquidation, for example, told the Finance Ministry that the Merchant Marine "can rather quickly figure out *its credits*," but "as to its debts, it has no idea of the total amount, and the Americans will have to straighten it out to present their bill. They will have difficulty doing that, and thus, it seems that we shall be in a good position to obtain an advantageous payment." As we shall see, the confusion resulted in settlements disadvantageous to the French government. In any event, the Finance Ministry expected to establish a credit of possibly $100 million. French Commissioner for Franco-American Affairs in New York, Maurice Casenave, cabled after consulting with Norman Davis at the U.S. Treasury that $29 million appeared closer to the mark. The Finance Ministry had "forgotten" that the United States government held a 688 million franc credit in a Paris bank account.[40]

Some of the settlements relating to the Franco-American balance were routine. The French Finance Ministry was satisfied with the Bayne-Voisin, Delano-LeHenaff, and Ignace-Parker accords because they appeared advantageous to the French government. But the Morel-Parker agreement and the Casenave-Mellon accord produced hard feelings between the two governments during and long after the negotiations.[41]

In October 1919 the United States Liquidation Commission (War Department), headed by Judge Edwin B. Parker, arrived in Paris for negotiations with Paul Morel, under secretary of state for finance with responsibility for liquidation of war stocks. The American Commission for Peace headquartered at the Hotel Crillon implied that the sooner France settled her accounts the sooner American bankers would lend her more money. Rathbone, representing the U.S. Treasury in Paris, rejected the French contention that the rate of exchange prevailing when the goods were delivered should be written into the final settlement of accounts. The United States government certainly did not wish to make a profit on French exchange depreciation, but neither did it think France should now benefit from the artificially high franc exchange at the time of delivery, supported largely through American loans to France. The French countered with the observation that the price of American goods sold to France during the war had also been artificially high. "It is thus absolutely impossible in fairness to retain the prices fixed in 1917 or 1918," argued the Finance Ministry, "and to apply to the settlement of these transactions a subsequent rate of exchange."[42] The Americans, of course, were simply able negotiators—they wished to obtain the highest possible price for American goods, and the worst possible rate for the franc.

The Parker Commission and Morel could reach no agreement on critical issues, and the Parker-Morel accord dated 25 November 1919 contained no clause fixing the exchange rate for franc-dollar conversion. The absence of such a clause rendered the agreement virtually useless, since there was no way to determine the actual credit due France. After the agreement was signed by Parker and Morel, the French Office of Liquidation found "errors to our detriment, whose total reaches *10 millions of dollars.*" Finance Minister Klotz, moreover, claimed the contract had never been submitted to him or anyone else in the Finance Ministry prior to signing. In a blistering note to Morel, Klotz exclaimed that "I can only indicate my astonishment that a document of this importance, which engages the finances of the State, could have been signed without my prior opinion. I will add that, had I been consulted, I would have been opposed to its conclusion in its present form, which, leaving aside completely the question of exchange, threatens to disarm us vis-à-vis the Americans in conversations to follow." Klotz ordered Morel to arrange another meeting with Parker before the American Commission left Paris. The contract, he said, must be "completed" by an exchange of letters adding a clause expressly reserving the question of exchange, and making the conclusion of a definitive settlement conditional upon the adoption of a satisfactory rate of exchange. Morel did arrange another meeting with the Parker Commission, but it proved inconclusive and Parker then left Paris for Washington.[43]

Klotz expected to rectify the deficiencies of the Parker-Morel accord in the definitive settlement of the Franco-American balance. The Casenave-Mellon accord, however, was not concluded until 28 June 1921. During the interim, François-Marsal succeeded Klotz at the Finance Ministry, Morel was dismissed and replaced by Yves Le Troquer, and the Wilson administration gave way to the Harding administration. These personnel changes made no difference in the negotiating position of either side.

Negotiations for the Casenave-Mellon agreement consumed fourteen months. François-Marsal, determined to "rectify" the errors in the Parker-Morel accord, attempted to centralize the negotiating process so as to produce a "contract which shall be established under the stamp of the Minister of Finance." The Finance Ministry invited the United States government to send representatives to Paris to conclude a definitive agreement on the Franco-American balance. The American response stunned the French. Judge Parker refused to amend the balance agreed to in the Parker-Morel accord, and the U.S. Treasury considered the Parker-Morel contract as "absolutely definitive." American Treasury officials recognized as valid the French claims of errors to the detriment of France, but refused to reopen the matter.[44]

Discussions centering on the exchange rate continued during the later months of 1920 and into 1921. In February 1921, shortly before the change of administration in Washington, the U.S. Treasury offered an exchange rate in the vicinity of 6 francs to the dollar, when the current rate was 15. The director of the Office of Liquidation, Mathieu de Vienne, advised Parmentier to accept the American offer before a new administration could offer less favorable terms. At the 6-franc rate, the French credit corresponded more or less to an American deposit of 630 million francs at the French Treasury. The Franco-American account could thus be settled simply by having the United States turn over its deposit to the French government.[45]

The solution envisioned by de Vienne ruled out any dollar payment by the United States government in settlement of its account. As de Vienne himself pointed out, "It is evident that the cancellation of obligations which our government has no intention of repaying immediately and for which it pays no interest [he referred here to credit against wartime advances from the U.S. Treasury which France would receive in settlement of the Franco-American balance] is not a very great advantage." France, he thought, could reap a much greater advantage by attempting to cancel its recent contract for purchase of surplus American war stocks, on which the government was paying heavy interest.[46]

Despite reservations, the French Finance Ministry concluded that it was wise to settle promptly before the Harding administration took office. Casenave wired Paris that he expected to sign an agreement on 3 March, the day before Harding took control. Then, the entire package fell apart. Casenave went to Washington expecting to sign the agreement. Instead, he reported to Paris, "we are sorry to have to inform you of the deception which awaited us in Washington . . . at the last moment, Mr. Baker, Secretary of War, so concerned with scruples, refused to accept the exchange rate of six francs for the dollar which had been agreed by us and by the Treasury Department as the principal condition of the contract." Despite the insistence of Secretary of the Treasury Houston, Baker refused to sign and held to his position that the exchange rate should be that of the day of final settlement—the current rate.[47]

Eliot Wadsworth, the new assistant secretary of the treasury in the Harding administration, now informed the French government that settlement of the Franco-American balance must give France a credit which precisely balanced the American deposit at the French Treasury, the so-called "Major Eddy account." By equalizing the accounts in this manner, it would appear as though the United States owed France nothing, and that, believed Wadsworth, would make the agreement more pallatable to Congress. An exchange rate of 6 francs would give France a credit equal to the Major Eddy account. The French were willing to accept Wadsworth's proposition, but the United States for some reason suddenly drew down its account at the French Treasury by about 30 million francs between February 1921, when Wadsworth made his proposal, and June, when the accord was signed. Instead of over 640 million francs, there was now only about 610 million francs in the American account. To balance this new amount, Wadsworth now insisted that the exchange rate would have to be raised to about 6.20 francs for the dollar. France demanded that the 15 February balance of 640 million francs be used in calculating the exchange rate—bringing it to 6 francs.[48]

After difficult negotiations dating back to the autumn of 1919, Maurice Casenave and Andrew Mellon signed an agreement establishing a definitive Franco-American balance on 28 June 1921. The accord fixed a French credit of 1,988,104,376 francs, balanced by a French debt of $233,014,570.94. At an exchange rate of 6.13459636-40558 francs to the dollar, the accounts balanced precisely after the transfer to France of the Major Eddy account at the French Treasury.[49] The Casenave-Mellon accord put to rest one of the most vexing financial issues troubling Franco-American relations. But during the course of the negotiations, another sore point had been raised. The French government concluded that the $400 million contract signed 1 August 1919 for the purchase of surplus American war stock ought to be either revised or canceled.

French officials believed the Americans had driven an unfair bargain on the war stock contract. The United States originally asked what the French considered the outrageous sum of 6 billion francs. France countered with a first offer of 1.5 billion francs. The amount ultimately fixed in the contract was $400 million (just over 2 billion francs at prewar exchange rates), due in ten years with interest of 5 percent per annum. The French government obligated itself for semiannual interest payments of $10 million, beginning 1 August 1920. As in the case of another contract judged unsatisfactory by the French Finance Ministry, the surplus war stock agreement was negotiated by Judge Edwin Parker and Paul Morel.

Morel was probably incompetent, and he handled negotiations for the war stock contract in the same secretive manner which characterized his conduct in the Parker-Morel contract. On at least seven occasions during June, July, and August 1919, Alexandre Célier, director of the Mouvement général des fonds at the Finance Ministry, asked Morel for information on the war stock negotiations. There seems to have been no response. Célier was not informed of the terms offered by Judge Parker, and concluded that "it is certain that we have little chance of arriving at a satisfactory result if the negotiations are not conducted in a more rigorous manner."

Only after it was signed did the $400 million war stock contract come under the scrutiny of French government agencies. When a bureau of control at the Finance Ministry, disturbed by the terms of the contract, asked Célier for the correspondence between Morel and Parker and transcripts of the negotiating sessions, they discovered that the Finance Ministry possessed no such documents. Lacking such information, Célier observed, there was no way to evaluate the contract, "particularly the price France agreed to pay." "I was consulted," Célier claimed, "only on the methods by which we could acquit ourselves of the payments." Finance Ministry officials also charged that American authorities sold for their own profit or transported to "unknown destinations" war surplus that under the contract belonged to France. Fire and theft further reduced the amount of material actually delivered to the French government. The director of the Office of Liquidation urged that legal action be taken against a number of agents of the United States army.[50]

The French government sold the American war stocks to various purchasers for only $220 million, but still owed the United States the full $400 million. The Office of Liquidation conceded that some problems connected with the resale of the stocks arose not from incompetence or criminal activity, but from broad economic and financial considerations. The recession of 1920–21 arrived just as the French government was attempting to dispose of the stocks. France had been forced to buy dear and sell cheap. In this instance, the fall in prices benefited the public at the expense of the Treasury. In the end, the taxpayers and lenders made up the difference.

To the detriment of France, the surplus war stock contract with the United States provided for payment in dollars. As the franc depreciated, the cost of the payments increased. Moreover, the French Treasury permitted French purchasers of war surplus to pay with "war damage bonds." Ultimately, these bonds were to be redeemed out of German reparation payments, but in the meantime the French Treasury deprived itself of much-needed cash. More often than not, the deficiency was made good by further advances from the Bank of France. The finance minister attempted to discontinue acceptance of war damage bonds in 1921, but political pressure from the innocent victims of German aggression forced him to back down. Sound politics inevitably triumphs over sound finance.[51]

Within the government, some officials recommended that France renegotiate the surplus war stock contract. Jean Parmentier, now director of the Mouvement général des fonds in the Finance Ministry, pointed out that the contract promised delivery by the United States government "without guarantee of quantity, of quality, or of present condition"—another negotiating triumph for Morel. France, he added, could not afford to alienate American opinion by renouncing a contract, especially when they were still trying to negotiate a settlement on the Franco-American balance.[52] This was one obligation the French would have to learn to live with.

While negotiations were in progress for the war stocks contract and the Casenave-Mellon accord on the Franco-American balance, the 1915 $500 million Anglo-French loan came due in 1920. Britain and France each had to repay the United States approximately $250 million. France intended to pay $31 million of the amount due in gold. But when it developed that the gold in question apparently belonged to the prerevolutionary State Bank of Russia, another crisis in Franco-American financial relations quickly erupted. The United States government assumed what it considered a proper legal and ethical position—it would accept no gold which legally belonged to a third party. The legal questions involved in this dispute were complex. The Bank of France held approximately $62 million in "Russian gold" in its vaults. To what extent did the Bank, the French government, and the Allied powers have authority to dispose of that gold?

Under the Treaty of Brest-Litovsk (3 March 1918) Soviet Russian authorities handed over to Germany substantial sums in money and gold. Under Article 19 of the Armistice, Germany placed this Russian gold in the hands of the Allied governments pending the signature of a definitive peace treaty. This provisional regime ended with the signing of the Treaty of Versailles, Article 259 of which, as interpreted by the French government, clearly established the fate of the Russian gold.

Article 259 required Germany to transfer to the Principal Allied and Associated Powers (PAAP) all of the monetary and specie instruments received from Russia under the Brest-Litovsk agreement. The PAAP were to employ these sums in a manner to be determined by them at a later date. Meanwhile, the gold was deposited at the Bank of France, which served as depository and fideicommissary. It was under this mandate conferred by the Versailles Treaty that Britain and France, with the consent of Italy, envisaged the use of Russian gold to pay off a portion of the Anglo-French loan.

France claimed $100 million of the $500 million had been borrowed for Russia through the agency of the British and French governments. As agents, these governments now had the right to cover responsibilities they had assumed for Russia by utilizing the $62 million in Russian gold. In principle, British Treasury officials agreed with the French position. Chamberlain told Geddes that the Russian gold should be used "in part of satisfaction of what is in fact though not in form a Russian obligation to citizens of the United States of America." Washington, however, wanted no part of any gold which might be claimed by a Russian government, either present or future. President Wilson informed the State Department that it was "contrary to his conscience" to accept Russian gold in repayment of the Anglo-French loan. U.S. Treasury officials, however, told Ambassador Geddes that if the gold arrived in New York, the assay office would not inquire into its origin. Britain and France paid off the Anglo-French loan by 15 October 1920—without the aid of Russian gold. The Bank of France agreed to put up $20 million of its own gold.[53]

Compared to the sums involved in the Franco-American balance, the surplus war stock contract, and the Anglo-French loan, the U.S. Treasury advances to be discussed with the WWDFC were enormous—$3 billion. Any mistake here could cripple French finances for decades to come. This matter had been on the back burner at both Treasuries since August 1919, when Under Secretaries Leffingwell and Davis had instructed Rathbone to inform French financial officials of the Treasury's desire to proceed with funding talks without delay. Rathbone told the French it was up to them to make specific propositions, and gave them a memorandum outlining the legal limits within which the French government's sight obligations could be converted into long-term bonds.[54]

Because Finance Minister Klotz concurred in the advisability of prompt funding of France's debt to both the United States and Britain, one might have expected the matter to have been settled long before Congress created the WWDFC in 1922. But like his British counterparts, Klotz sought a "general and simultaneous settlement" of inter-allied debts. He wrote to his financial representative in London, "We have the greatest interest in linking the consolidation of American advances to the settlement of British advances, whose repayment, in the present state of things, must come, in principle, during the three years following the signing of the Peace Treaty."[55] Klotz thus established the "linkage" of France's repayment of debts to the United States with a satisfactory settlement of her debt to Britain.

Klotz's notion of a simultaneous settlement with the United States and Britain boiled down to a request that the U.S. Treasury delay a funding operation and suspend interest payments for at least three years. Klotz counted on the U.S. Treasury not to demand repayment of France's sight obligations when she was so obviously unable to pay. But France's obligations to Britain were due during the three years following the signature of peace, and it was not at all clear in the fall of 1919 that the British Treasury was willing to change that arrangement. Klotz thus assumed that all French resources during the coming years would be absorbed by payments to Britain, leaving nothing for the United States. How unfair it was, he remarked, to treat such good allies so unequally! In view of coming financial negotiations with Britain, Klotz suggested that French financial representatives in New York request American "friendly intervention" by "facilitating our situation in London."[56]

While Klotz was pursuing American support in dealing with the British Treasury, he also sought to obtain British assistance in negotiations with the United States Treasury. He aimed to establish a common Anglo-French front against the American Treasury. Klotz indicated to the British Treasury his conviction that there was "a powerful interest that the French and English governments get together on the response to the American propositions." The two Allies could strengthen their united front against the United States if they first agreed on a settlement of the French debt to Britain. Assuming fair treatment for France in such a settlement, the Allies could then approach the United States Treasury and demand an agreement along similar lines. Klotz considered the general conditions for an American settlement as set down in Rathbone's August 1919 memorandum "acceptable," so long as France obtained a three-year postponement of interest payments.[57]

Sensing Klotz's maneuvers to form an Anglo-French debtors' coalition, the U.S. Treasury sent Rathbone to Paris on 1 October 1919 to conclude funding agreements with the European debtors. Rathbone was coming to Paris to prevent any prior arrangement between the British and French Treasuries. As we have seen above, Rathbone's discussions with the two Treasuries in Paris and London broke down in June after Rathbone made propositions with Blackett termed "preposterous." For France, the collapse of the funding talks came as an unwelcome development. On the eve of Rathbone's arrival in Paris, the Finance Ministry had informed the French financial representative in London, Joseph Avenol, that the funding talks were critical. France could no longer obtain credit in the American financial market owing to bankers' reluctance to make further commitments so long as $3 billion in sight obligations threatened the French Treasury.[58]

Collapse of the Rathbone negotiations opened the way for another attempt at an Anglo-French financial coalition against America. The joint Anglo-French communiqué issued after the Hythe conference of 16 May 1920 called for simultaneous settlement of inter-Allied war debts and German reparations. When Warren G. Harding stated as candidate for the presidency that the Allies would have to pay under any circumstances, French Finance Minister François-Marsal observed that Harding's position contradicted the Hythe pronouncement, "to which we must hold firm." He advised the French premier, Alexandre Millerand, that "we can be required to pay our war debts only to the extent that we realize the rights which the Treaties signed by all the Allies confer upon us."[59]

Millerand's successor, Georges Leygues, forwarded François-Marsal's war debt interpretation to Ambassador Jusserand, urging him to contact members of the soon-to-be Harding administration and "enlighten them on our point of view in this matter." Instead, Jusserand spoke with officials at the U.S. Treasury, who bluntly told him that the Hythe conference had been nothing more than a conversation between debtors in the absence of the creditors. Secretary of the Treasury Houston advised France to fund promptly and Jusserand advised his government to take this counsel seriously.[60]

The British cabinet's decision in December 1920 to send the Chalmers mission to Washington for funding talks threatened the Anglo-French "understanding." Should the French Finance Ministry bow to Houston's pressure and fund its debt before the Democratic administration left office? The answer, in the words of a Finance Ministry memorandum, was simple: "We made a dilatory response to these suggestions." The Finance Ministry instructed Casenave in New York "not to lose contact" with the U.S. Treasury, to inform them of France's difficulties resulting from wartime devastation, "always with the objective of never engaging in any discussions which might lead you in the near future to any serious negotiations."[61] This was the French version of the British policy of delay.

Britain canceled the Chalmers mission, but mutual suspicion that one or the other was about to make a deal in Washington continued to haunt Anglo-French relations. Neither government wished to be the first to settle up with the United States, but neither wished the other to preempt a favorable position by taking the lead. The British Foreign Office took seriously the wildest rumors concerning French intentions. Ambassador Geddes reported a French offer of the use of French ports as American submarine bases in the event of an American attack on Britain. He later reported Washington stories that Briand had offered to cede to the United States the colonies of French Guiana and the French West Indies in return for a significant reduction in French debt to America. Former Premier

René Viviani was rumored to have proposed to President Harding that the United States pay France a sum equal to the full value of reparations due France, and then collect from Germany. This deal was also contingent on American use of French ports as wartime bases.[62]

France and Britain were running out of time, for in June 1921 the United States government was preparing to compel the European states to fund their debts. French financial representative Casenave learned of a meeting between J. P. Morgan & Co. partners Thomas W. Lamont and Dwight W. Morrow and Secretary of State Hughes, Secretary of the Treasury Mellon, and Secretary of Commerce Hoover. The meeting established some basic principles for the impending funding negotiations. The administration would ask Congress for wide latitude in negotiating terms for each of the debtor states. France would not be asked to come to terms before Britain had concluded a funding agreement, "everyone agreeing that the two nations cannot have the same treatment, given the enormous difference in their financial situations and the burden imposed by the war." Casenave's view, which he passed on to his superiors in Paris, reflected the intent of the Harding administration. He told the Belgian ambassador in Washington that France would not begin negotiations before Britain had concluded its, because "we have, indeed, some chance of being treated better."[63]

In Paris, the Finance Ministry continued to believe it was "expedient" to put off solution of this "delicate problem" until Washington authorities expressly requested France to negotiate. It was not in the interest of France to convert to long-term securities with specified maturity dates the existing sight obligations "whose danger of demand is balanced by the very size of the debt." There remained the possibility of cancellation, but on that question the Finance Ministry "always agreed with our Ambassador in Washington that the policy of silence was the most fruitful." François-Marsal explicitly told Casenave in New York that "I can only advise you in the clearest manner against engaging in even unofficial conversations on this point with an official of the Treasury." "Our clearest interest," he wrote, "commands us not to provoke a fresh examination of the problem and in particular to refrain from any initiative or statement" which might prejudice France's position when American authorities eventually raised the issue of the debt.[64]

As the upcoming Washington Disarmament conference loomed ahead during the autumn of 1921, French Premier and Foreign Minister Aristide Briand asked the Finance Ministry for its views "in anticipation of confidential conversations which might come up in the course of the Washington conference on the subject of debts contracted by the Allies" with the American government. Finance Minister Paul Doumer apparently preferred not to discuss French debts at the Washington conference. He informed Briand that he was sending only one financial representative, Jean de Sièyes, "given the interest we have . . . that the essential problems impinging on the relations of the two Treasuries should not be raised in the course of the coming conference." Sièyes, Doumer cautioned, would discuss nothing with the American delegates; his sole mission was to establish liaison between the French Finance Ministry and the rest of the French delegation. Nevertheless, following Briand's request, Doumer asked Parmentier to draw up a memorandum detailing France's position on funding the debt. Known as the "Note Parmentier," its thesis was accepted by Doumer, who passed it on to Briand with the Finance Ministry's stamp of approval.

Parmentier's message was simple and clear. *Legally*, France owed money to Britain and the United States, but *"in fairness*, our country owes nothing, in any form, to any of the Allied governments." France had already made the greatest sacrifice in blood, and even if her foreign debts were canceled, France would still have the "privilege" of making the heaviest sacrifice. The U.S. Treasury, he conceded, would undoubtedly tell the French they had to honor their signature. In that event, France must agree to no funding plan until Germany's reparation obligation had been settled definitively. Even then, France should discuss her debts only as part of a general settlement of all wartime debts. Parmentier advised his government to undertake no obligations with respect to war debts at the Washington Conference unless the Allies offered compensating advantages that the French government considered acceptable.[65]

With the American invitation to send representatives to Washington for funding talks, France's policy of silence had apparently reached its limit. American Ambassador Myron T. Herrick communicated the invitation in a letter expressing the WWDFC's "desire to receive propositions or observations which the French Government might wish to address to it relative to the settlement or consolidation of debts which it contracted with the American Government." Raymond Poincaré, now president of the Council and foreign minister, passed the invitation on to his finance minister, Charles de Lasteyrie. Lasteyrie advised Poincaré to inform the United States government that "the French Government is prepared to send to the United States a delegation charged with furnishing the World War Debt Commission all the information it might desire." He would designate for such a mission the director of the Mouvement général des fonds, Jean Parmentier.[66]

The French government notified Ambassador Herrick on 16 May 1922 that Parmentier would go to Washington for the purpose of providing information to the WWDFC. In a note to Lasteyrie, Poincaré referred with satisfaction to "the decision taken by us which consists solely in showing our good will to the American Government."[67] The United States government, of course, expected from Parmentier something more than "information" and a show of "good will." If the French came to Washington simply to delay, while the British came to talk seriously about funding, Franco-American relations could take a disastrous turn. The British Treasury and the French Finance Ministry were each anxious to know precisely what the other intended to do in Washington. The intensity of mutual suspicion grew with each passing day.

On 26 May, Poincaré asked his ambassador in London, Auguste Félix de Saint-Aulaire, how the British intended to respond to the invitation for funding talks. The French financial delegate in London, Joseph Avenol, had several lengthy discussions of the Parmentier mission with Basil Blackett at the Treasury, and his reports of these conversations dramatically emphasized the tension between London and Paris on the debt funding issue.

Blackett first asked Avenol "with incredulity" if the note announcing Parmentier's mission was authentic. He told Avenol that France had made a mistake in responding to the American invitation without first consulting the British Treasury. Blackett's sudden taste for consultation with the French seems somewhat disingenuous in view of Britain's haste in dismantling the wartime financial entente. Avenol, however, concurred in the advisability of consultation, "but this logical procedure was not favored by circumstances." By this Avenol meant that the British Foreign Office had declined to respond to French inquiries as to whether Britain planned to send a delegation to Washington. The Foreign Office claimed that questions of reparations and inter-Allied debts were "treated entirely and directly by the Treasury." While this was technically correct, the Foreign Office must have known or been able to determine whether Britain intended to discuss debts with the WWDFC. In any event, Avenol was unable to consult responsible Treasury officials, because Chancellor of the Exchequer Sir Robert Horne and Blackett were attending the Genoa Conference. Unable to obtain any information from London, Poincaré had decided to go ahead with the Parmentier mission.[68]

Blackett now explained to Avenol the position of the British Treasury. Ambassador Geddes had urged Britain to send a delegation, but Blackett and Horne preferred the existing sight obligations to "a rigorous and definitive system of obligations." The French mission "would have the effect of attracting attention to a question for which, given the lack of a good solution, the best policy is silence." Had France made no response to the invitation, Blackett reasoned, the chances of amending the debt funding law would have been better.[69]

Avenol came away from his conversations with Blackett convinced that France must act independently of the British Treasury. He advised the Finance Ministry to withhold from the British government information concerning the position France intended to take in the forthcoming funding talks. "We must," he observed, "preserve completely the autonomy of our relations with her [Britain], without giving or offering the British Government the occasion to advise us or to criticize us." Britain's debt to the United States exceeded that of France, and Britain certainly could not plead inability to pay. These facts led Avenol to the conclusion that as a debtor of the United States, the British government "is certainly in a position less favorable than ours; thus we must carefully avoid joining our fates." As a debtor of both Britain and the United States, France had to try to obtain the best terms from both, had to try to find "a difficult position of balance" between the two creditors.

Avenol's 30 May 1922 letter to the finance minister constituted both a plea for an independent French financial policy and a critical assessment of British financial policy since the Armistice, which he characterized as ambivalent, contradictory, and timid. France, he argued, should never have tied itself to British financial diplomacy, should never have left the initiative to Britain, should never have allowed Britain to dictate a policy of waiting silently for a general settlement of intergovernmental war debts. But that was all in the past. Now, contended Avenol, France was compounding its error by changing policy in mid-stream. The Parmentier mission was a mistake. France should negotiate with the creditor most likely to offer satisfactory terms, and that creditor, believed Avenol, was Britain. A French success in Washington, on the other hand, would only raise anti-French sentiment in London, and Britain would call in the French debt. France, advised Avenol, should reject Washington's invitation and instead press Britain for a reasonable settlement in what he believed was a favorable moment for France.[70]

Avenol's letter to the finance minister pointed up the incredible complexity of the debt situation, emphasized the intricate tactical problems involved in developing a sound program of postwar financial diplomacy, and gave new evidence that the wartime financial entente had degenerated into mutual suspicion. Avenol's arguments may have caused the French government to reconsider its decision to send Parmentier. Poincaré informed Herrick on 16 May of Parmentier's impending mission, but Parmentier did not leave for America until the first week in July. This delay prompted Herrick to send an emissary, a Mr. Whitehouse, to visit Poincaré on 6 June, asking that Parmentier be sent to Washington as soon as possible. This was the second visit from the American embassy in less than a week, and Poincaré was beginning to understand the message.

Poincaré now urged Parmentier to hasten his departure for Washington; if he would be delayed for more than another month, it would be preferable to send someone else and join the mission when he could. He told Parmentier that the United States government was preoccupied with showing the American public some results on the debt question before the next elections. France, observed the premier, actually benefited from America's "pressure to accede to a wish so insistently expressed." If France was going to have to pay, it served Poincaré's political fortunes to have it appear that it was forced to pay by greedy American creditors.[71]

Parmentier's instructions from Poincaré and Lasteyrie circumscribed his authority just as the debt funding bill restricted the latitude of the WWDFC. He was to conduct himself "in such a manner that the Government of the United States cannot at any time conclude from your one meeting with the WWDFC, or even from your silence, that France has tacitly accepted the principles of the federal law of 19 February 1922." He had "no power to negotiate an arrangement of any nature, nor to acquiesce in any formula concerning the consolidation of our debt."[72] Parmentier was to do nothing but show the WWDFC why France could not pay. As we shall see, he performed his mission only too well.

On the eve of Parmentier's departure for Washington, Lloyd George let it be known that Britain reserved the right to ask the Allies to begin interest payments on their debts as the three-year moratorium expired in October 1922. Generally viewed as Britain's response to America's insistence that Europe fund its debts, this move was equally a warning to the French against sending Parmentier to conclude a deal in Washington. Alarmed at Britain's financial pressure, Lasteyrie and Poincaré instructed Avenol and Saint-Aulaire to explain to the British Treasury and Foreign Office that Parmentier was not empowered to make any settlement. Avenol briefed Horne and Blackett. Blackett told Avenol that if the United States would facilitate a general international debt settlement, Britain would renounce debts owed by her Allies as well as German reparation payments. In view of American opposition to a general settlement, Blackett favored British funding of its debt to the United States, followed by a British initiative for a general settlement in Europe without American participation. "Obviously," wrote Avenol, "the ministers are less daring."[73]

Ambassador Saint-Aulaire learned what the British cabinet had in mind in his interview with Lord Balfour, lord president of the council and acting foreign minister. The ambassador carefully explained to Balfour the nature of Parmentier's mission and laid out the French position on inter-Allied debts—which coincided rather closely with the British position. Balfour agreed that a general settlement of all war debts was the best solution, but that clearly was not in the cards. Balfour then informed Saint-Aulaire of his intention to send to France and the other debtors of Britain "a note exposing the principles of British policy in this matter," and proceeded to give the ambassador a preview of the forthcoming Balfour Note of 1 August 1922. In the same measure as Britain was discharged from its debt to the United States, Britain would renounce debts owing to it. The cabinet would also declare that they were "prepared to consider" abandoning a portion of Britain's credit on Germany if such a sacrifice would facilitate a general settlement.[74] As read by the Allied debtors, the Balfour Note was a threat that Britain would collect its debts from Europe in order to pay its debts in America.

The British government apparently intended the Balfour Note as both a move to wreck the Parmentier mission and an attempt to shame the United States into joining Britain in a generous settlement of intergovernmental war debts. In the first instance the Note was unnecessary, and in the second it was misguided. The Balfour Note was a political document sent forth against the counsel of financial experts at both the Bank and the Treasury. The Bank warned of the "bad impression" the Note was likely to make in Europe and America. At the Treasury, Blackett shared the Bank's misgivings. In a 12 July memorandum to Horne, he described the policy adopted by the cabinet as "fundamentally insincere." France would tell Britain it could not pay unless the Germans paid up on reparations, and Blackett conceded that "the French budget can perhaps never be balanced on less." Britain's policy was indefensible. "Our policy being to persuade France to agree to a big reduction in the total of Reparations in the interest of European civilization," reasoned Blackett, "can we reasonably pretend that we expect Europe to provide what we pay to the United States of America?"[75]

Blackett was not quite the idealist he appeared to be in his 12 July memorandum. He would not ask the Dominions to forego their share of German reparations, because these payments would enable them to continue interest payments to the Treasury on £150 million in wartime advances. A generous Britain would cancel bad debts, but not the good ones. Blackett's colleague at the Treasury, Sir Otto Niemeyer, proposed that France and Italy provide Britain some compensation for canceled debts. They might, for example, surrender the gold they had deposited at the Bank of England as collateral for wartime advances.[76]

Balfour's Note had once again established Britain—not the United States—as France's most pressing creditor. It was thus Poincaré who most vigorously attacked the Balfour Note. He implied it was Britain's fault if the hoped-for general settlement of war debts had proved elusive. In any event, reparation of damage done by the Germans took precedence over any other debt. Once Germany had paid off her obligation, France would not object to a general settlement of other debts. France's debt to Britain, Poincaré argued, had been inflated by inequitable overcharges and improper methods of determining costs. America, he thought, held a higher claim to repayment than did Britain because the Americans came into the war not to defend their very existence or protect their interests, but "to defend, with their honor, the basic principles of civilization." Poincaré, like Mellon and Avenol, rejected Balfour's implication that Britain had borrowed for the French and had guaranteed some of the credits France had received from the U.S. Treasury. The British Foreign Office registered its displeasure with Poincaré's response. One assistant foreign secretary characterized his note as an "outrage," and referred to "the gratuitous and senseless nature of his [Poincaré's] latest impertinence" which went so far as to contain "charges of extortion."[77]

French intransigence on the reparation issue merely stiffened following the Balfour Note. At the 7–14 August London conference of the prime ministers, Poincaré informed Lloyd George that in view of Britain's position in the Balfour Note, "it was impossible for the French government to consider for the time being the question of the reduction of German reparation debt."[78] Meanwhile, Parmentier's mission went ahead as scheduled. He arrived in New York on 12 July, journeyed to Washington on the 13th, but did not meet with the WWDFC until the end of July, as the Balfour Note was being prepared and issued. Parmentier met twice with Secretary Mellon on 14 July. Eliot Wadsworth, a Treasury under secretary who also served as executive secretary of the WWDFC, was on vacation until the end of July after his recent marriage. Mellon was anxious to proceed, and asked Parmentier "what were the suggestions of the French government with respect to consolidation of the debt." Parmentier replied that France was in no condition to make payments or to even agree to make payments on any particular terms at the moment. Mellon then asked the envoy to provide him with relevant information in writing, after which he would present Parmentier to the WWDFC.[79]

Two weeks passed before Parmentier met with the WWDFC. Meanwhile, the U.S. Treasury paid him no heed. Wadsworth's absence, he observed in a report to Lasteyrie, "has deprived me up to now of continuous and intimate relations with the Treasury, Mr. Mellon and Mr. [Parker] Gilbert holding to a nearly absolute silence from which they consent to emerge only to discuss unimportant details." When Parmentier finally met with the WWDFC on 28 July he handed the Commission a lengthy "Memorandum on the French Financial Situation."

Conforming to instructions from Poincaré and Lasteyrie, Parmentier's memorandum presented a mass of statistics purporting to demonstrate that, owing to Germany's aggression, France was in no condition to pay. She wanted to pay, but to attempt to do so now "would fatally result in imperiling the economic life of the country" and must produce "a financial and economic catastrophe, with inevitable repercussions on the general world situation." In the short run, France had to rely on short-term securities and Treasury bills in order to survive. So far, the French public had accepted these securities, but American demands for immediate repayment might erode the public's confidence in the French Treasury's ability to redeem its obligations. "Monetary catastrophe would be likely to follow," precipitating a complete "breakdown of the franc."[80]

Had Parmentier overdone his bleak picture of France's financial situation? The plan, after all, was to portray France's situation as serious, but not hopeless. No one in the Finance Ministry wished to cause a panic in Paris. Parmentier himself recognized that he might have gone too far. In his report of 3 August he observed that it was "dangerous to make public declarations presenting our financial situation as desperate. Such declarations would certainly have a deplorable repercussion abroad and even in France."[81] The WWDFC, however, seems to have ignored Parmentier's memorandum. Parmentier "had the impression they had only partially acquainted themselves" with the document. The Committee's questions to the envoy were "clearly improvised, showing a great concern to deal tactfully with American public opinion."[82]

Parmentier and the French government in general were fixated on the problem of American public opinion. They continued to believe that the United States government and the WWDFC pressed for funding and payment of the debt only because they were forced to do so by the pressure of public opinion. If the French waited long enough, perhaps they could turn American public opinion to their side. In the meantime, wrote Parmentier, the Harding administration simply did not wish to offend the voters. Mellon and the WWDFC, he believed, hoped France would suggest a settlement "whose realization might be far off and the chances of execution minimal, but which public opinion would regard as a tangible result" of the meetings.[83]

It is not clear from the record that the U.S. Treasury and the WWDFC simply wanted a cosmetic agreement that would give the impression of progress toward payment of the debt. On two separate occasions, Mellon and Smoot asked Parmentier for concrete propositions. He responded that France could make no immediate payments, and could conclude no agreement whose execution depended upon factors beyond the control of the French government—receipt of German reparation payments. Hoover took exception to France's claim of incapacity to pay. He argued, according to Parmentier, that a state's capacity for external payment had little to do with its internal financial condition. In any event, Hoover contended, French exports now exceeded imports, and it could pay with the surplus in its trade balance, augmented by any reparation payments it might receive. To this Parmentier replied that the current trade surplus, if any, was very fragile, and any surplus would go toward repayment of short-term credits obtained during 1919 and 1920.[84]

Following his initial meeting with the WWDFC, Parmentier suggested to Poincaré that France should simply tell the Commission that its financial position was "too uncertain" to permit a definitive debt funding commitment. Noting that the Commission's mandate expired 9 February 1925, Parmentier proposed that France ask for an adjournment of negotiations until late 1924, providing time for the "uncertainties" to dissipate. Perhaps American public opinion would be more favorable, but most important, Washington would be able to stand up and do the right thing—forgetting political expediency—after the 1924 elections.[85]

Poincaré approved Parmentier's suggestion for "adjournment" of the negotiations, stipulating only that it "must be presented in conditions such that it cannot be interpreted in any way as an implicit recognition of the collectibility of our debt at the expiration of the adjournment." The debt to the U.S. Treasury, he emphasized, could not be made payable until Germany had repaid all advances France had made on her reparation account.[86] The WWDFC was not surprised when Parmentier presented the adjournment plan at the 11 August meeting. Hughes, Smoot, and Burton warned that such a delay would imperil Franco-American relations. Burton went so far as to suggest that "adjournment" until late 1924 looked like "disguised repudiation." Parmentier rather undiplomatically observed that American opinion need not be enraged if the Commission would present the adjournment in the proper light. He continued, as he reported to Poincaré, "by developing the arguments previously furnished and especially by pointing out the difference between a signature given during the war, under pressure of the most imperative necessity, and a signature which might be given today, deliberately and with full knowledge of future uncertainties."[87]

Parmentier's statement left an unfavorable impression with the WWDFC and created an uproar in the Parisian press when it leaked out in September. *La Figaro* portrayed Parmentier as insinuating that France had signed obligations under the pressure of war with no intention of honoring them later, and preferred not to sign in 1922 new obligations that she would have to honor. *L'Oeuvre* bluntly accused Parmentier of telling the WWDFC that "engagements made in time of war are nothing but useless scraps of paper."[88] However one chose to interpret Parmentier's remarks, the Commission's response made it clear that a two-year postponement was out of the question. Burton had spoken of a possible extension of two or three months. Parmentier now believed that the Balfour Note had impelled the WWFDC to press France for an immediate funding agreement, before the French economy collapsed under the weight of British demands for payment.[89]

Parmentier could now see only two alternatives for France. It must either break off negotiations immediately, or sign an agreement conforming to the rules laid down in the debt funding law. Poincaré and Lasteyrie concurred that the WWDFC's rejection of a formal adjournment of talks forced France to move for what they termed an "adjournment *de fait.*" Parmentier would cite the need to return to Paris to update the government and parliament on the views of the WWDFC. Prior to his departure from Washington, Parmentier was to "indicate that you do not consider the conversations as terminated, but as simply interrupted."[90]

As he prepared to depart for Paris, Parmentier began to have second thoughts about the long-term implications of breaking off the talks. He would do everything possible to make the breakdown appear as normal as possible, and Mellon would help out by issuing a communiqué describing his return to Paris as a "useful" move. His exit from Washington would coincide with an interruption in the WWDFC's work caused by the projected trips of Hughes to Brazil and Burton to Europe. But, Parmentier warned Poincaré, unless France resumed the talks soon, the prospect of obtaining just and generous terms would be diminished further.[91]

Reversing his position, Parmentier now advised his government to sign a funding agreement conforming to the debt funding law, provided it included a long postponement of the initial payment. Parmentier recognized the "serious problems" such a move would cause the government among the French electorate, but the political damage could be minimized if the contract were forced upon France by the WWDFC. Limited as were the powers of the WWDFC, it was, claimed Parmentier, empowered to offer terms "singularly more favorable than those set forth in our obligations themselves." A funding agreement would commit the French government to no new obligations—"it will simply have chosen conditions relatively more favorable." If authorized to do so by Poincaré and Lasteyrie, Parmentier would ask Mellon to draw up a proposal, "purely unofficial and with no commitment on one side or the other." Such a document would clarify France's position and would facilitate the eventual resumption of negotiations.[92]

By the next morning, the 18th of August, Parmentier had changed his mind. "In the current circumstances," he cabled Lasteyrie, "I consider it necessary to hasten my departure as much as possible." He proposed to leave Washington on 23 August. Parmentier had concluded "on reflection" that asking the U.S. Treasury to draw up even an "unofficial" document might give the impression that the French Finance Ministry approved the move in principle. He thus decided to ask merely that French legal officers in Washington prepare a text for internal use only; ultimately, it might be communicated to U.S. Treasury lawyers.[93]

Lasteyrie had already authorized Parmentier to consult with Treasury officials about conditions which might be incorporated in a funding agreement. Only Parmentier and the Treasury officials intimately involved should know of these talks, and in any event Parmentier was to leave Washington no later than the 23rd. Within twenty-four hours, Lasteyrie had a change of mind and cabled Parmentier to forget about further consultation and leave Washington forthwith. Parmentier left Washington on 23 August 1922, his mission a shambles.[94] Blackett's warning against sending a mission had proved accurate. Parmentier's career at the Finance Ministry was destroyed, though he did not resign until March 1923.

Lasteyrie and Parmentier had the unpleasant task of explaining to Poincaré precisely where France now stood in the debt question. Using Parmentier's final report as a basis, Lasteyrie told the premier that the WWDFC seemed convinced of France's present inability to pay anything, and seemed disposed to grant a moratorium. But the debt funding law required the WWDFC to ask France to sign a funding agreement. With an eye to the forthcoming November elections, the WWDFC had to prove itself to the American electorate by at least getting negotiations under way.

Parmentier had hoped for a two-year adjournment, but the furor caused by the Balfour Note destroyed any hope for that. The U.S. Treasury had gone along with the "interruption" caused by Parmentier's return to Paris, but would most likely request a resumption of negotiations before long. When that request came, Lasteyrie advised, France should reiterate her incapacity to pay, and force the U.S. Treasury to demand that France either fund or pay up in full. This tactic would at least convince French voters that their government had offered nothing to the Americans.[95]

France desired a general settlement of reparations and inter-Allied debts. Lasteyrie accepted Parmentier's suggestion for a scheme to force just such a general settlement. France could declare herself a debtor unable to pay the interest on her debts. As a virtual bankrupt, France could then claim inability to renounce any of her credit on Germany without the formal consent of each of her own creditors. Aside from a declaration of bankruptcy, Parmentier could recommend only reversion to old wait-and-see policy.[96]

British Foreign Office officials were not in the least disturbed by this latest French embarrassment. From the outset they had hoped Parmentier's mission would fail. They believed the French mission "appears to have been prompted solely by a desire to anticipate us." Britain felt that if the WWDFC intended to deal with each debtor nation separately, being first brought some advantages. Having lost that advantage as Parmentier was preparing to go to Washington, the Foreign Office "hoped that the French will adopt a *non possumus* attitude and so leave the field clear for us." This, of course, is precisely what happened, and the British government wasted no time retrieving the initiative. They announced their own mission to Washington, scheduled from October 1922.

The British were anxious to avoid the mistakes of their French comrades. Many observers believed France had sent the wrong man for the job. *Le Petit Bleu*, for example, referred to American "stupefaction" on learning that "we attach so little importance to negotiating with them that we send them a representative with no stature and no experience." To deal with Mellon, France sent "only a little young man, presumptuous and without authority" to conclude an agreement. One can argue Parmentier's qualifications—Schuker refers to him as "universally held in high regard for his technical competence"—but the French press did raise serious questions concerning his prestige and honesty.[97]

Britain, on the other hand, selected for its mission the two most powerful financial authorities, Chancellor of the Exchequer Sir Robert Horne and Governor of the Bank of England Montagu Norman. As Grenfell explained to Lamont, this was a deliberate move. "We are sending our two most important people," he wrote, "so that there should not be the slightest feeling on your side that due honor is not being paid to the President and Mr. Mellon."[98] But as Lloyd George's Coalition government began to disintegrate in October 1922, Horne postponed his departure for Washington.

British financiers who supported prompt funding of the debt expressed disappointment at yet another delay and the possibility of continuing international financial chaos. As Grenfell told Lamont, a debt settlement would bring America and Britain closer together. The two nations, he held, should "work jointly and stop pinpricking, then the rest of the world would have a combination to whom they would have to pay attention. At present everyone can play their own game which means that nothing can be done and then bolshevism becomes a real menace."[99] Three days after Grenfell's observations, the Unionists withdrew their support and Lloyd George's Coalition cabinet fell on 19 October 1922. Andrew Bonar Law, a Conservative, formed a new government in which Stanley Baldwin served as chancellor of the exchequer.

Baldwin's assumption of the chancellorship produced some changes in style but none in substance so far as funding of the American debt was concerned. In 1931, Lloyd George accused Baldwin of contributing to Britain's depression-era financial problems by initiating funding negotiations that resulted in adverse terms. The charge against Baldwin lacked substance. Lloyd George himself had published an article in *The Times* in February 1923, in which he approved the terms Baldwin had obtained after the conclusion of the Anglo-American funding agreement. Provoked by a heated exchange between Lloyd George and *The Times* in 1931, Sir Robert Horne, the last chancellor in Lloyd George's Coalition government, took up Baldwin's cause. He pointed out that the decision to face the obligation to the United States was taken during the final days of Lloyd George's regime. The former prime minister could not accuse Baldwin of breaking the common front with the Allies and negotiating a separate agreement. Perhaps Baldwin might have obtained better terms, but Horne, who was in the United States in an unofficial capacity during Baldwin's negotiations, believed the chancellor had extracted the best terms the WWDFC would settle for.[100]

Baldwin simply carried out a decision already taken by the Lloyd George government, but his negotiating style helped to insure a successful result. Parmentier's mission had demonstrated the importance of choosing proper tactics. Perhaps the British were overly concerned with style—Norman, for example, observed that "Sir Robert Horne was a bachelor, while the present Chancellor will be accompanied by Mrs. Baldwin, which may or may not help matters"—but Baldwin's conduct was beyond reproach. Horne had planned to try to convert American opinion and influence the WWDFC with speeches to "suitable audiences" upon his arrival, but "Baldwin has no such illusions and means to do his talking with the Commission and to spend the rest of his time in the comparative quiet of the Shoreham Hotel."[101]

British financiers seemed uncertain of the possibility of truly "negotiating" within the strict limits of the funding law. As Grenfell observed to Lamont when Horne's projected mission was announced in October 1922, "The powers of your Committee are not clear to us as to how far they can modify the Act, and if there is no possibility of varying the interest and the date due our emissaries have a difficult task." The Commission, of course, had no power to "modify the Act," and Lamont believed that "it seems to me that the Chancellor will . . . have to sign on the dotted line, or pretty nearly to it." Lamont did suggest ways in which Britain might obtain concessions within the framework of the law through the privilege of discounting maturities at any time to take advantage of "easy money conditions," and by refunding a large portion of its debt in the form of long-term, low-interest securities sold to American investors. Placing the debt in the hands of private investors would remove "a serious handicap to the friendly relations between the two countries" and relieve some of the financial burden on the British Treasury.[102] The war debt, however, was a powerful diplomatic lever which neither government wished to give up to private interests.

Baldwin and Norman arrived in Washington on 4 January 1923. While they were en route to the United States, President Harding addressed to Senator Henry Cabot Lodge a letter concerning Senator William Borah's resolution calling for a general economic conference in Washington. Lamont told Grenfell he presumed the letter had been drawn up for the president by Secretary of State Hughes, but "the point is that Harding suggests to Congress that Congress free the hands of the Debt Commission so as to enable it to deal adequately with the inter-allied debt situation." Other sources indicate that Harding instructed the WWDFC not to consider itself bound by the terms of the debt funding law.[103]

The negotiations nearly failed, but by 19 January 1923 Baldwin and the WWDFC had reached an agreement. Britain was to pay the full sum of $4.6 billion in sixty-two annual installments at 3 percent for the first ten years and 3.5 percent for the remainder of the contract. Annual payments of about £33 million during the first ten years would rise to £38 million thereafter.[104]

American financiers disagreed on the implications of the British funding agreement. Strong told Norman that "with the debt settlement concluded, I am coming to feel that the future, in many respects, is more in your hands than ours." Strong believed the agreement hastened the resurrection of the gold standard, under which the world's financial problems would straighten themselves out in a self-correcting process. London would regain its former position as the financial capital of the world.[105]

Lamont, however, considered the settlement a disaster. His newspaper, the *New York Evening Post*, blasted an unreasonable Congress and a timid president. The same Congress which refused concessions to the British debtor "will probably continue to grumble against the wicked French for refusing to be reasonable with a German debtor in difficulties." The ultimate culprit, however, was Hoover and his claim that Europe could pay. "We cannot emphasize too often the mischief for the European situation to-day wrought by Herbert Hoover's assertion that 95 percent of America's claims on the continent are good," the *Post* editorialized. "If Hoover and Congress are confident that England and the Continent will get well enough to pay up if they have to, France has every reason for demanding that Germany will get well enough to pay up if she has to. If there is no reason for being sentimental about the debts there is no reason for being sentimental about reparations."[106]

Among the British, Baldwin and Norman supported the agreement they had negotiated, but Prime Minister Bonar Law, backed by the banker McKenna and the economist Keynes, opposed it. Baldwin had in fact argued in his first meeting with the WWDFC on 8 January that American labor, business, and the U.S. Treasury itself (through tax revenues) had already profited nicely from the wartime advances to Britain. Owing to abnormally high wartime prices, Britain was now being asked to repay greater value than she had received. Britain wished to pay, but could not do so because American tariffs kept British goods out.[107] Baldwin's arguments sounded much like those employed by the French. The United States wanted the best of all possible worlds. Americans wanted no foreign competition in domestic markets, they wished to continue to sell goods in Europe, and they wanted the Europeans to repay their debts.

Baldwin accepted the settlement only because he believed the Congress then in session would accept no other terms. Lamont's conversations with Hughes and Melon confirmed Baldwin's judgment— "they felt as Baldwin did, that if the matter were allowed to run over for another twelve months or so, it might assume phases much less favorable." Baldwin, however, was uncertain of his ability to convince the British cabinet to accept the terms.[108] Because the agreement's terms fell outside the guidelines fixed by the funding law, President Harding had to submit the accord to Congress for ratification. He urged acceptance of the Commission's work in a special address to Congress on 7 February 1923. Britain, he said, could not conform to the limitations on time and interest rates provided in the law, but "there was a nation acknowledging its obligations and seeking terms in which it might repay. So your commission proceeded to negotiate in a business way for a fair and just settlement."[109]

With these words from President Harding, Congress accepted the British settlement negotiated by the WWDFC. The logjam of international debts had apparently been broken, and the way toward reconstruction of the international financial system now appeared open. But France was more than ever financially and diplomatically isolated. It would be pressed to follow Britain's lead and fund its debt to the United States, and would in turn press Germany to honor its obligations under the Treaty of Versailles.

France continued to insist that it could not meet its obligations to the United States and Britain without German reparation payments. The idea of a French occupation of the Ruhr, actually carried out on 11 January 1923, commanded serious attention in French government and financial circles as early as the spring of 1921. Conversations with French Premier Briand and former Premier Millerand convinced Lamont in April 1921 that both leaders considered "immediate occupation" of the Ruhr a necessity. Many conservative French bankers agreed.[110] By the summer of 1922, British Chancellor of the Exchequer Horne found it "puzzling" that "a nation with such immense potentialities as Germany could not pay more," but concluded that Germany should be granted a moratorium on payments. Rather than force Germany to pay, one had to attract wealth back to Germany and make Germany "a country fit for capitalists to live in."[111]

So long as Horne remained as chancellor, Britain and France were on a collision course. A German default in payments would disrupt European finances and the consequences for Britain would be "most serious." Impressed with the sincerity, strength of character, and ability of Germany's Foreign Minister Walter Rathenau (characteristics most British officials found lacking in French leadership), Horne was inclined toward a moratorium until the Germans could straighten out their finances. If France objected, there were ways to pressure the French government. British Foreign Secretary Curzon, however, urged Britain to make every effort to *convince* the French government of the need for a moratorium, possibly offering to compensate France for any losses she might incur.[112]

Curzon and his under secretary, Sir Eyre Crowe, sought to couple a moratorium on German payments with financial assistance to France. In the absence of some quid pro quo, the Anglo-French entente which Crowe considered "of supreme importance" might be destroyed. Crowe dismissed "some of the Treasury and Downing Street tendencies . . . towards the substitution of an entente with Germany for that of France" as "a chimera under present conditions and must remain so for a long time." At its meeting of 16 December 1921 the British cabinet ruled out financial concessions to France in return for support for a moratorium. France's financial problems were the result of its own unsound financial policies, not Germany's failure to pay reparations. "So long as she refused to economise," the cabinet agreed, "it would be mistaken policy for Great Britain to deal tenderly with her on the reparation question."[113]

As Parmentier was meeting with the WWDFC in Washington, and the day before the Balfour Note was to be released, the Finance Committee of the British cabinet held a thorough discussion of German reparations and the inter-Allied debts. This meeting pointed toward the total impasse between Lloyd George and Poincaré during the London conferences of August and December 1922. At the Finance Committee meeting of 31 July, Lloyd George "objected very strongly to being placed in the situation of having to pose as the friend and pleader for Germany." The prime minister "had no wish to let Germany off." It was responsible for Europe's present financial chaos and should be treated by its "innocent creditors" as "a willful and dangerous debtor." To forgive Germany's reparation obligation would be politically fatal to the British government. "We should look very foolish," observed the prime minister, "if Germany were to revive financially practically free from debt . . . while we were still staggering under a vast burden of war debt." Referring to German and French obligations to Britain, Lloyd George added that "he objected strongly to the suggestion that whoever else failed to pay, Great Britain should on every occasion meet her obligations."[114]

Lloyd George carefully distinguished Germany's legitimate refusal to pay France's illegitimate reparation claims and its illegitimate refusal to pay Britain's legitimate demands. Britain's claim, he argued, had been "carefully and fairly prepared," while France's claim was "grossly exaggerated." France had "inserted" a figure of over 2,000 million francs for the devastated regions alone, more than the total prewar estimated value of the territories. "M. Poincaré," the prime minister acidly commented, "wished to make a profit out of reparations at the expense of France's other allies."[115]

British Treasury representative on the Reparation Commission Sir John Bradbury envisioned a general writing-down of German reparation obligations and inter-Allied debts as inevitable. If Britain and the United States were to treat the debt owed by France as a pure business proposition, they first had to know the value of France's assets in order to determine what it could reasonably pay. One of those French assets was their claim to German reparations. Bradbury clearly expected sums paid to France by Germany to find their way to the British and American Treasuries. Britain, he cautioned Horne, should write-off or write-down no inter-Allied debts without first considering German reparation payments. "The first step," he wrote, "is to find out what we, the Allies, generally can in fact extract from Germany as a business proposition." Bradbury urged his government to use the financial weapon against French intransigence. "Not a penny or a cent (either in respect of the inter-Allied debts or British and American claims against Germany)," he advised Horne, "ought to be given or promised to France until we and America are quite sure that a concession will result in a general settlement . . . if we tell them firmly that a provisional settlement with Germany is an indispensable preliminary to any discussion of inter-Allied debts, it will not be long before they become practical."[116]

Poincaré did not consider as "practical" a settlement under which France merely served as a conduit for passing on German payments to London and Washington. Conferences in London on 7–14 August 1922 between Poincaré and Lloyd George and 9–11 December between Poincaré and the new prime minister, Bonar Law, produced no solution to the impasse. At the August meeting, Poincaré pointed out that French taxpayers had "advanced" 108.5 billion francs to Germany, the interest charge on which created a budget deficit equal to the amount in the ordinary budget. Everyone was concerned with Germany's "hopeless" situation, but France was hardly better off. As the December conference broke up, it seemed certain that France had decided on an occupation of the Ruhr as the only means of collecting Germany's obligation and balancing the French budget.[117]

Britain had resisted outright cancellation of French debts or linking reparation payments to inter-Allied debts partly out of fear that to do so would give France the freedom to pursue ventures such as the Ruhr occupation. The debt was the best weapon the British Foreign Office held against an independent French foreign policy. Alarmed at French threats to occupy the Ruhr, South African Prime Minister Jan Christiaan Smuts suggested a joint statement from all British Empire nations warning that they would "disassociate" themselves from France if an occupation took place. He proposed a policy of "appeasement" toward Germany combined with a forceful attitude toward the French, whom he accused of "practically tearing up [the] Peace Treaty" with their threatened occupation of Germany. So long as France threatened the peace of Europe, "no concession should be made in respect of her war loan liability. War debts of Allies should be used as a weapon to secure policy of real appeasement in Europe and should only be foregone for that purpose and in that event." The Allies, Smuts believed, must reduce Germany's reparation obligation and grant it a moratorium on payment. But "any remission of war debts which the British Government may be disposed to make should be conditional on France desisting from isolated coercive measures and agreeing with the Allies to a policy of appeasement."[118]

Within the British government, opinion on the Ruhr occupation was not quite so negative as one might assume. Under certain conditions, the British might have supported France. Everything hinged on whether France's demands on Germany were judged reasonable. Treasury officials such as Bradbury believed Britain should back French demands for reasonable German payments. He told Horne in June 1922 that "we must make it clear to them that if they are prepared to treat the German situation on business lines we will back them up in the necessary pressure upon Germany—even up to the point of a Ruhr occupation in the event of real recalcitrance. I have felt much sympathy with German resistance while it has been resistance to impossible demands, but as soon as it becomes resistance to a tolerable settlement it is mischievous."[119]

Some Treasury officials believed French control over the Ruhr's coal and Lorraine's iron ore would pose a threat to Britain's steel industry, but at the Foreign Office Sir Eyre Crowe viewed occupation of the Ruhr as "an effective means of coercing Germany into the acceptance and fulfillment of reasonable demands; that, therefore, provided such reasonable demands can be formulated, we should not refuse our associating ourselves with the occupation in the case of Germany not carrying out what she might be induced to promise."[120] R. H. Brand, the British financier who had served on the Experts Committee appointed by the Reparation Commission to investigate German finances in May and June, proposed that the Allies set a reasonable sum for reparations, give up the policy of force, persuade Germany to accept financial reform, and, if the French would agree to all this, cancel their debt to Britain. If France would not agree, Britain would have to enlist American support to pressure the French government. American help, Brand conceded, probably would not be forthcoming, and Britain would have to let France collect as it saw fit, "first in the Ruhr and perhaps if she does not find it there, even in Berlin."[121]

Brand considered the United States Treasury as the ultimate villain in the case. How could France agree to a reasonable reparation figure so long as the United States demanded repayment of the full amount of the French debt? Brand apparently convinced some officials in the Foreign Office. Miles W. Lampson, who had lunched with Brand, observed that "the French must have their pledges— and those pledges are to be the Ruhr coal mines. Will France be prepared to give up that demand in return for the offer of remission of debt? That is really the whole point." "Personally," Lampson concluded, "I very much doubt whether in any circumstances Poincaré will abandon his Ruhr scheme."[122]

Lampson was correct. Poincaré would not abandon his Ruhr scheme. In a 14 December 1922 meeting with the French premier, Britain's ambassador, Lord Hardinge, gathered that what Poincaré sought from either the Rhineland or the Ruhr was money—immediate financial resources. Cancellation of French debts would add nothing to current government revenue.[123] Far from providing resources for the French Treasury, the Ruhr occupation proved costly to the government and disastrous for the French franc, which soon sank to new lows. The occupation, which began on 11 January 1923, immediately led to German passive resistance. In November, passive resistance ended and the French government concluded an agreement with the Ruhr mine operators to secure coal deliveries. On 14 January 1924 the Dawes Committee began deliberations that produced the Dawes Plan for German reparation payments on 9 April

1924. Seven days later the German government accepted the Dawes Plan, and a month-long London conference from 16 July to 16 August gave its seal of approval.

Poincaré failed to survive the Ruhr fiasco. Edouard Herriot succeeded him in June 1924 after elections in May had given the parliamentary majority to the *Cartel des Gauches*. Before he stepped down, Poincaré, who "was not really at home in the complicated world of postwar finance," attempted to retrieve control over monetary and financial policy from his finance minister, Lasteyrie.[124] In a lengthy letter to Lasteyrie, Poincaré analyzed France's desperate financial situation. He concluded that nothing could be done to improve it until France funded its debt to the United States Treasury.

Too late to save himself, Poincaré had arrived at the realistic attitude so long demanded by the British and Americans. Should the Dawes Plan favor France, payments from Germany could not be expected for some time to come, "but the French Treasury needs immediate resources." As soon as a reparation settlement loomed in sight, he believed, France must place a foreign loan to tide over the Treasury and stabilize the franc until German payments began to come in. Under current conditions, Poincaré understood, such a loan could not be placed. The American market was effectively closed to French securities, and in any event was too costly. That left only London, "which is particularly badly disposed toward us at the moment." If the Dawes Committee settled the reparations issue, Germany's financial requirements in the international financial markets would affect adversely French prospects for floating a loan.

Poincaré asked Lasteyrie to make all of the necessary preliminary studies so that France would be prepared to move for a loan when market conditions improved. "It follows," he continued, "that nothing of this sort is possible if we do not broach with the United States conversations on the subject of our debts." Poincaré noted Mellon's statement as Parmentier left Washington two years earlier that the talks were merely adjourned, not definitively broken off. The policy of silence had ended.

On the matter of debts, Poincaré feared the British more than the Americans. To insure that "we could not obtain from the English less favorable conditions," he suggested that France reach a "separate and advantageous agreement" with the United States before beginning talks in London. The original term of the WWDFC expired 9 February 1925. To avoid being caught in a last-minute rush, Poincaré recommended that France take the initiative for an early settlement. He impressed upon Lasteyrie his belief that "these important matters must be studied with the greatest care; they determine our foreign policy."

Poincaré asked the Finance Ministry to collaborate with the Foreign Ministry in the preparation of precise recommendations for consideration by the cabinet. He named as his personal representative for this task Jacques Seydoux, assistant director for commercial affairs at the Foreign Ministry, described by Schuker as the "chief specialist in economic affairs at the Quai d'Orsay and by far the most lucid mind among senior French bureaucrats in the 1920's." Lasteyrie was asked to designate someone from the Finance Ministry to meet with Seydoux as soon as possible.[125]

To Poincaré's urgent plea for action on the American debt, the Finance Ministry responded with the old policy of delay. Pierre de Mouÿ, the new director of the Mouvement général des fonds, advised Lasteyrie to consult with Jean Boyer, the French financial attaché in the United States, prior to beginning any consultations with Seydoux. Poincaré's 21 January 1924 letter to Lasteyrie remained unanswered on 16 February, when Poincaré sent a second message reminding Lasteyrie that he was to appoint a deputy to work with Seydoux. Lasteyrie finally responded on 20 February, informing the premier that nothing could be done until Boyer sent up-to-date, in-depth information on American public opinion. In November, after Poincaré's fall from power, Mouÿ was still recommending delay. It would be "imprudent," he said, for France to accept any settlement of inter-Allied debts prior to a "definitive determination of our claim on Germany." The Dawes Plan had been approved, but no one really knew exactly how much it was worth to France, or precisely how the Germans would make the payments.[126]

Ultimately, the French government sent Joseph Caillaux to London where he worked out a tentative settlement of France's debt to England during the summer of 1925. Then he proceeded to Washington, where two of his proposals for funding were rejected by the WWDFC, whose mandate Congress had renewed for another two years. The Commission also rejected Caillaux's demand for a so-called "safeguard clause," under which French payments would be reduced if Germany failed to make its payments as prescribed in the

Dawes Plan. The WWDFC countered with a proposal that France pay $40 million annually for the next five years, when the entire matter would be reviewed. Caillaux returned to Paris.[127]

Not until 20 April 1926 did Henry Bérenger, French ambassador and plenipotentiary to the United States, sign an agreement with Secretary of the Treasury Andrew Mellon in settlement of the French war debt to the United States. The pact fixed the principal at $4.076 billion, payable in fluctuating annual payments over sixty-two years, at interest rates varying from 1 percent to 3.5 percent. Although France had to abandon the safeguard clause as well as her demand to postpone initial payment, her capacity to pay appears to have been considered in the final settlement. The United States government contended that the agreement in effect reduced France's total debt to America by 60 prcent, if one calculated the impact of the reduced interest rates (from the original 5 percent) and the exclusion of $2.3 billion advanced to France after hostilities had ceased.

The French government considered the American calculations invalid, based as they were on an assumed interest rate of 5 percent over the entire sixty-two-year period. To the French, who believed prevailing world interest rates would be closer to 3 percent over the long run, the actual reduction in their debt appeared far smaller than that claimed by the United States. The French parliament was displeased with the settlement, and withheld ratification until July 1929.[128]

For France, satisfactory resolution of the inter-Allied debt provided the acid test of the vitality of the wartime alliance. By 1923, France believed the entente had failed to pass the test. The financial entente had in fact disintegrated when the United States and Britain unpegged the pound and the franc in March 1919. France left the Paris Peace conference believing the Versailles Treaty failed to meet either its security or its financial requirements, a belief soon reinforced when the United States and Britain failed to ratify mutual defense pacts with France. At the Washington armaments conference of 1922, Britain and the United States treated France as a third-rate power, on a par with Italy. In negotiations concerning inter-Allied debts and German reparations, France was just another debtor nation, and not the most preferred debtor at that.

Perhaps this was the inevitable outcome of a marriage of convenience between incompatible allies. In his history of the 1922

Genoa Conference, J. Saxon Mills portrayed Britain and France as representing inharmonious mental processes and material interests. "The French," he wrote, "are intensely logical and syllogistic in their habits of thought. They will build a logical structure on premises which may be quite unsound, and they will defend and maintain it with the utmost obstinacy. They will push a questionable proposition or theory to its logical issue as though it enshrined ultimate truth."

The British, on the other hand, "deal less with generalizations and syllogisms. They are practical and empirical. They know by experience that if they do certain things certain other things will follow, whether it be logical for them to follow or not." We are confronted, Mills believed, by "a radical difference in positive interest and in psychological character which had been suspended during the storm and stress of actual conflict, but re-asserted its influence when the work of political, industrial, and commercial reconstruction in a war-broken world had begun." For Mills, then, "it is not surprising, therefore, that the two countries . . . should have found it difficult to continue that intimate wartime accord into the days of peace."[129]

Innate differences in mental processes and material interests surely separated Britain and France, but these differences were amplified by concrete actions taken by members of the entente during the first months and years of peace. In the matter of reparations and inter-Allied debts, Mills's analysis fails to comprehend one of the major protagonists, the United States government. No matter how loudly the United States protested that the two matters bore no relationship to one another, one cannot overlook the connection between French "intransigence" on the reparation issue and American "obstinacy" concerning payment of inter-Allied debts. The United States refused to cancel any portion of the inter-Allied debt, and France refused to concede any reduction in Germany's reparation obligation. As so often they had in the past, the British stood somewhere in the middle. As was their custom, they played the role of the moderate party, willing to accept any reasonable compromise in either question, so long as the arrangement did not deflect Britain's drive to return to gold at $4.86.

6

J. P. Morgan & Co.
and the French Finance Ministry

ON THE TWENTY-NINTH OF MAY 1920, Finance Minister François-Marsal advised French premier Alexandre Millerand against granting the Legion of Honor to a Buenos Aires banker whose services to the republic appeared insufficient to merit such a high distinction. But he urged Millerand that "on the condition that they be employed in a judicious manner, the attribution of honorific distinctions to financial personalities of countries where we have operations to conclude is a means of action we should not neglect."[1] Five months later, the president of the French Republic awarded a certificate of the Legion of Honor to J. P. Morgan, Jr., senior partner of J. P. Morgan & Co., in recognition of services performed for the French government during the First World War.

J. P. Morgan & Co. was an important component in the financial and monetary entente that enabled the Allied and Associated Powers to survive the four-year contest with the Central Powers. During the war, Morgan's served as the commercial and financial agent of the French and British governments in America. But the relationship between the French Finance Ministry and Morgan's involved much more than the mere purchase of services. During and after the war, the Finance Ministry made important financial decisions only after consultation with Morgan's, and it was not always clear whether the Finance Ministry or Morgan's had the final word. The agent in fact exercised great control over the financial and monetary policies adopted by the French government.

What role did J. P. Morgan & Co. play in the development of France's postwar financial and monetary crisis and the failure of the government to resolve it? In his recent book, Stephen Schuker reflects the generally accepted thesis of French incompetence and lack of "realism." Deficiencies in French fiscal, financial, and monetary policy, according to Schuker, reflected outdated and simplistic economic theories that hardly applied to the new postwar situation. On the other hand, Schuker notes, "In retrospect, the Wall Street bankers, chief among them J. P. Morgan & Co., stand out as a remarkably able and farsighted group."[2]

The French Finance Ministry made many of its crucial decisions either at the suggestion of or with the concurrence of Morgan's. Some of the alternatives suggested by Morgan's seem no more "realistic" than the policies adopted by the French government. J. P. Morgan & Co., moreover, along with other Wall Street bankers, profited significantly on the servicing of France's massive public debt. Examination of the relationship between Morgan's and the French Finance Ministry must emphasize the point that "the bankers found themselves faced with potential conflicts between their private and quasi-public responsibilities—conflicts which, in the absence of public accountability, they could only imperfectly resolve."[3] J. P. Morgan & Co. faced the ethical dilemma of attempting to serve three potentially conflicting interests—those of the French government, the American investing public, and the partners in a profitmaking investment house. How well the firm succeeded in balancing those interests will be left to the reader to decide.

Whether the client be a corporation or a government, the relationship between the investment banker and those on whose behalf he has issued securities is both important and interesting to students of the financial process. Investment banks traditionally have maintained intimate relationships with their clients. It is clearly in the interest of both the investment house and the client that the flotation of a new issue be successful. To insure investor interest, investment bankers often assume management functions in the corporations whose bonds they sell. A 1929 study of investment banking observed that "this kind of power over the affairs of the borrowing enterprise represents the correlative of the moral responsibility which he has assumed toward the holder of bonds or stock he has sold."[4] What makes the case under consideration in this study particularly interesting is the fact that an investment banker assumed management functions not within a corporation, but within the Finance Ministry of a major European nation.

The character and reputation of the house of issue generally proves an important consideration in inducing the bond buyer to part with his money. This was particularly true in the case of foreign securities with which the American public in the 1920s was little familiar. Morgan's reputation was the best during the decade of the 1920s, and to maintain it the firm had to select its foreign issues with great care. Thus, the firm was not always in a position to satisfy the immediate requirements of the French Treasury for dollar resources. The French Finance Ministry, nevertheless, came to depend solely on the House of Morgan for advice and assistance in selling government securities in the American capital market.

Even in normal times, foreign governments must ascertain whether a market exists for their bonds. The extent to which those governments utilize the services of American investment houses depends upon the credit of the borrower. After the First World War, even old borrowers such as France, more or less well known to the American capital market, could float issues in New York only with the greatest difficulty. A banker who once successfully floats an issue of a client's securities generally becomes affiliated with that client's future issues, and there is a good chance that the connection may become permanent. During the 1920s, foreign borrowers in the United States capital market found it difficult to obtain new loans in periods of high money rates or of a poor bond market, particularly if they had scattered their old loans among various banking houses. Certain foreign governments thus made it a practice to sell their securities through a single American firm, on whose assistance they might rely when markets were adverse to foreign loans. Houses with a large measure of prestige were best suited for this function. J. P. Morgan & Co. was regarded as the official banker in the United States for the governments of Britain, France, and Italy.[5]

If the French government's dubious postwar financial position led it to seek the services of the strongest New York investment banker, then Morgan's was the logical choice. Morgan's expertise and specialization as originator of new issues placed the firm practically in a league of its own. In the United States during the 1920s there were only two exclusively wholesale general investment houses—J. P. Morgan & Co., and Kuhn, Loeb & Co. Other houses found it necessary or advantageous to supplement their originating activities with a selling organization, whereas Morgan's relied on approximately

1,000 retailers associated with them in selling new offerings. Of all the major American investment houses, Morgan's was the only one which never joined a syndicate merely as participant.

Given France's questionable postwar financial condition owing to its massive public debt, and Morgan's unquestioned leadership among American investment bankers, the close postwar working relationship between the Finance Ministry and J. P. Morgan & Co. was by no means unusual. When that relationship became one of almost total dependency—to the point where France's financial survival appeared to depend upon the efficacy of Morgan's efforts in New York—the association assumed quite unusual dimensions.

Morgan's relationship with the French government had solidified during the war, when the firm expedited the purchase of war material and foodstuffs in the United States, facilitated loans in the American capital market, and advanced funds from the firm's own resources.[6] Precisely how much Morgan's services as purchasing agent and facilitator cost the French government (or, conversely, how much Morgan's made on these transactions) is difficult to determine from the available public records. During the 1920s, it was the rule that "investment houses never make their statements public, neither balance sheet nor income account," and government regulating authorities required no such statements.[7] The sums involved, however, are clearly significant.

Between early 1915 and May 1917, when Morgan's received a 2 percent (1 percent after the first $50 million in contracts) commission on purchases handled by the firm, and 1/8 of 1 percent on other purchases, the contracts handled by Morgan's came to $949 million. The firm presumably made a commission of at least $10 million on those transactions alone. Between 1 May 1917 and 31 December 1918, when Morgan's received a commission of 1/2 of 1 percent on at least a portion of the contracts, the French government purchased in America supplies in the amount of $2,509,900,000.[8] Aside from Morgan's direct involvement in French war contracts, there were other sources of a potential conflict of interest. Herman Harjes, president of Morgan, Harjes et Cie. (Paris), and N. Dean Jay, a senior member of the same firm, both served in the United States army, Office of the General Purchasing Agent, American Expeditionary Force, under Brigadier General Charles G. Dawes. As lieutenant colonels, they had extensive dealings with the French government in Paris. There was, finally, the delicate issue of holdings of Morgan's or Morgan's partners and employees in American firms with which either the British or French governments made contracts through Morgan's. Edward R. Stettinius, for example, formerly a vice-president of Babcox and Wilcox Co., claimed he had sold his stock in the manufacturing firm before any contracts were concluded.[9]

By the end of the war, Morgan's role had become that of American banker to the French government. This function assumed added importance as France's dollar requirements for purchases of foodstuffs and reconstruction materials continued at a high level after the war. Further assistance from the United States Treasury and federally chartered institutions such as the Grain Corporation and the War Finance Corporation became problematical at best. Only a month after the signing of the Armistice, Joseph Simon, representing the Contrôle central du Trésor in the office of the French high commissioner in Washington, questioned the wisdom of continuing French dependence on the benevolence of the American Treasury. He estimated, too optimistically, that France might have to rely on the United States Treasury for a portion of its dollar requirements during the first six-to-eight months of 1919. He advised the Finance Ministry to begin an immediate move toward reestablishing contact with America's private capital market.[10]

Simon believed the prestige of France's victory in war, the confidence inspired by France's wartime financial effort, and the sympathy for France generated by close wartime cooperation would all combine to render American bankers more than willing to support France's postwar dollar requirements. Baron Jacques de Neuflize, representing the Bank of France in New York, shared Simon's optimism. In a letter to the Exchange Commission of the Finance Ministry, he gave assurances that the American financial system "is at our disposal" for all types of borrowing. American businessmen would find ways to finance French reconstruction "because they need our orders." Secretary of the Treasury McAdoo, said Neuflize, had provided assurances that private operations in American capital markets could accommodate the requirements of friendly nations in the settlement of their debts in the United States.

Neuflize thus joined Simon in recommending that France break its dependence on the United States Treasury. Given the availability of private resources, he believed, "we have thus become very independent of the American Treasury . . . [but] out of habit we continue to solicit her support."[11] In New York, French financial representatives learned from "some of our banker friends" that "the day when we wish to or are able to follow our own way and detach ourselves from the tutelary support of the United States Treasury, the French government as well as our major firms will easily find adequate facilities on the New York market."[12]

Did it make any difference whether France borrowed from the Federal Treasury or in private financial markets? There was one advantage in borrowing from the Treasury—lower interest rates. Whereas the Federal Treasury had been charging 5 percent on its advances to France, the Finance Ministry could expect to pay private banks in New York at least 5.5 percent. But in Simon's opinion, money saved in lower interest rates was no compensation for the political risk implied by French dependence on the American Treasury. Simon pointed to a long list of controls the U.S. Treasury either had imposed or might impose on French monetary and financial policy: American dollars could not be used for purchases in neutral countries; orders for American goods had to be submitted to an American agency for approval (to insure against "extravagant" purchases); French dollar resources beyond a normal amount (defined as $30–40 million) might have to be employed to reduce French debt in the United States; Treasury authorization would be required for any significant French credit operation in American financial markets; and the Federal Treasury would be in a position to dictate exchange rates, to the detriment of the French franc.[13]

Would not an appeal to American financial markets equally deliver France into the hands of a few American bankers? Simon warned of just such a possibility. The Morgan bank in particular sought France's business, he reported. Morgan's seemed bent on obtaining a monopoly on all future borrowing by the French government. American financial institutions such as Morgan's, Bonbright and Co., and the Title Guaranty and Trust Co. had submitted plans for the rehabilitation of French finances. All of them, warned Simon, presented clear dangers for the integrity of the French nation.[14]

Simon bluntly cautioned that before dealing with American bankers, the French government would have to make clear to them that there could be no question of mortgaging France to American bankers as the price of their financial assistance. The French government could not permit a monopoly on French credit operations by any single Wall Street firm. Propositions from American financiers containing exchange rate clauses tending to maintain the depreciation of the French franc would be rejected. Simon believed France could enforce these demands because American bankers would be competing for the business of French borrowers. France would choose only the most favorable propositions.[15]

By the spring of 1919, it was clear that France could no longer rely on the U.S. Treasury. Describing his cordial greeting at the Treasury Department in July 1919, Neuflize reported that "the disposition of America toward France is *theoretically* excellent, but in practice we are still rather far from obtaining new concrete aid."[16] Like it or not, the French government was forced to seek help from the Wall Street bankers. Working with the Wall Street bankers proved to be no easy task either for the Finance Ministry or the bankers. Relations were strained. Finding the money was not so easy as everyone had said it would be. Morgan's often felt the Finance Ministry demanded the impossible, while the Finance Ministry sometimes doubted Morgan's sincerity in serving the interests of the French Treasury.

Dollar resources were not always available in the New York financial market, and when they were available the terms were often more severe than the Finance Ministry wished to accept. Claiming France could not pay its debt to the United States, the French government painted a bleak picture of French finances. Maurice Casenave warned his superiors in Paris that alarmist statements made by government officials were frightening potential foreign leaders. The Finance Ministry, he advised, should demonstrate that France's position was difficult, but not desperate. But France was only part of the general picture of European financial chaos. The governor of the Federal Reserve Board, Warren P. G. Harding, told a group of French financiers and industrialists that in view of the condition of Europe, they should be pleased to get money in America at 12 percent.[17]

Inexperienced American investors viewed foreign securities with suspicion and skepticism. When Finance Ministry officials inquired about the possibility of issuing French "lottery bonds" in New York, they were told such issues were illegal under both federal and New York state law. Assistant Secretary of the Treasury Leffingwell agreed that placement of foreign securities in America would be difficult. American investors were not interested in bonds paying 6 percent or less, but most of the borrowing countries could not afford to pay more than 6 percent. Leffingwell encouraged the Finance Ministry to list French securities in New York, but only on the condition that they be payable in either francs or dollars, following the tendency of exchange rates. From Leffingwell's remarks, Baron Émile du Marais concluded that "only the attraction of exchange can convince Americans to subscribe to foreign issues."[18]

American investors in French securities were merely speculating in exchange. Morgan's shared Leffingwell's opinion, and generally included an exchange option clause (payable in either French francs or dollars) in propositions for French credit operations in New York. Finance Minister Klotz complained to Clemenceau that Morgan's conditions were "extremely rigorous," because they included "an exchange option beneficial to the leaders . . . which would in effect consecrate officially and to a large extent consolidate the heavy depreciation presently experienced by our exchange."[19] Klotz and each of his successors at the Finance Ministry rejected Morgan's demands for exchange option clauses in French obligations issued in the United States.

Successful flotation of French securities in America also depended on a definitive, realistic settlement of German reparations. Assistant Secretary of the Treasury Norman Davis told French financiers and industrialists that American investors would not subscribe to French securities without assurance that Germany's debt to France was likely to be paid. The French government's refusal to reduce its claim on Germany, and its reluctance to discuss its debt to the United States, complicated Morgan's efforts to place French loans in the American market.[20]

Given the high level of American resistance to French issues, Morgan's found it difficult to open the United States financial market to the French government during 1919 and the first half of 1920. This was, however, a critical period for the French Finance Ministry, whose dollar requirements swelled considerably owing to reconstruction costs and the maturation of war loans. As the war ended, the Finance Ministry's major source of dollars consisted of compensation from the U.S. Treasury for francs advanced by the French government for use by the American forces in France. The French government obtained these francs in the first instance by borrowing them from the Bank of France. This dubious procedure merely inflated the French money supply, and constituted a financial burden on the French people. But the United States argued that American forces in France created no real charge to the French government, because the francs spent by American troops remained in France, enriched French commerce, and created purchasing power for French investors who subscribed to French government loans. Neither Leffingwell nor Oscar Crosby, acting secretary of the treasury during McAdoo's illness, understood the inflationary impact and pressure on French exchange caused by this procedure.[21]

Whatever the merits of the practice, the rapid withdrawal of American troops after the Armistice produced a sharp decline in American requirements for francs during the first months of 1919. This meant, of course, fewer American dollars for the French Treasury. The Finance Ministry was alarmed, but when the director of the Mouvement général des fonds, Alexandre Célier, asked Norman Davis for an estimate of future franc requirements for U.S. troops, Davis indicated that "the needs will be clearly much lower than the figures originally envisaged by the American services themselves."[22] This was not good news for the French Treasury, in view of the approaching 1 November 1919 maturity of the so-called Three Cities Loan (Bordeaux, Lyon, and Marseilles). Célier told the mayors of the cities involved that the loan would have to be renewed because there were no dollar funds with which to repay it on the maturity date.

Kuhn, Loeb & Co. had underwritten the original Three Cities issue, but the Finance Ministry now held conversations with both Kuhn, Loeb and Morgan's on terms for a renewal. Morgan partner Edward R. Stettinius indicated that a Three Cities renewal would have to be linked to a wider operation involving other cities. Morgan's was obviously reluctant to become involved in an operation whose success appeared doubtful. Stettinius asked the Finance Ministry to consider Morgan's proposition, but he also advised Célier to follow up without delay his conversations with Kuhn, Loeb & Co.

Kuhn, Loeb did handle the $45 million renewal issue, and only about one-third of it was taken up by the public. Morgan's reluctance seemed to be justified.[23]

While awaiting the proceeds of the Three Cities renewal issue, the Finance Ministry needed $20 million to meet its immediate obligations in the United States. Célier cabled the French financial agency in New York that "it seems to me that Kuhn, Loeb is more appropriate than anyone else to make us the advance," and instructed his agents to try to reach an agreement on terms. Célier indicated that Morgan's had also offered to advance the $20 million, without any engagement by the Finance Ministry to give Morgan's a major operation later. "I do not deny that acceptance of the offer implies a certain moral engagement on our part," observed Célier, "but I am inclined to accept in the event Kuhn, Loeb is unable to give us the advance."[24]

Morgan's seemingly irresolute response to France's dollar requirements for the Three Cities Loan created dissatisfaction in French financial circles and provoked some unfavorable commentary from the U.S. Treasury as well. Jacques Neuflize complained as early as 18 July 1919 that nothing had been arranged for the provision of French dollar requirements. The problem, he believed, was Morgan's desire to lead the column in all matters concerning the financing of Europe. "They are more interested," he reported, "that nothing shall happen without them, than in doing something themselves. Their desire to do something is none the less very sincere, but it is dominated by a preoccupation with protecting their place in the field."[25]

Leffingwell addressed members of a French financial mission touring the United States in terms highly critical of the Morgan group, "whom he accused of lacking imagination and of being extremely timid."[26] Neuflize believed the U.S. Treasury conceded Morgan's expertise in European financial matters, but did not wish to see Morgan's or any other Wall Street firm monopolize Europe's operations in the American financial market. According to Neuflize, the Treasury favored the creation of a large number of independent syndicates or groups of exporters. The Wall Street bankers, forming only a small part of the total edifice, would "disappear in the mass."[27]

Neuflize doubted such a decentralized scheme could function effectively to meet French dollar requirements. In this conclusion he seems to have reflected a general feeling among French financiers that the alternatives to dealing with Morgan's were unsatisfactory. Morgan's Wall Street competitors offered the French Finance Ministry propositions no more inviting than those offered by Morgan's, and lacking the vast influence, power, and wide range of expertise provided by the Morgan establishment. Reacting to Morgan's refusal to lead the Three Cities renewal issue, Baron du Marais wrote to the president of the Republic, Raymond Poincaré, that "I have the impression that Morgan's has put together here a group which includes all the necessary elements for the placement of securities, and that one can in no way manage without their support. This is a fact about which we can do absolutely nothing. In these conditions, wisdom seems to dictate that we accept the fait accompli, and try to give Morgan's the impression that we have full confidence in them."[28]

In 1919, the French Finance Ministry was not prepared to admit that it was a captive of J. P. Morgan & Co. Célier discussed this problem with Joseph Avenol, France's financial delegate in London. In conversations with Blackett at the British Treasury, Blackett had questioned the relationship of the two Treasuries with Morgan's and Kuhn, Loeb & Co. "I understand very well," wrote Célier, "that the British Treasury desires to break free of the hold of the Morgan firm . . . For our part, we have sought on several occasions to affirm our independence by concluding certain operations with Kuhn, Loeb." Célier suspected that Blackett sought to "reserve exclusively for himself the right to treat with Morgan's by directing us to Kuhn, Loeb," an arrangement Célier was quick to reject. "Blackett," he advised Avenol, "cannot fail to appreciate with us how desirable it is to establish relations with all the American firms who wish to work with Europe."[29]

Did any American firms wish to work with Europe? Speaking for Morgan's in September 1919, Stettinius told Célier that the U.S. Senate's delay (and eventual refusal) in ratifying the peace treaty had produced "a complete stoppage of any comprehensive plan for the financing of France's requirements in America." Morgan's could offer little assistance to the Finance Ministry in these circumstances. "As to the immediate future," wrote Stettinius, "we see no solving of the situation so as to enable us to undertake any comprehensive scheme of finance, but we are inclined to believe that it will be possible to obtain moderate amounts in isolated operations which we are now actively investigating." Stettinius saw little possibility of even stopgap measures such as the sale of French Treasury bills in New York. "With reference to French Treasury bills," he observed, "the American market is now in a position where supply is inclined to exceed demand, and we are hardly able to foresee any favorable development in that regard in the near future."[30]

Stettinius honestly believed America's financial markets were closed temporarily to French issues. He advised Morgan's Paris correspondent, Morgan, Harjes et Cie., that "our market for French government securities is today in a very delicate situation. The general investing public appreciates in theory the necessity for foreign credits, but each time an investment in such securities has been made, the market has shown an immediate loss and the result is that one is disposed to let someone else take up the burden."[31] During the fall of 1919, then, Morgan's was apparently content to see the French government account pass, more or less, to any Wall Street firm willing to assume the risk.

The Finance Ministry now concluded that the only way France could meet its dollar obligations in the United States was through the sale of dollar-denominated French Treasury bills in New York. Célier consulted with French Treasury representative in Washington Joseph Simon and Morgan partner Thomas W. Lamont in June 1919, and "in agreement with them" decided to proceed with Treasury bill sales. The U.S. Treasury indicated it had no objection to such sales. Célier had in mind a $50 million issue.[32]

Morgan's agreed reluctantly to handle the Treasury bill issue. It was a risky venture, for where would the French Treasury obtain dollars if renewals failed to keep pace with maturities? Morgan's presumably covered that possibility by undertaking to form a syndicate of bankers to guarantee the purchase of up to $20 million in French Treasury bills if renewals should fail to meet maturities. In addition to the regular annual commission of ½ of 1 percent on the face value of bills outstanding, the Finance Ministry agreed to pay an additional commission of ½ of 1 percent on the $20 million guaranteed by the syndicate, whether or not the syndicate actually purchased any bills. This type of "insurance premium" was not an uncommon feature in new issues floated by American corporations, but it was costly. In accepting the stipulation, Célier told Casenave that "this supplementary charge seems to me to be compensated by the guarantee which is thereby assured to us against overly precipitous demands for reimbursement." With this guarantee, Célier instructed Casenave to raise the upper limit of issue to $75 million rather than the $50 million previously discussed.[33]

The final contract accepted by Finance Minister Klotz empowered Morgan's to issue a maximum of $75 million in sixty- and ninety-day dollar-denominated French Treasury bills. The interest rate was to be determined by Morgan's according to market conditions. At Morgan's suggestion, the Finance Ministry set up an account sufficient to permit Morgan's to repurchase up to 10 percent of the outstanding bills in order to maintain a market. No mention of this disposition was to be made to the public. Klotz stipulated informally that for the time being, no more than $50 million would be issued, with a maximum weekly maturity of $5 million. The one-year contract expired 13 July 1920.[34]

From the outset, the sale of French Treasury bills in New York disappointed the Finance Ministry's expectations. Emmanuel Vergé, an inspector of finance posted in New York, reported that sales for the first month ending 30 September 1919 produced only $4.6 million rather than the expected $25 million. He attributed the slow sales to rising New York "call money" rates, which had reached 15 percent in September, and warned the Finance Ministry not to expect these high rates to decline any time soon.[35] The 5.5 percent Treasury bill rate initially fixed by Morgan's proved insufficient to attract American investors.

Treasury bill sales increased in October, but sales during the first week of November came to only $4,325,000, or $675,000 less than the $5 million in maturing bills. This problem persisted. In February 1921, the Finance Ministry conceded that "renewals were almost always less than reimbursements," a situation which imposed a heavy drain on France's limited dollar resources in New York. The syndicate guarantee was no help "because Morgan's, despite our insistence, always dissuaded us from appealing to the syndicate, which has never been used."[36] To cover the Treasury bill deficit, the Finance Ministry simply drew upon its dollar deposits in New York banks. Klotz reminded Casenave that this procedure did not conform to the arrangement made with Morgan's for the purchase of bills by a guarantee syndicate. "Under these conditions," wrote

Klotz, "I do not understand how you could have been led to draw upon your cash balance for the repayment of part of the first portion of bills issued." The Finance Minister wanted an explanation of the reasons causing his New York financial agents to "renounce the application of the agreement."[37]

For the month of December 1919, the deficit in the Treasury bill account came to about $1 million, all of which was again covered from the cash balance of the French financial agency in New York. Klotz again ordered the syndicate guarantee invoked, but Morgan's told Vergé that to do so would produce a "deplorable" effect on the New York market for French securities.[38] This was no doubt quite true—if word circulated that France could not finance its own Treasury bill sales in New York, the impact on French credit would be disastrous. But, if the guarantee could not be invoked, why did Morgan's not tell this to the Finance Ministry from the beginning? Had the guarantee syndicate accepted its ½ of 1 percent commission with no intention of meeting its obligation?

For the moment Klotz resigned himself to bailing out the Treasury bill account with Treasury resources, but he made it clear to both his own staff and Morgan's that there could be no question of the right of the Finance Ministry to demand that the syndicate take up the Treasury bills. The principle was well established, and it was up to Finance Ministry officials on the spot in New York to decide when to invoke the guarantee. Klotz acknowledged the "serious disadvantages" of renewing Treasury bills through the syndicate, but why was the French government paying the additional ½ of 1 percent commission? The payment of that commission, observed Klotz, "can only be explained if it provides the Treasury with the certainty of obtaining the renewal of bills up to the limit of $20 million on which this commission is based."[39]

On 29 January 1920 the new finance minister, François-Marsal, ordered his New York agents to ask Morgan's to raise the Treasury bill rate to 6.5 percent. Under no conditions were they to meet the deficit from their own funds. "If Morgan's intends to cover the deficit," he cabled, "I suppose they will agree it is time to go to the syndicate." The finance minister was wrong. Morgan's refused to either raise the rate or go to the syndicate. The situation was now reaching crisis proportions. Treasury bill maturities during the final week of January came to $4,190,000, but sales to the public amounted to only $160,000. By the end of January the deficit in the account had reached $5,835,000. Vergé now refused to cover the deficit from his New York bank accounts. His refusal produced a meeting with Henry P. Davison at Morgan's on 28 January.[40]

Morgan's held to the position that raising the rate or appealing to the syndicate would damage France's credit in the United States and undermine its chances of floating large issues on the New York market at a later date. J. P. Morgan & Co. could rightly claim the firm was only trying to protect the long-run interests of the French Finance Ministry, but if ever there was an appropriate moment for Keynes's dictum that "in the long run we are all dead," this was it. The French Treasury needed dollars immediately, but Brown Brothers & Co. confirmed Morgan's opinion that the American market was as good as closed to foreign securities. American investors were going into municipal bonds and other tax-exempt issues to escape the "excessive" level of the income tax.[41]

During the meeting of 28 January 1920, Davidson told Vergé and Casenave that with the support of a small group of bankers (not the forty-two-member guarantee syndicate), Morgan's would subscribe to an amount of Treasury bills sufficient to cover the deficit in the account. By avoiding a public appeal to the syndicate, France's credit rating would be protected. Casenave and Vergé still wished to go to the syndicate, but Morgan's refused. Instead, Morgan's, the First National Bank of New York, the National City Bank, and Brown Brothers & Co. agreed to put up the funds. Morgan's warned, however, that such assistance could not continue indefinitely. During the six-to-eight weeks before a major credit operation would be possible, "the French government must count completely on the help of the Bank of France or another source unknown to us."[42]

The bankers made good an $8,520,000 deficit in February 1920. That was the limit. Morgan's sent Davison to Paris, where he insisted that French credit would suffer if the Finance Ministry failed to repay Treasury bills not renewed at maturity. Davison convinced Célier, who informed Casenave in New York that the Finance Ministry was placing $10 million at his disposal immediately. Casenave was to assure payment on an additional $10,235,000 in Treasury bills due to mature about 9 July and 30 July. Célier promised to see to the mobilization of the necessary dollar resources.[43]

In March 1920, the Finance Ministry again asked Morgan's to

raise the Treasury bill rate to 6.5 percent. Morgan's still advised against such action, but when Treasury bill sales during the last week in March amounted to only $5,000, Casenave and Vergé again insisted on raising the rate. Morgan's finally conceded, and "agreed to go with the exigencies of the market." At 6.5 percent, sales rose dramatically, apparently justifying the Finance Ministry's position against Morgan's intransigence. April's sales of $9 million covered reimbursements; sales in May were still better at $14,915,000, and again covered repayments. Between 28 March and 31 July, bills in circulation increased from $15,842,000 to $25 million. But by July, the balance began to turn against the Finance Ministry again as reimbursements totaled $10,585,000 against sales of only $10,117,752.[44]

With the expiration of the one-year Treasury bill contract on 31 July 1920, the guarantee syndicate was dissolved. Morgan's agreed to continue to handle French Treasury bills, but to replace the never-used syndicate the firm required the Finance Ministry to establish at Morgan's a special $3 million account to serve as a guarantee for maturing bills. Morgan's agreed to pay the French government interest of 3 percent on the unused portion of the fund.[45]

France's financial position in the United States remained precarious during the summer of 1920. By November, the situation was desperate. On 15 October, France had repaid to the United States her $250 million share of the $500 million Anglo-French loan of 1915. Under normal conditions, timely repayment of a major dollar loan would have been a triumph for French finance. But France had repaid only under strong pressure from the United States and Britain. In April, Morgan partner Henry P. Davison warned Casenave that no further French credit operations would be possible in America unless and until the Anglo-French loan was repaid.[46] The British Treasury was anxious to repay its share to prove to the world that its finance was sound. France could hardly refuse to pay without disastrous effects for the French franc and French finance in general. The French, however, were in an impossible position, for there was no way they could raise $250 million without provoking another disaster of almost equal proportions. This became clear to the Finance Ministry and Morgan's only after the damage had been done.

Speaking in Strasbourg on 20 October 1920, at a rally for the 6 percent internal loan to be issued 16 December, Finance Minister François-Marsal told his audience that a portion of the proceeds of the new loan would be used to pay off old debt. France, he said, must pay off its war debt in order to regain its position as "one of the world's bankers." Pointing proudly to the repayment of the Anglo-French loan five days earlier, he noted that three-fifths of it had been repaid "definitively," while two-fifths of the $250 million had been raised through a long-term loan, which itself would have to be repaid eventually.[47] There was no hint of alarm in the finance minister's words, and one must conclude that François-Marsal did not at the time realize how dangerous were the methods which had been employed to raise the $250 million for repayment of the loan.

The long-term loan whose proceeds provided dollars for repayment of the Anglo-French loan was the Twenty-Five-Year External Gold Loan, formally issued on 15 September 1920 at 8 percent. The loan was a great success on the New York market, and as a result Morgan's received much praise and 6 percent of the $100 million raised. The French Treasury was credited with the remaining $94 million. The price for this success, however, was high, and the French Finance Ministry was not quite so pleased with the result as was Morgan's. The loan was "well over-subscribed," and Morgan's was "delighted with the wonderful success of the New French loan." As Morgan partner Dwight Morrow told Lamont, "Everything broke in our favor. The Polish news continued good up until the safety of the loan was assured." And the small investment market had shown great interest in the issue, apparently out of ignorance. Morrow observed that the small investor apparently "would rather buy an 8 percent bond at par than a 6 percent bond on an 8 percent basis. Perhaps this is due to the fact that he does not carry a bond table around in his pocket."[48]

In Paris, however, the astounding success of the 8 percent loan merely indicated that Morgan's had offered too much to the investors. Morrow conceded that "we feared a little bit that the French might feel (however unreasonable such a feeling would be) that the success of the loan showed that we had exacted too high a rate. We all think that the rate was just right under all the circumstances." Noting some comment on the fact that American investors had received very favorable terms on interest and redemption, Lamont responded that "the bankers who were responsible for bringing out this loan on terms that would insure success for France at the present critical juncture would much prefer to be criticized for too much success rather than for failure."[49]

Negotiations between Morgan's and the Finance Ministry for the 8 percent loan had not gone smoothly. François-Marsal sent the deputy director of the Mouvement général des fonds to negotiate in New York. His instructions were to obtain a $125 million loan with a syndicate guarantee for the entire amount. Morgan's proposed a loan of only $100 million, only half of which would be guaranteed. It would be issued at 100, bearing a nominal rate of 8 percent. The actual cost to the Finance Ministry, however, would be higher owing to provision for reimbursement at 115 through drawings, and a 6 percent commission for Morgan's. As the Finance Ministry understood Morgan's proposal, the interest was to be paid in advance.[50]

Upon learning of Morgan's terms, François-Marsal cabled Parmentier that "I do not have to tell you how exhorbitant these conditions seem to us." He was particularly upset because New York bankers had assured him that if the Finance Ministry could repay half of its share of the Anglo-French loan "by proper means," a credit operation for the balance could easily be arranged "on reasonable terms." The finance minister claimed he had done what the bankers had suggested, and "in return they offer us an operation coming to 10 percent, of which the entire placement is not even guaranteed." The finance minister was incredulous. "I wonder," he wrote, "if Morgan's has completely understood the situation."[51]

François-Marsal told Parmentier that if Morgan's could not offer acceptable terms, France could do without any long-term financing. Citing what he termed "the continuing improvement of our financial situation," he instructed Parmentier to submit a counterproposal for a short-term loan under which American bankers would give the Finance Ministry an advance of $100 million, repayable in nine equal installments beginning 31 December 1922.[52] The finance minister soon returned to his senses, and a few days later he was discussing terms for a long-term loan with Herman Harjes, president of Morgan, Harjes et Cie. He continued to hold out for $125 million. If the loan had to be cut to $100 million, he suggested to Harjes that the additional $25 million be raised either through a bankers' syndicate or by issuing more French Treasury bills in New York.[53]

To supplement the $100 million 8 percent loan, Morgan's did undertake to place $35 million in French Treasury bills as part of the package for repayment of the Anglo-French loan. The British Treasury at the same time agreed to purchase $10 million in French Treasury bills, half at sixty days, half at ninety days. To complete the resources required for repayment of the Anglo-French loan, the Bank of France, under pressure from the government, put up $20 million in gold, probably Russian gold. Dollar purchases in world money markets and the sale of foreign securities held by the French Treasury added to the funds required for the Anglo-French repayment. Beginning 24 June 1920, the Finance Ministry systematically purchased dollars to a total of $66,252,000. For the entire calendar year 1920, Morgan's dollar exchange purchases on behalf of the French government came to $200,626,634.12. Additionally, French government accounts throughout the world, particularly those in Buenos Aires, Montevideo, and Rio de Janeiro, were stripped of every available dollar, leaving them without means of paying French debts in Latin America.[54]

Dollar exchange purchases naturally depressed French exchange, but it was the additional Treasury bill issue which ultimately proved disastrous to the Finance Ministry. With the repayment of the Anglo-French loan, French Treasury bills outstanding in New York mushroomed to record levels. On 15 September, the total stood at approximately $49 million, but the "unprecedented success" of the 8 percent loan led to overconfidence at both the Finance Ministry and Morgan's. Morgan's agreed to increase the weekly issue of ninety-day bills from $3 million to $7.5 million for each of the following five weeks. So successful was this move that by 23 October, outstanding French Treasury bills in New York came to $74,445,000 —$80,215,240 if the British Treasury purchase was included.[55]

The bubble burst quickly. When Morgan's agreed to increase the Treasury bill issue on 16 September, Dwight W. Morrow had assured Parmentier that Morgan's would do everything in their power to obtain renewals putting off repayment at least until the spring of 1921. By that time, Morgan's believed, a major consolidation would be possible. To protect themselves, however, the firm asked the Finance Ministry to increase its special account at Morgan's from $3 million to $7 million, to cover any large "unforeseen" repayments. Repayments began to outstrip new purchases and renewals by 29 October 1920, "despite the encouraging words of J. P. Morgan & Co." To cover the deficit, the French Treasury purchased dollars,

$18 million in November and $40 million in December. Despite these ominous signs, François-Marsal confidently looked forward to a major New York credit operation in 1921 "to give our Treasury a little elasticity." He felt certain that "the situation will not be too difficult if we can count on the support promised by Morgan's."[56]

The Finance Ministry probably overestimated Morgan's power in the American financial market, and it remained a constant concern for the Morgan partners to try to impose a more realistic view on the rue de Rivoli. During the French financial crisis of 1924, Finance Minister Étienne Clémentel counted on Morgan's to meet the Treasury's dollar requirements. Herman Harjes observed to Morrow that "What worries me in this whole situation is that your friend M. Clémentel is reposing absolute confidence in the House of Morgan and really expects it to do wonders for him—I am afraid he will get quite a jolt if we do not come across."[57]

Morgan's did attempt to alert the Finance Ministry to a potential crisis in November 1920. When Parmentier informed Morgan's that the Treasury would require $236 million to meet its dollar requirements during the next twelve months—$73 million simply to cover maturing Treasury bills—Morgan's strongly urged the Finance Ministry to ship immediately $25 million in gold earmarked for redemption of Treasury bills. The Treasury bill position, Morgan's warned, might worsen owing to the condition of American financial markets. The finance Ministry was unwilling to part with any French gold, but Parmentier did suggest to Francois-Marsal that "possibly we should consider again shipping Russian gold which remains unproductive in the Bank of France." France, in any case, had reached its limit on short-term borrowing and would have to find some other source of dollar funds.[58]

As an alternative to the shipment of gold, the Finance Ministry suggested a number of small New York credit operations involving French municipalities, departments, railroads, and colonies such as Algeria. Morgan's consistently discouraged such minor operations, because they would only detract from the success of subsequent large issues. As the Treasury bill crisis deepened in December 1920, Casenave held conversations at Morgan's with Stettinius, Thomas Cochran, George Whitney, and N. Dean Jay. He relayed the message from Paris that there was no question of shipping gold and that the Finance Ministry was counting on Morgan's assistance to pull them through the crisis. Morgan's indicated they might have to raise the Treasury bill rate to 8 percent until March 1921, when a major credit operation might be possible. Recognizing the adverse impact of an 8 percent rate on French credit. Casenave now came around to Morgan's position. He advised the Finance Ministry to persuade the British Treasury to renew the Treasury bills it held, and urged his government to reconsider the shipment of Russian gold.[59]

The only permanent solution to France's Treasury bill and dollar crisis was a major consolidation issue in the New York market, but Morgan's maintained that the market would not sustain such an operation. At last Morgan's relented conditionally, and Casenave cabled Paris on 22 December 1920 that the firm was prepared to handle a large issue early in 1921 if the market had improved. But by 11 January 1921 Morgan's had reversed its position and informed Casenave that they did not wish to direct any major French loan during 1921. They advised the Finance Ministry to purchase foreign exchange to cover its dollar requirements. To cover dollar requirements for the next ninety days, the best course was to ship gold.[60]

Acting in good faith, J. P. Morgan & Co. believed it was protecting the interests of its client by refusing to underwrite French loans in a doubtful American market. The French Treasury, of course, needed dollars immediately, and Morgan's might have been able to procure them in the marketplace had they been willing to sacrifice the Finance Ministry's long-term interests for a short-term gain. Dwight W. Morrow conceded to a French Treasury official on loan to the Inter-Allied Commission for Bulgaria that "it is sometimes possible by paying exhorbitant rates to secure bankers to sell a loan to the public even though there is not perhaps a general demand for it. Our firm has always been unwilling to offer a loan for a country if the rate had to be one which would be discreditable to the country whose bonds we were selling."[61]

The head of the French financial agency in New York, Jean de Sieyès, confirmed Morgan's assessment of prospects for foreign loans on the New York market. The 6 percent perpetual issue of December 1920 had netted only $3,158,173. More disturbing was the fact that whereas fifty-seven banks had participated in the 5 percent issue of 19 February 1920, only twenty-six had offered to participate in the December issue. The American market, warned Sieyès, was already overtaxed with demands from other European bor-

rowers. A crisis approaching panic proportions had hit simultaneously American agriculture, industry, and finance, foreign exchanges
had dropped sharply, and the entire financial situation was complicated by the presidential election coming in November 1920.[62]

At the Finance Ministry, however, Parmentier, now director of
the Mouvement général des fonds, saw no extenuating circumstances. In a memorandum dated 5 February 1921 he criticized
Morgan's in most unflattering terms. Morgan's, he claimed, had
underwritten the highly successful 8 percent issue of September 1920
"only with reluctance." Assurances from Morrow and Whitney that
there would be no problems with Treasury bill renewals turned out
to be worthless. Parmentier actually accused Morgan's of failing to
represent the interest of its client, the French Finance Ministry.
Treasury bills were not being sold because "we learn from a trustworthy source that our Wall Street 'friends' have, at least in one instance, refused a request from a New York establishment to purchase
our Treasury bills."[63] From his point of view, Parmentier had a valid
complaint. But as both underwriter and seller of securities, Morgan's
had responsibilities to clients who purchased securities as well as
those who issued the loans. It was the classic conflict of interest confronting every investment banker.

When Morgan's finally handed Casenave a proposal for a $100
million issue for 1921, complained Parmentier, it contained conditions much more severe than those offered to the Belgian government at the same time. No matter, though, because when the cabinet
of Georges Leygues fell on 12 January 1921, Morgan's withdrew its
proposition. Looking at France's assets and liabilities, wrote Parmentier, "one can see the tragic situation in which Morgan's, with full
knowledge of the facts, has abandoned us." During the three weeks
between 6 and 28 January, France had to cover a deficit of $33,-
260,000 in its American accounts. Growing exchange problems ruled
out further dollar purchases. France had either to ship gold, which
Morgan's had been recommending for months, or "place ourselves
completely in the hands of this establishment [Morgan's], begging
them to save the French state from bankruptcy."[64]

The combination of an unexpected improvement in the franc
exchange, strict compression of French expenditures, and a $12 mil-
lion credit from the National Bank of Commerce provided the Finance Ministry the dollar resources required to meet its 28 January

obligations, "to the poorly disguised surprise of Morgan's." "Up to the last moment," Parmentier charged, "the heads of Morgan's refused us the least bit of help." With the 28 January crisis behind them, Morgan's then refused to issue additional Treasury bills or cover maturities on outstanding bills. Morgan's attitude toward the French government, observed Parmentier, "found its definitive expression on 2 February 1921, when these gentlemen informed us that in the absence of any subscriptions inscribed in their books, we would have to take measures to reimburse at maturity the $35 million in outstanding Treasury bills."[65]

The Finance Ministry, Parmentier implied, now contemplated replacing Morgan's as its financial agent in the United States. Certain American bankers who presumably wished to break Morgan's near-monopoly on servicing the French debt in the United States had submitted propositions for the issue of large dollar loans in New York. "Desiring to furnish our Wall Street friends a new opportunity to demonstrate to us a more favorable disposition," the Finance Ministry notified Morgan's on 2 February 1921 that it was still disposed to effect a large operation with Morgan's as underwriter. But given the great number of other interesting offers, Morgan's would have to give the Finance Ministry a definitive response very soon.[66]

Morgan's insisted that American lenders doubted France's capacity to repay loans without help from Germany. They advised the French to put off operations in the New York market until April or May 1921, when, they believed, the terms of the German indemnity would have been fixed definitively. They informed Morgan, Harjes et Cie. that Americans were fed up with the lack of progress in the reparations discussions, implying that French intransigence was holding up a reasonable settlement. Assuring the Finance Ministry of their appreciation of the extent of the Treasury bill problem, Morgan's again suggested purchasing dollars or shipping gold.[67]

Parmentier was by now exasperated. In a 14 February conference with representatives of Morgan, Harjes et Cie. he wondered "What would J. P. Morgan & Co. have me do? The French government must provide approximately $47 million between now and 1 May, of which about $30 million is in Treasury bills." Parmentier "stated that he was in a very difficult position, that it was quite impossible to consider shipping gold . . . and that he sincerely hoped Morgan's could find some means of providing for a renewal of these bills."[68]

Responding to Parmentier's threat to place issues with other New York firms, Stettinius sat down with Casenave and Sieyès for two days of consultations, systematically examining the reasons why a large operation for the French government was impossible. He stressed Morgan's concern with establishing France's long-term credit in the United States on a broad, firm basis, and that would require careful planning over a long period of time. Other Wall Street firms might offer propositions for small issues of municipal and railroad bonds, but these were short-term solutions calculated to profit the firms rather than the French government.[69] By April 1921 Parmentier was still holding out for a major credit operation of at least $100 million. Morgan's finally offered a Loan Against French Indemnity Annuities, but the proposition included a clause allowing payment in either French francs or dollars, at the discretion of the lender. Parmentier rejected the proposition because the exchange clause "might prove embarrassing in the future and would be difficult to explain to the Chamber."[70]

Although the critical reparation settlement—the London Schedule of Payments—was just around the corner, Morgan's was extremely pessimistic about prospects for an agreement. In London en route to Paris, Thomas W. Lamont cabled Herman Harjes that a large French loan was still "out of the question." "After talking with members of the Government here," he confided, "I am rather hopeless of any early settlement of the Reparations question." Lamont predicted that the French would take vigorous action if a settlement were not reached. "Does it not appear almost certain," he observed, "that France will occupy the Ruhr early in May? And certainly another such expedition, no matter how fully warranted, is not likely to improve French Government credit in the American market." Back in New York, Lamont's partners shared his fear of an imminent French occupation of the Ruhr. Responding to Lamont's request for the latest information on American market conditions, Morgan's noted that "in fact if the Reparations situation got into a worse position such as might be the case if the French had to call out a whole army class for an invasion of Germany, it might make it impossible for us to do anything" about a French loan.[71]

After a month of hard bargaining, Morgan's and the Finance Ministry signed an agreement to issue a $100 million loan at 7.5 percent in June 1921. At the end of April, a major issue by the

Burlington Railroad was slightly oversubscribed at $234 million, but Morgan's believed Burlington's success "did not leave a large margin of safety" and demonstrated that "money is not as plentiful as it had been" considering the very attractive terms of the loan. The Burlington issue, moreover, was bound to be followed by other large domestic issues that would drain American financial markets temporarily. Nevertheless, J. P. Morgan & Co. decided in early May that a French operation for $100 million could be handled during the next sixty days.[72]

Having agreed in principle to underwrite a major French issue, Morgan's now had to come up with terms suitable to the Finance Ministry. Morgan's hesitated to present any terms because "conditions change rapidly" in European financial affairs. Volatile markets for foreign securities and fluctuating exchange rates tended to make investment in foreign securities nothing more than speculation in exchange. Morgan's hoped to work out something more favorable to the French government than the 1920 8 percent issue. To strengthen the market for a large French operation, Morgan's offered to form a small banking group to provide the French government with $15 million with which it could purchase outstanding City of Paris Sixes and French Government Eights prior to the $100 million issue.

The critical issue in any French securities operation was the depreciating French franc. On 10 May, Morgan's suggested a fifteen-year noncallable 8 percent (7.5 percent if conditions improved prior to the issue) issue, convertible into an internal franc bond on the basis of a 9-cent franc (current rate was 8.15). The Finance Ministry assumed the franc would improve, and refused to fix such an adverse rate into its securities for the next fifteen years. The Finance Ministry rejected any conversion plan "unless at some figure that is manifestly defensible and advantageous," such as 12.5 cents per franc. Morgan's countered with a suggestion for conversion in stages—9 cents during the first five-year period, 11 cents the second, and 13 cents the third. The British government, according to Morgan's, "liked very much" the automatic conversion privilege because it resulted in a "cancellation of external debt and the substitution of a lower interest bearing internal debt." The translation of external into internal debt, argued Morgan's, was well worth any initial loss on exchange.

Another feature proposed by Morgan's stipulated that the French government would constitute a fund at Morgan's for the repurchase of a portion of the issue during the first five years of the loan. To maintain the purchase fund, the Finance Ministry would make a monthly deposit of $1 million with Morgan's. Any balance outstanding after the first five years would be repayable to the lenders during the twentieth year. Parmentier rejected this arrangement. The French Treasury could not afford monthly payments in excess of $750,000. He also demanded that the bonds be callable after five years. Morgan's refused to underwrite a callable issue, because American investors were not interested in a five-year investment. "No matter how attractive the rate is made," observed Morrow, "there is a great deal of money of the small investor that will not go into the bond if it is likely to be taken away from him in less than twenty years." Parmentier insisted on the callable feature in order to permit the Finance Ministry to take advantage of a rise in the franc or a decline in interest rates.

Dissatisfied with the terms offered by Morgan's, the Finance Ministry indicated it "is really not now urgently desirous of a loan" because its position in the United States had improved. The French government was determined to balance the 1922 budget even if it had to double tax rates. Germany accepted the terms of the London Schedule of Payments on 11 May, apparently assuring France of some reparation payments during the coming year. While neither the French government nor the parliamentary opposition was pleased with the terms of the London Schedule, Morgan's advised them that an unduly strong condemnation of the settlement would have an unfavorable effect on the projected loan issue in the United States.

Morgan's advised the Finance Ministry, which now thought it could do with a $50 million issue, to go immediately for $100 million "on the ground that it was better to go while the going was good and get a substantial sum in hand for contingencies." There was, however, another reason for Morgan's interest in concluding a prompt agreement for a major French operation. On 11 May, the firm cabled Morgan, Harjes et Cie. and Lamont (who was in Paris at the time) that "Otto Kahn [of Kuhn, Loeb & Co.] is on his way to Paris and we have received an intimation that he may be desiring to arrange a new City of Paris loan as opposed to a French Government loan."

Negotiations continued to drag through May, held up by attempts to reduce Morgan's spread from 6 percent to 5 percent, and a dispute on the actual cost of the loan to the French government. Morgan's put the actual cost at 8.86 percent, but after days of calculating, the Finance Ministry came up with a figure of 9.19 or 9.20 percent. The precise cost was in fact not agreed upon prior to the signature of the underwriting agreement. But when Morgan's offered a guarantee that bonds repurchased with the first three months' installments would not cost the French government an average of more than 96 plus interest—thus reducing the cost—Finance Minister Paul Doumer authorized his agents in New York to sign the contract on 21 May 1921. Morgan's cabled Lamont that the guarantee would cost the firm nothing, because it would come into play only if the "loan would be an amazing success." J. P. Morgan & Co. apparently held no such high expectations for the issue.

In the final underwriting contract, Parmentier obtained most of the concessions he sought. Though the issue was not callable, it did not contain provision for conversion at a preselected exchange rate. It was a noncallable issued at 7.5 percent, with a syndicate guarantee for the entire $100 million. Payments for the repurchase fund were set at $750,000 per month during the first five years. The loan was issued in June 1921, and after deductions for expenses, the French government account in New York was credited with $90,125,000. The account furnished the resources for repayment of outstanding French Treasury bills.[73]

Success with the 7.5 percent loan of June 1921 resolved for the moment the French Treasury bill and dollar crisis. But the strained relationship between the Morgan organization and the French government was only smoothed over. The refusal of Morgan, Harjes et Cie. to participate in a loan for Verdun, "simply because we were not particularly attracted by some of the French issuing banks," drew a sharp reaction from Minister of Liberated Regions Louis Loucheur. Loucheur went to Herman Harjes and threatened "that he would never shake me by the hand again, that he would never bow to my wife when he saw her in the street and that he would absolutely have nothing more to do with the firm unless we allowed our name to appear on the circular!" Harjes relented.[74] At the Finance Ministry, however, Doumer had nothing but praise for Morgan's handling of the 1921 7.5 percent loan. "The success of such a large credit operation, in the midst of particularly difficult political and financial conditions," he wrote Morgan's, "gives us new proof of the power of your organization as well as of your devotion to French interests."[75]

If the 1921 loan temporarily solved the Finance Ministry's dollar crisis, it exacerbated the Finance Ministry's political relations with the French Parliament. The president of the Senate Finance Commission termed the loan part of the "extra-legal regime . . . left to us by the war," because the Finance Ministry had not bothered to consult parliament on the terms of the underwriting contract with Morgan's. Parmentier pointed out that the law of 29 September 1917 empowered the government to issue loans in the United States without special legislative authorization. Unstable conditions in both European and American financial markets made rapid negotiations imperative, leaving no time for parliamentary consultation or approval. Today's opportunity for placement might disappear tomorrow. Had not Morgan's withdrawn an offer in January?[76] Parmentier seemed to be saying that so long as the financial crisis continued, the French parliament would have to relinquish some of its control over a portion of the national debt.

French dollar requirements in the United States continued to plague the Finance Ministry. The Finance Ministry notified Casenave in New York that J. P. Morgan & Co. would issue no additional Treasury bills after the conclusion of the June 1921 loan, but the Treasury bill issue was not yet dead. In October, Parmentier directed Casenave to incinerate the $235 million in Treasury bills redeemed since the inception of sales, but added that "as to the $45 million in bills signed but never issued, they should be left on deposit with Morgan's. We have always considered that the operation in question was only provisionally halted, not definitively closed out." One year later, the Finance Ministry sought to resume Treasury bill sales in New York, but Morgan's warned that such a move "would be construed as a confession of weakness as to the French position."[77]

The French Treasury bill and dollar crisis of 1920–21 discloses an intimate but complex relationship between the French Finance Ministry and J. P. Morgan & Co. It would be unjust to describe the Finance Ministry as a captive of Morgan's. Other governments relied on the House of Morgan for assistance in the United States, and as N. Dean Jay pointed out to Herman Harjes, "certainly the British

Government have found it to their advantage to conduct all their financial transactions [in the United States] through J. P. Morgan & Co."[78] The relationship between Morgan's and the Finance Ministry held definite advantages for both parties. For Morgan's, the profits were large. For the Finance Ministry, there was the power of Morgan's organization, combined with their experience and knowledge of American and European financial markets. But in addition to the material bond between the two actors in this drama, there existed a kind of spiritual kinship that helped to override the occasional differences over tactics and terms.

Against a background of Anglo-Saxon opinion that almost unanimously condemned French finance as incompetent, the Morgan partners consistently supported and praised French efforts to deal with the financial and monetary legacy of the war. Lamont told the annual meeting of the American Bankers Association in 1922 that the French people deserved great credit for investing 100 billion francs in French government securities since the war, and reducing their trade deficit from 23 billion francs to only 2 billion in the course of the preceding year. Morrow conceded to Lamont that "not only me but some of the other partners feel that France's foreign obligations are much better than we thought they were," and he promised to "devote some time to putting the very strong French position before the public." N. Dean Jay told the Bond Club of New York that "in taxation France has been constructive and bold," and as a nation which had never repudiated her debts, France was "an excellent moral risk."[79]

J. P. Morgan & Co. was more than a banker to the French Finance Ministry. As Lamont observed to Morrow, in times of easy money "almost anybody" could do a decent job of financing for the French government. "Therefore the contact that we have with the Government," he wrote, "depends upon something more personal and intimate—that is to say, counselling with the Finance Minister from time to time, holding his hand and letting him feel that he has someone in America to whom he can turn for general counsel. That is the strength of our position today, and if we fail to maintain that contact we shall lose our position."[80]

It was J. P. Morgan, Jr., himself who took the lead in defending France against its critics in America. In March 1922, Parmentier expressed to Herman Harjes his concern that large French balances in American banks might cause certain unfriendly politicians in Washington to ask why France should not use some of those dollars to repay its debt to the United States. Harjes mentioned this to Jay, and Jay spoke directly with Morgan. By Jay's account, "he stated that no one in this country or elsewhere had any right to demand what if any balance anyone had with J. P. Morgan & Co., and that should anyone ask, he would be told it was none of his business."[81] Where would the French Finance Ministry find a better friend than J. P. Morgan & Co.? Morgan's guidance, self-interested as it was, helped the French government through the financial and monetary crisis of the early postwar years.

7

Reconstructing
International Trade

America must assume the responsibility for the direction of
the world and its economic reconstruction.
                    —Warren F. Hickernell,
                        The Alexander Hamilton Institute, 1921

The United States could not, if it would, assume the burdens of all the earth. It cannot undertake to finance the
requirements of Europe . . . nor can the Government of the
United States tax the American people to subsidize the business of our exporters.
                    —Carter Glass,
                        secretary of the treasury, 1920

By 1919, the old international economy was nothing but a distant
memory. The war had shattered traditional trading patterns, and
Central Europe and Russia had been separated from the international commercial system. The gold standard was gone, and international debt had reached such proportions that credit was unobtainable for most members of the international trading community.
The international economy had to be reconstructed, and the first
stage involved reviving the international credit system, without
which goods could not be moved from one country to another. The
second step required the rehabilitation and reintegration of Central
Europe and Russia into the international economy. Without the
participation of these areas, the economies of Western Europe could
not hope to achieve full employment. The third operation, tied
closely to the second, centered on the need to assure each of the industrial nations adequate supplies of raw material and fuel. The end
of the "hot war" brought the beginning of a "cold war" in which the
Great Powers contended for control of coal, oil, and other resources.

Efforts by the United States, Britain, and France to reconstruct the international economy fell short of the objective. It was fashionable at the time, and remains so today, to attribute the world's interwar economic disasters to the failure of American financial leadership. Thus, it was natural for a ranking official in the British Foreign Office to describe American economic policy toward Europe in 1922 as "incredibly mean and contemptible."[1] An alternative theory suggests that sheer incompetence and inability to understand the issues underlay the failure to reconstruct the international economy during the early postwar years.

Whatever the value of traditional explanations implying incompetence or malevolence, they fail to explore the complexity of the economic situation facing Europe and America in 1919. The awesome task of creating new international financial institutions required a degree of wisdom and sacrifice seldom if ever seen in the age of modern, industrial, nationalistic capitalism. Legitimate national interests often conflicted with the requirements of international welfare, and rational programs for international reconstruction often ran aground on domestic political and economic interests.

Reconstruction of an international credit system was the key to the revival of international trade. By 1919, the United States had become the world's ultimate creditor. Britain, now a debtor as well as a creditor, could no longer conduct business with continental importers without support from America. The chairman of Lloyd's Bank, Robert H. Brand, told Morgan partner Thomas Lamont that Britain could not pay cash for raw material from the Empire and then reexport finished products on credit unless the United States gave financial assistance. Brand assured Lamont that "if Great Britain has reasonable security that she can obtain sufficient credit in the United States, she can grant credit elsewhere." It was essential, added Brand, that American credits be granted with the understanding that they could be spent outside the United States.[2]

Lamont's response foreshadowed America's noncommittal attitude in the credit question. The European states had not presented any "reasonable estimate" of their dollar requirements. When they studied their needs carefully, the Europeans would find they required less assistance than they thought. In any event, Lamont thought it highly improbable that American credits would be made available except for the purchase of supplies in the United States.

Despite the ravages of war and the chaos of revolution, many Americans doubted Europe's need for massive postwar assistance. Herbert Hoover's 3 July 1919 "Memorandum on the Economic Situation of Europe" conceded only that America might have to grant credit and devote its surplus productivity to European needs during a "certain temporary period." The Europeans would have to restore themselves through harder work, more saving, and fewer imports. American aid, Hoover stipulated, carried the condition that the recipients set their internal financial and political houses in order, curtail consumption of luxuries and expenditures on armaments, and work for peace. If these conditions were met, Hoover estimated that "the economic burden upon the West should not last over a year and can be carried and will be repaid."[3]

By early 1920, the United States Treasury and the Federal Reserve Board had adopted Hoover's position. Secretary of the Treasury Carter Glass announced that "the Treasury is opposed to further government aid . . . The governments of the world must now get out of banking and trade." Glass believed "the need of Europe for financial assistance, very great and very real thought it is, has been much exaggerated both here and abroad." He cautioned that "we must not allow our sympathy to warp our judgment and, by exaggerating Europe's financial needs, make it more difficult to fill them." Europe had to tax itself, balance its budgets, and ship gold to the United States to pay its debts. America, like Britain, could not continue to sell on credit to Europe when it had to pay cash for imports from Central and South America and the Far East.

Glass contended that the task of financing European restoration "belongs primarily to our exporters." Those who would reap the profits should take the risks. The United States government, Glass stated, would not participate in any international financial conference unless the "scope and character and limitations of such a Conference as well as the impossibility of United States Government action are clearly understood. Following Glass's lead, British Chancellor of the Exchequer Austen Chamberlain announced that if Britain participated in an international finanical conference, it would be on the condition that Britain could undertake no new financial liabilities on behalf of any other nation.[4]

The French Finance Ministry agreed in theory with Carter Glass's position that the only "final solution" to Europe's credit crisis lay in balanced budgets reflecting reduced expenditures and higher taxes. But as the Belgian delegate to the 1920 Brussels financial conference observed, restoration of domestic financial integrity was a long-term process and "while waiting for the results, we have to live." The director of the Mouvement général des fonds, Alexandre Célier, always mindful of the French Treasury's precarious situation, nevertheless expressed reservations about accepting credits guaranteed by foreign governments. Debtor nations might easily lose their financial independence under international controls imposed by the lenders.[5]

Some influential American financiers and Treasury officials doubted from the beginning the adequacy of private credit facilities for the gargantuan task of revitalizing Europe and reconstructing normal trade patterns. Thomas W. Lamont and Norman Davis, members of the American financial delegation at the Paris Peace conference, urged President Wilson and Assistant Secretary of the Treasury Russell C. Leffingwell to extend American credit to Europe without restriction. They urged in particular a much-expanded role for the War Finance Corporation, suggesting that the WFC be empowered to make direct advances to Western European nations experiencing the most pressing difficulties.[6]

Export-import credit schemes involving official agencies such as the WFC and the Grain Corporation soon proved inadequate. Lamont admitted that the law authorizing WFC loans "is simply not one to attract our exporters at all," and Secretary of Commerce William C. Redfield observed that "nobody wants to borrow money under the conditions set forth." By February 1920, the WFC had advanced only $27 million of the authorized $1 billion, and in May the agency ceased its export subsidies because it seemed "illogical that a government agency such as the WFC continue to do indirectly what the American government refused to do directly."[7]

Lacking either advances from the United States Treasury or credits from official American agencies, France turned in desperation to London for sterling advances with which to pay for grain imports from the United States. The City, however, refused to provide credit to finance American exports. One London financial establishment, Hudson's Bay House, advised France that the Americans "will probably decline to take their share of the common burden" so long as Europeans continued to finance imports through dollar purchases in the money markets. If France simply refused to pay its bills, American policy would have to change.[8]

Turned away by London, the French Finance Ministry resumed its search in America for credits on which to import food and fuel. The U.S. Treasury directed the French to the Grain Corporation, but on 29 January 1920 French financial representatives in New York reported that "approaches made to the director of the Corporation for a three-year credit have gone without any result." The Grain Corporation, it seemed, was empowered to authorize foreign grain sales only when there existed a surplus that could not be disposed of on the American market, and when the price fell below $26 per bushel. Neither of these conditions had been met during 1919, and the French representatives believed nothing short of personal intervention by President Wilson could help them.[9]

French attempts to negotiate medium- or long-term credits with private American suppliers and financial institutions encountered opposition from the Federal Reserve Board. Bonbright & Co. set up a credit arrangement for Creusot and some other French industrialists, and Standard Oil seemed favorably disposed toward granting a two-year credit (six-month credit, renewable up to two years) for $10 million in kerosene and gasoline and the cost of shipping. But the Federal Reserve Board quashed these plans, ruling that such schemes were merely attempts to disguise long-term credits as short-term credits. As long-term loans, they were ineligible for discount at federal banks. The governor of the Federal Reserve Board, W. P. G. Harding, personally directed his legal counsel to explain to French representatives that only ninety-day paper was eligible for rediscount by a Federal Reserve bank. The Board prohibited renewal of ninety-day paper, and the banks had been so notified. The Board did not wish to "immobilize" banking resources in long-term placements. Only in May 1921, when the recession began to hurt American exporters, did the Federal Reserve Board relax its position and accept six-month commercial paper for rediscount at Federal Reserve banks.[10]

As a Great Power unable to obtain credit in either Britain or the United States, France had lost her predominance in Europe long before the financial crisis of 1924 and the adoption of the Dawes Plan. Turning to lesser powers such as Argentina, Uruguay, and

Spain for credits, France often found the terms unfavorable. So long as France remained a debtor to these smaller powers, French foreign policy was dictated by financial considerations. The Finance Ministry could not repay wartime credits opened with Argentina and Uruguay, but as the war ended France desperately needed additional foodstuffs. Argentina demanded that Britain participate in any operation for additional credits, but the British Treasury refused. By the end of 1920, as Argentina's grain trade began to suffer from a combination of worldwide recession and a glut on the grain market, the Argentine government demanded repayment of past-due credits unless France agreed to open new credits for additional grain purchases. By that time, however, France did not need the additional grain. Its trade deficit with Argentina, 263 million francs for the first two months of 1920, fell to only 60 million francs for the first two months of 1921.

France told the Argentine government it could not pay, and the Argentine government extended the credit one year at a time. In 1922, the Argentines suggested that the French government purchase a railway company owned by the province of Buenos Aires, and turn it over to the Argentine government in payment of its debt. Finance Minister Lasteyrie rejected the plan. In January 1923, the Argentine government asked that France at least pay the interest on its debt. Parmentier advised the finance minister that they should accede to the request, since the Argentines had been so accommodating in extending the credits.[11]

If France escaped Argentine financial and diplomatic pressure, it was owing to a postwar surplus on world grain markets which placed Argentina in a less favorable position. But France's problems with other creditors, such as Spain and Switzerland, caused more persistent difficulties for the Finance Ministry and Ministry of Foreign Affairs. In the case of Spain, the financial problem was tied to a diplomatic test of strength over Morocco. Under an agreement of 6 March 1918 Spain had granted France a one-year credit of 455 million pesetas. When the initial credit expired, it was extended and enlarged. By July 1919, France owed 533,285,000 pesetas, of which 113 million was past due.

France undertook negotiations for a new agreement when Finance Minister Klotz told Foreign Minister Stephen Pichon that a simple renewal of credits would not suffice. France needed a general import-export agreement with Spain, assuring her an additional monthly credit of 35 million pesetas. This additional credit would be used to maintain exchange stability between the two countries without forcing France into the money markets. Klotz required another advance of 50 million pesetas to pay for a previously agreed transaction—a large French purchase of Spanish *vins du ravitaillement*. To interest the Spanish government, Klotz suggested that France might offer Spain some of the anticipated German reparation obligations. A neutral country would thus acquire a direct interest in seeing to it that Germany paid up.[12]

Financial negotiations with Spain soon bogged down. According to the French chargé d'affaires in Madrid, it was the Moroccan situation which "paralyses the success of our financial projects" with Spain. After Under-Secretary of State for Finance Charles Sergent conferred in Paris with the French ambassador to Madrid, Klotz conceded that "no negotiation with Spain has any chance of success so long as the Moroccan question is not settled." Spain had become one of France's largest creditors, and the Finance Ministry needed the cooperation of the royal government in Madrid.[13]

Cooperation was not forthcoming, as the Spanish government had decided to use the financial negotiations as leverage for some sort of political concessions in North Africa. The French Ministry of Foreign Affairs apparently wished to handle the affair as any Great Power would—by refusing to accede to any Spanish demands. Some Finance Ministry officials, such as the director-general of customs, suggested that France retaliate by prohibiting the importation of Spanish wines and oranges if Spain offered unacceptable credit terms. But in December 1919, the financial negotiations appeared to be moving ahead as Spain granted an additional credit of 35 million pesetas. Célier, director of the Mouvement général des fonds, thus counseled that it was an "inopportune moment" for measures "which would be considered by the Spanish government as unfriendly." But the threat of retaliation, he conceded, could pressure Spain into granting the desired financial concessions.[14]

The French were about to learn that in the postwar game of power politics, Spain held the high cards. In conversations with King Alphonso XIII, the French chargé d'affaires in Madrid learned in February 1920 that "our credits could only be prolonged on condition of according Spain political compensation in Morocco."

France tried to keep the negotiations on strictly economic and financial terrain. Finance Minister François-Marsal suggested that the Moroccan question not be broached, and asked the press to "observe the greatest reserve on this subject." Admitting he was unqualified to evaluate Spain's political demands in Morocco, the finance minister asked the premier and foreign minister, Millerand, to consider France's very important financial and economic requirements in any discussions regarding the Tangier regime or the respective frontiers of French and Spanish Morocco. France's financial requirements, he estimated, might well outweigh any advantages in territory or prestige France could extract from Spain.[15]

During the spring and summer of 1920, the conflict between the Finance Ministry and the M.A.E. (Ministry of Foreign Affairs) over the handling of the Spanish/Moroccan question deepened. The attitude of the M.A.E. stiffened, while the Finance Ministry argued that the country's financial position precluded an adventurous foreign policy directed against Spanish interests in Morocco. The precarious nature of France's financial position became obvious when a Spanish deputy from Barcelona named Lerroux sent François-Marsal his proposal to negotiate a 40 million peseta debt-consolidation loan in Spain. To obtain the loan, France would have to declare her commitment to respect the 1906 Act of Algeciras and pledge to maintain the Morrocan regimes established by the terms of that act. The finance minister advised Millerand against rejecting Lerroux's proposition out of hand. "I think," he cautioned, "it is not without danger to excite Spanish susceptibilities and disturb her African ambitions, especially since our financial difficulties place us at the mercy of her good will and in any event prevent us from exploiting any territorial advantages we might eventually obtain."[16]

Following the advice of his ambassador in Madrid, Count Auguste Félix de Saint-Aulaire, Millerand suggested a cut-off of French phosphate exports to Spain and the closing of the French border to all imports from Spain. At the same time, France might make a gesture of good faith by paying the debt installment due in June 1920. François-Marsal pointed out that the French Treasury could not afford to make the June payment. In any event, it was unnecessary because Spanish bankers had already indicated their desire to renew the credits. France's problems with Spain, observed the finance minister, were political, not financial. He advised Millerand to order Saint-Aulaire to continue the financial negotiations. Célier also believed the political obstacles to a financial settlement with Spain would disappear if France let it be understood that she envisaged no impending change in the status of Tangier and the Spanish zone of Morocco.[17]

As the Spanish financial negotiations continued, Millerand ordered the Finance Ministry to make an initial payment on the debt. François-Marsal insisted the Treasury needed all the resources at its disposal to make the repayment of the Anglo-French loan from the United States. Deposits in Madrid had been increased to 35 million pesetas, approximately the same amount as the initial payment due Spain, but that sum was to be converted into dollars for the Anglo-French repayment. Under no circumstances, said the finance minister, could it be used to pay off debts to Spain. To facilitate the ambassador's negotiations, however, François-Marsal agreed to delay the conversion as long as possible, "to leave the Peninsular Government in uncertainty as to our true intentions."[18]

The threatened tariff war had already begun on the French-Spanish border. A sweeping French decree of 23 April 1920 had reduced imports from all nations, including Spanish wines and liquors. Spain had retaliated, and by November trade between the two countries stood at a practical standstill. François-Marsal now agreed that if the Spanish government refused to accept a "sensible" plan on credits, France should threaten to restrict imports further and to cut off the supply of phosphates. But Célier urged the finance minister to back down. France, he believed, should take the initiative to end the tariff war. Closing the peninsula to French products only benefited British and German exporters. France could not afford this setback just at the moment when her trade balance was beginning to straighten out. To delay a settlement would "lead to a complete economic rupture with Spain, for which we would bear the entire responsibility." The French Treasury, he warned, could not bear the financial consequences of an economic war with Spain.[19] Clearly, the end of French power in Europe had arrived in a most humiliating guise. To settle its debt to Spain, France had to give up its anti-Spanish pretensions in Morocco.

The confrontation between France and Spain was only one indication that Woodrow Wilson's spirit of internationalism had failed to conquer postwar Europe and America. Proposals for autarchy, corporatism, export cartels, and tariff barriers became common currency during the years immediately following the war. International cooperation withered away as the United States, the United Kingdom, and France each established national programs to facilitate their own exports. Wilson's ideals were easily perverted. The London banker Frederick Goodenough observed in 1922 that "the theory of self-determination, however necessary or desirable it may have been as a political ideal, has served to raise tariff barriers."[20] To facilitate exports, the United States created special banks to finance exports under the Edge Act, France established a National Export Bank, and Britain set aside a £26 million fund in the Overseas Trade (Credit and Insurance) Act of 1920 to provide credit and insurance for exports to eastern Europe and the Black Sea region. As the recession of 1920 wiped out the postwar boom, protectionist fever hit all of the major trading nations.

The war had taught all of the belligerents the value of self-sufficiency. By 1919, autarchy, efficiency, and organization had become the watchwords for those most interested in national economic survival in a hostile postwar environment. Nowhere was this sentiment stronger than in France. Early corporatists such as Pierre d'Autremont argued the need for a French plan for the coming combat for international markets and resources. French commerce must be considered as a corporative, national enterprise, organized in "living cells, organic and powerful, capable of confronting international rivals." Autremont carefully disassociated himself from "narrow economic nationalism," but warned that France must face its competitors as a united nation. The cartel, he argued, must replace "the absurd regime of individual competition." The state should determine what to produce and the quantities required. The nation must possess a merchant fleet capable of handling its export trade, and France must be represented abroad by an army of competent officials promoting the growth of French commerce. The creation of an Office central de l'expansion nationale under Edmond Chaix was a good move in the right direction, but it remained to be seen whether the bureau would receive adequate funding.[21]

France's impecunious Treasury could not afford to spend funds for the promotion of French economic interests abroad. The government rejected a plan to establish a New York publicity bureau to counter anti-French publications in America, and the Finance Ministry closed down the French financial agency in New York in 1922. François-Marsal vetoed a proposal supported by both the French ambassador in Washington and the French consul-general in New York, calling for creation of an Office National Économique Francais aux Etats-Unis. Instead, he supported the ministers for commerce and foreign affairs, who were content to create a new post for a commercial attaché in New York.[22]

Postwar nationalism and the collapse of the boom in 1920 produced tariffs and exclusionary legislation which hampered the revival of an international economic system. It is not clear that actual world market conditions justified these trade barriers. Justified or not, by the end of 1920 the British parliament had enacted legislation protecting textile colorants and pharmaceuticals from German competition. Then came tariffs to protect "essential industries" and a heavy duty on goods "dumped" in Britain at prices below those prevailing in the country of origin, production costs below those prevailing in Britain, or prices unduly reduced owing to depreciation of the currency of the country of origin.[23]

American commercial policy during the early 1920s caused deep concern in Europe. The Edge Act and the Webb Act provided export credits and modified American law concerning trusts and cartels in order to facilitate cooperative export ventures. Though these acts supposedly operated to promote the revival of international trade, the French Finance Ministry warned that "we must watch carefully the repercussions on the French market of attempts at 'dumping' which might arise under the cover of the new legislation."[24] But it was the Fordney-McCumber tariff of 1922 which represented "the first heavy blow directed against any hope of effectively restoring a world trading system." For the French government, this tariff posed a particularly severe problem. Congress was demanding repayment of all inter-Allied war debts, but "the tariff under discussion [Fordney-McCumber] would render this mode of liberation from debt nearly impossible." France could pay only with exports, and the tariff closed off that avenue.[25]

During the period of industrial and agricultural reconstruction, France was not in a position to export—and the country was inundated with imports. Hoping to slow the decline of the French franc, France concluded a reciprocal import-limitation agreement with Switzerland in March 1920. French officials dissatisfied with the terms went so far as to recommend unilateral denunciation of the agreement. Others suggested prohibiting imports of Swiss embroidery and watches and halting French coal shipments if the Swiss government refused to renegotiate the accord.[26]

The Swiss problem, however, was only the tip of the iceberg. In a mood of desperation, the French government issued on 23 April 1920 a decree prohibiting the importation of hundreds of articles from all nations of the world. As a means of strengthening both the French franc and domestic industries this measure was probably ineffective at best and counterproductive at worst. Premier Millerand admitted that the prohibited articles accounted for only 3 percent of total imports. Officials in the M.A.E. particularly opposed the prohibitions, pointing out that interdiction of British products would make London bankers even less willing to open new credits for France. Millerand believed retaliation against French exports would wipe out any gains from import restrictions. France, he noted, exported mostly luxury articles which other nations could easily do without. France's problem was her inability to export sufficient quantities of "products of primary necessity" such as phosphates and iron ore. Such exports, Millerand argued, would enable France "to impose our will as can England or the United States, who have coal, wool, wheat, and cotton."[27]

The Finance Ministry was in fact developing an interest in utilizing French exports OPEC-style as a weapon against her competitors. On 4 April 1920, the director-general of customs summoned a meeting of Finance Ministry officials to discuss "certain raw materials which we export to countries with elevated exchange and which could serve as a basis for economic pressure." He observed that in the existing situation of shortages, countries producing raw materials tended to use them as a sort of currency of exchange. At the same time, François-Marsal asked Célier for his views on "measures to take with a view to maximum use for purposes of economic pressure the products we possess and which could be withheld from other countries." To the finance minister's list including iron ore, potash, phosphates, and bauxite, the director-general of customs added potatoes and dried vegetables.[28]

French attempts to use export-import quotas as a weapon against intransigent creditors and debtors failed. Countries with strong exchange could obtain commodities elsewhere—export restrictions alone could not raise the value of the franc. Nor could import restrictions alone prevent the fall of the franc. François-Marsal argued vehemently that any foreign exchange France held must be "reserved for the essential needs of the country," but the French chargé d'affaires in London responded to the import restrictions of 23 April with the observation that "decrees will not halt the depreciation of the franc." The M.A.E. eventually prevailed against the Finance Ministry, and a decree of 22 July 1920 reduced the number of articles prohibited from entering France.[29]

Everyone agreed on the need for economic reconstruction, but national interest determined where the process should begin. Economists and politicians emphasized schemes to revive traditional prewar patterns of international trade (which favored Britain) through the employment of conservative financial means. Thus, British concern for the rehabilitation of Central and Eastern Europe and Russia was very great, and represented a priority much higher than the reconstruction of France. The British economist J. H. Clapham suggested that ideally "for the comfort and peace of the world a universal restart is desirable,"[30] but it was clearly beyond the means of the vanquished victors to make a fresh start everywhere at once. French experts thought the reconstruction of Europe's financial and monetary system should begin in France, but the British had other ideas. Keynes believed the priority lay in the economic reconstruction of the enemy, Germany, while Montagu Norman's first objective was the financial reconstruction of the other enemy, Austria. Lloyd George had decided by 1922 that the financial rehabilitation of Soviet Russia required immediate attention. In any case, the requirements of Germans and Bolsheviks took precedence over the needs of the French.

In 1919, the French government was forced to look to Central Europe, Eastern Europe, and Russia out of sheer necessity. Finance Minister Klotz "had already stated in the French Chamber that he would not pay high prices to British manufacturers for goods which could be bought cheaply in Germany." Klotz had indeed alerted Clemenceau in October 1919 that a lack of dollar resources forced France to reduce purchases in the United States and seek alternate suppliers of cereals in Central Europe, Roumania, and southern

Russia. Machinery and manufactured goods, Klotz believed, "can be obtained in countries where we have means of payment, particularly in Germany and Austria."[31]

Klotz's "buy German" program was intended as nothing more than a temporary expedient to help France surmount the immediate postwar reconstruction and credit crisis. British officials, on the other hand, viewed the financial reconstruction of Germany and Austria as both a vital stage in the reconstruction of international trade and a critical step in the containment of Soviet Bolshevism. Montagu Norman and Winston Churchill took a strong anti-Bolshevik line, while Lloyd George held tenaciously to his view that only the revival of trade and investment in Russia—no matter who governed the country—could resurrect the slumping British economy. As the prime minister pressed for a rapprochement with Soviet Russia between 1920 and 1922, he split the Coalition cabinet, undermined his political authority, and opened new rifts with the French government, which did not share his estimate of the value or wisdom of dealing with the Bolsheviks.[32]

Prewar British and French investments in Russia were significant and both countries considered the massive Russian market an important element in their overall trade picture. With the Bolshevik seizure of power in 1917, the Russian trade collapsed and the new Soviet government nationalized investment properties held by foreigners. Western attempts to resume trade and renew investments with a government avowedly hostile to capitalism and the notion of private property produced a division of opinion based on one's perception of the national interest and the extent to which one stressed principles or expediency in framing national economic policy.

Britain appeared to need Soviet trade and investments more than did France during the early 1920s. During the contraction of 1920–21, British industrial production fell by over 18 percent and unemployment rose to 22 percent of those insured. Many experts believed revival of Britain's export trade held the key to her economic revival, but at the end of 1924 her exports were still 25 percent below the 1913 level. In France, domestic reconstruction requirements ruled out high unemployment rates. France required no foreign investment outlets to take up surplus capital, because France had no surplus capital. By the first quarter of 1921, France could show an export surplus of about 5 percent. France, in other words, was able to restructure its postwar economic and financial posture without recourse to the Russian expedient.[33]

Russia's former Allies generally considered postrevolution Russia as a nation outside the law and the fanatic Bolsheviks governing the country as enemies of western civilization. But in Britain, where pragmatism often outweighed theoretical considerations, the financial leadership soon began to view Russia's vast markets and investment possibilities with increasing interest. Not even during the boom of 1919–20 could one ignore a country that had provided Britain a £27 million market. In June 1919, *The Economist* urged immediate resumption of economic relations with Russia. Reopening commercial relations with such a regime presented "enormous" difficulties, "but the importance to British merchants of getting a foothold in the Russian market is so great that every effort should be made to overcome the difficulties."[34]

The government had already begun to move. The Board of Trade's War Risk Insurance Office offered to insure British goods exported to Russia and Russian goods exported to Britain. The Board of Trade had arranged with major London banks, including Lloyds, London County Westminster and Parr's, and the National Provincial and Union Bank, to grant advances against goods exported to Russia and insured under the Board of Trade program. Four steamship lines including Cunard had agreed to provide regular service to Russian ports. These arrangements applied only to southeastern portions of Russia and the northern Caucasus. Because Soviet currency was not acceptable in Britain—or in most of Russia for that matter—all transactions were to be straight barter arrangements.[35]

On 16 March 1921, Sir Robert Horne, president of the Board of Trade, and Leonid Krasin, commissar of foreign trade, signed the first official trade agreement between the Soviet government and a major western power. One aspect of Lenin's New Economic Policy, this opening to the West was followed by a similar pact with Germany on 6 May. The origins of the Anglo-Soviet trade agreement can be traced back to October 1919, when the European neutrals rebuffed a request by the Allied Supreme Council that they honor the blockade on Bolshevik Russia. Both the Soviet and British governments seized the opportunity to exploit the disintegration of the anti-Bolshevik front.

Lloyd George responded to the breakdown of the Russian blockade during mid-November of 1919. So long as the postwar boom continued, he stressed Russia's importance as a supplier of food and raw material rather than as a market for British goods. In January 1920, the Allied Supreme Economic Council indicated its willingness to reopen trade with Russia through the Russian Cooperative Organization, thereby avoiding contact with the Soviet government. In a statement issued 23 February, the full Allied Supreme Council ruled out resumption of diplomatic relations with Russia until "Bolshevist horrors have come to an end, and the Government of Moscow is ready to conform its methods to those of all civilized governments." But the Supreme Council allowed that "commerce between Russia and the rest of Europe, which is so essential for the improvement of economic conditions, not only in Russia, but in the rest of the world, will be encouraged to the utmost degree possible without the relaxation of the attitude described above."[36]

Under French leadership, the neutrals appeared to take the lead in breaking into the Russian market. At the suggestion of France, delegations from Holland, Denmark, Norway, Sweden, and Switzerland met in Geneva and on 17 April 1920 issued a statement outlining a common policy in establishing commercial relations with Russia.[37] Realizing that trade with Soviet Russia was about to resume, British industrialists and financiers wished to get their share. But how would Russia pay for imports from the West?

Under a Swedish contract of 15 May 1920 for agricultural, railway, and telephone equipment valued at 100 million kroner, the Soviets agreed to pay a quarter of the total in gold held by the Soviet government. The Soviets held about $500 million in gold bullion and coin inherited from the Tsarist regime. Because western governments refused to accept any of this gold, the Swedish contract represented an important breakthrough for the Soviet government. E. F. Wise, the British representative on the Supreme Economic Council, on several occasions advised his government that the Russians were prepared to pay in gold and platinum, and "if we refuse to trade the result will merely be that the gold and platinum will go elsewhere."[38]

At the invitation of Lloyd George, passed on by Wise, a four-man Soviet trade delegation led by Krasin arrived in London on 26 May 1920. During the subsequent talks, Krasin's position was strengthened by a decree of 11 June 1920 converting the Commissariat of

Trade and Industry into the Commissariat of Foreign Trade, headed by Krasin. Thus bolstered with new authority over all aspects of foreign trade, Krasin negotiated until the beginning of July, when the London talks were temporarily broken off. When they resumed in August, Krasin, accompanied by Lev B. Kamenev and V. P. Miliutin, returned to London.[39]

Britain greeted these Bolsheviks with great apprehension. Each delegate was asked to sign a statement agreeing to refrain from interference in British politics and internal affairs and to refuse all press interviews unless approved by the British government. All but Krasin signed the statement, and Krasin gave his verbal assurance. When they arrived in August, Kamenev and Miliutin refused to sign, but also gave their verbal consent. Paradoxically, the Soviet government suspected Krasin for entirely different reasons. They believed, according to Wise, that Krasin was "too much a business man and too little a revolutionary communist, and that Litvinov was necessary to watch him and keep him straight."[40]

As the trade discussions began, it was not clear who most needed an agreement—Lenin or Lloyd George. By inaugurating the NEP, Lenin admitted the importance of foreign investment and trade in rehabilitating the Russian economy. But as Wise had pointed out to Lloyd George, Europe's economic situation was "going from bad to worse," and it seemed "quite clear the only substantial hope of improvement lies in the re-starting of trade relations with Russia." There was, claimed Wise, a direct connection between "the Russian problem" and Britain's high cost of living. If the trade talks failed, Lloyd George would be hard pressed to explain it to a British public anxiously awaiting cheap Russian grain.[41]

Before trade negotiations got underway, it was obvious that each side intended to use the discussions to force political concessions from the other. If Britain insisted on Soviet recognition of the right of private property in Russia, the Soviets were equally determined to press for de facto recognition. British private interests claimed compensation for war damage to their Russian investments and for investment property nationalized by the Soviet government. Russian goods shipped to Britain under a trade pact might be tied up in British courts under legal proceedings brought by Britons holding claims against the Soviets. Without a settlement of the claims question, Wise cautioned, the Soviets could not raise credit abroad.

And without credit, the Soviets could not trade with the West.[42]

The questions of private property and compensation for nationalized property were only a small portion of the larger basket of political issues that might be raised. A group of four ranking officials of the Board of Trade and the Treasury, along with Wise, recommended that Lloyd George take up with the Soviet delegates the question of Allied prisoners held in Russia, problems in Persia, Afghanistan, and the Caucasus, antiwestern Soviet propaganda, the activities of General Wrangel, the Poles, and the Ukranians, points raised by the Admiralty concerning the Baltic, the Black Sea, and the Caspian Sea, and the matter of Russia's prewar debts to Britain. Oddly enough, this proposed shopping list did not include the presumed purpose of the meetings with the Soviet delegation—conclusion of an Anglo-Soviet trade agreement.[43]

From influential British political figures—some of whom were members of his Coalition cabinet—and from Britain's friends and Allies abroad Lloyd George received warnings against any dealings with the Bolsheviks. French Premier Millerand feared the talks would imply diplomatic recognition of the outlaw regime. He suggested that Krasin be permitted to negotiate with none but technical financial experts. "The intervention of members of the Government or Ambassadors," cautioned Millerand, "would modify the character which such conversations must conserve and would give them that character which they must not have, that of negotiations between one Government and another."[44]

While the French government desired a common front with the British in dealing with the Soviet regime, it differed with the British on concrete plans for establishing commercial relations. Paris wanted international supervision over the Russian economy, in much the same manner in which she sought international—meaning French —control over the German economy. Prior to any resumption of commercial relations with Russia, the Soviets had to settle up old debts, and the settlement had to include "guarantees." From the Russians, the French did not want money. They sought "the peaceful conquest of Russia's resources."[45]

Within his cabinet, Lloyd George met opposition from Lord Curzon and Winston Churchill. Outside the cabinet, Sir Samuel Hoare presented the prime minister with one of the most cogently argued pleas against negotiating with Krasin. Hoare agreed on the need to reestablish peace in Eastern Europe and bring Russian resources back into the world market. "It is about the methods that are being adopted," he wrote, "that I am genuinely anxious." Hoare's first concern was with the impact of the negotiations on the French, who were getting the impression that Britain was "merely interested in pinching the Russian market." Hoare referred to "the French bond holders' fury against anyone who gets any part of the Russian gold." French investors in prewar Russia felt they had first claim on Russian gold and that in accepting such gold the British government would become "the receiver of stolen goods."[46]

Hoare did not suggest "a permanent Chinese Wall against Bolshevik Russia," but he did insist upon "guarantees" from the Soviets that they would not use trade relations as an opportunity to incite British workers against their government. Hoare believed the Soviets were desperate for British trade and investment, and the prime minister should use trade negotiations to "force them into accepting some kind of general settlement" of the broad political issues separating the two governments. From the point of view of domestic politics, a "big appeal for a comprehensive settlement" would excite far less opposition than "a limited appeal to the material interests of British traders." The prime minister took serious political risks by undertaking negotiations from which "the Bolshevik Government will receive great moral support at the moment when economic chaos is making the collapse of Bolshevism inevitable."[47] The British prime minister, so it was being argued, was rescuing the Bolshevik outlaws just as their regime was on the verge of crumbling. The diametrically opposed intentions of the two negotiating governments, Hoare believed, must make any agreement that might be reached unstable and unworkable. The Prime minister was entering the talks "with the *arrière pensée* that by re-establishing normal life in Russia you will be destroying the Bolshevik Government, whilst the Bolshevik Government are frankly declaring that they regard the resumption of trade relations as a means for Bolshevik propaganda and for bringing nearer the day of world revolution which will destroy the British capitalist Government. How can any official agreement be stable when this is the mentality of the two contracting parties?"[48]

Lloyd George did not regard an Anglo-Soviet trade agreement as a "limited appeal to the material interests of British traders." He hoped it would provide the basis for a general economic rehabilitation of Europe, which in turn would insure the long-term interests of the entire British nation. The prime minister thus plunged ahead with negotiations with Krasin.

While these apparently unproductive negotiations continued, the United States government cautioned the British Foreign Office against any move that might imply recognition of the Soviet regime. The United States appreciated the "natural desire of the British Government to protect its interests in the Near East and to conclude, if possible, effective political arrangements with the elements at present in control of Russia," but Washington continued to view the Bolshevik regime as a temporary phenomenon undeserving of recognition as a legitimate government.[49] By the end of June, however, it appeared America's concerns were baseless, as the trade negotiations seemed to be collapsing. Krasin presented the Soviets' formal position in a 29 June statement, and it seemed to leave no room for agreement.[50]

Lloyd George prepared a countermemorandum listing Britain's conditions. He then left for an Allied meeting at Spa set for 7 July, at which the Polish situation was to be discussed. There the trade negotiations stood until August 1920. The Soviet government accepted Lloyd George's conditions on 7 July, but this acceptance did not lead to an early agreement.[51] The problem was Poland. The Red Army had turned the tide, taken the offensive, and evicted Polish forces from Kiev and the Ukraine. Both sides now assumed a more intransigent attitude in the matter of resumption of commercial relations.

When Krasin, accompanied by Kamenev, returned to London in August, anti-Soviet hysteria was sweeping London, and the cabinet was not immune. On 25 August, Winston Churchill, secretary of state for war, circulated to the cabinet a memorandum including a minute prepared by the chief of the imperial general staff, Sir Henry Wilson. From evidence presented by Wilson, Churchill concluded that "there is no doubt that Kamenev and Krassin are actively interfering in our internal affairs as well as in our relations with France . . . They disburse funds for revolutionary propaganda . . . No one can doubt that they are a foundation of conspiracy and corruption, having ceaselessly the purpose of paralyzing and overturning this country and isolating it from its Allies." On 2 September Lord

Curzon sent his own memorandum to the prime minister, Bonar Law, A. J. Balfour, Austen Chamberlain, and Churchill, charging the Soviet delegates with "abusing our hospitality" and urging their expulsion.[52]

Lloyd George, who was at the time in Lucerne, strongly opposed expulsion of the Soviets. He admitted the evidence against them was strong, but pointed out that most of it had been gathered by spying on the delegates and intercepting their telegrams. To expel the delegates the government would have to admit its illicit activities, and the British public would not stand for such behavior from its officials. It "looks like inviting men into your home and then opening their letters," he explained. In any case, crude Soviet propaganda would never impress the British working class. But most of all, stressed the prime minister, Britain needed Russian trade and access to the "infinite reserves of grain and raw materials." Germany was getting locomotive orders from Russia, and the Czechs had obtained orders for agricultural equipment. Britain needed manufacturing orders, too, and needed Russian grain to bring down the cost of food. "It is all very well," he observed, "for President Wilson to discourage dealings with Russia. He is a seller of corn; high prices suit him."[53]

Churchill and Curzon pressed their case, and Kamenev was expelled on 10 September. He had allegedly sold Russian crown jewels and platinum in London to subsidize communist propaganda in the *Daily Herald*, organized "councils of action" (soviets) to prepare a general strike, propagandized the army, and generally incited the British people to revolution. Churchill and Curzon continued to agitate for the expulsion of Krasin and the rest of the Soviet delegation, without success. Lloyd George was determined to reach an agreement and preserve a portion of the Russian bonanza for British exploitation. Hoping to take the heat off his own government, he suggested to President Wilson in a letter of 5 August that the bilateral discussions between Britain and the Soviet government be shifted to a general conference between the Soviets and the Allies. Wilson, hostile to the idea of any type of negotiations with the Bolsheviks, did not respond to Lloyd George's message until 3 November, the day after Harding's election to the presidency.

Wilson sharply criticized Lloyd George's Russian policy. "As to Russia," he wrote, "I cannot but feel that Bolshevism would have burned out long ago if let alone, and that no practicable and permanent settlement involving Russian territory and rights can be arrived at until the great Russian people can express themselves through a recognized Government of their own choice." This, of course, is what Wilson told the Germans before the November 1918 revolution overthrew the Kaiser. Wilson, not Lenin, may have been Europe's most dangerous revolutionary. Wilson, furthermore, had committed American troops in a confused attempt to intervene in the Russian civil war. He could hardly claim that the United States had pursued a hands-off policy while awaiting the collapse of the Bolshevik regime under its own incompetence. Wilson refused to send American representatives to an Allied conference designed to conclude a trade agreement with Russia "and, as I understand, subsequently extending recognition to the Soviet regime." Wilson was convinced that "no useful purpose can be served through official relations with the Soviets," and contended that negotiations simply tended to keep them in power.[54]

Wilson's parting shot at both Lloyd George and the Bolsheviks arrived in London just as trade negotiations were resuming. From November 1920 to March 1921, the discussions went reasonably well. The Anglo-Soviet trade agreement was signed on 16 March 1921. The signatories promised to take no hostile action or propaganda against each other either directly or in territories considered vital to their interests, such as India and Afghanistan. There would be no blockade against Russia. The British government would initiate no action to attach or take possession of gold, funds, securities, or commodities exported from Russia in payment for imports. Britain would not bar Russian precious metals or bullion. A separate "Declaration of Recognition of Claims" set aside settlement of claims of nationals of either country for a separate general peace treaty. Meanwhile, both governments recognized in principle their obligation to compensate private persons who had supplied goods or services for which they had not been paid. Such private claims, however, were not to take precedence over other classes of claims, such as Soviet claims for damages resulting from British and American occupation forces.[55]

How significant was the Anglo-Soviet trade agreement? To Benjamin Strong at the Federal Reserve Bank of New York, the pact looked more like a political ploy than a sound business venture. He doubted that any desirable business would result from it "with the possible exception of such limited sales of goods as may be paid for with the 'tainted' gold." At the Bank of England, Montagu Norman agreed that "the trade that will spring up as a direct consequence of it is likely to be small, but I think it may have considerable indirect results in helping to open up private trade and somewhat restore private property or ownership in Russia."[56]

The agreement constituted de facto recognition of the Soviet government by Great Britain, and thereby validated Soviet nationalization laws in the eyes of British courts. Traders would no longer have to worry about legal actions that might hold up their cargoes or gold payments. After 1921, governments as a rule did not interfere with Soviet trade. Soviet trade with the West, however, did not immediately take off. There were difficult organizational problems inherent in commerce between capitalist and noncapitalist systems. More to the point, the Soviet government's appetite for western imports was not matched by its ability to supply the exports desired by the manufacturing powers. It would take foreign capital to develop Russia's resources, capital which could be supplied only through a system of foreign concessions.[57]

During the period of war communism, foreign concessions could play no role in the Soviet economy. But as war communism gave way to the NEP, the psychological and practical barriers to the granting of leases to foreign capitalists began to dissolve. Lenin justified and explained the new concession policy to the tenth party congress in March 1921. Foreign technical assistance and equipment would not suffice to develop Russia's natural resources. It would take extensive concessions "to the most powerful imperialist syndicates" —"a quarter of Baku, a quarter of Grozny, a quarter of our best forests." Lenin later outlined the dual purpose of the concessions policy. It would speed the development of Russia's heavy industry, and improve the condition of the workers and peasants.[58]

The first concessions granted to western capitalists were more symbolic than real. On 14 May 1921 the Far Eastern Republic granted the American Sinclair Exploration Company rights to exploit oil in northern Sakhalin. But the concession had no value to Sinclair at the time because the island was occupied by the Japanese.[59] A permanent British commercial mission, as provided in the Anglo-Soviet trade agreement, opened in Moscow on 31 July 1921, but its presence did not seem to help any British capitalists to obtain concessions. The first few concessions granted went to Americans. In June 1922, the American United Drugs and Chemical Co. received a concession for the working of asbestos in the Urals. According to the head of the British commercial mission, R. M. Hodgson, American United was merely a front for the real recipient of the concession, Armand Hammer. Hodgson described Hammer as the son of an American socialist who had met and established a friendship with Lenin during Lenin's exile in Europe. Hammer had visited Russia during the autumn of 1921, and Soviet officials had greeted him warmly in the hope of attracting American capital. "He was given to understand," wrote Hodgson, "that any concessions which he might like to take up were within his grasp," and he ultimately chose the Alapayevsk asbestos property. Hammer was being used as bait to attract other foreign investors. "Lenin," reported Hodgson, "shows a lively interest in this undertaking, which has been established evidently not so much with the object of practical working but in order to create a precedent."[60]

If the early agreements were largely symbolic, the real test of Lenin's concessions policy came with the contract signed on 9 September 1922 by Krasin and Leslie Urquhart. A British mining engineer, Urquhart was an authority on Russian trade. Once the British vice-consul at Baku, he took over management of several important British firms in Russia in 1901, eventually becoming chairman of Russo-Asiatic Consolidated, Ltd. Prior to the revolution, Russo-Asiatic owned and worked a massive mining area in the Urals. The firm produced 60 percent of Russia's total output of lead, and significant amounts of gold, silver, copper, and zinc. The concession also included extensive forests, fisheries, coal deposits, and industrial plants. Maxim Litvinov estimated Urquhart's interest at practically 30 percent of all British claims against the Soviet government. After making contact with Krasin in June 1921, Urquhart traveled to Moscow in August to continue discussion of terms. He was determined to retrieve his concession.[61] Two German firms, Krupps and the Berlin bank of Mendelssohn, acquired an interest in Russo-Asiatic Consolidated, and with their assistance Urquhart reached agreement with Krasin in Berlin on 9 September 1922.[62]

The terms of the agreement were strikingly favorable to Urquhart. He received a ninety-nine-year concession, with all rights previously enjoyed, including control over the labor force. Royalty fees and taxation were limited to 8 percent, lighter than under the concession of the tsarist era. Estimated annual profit from copper, zinc, lead, gold, and silver was placed at £2,400,000. The Soviet government did not admit the right of compensation for loss of ownership and damage, but the government did pledge to invest up to 20 million gold rubles in the properties and gave Russo-Asiatic Consolidated an "advance" of £150,000. This, wrote E. H. Carr, was compensation in disguise. Lenin was willing to recognize compensation in some guise in return for additional foreign credits. He would approve the concession, according to Carr, "only on condition that a big loan is granted to us."[63]

According to Litvinov, Soviet Russia was prepared to make important economic concessions to Urquhart on the assumption that by satisfying one of her most important creditors, the Soviet government would improve relations with the British government and promote an overall final settlement of outstanding issues.[64] Although British newspapers such as the *Daily Telegraph* assumed that "Mr. Urquhart has not committed himself to sinking fresh capital in Russia without the knowledge and encouragement of the British Government," the Foreign Office in fact harbored deep reservations about the Urquhart agreement.[65] Two minutes written by Reginald W. A. Leeper, second secretary in the Northern Department of the Foreign Office, communicate the fear that Urquhart's deal represented a prelude to pressure from the Soviets for corresponding political concessions from the British government. Anything the Soviet government did was by definition suspicious. "In view of the duplicity of the Bolsheviks," wrote Leeper, "it is permissible to conjecture that there is a good deal more behind this agreement than meets the eye. It may well be another attempt to extract something from His Majesty's Government."

What might the Soviets want? Leeper wondered where the Russians intended to get the £150,000 in cash promised to Urquhart's firm. "Perhaps," he mused, "the sums to be paid are to be extracted from somebody else." Perhaps Urquhart was to persuade the British government to hand over sums due the former Russian government, on the argument that they would be employed to finance British interests in the Soviet Union. Leeper believed Urquhart "will move heaven and earth to get His Majesty's Government to induce the banks to give credit both to himself and to the Soviet Government." The Foreign Office, warned Leeper, must "resist any indirect attempt to raise credits, in which His Majesty's Government would be involved, until the Bolsheviks accept the full conditions put to them at Genoa and The Hague."[66] If the British government intended to follow Leeper's advice, then Lenin's condition for approving the Urquhart concession—large new credits—would not be met.

When he signed the contract with Krasin in Berlin, Urquhart told the press he had received no "guarantees" from the Soviets. The contract was based on nothing more than "good faith on both sides." Soviet authorities, he suggested, were prepared to make similar arrangements with anyone who would accept Soviet overtures as gestures of good faith. But if foreign nationals were to obtain favorable concessions, "it is up to the Governments of the nationals concerned to cooperate."[67]

The Soviet Politburo vetoed the Urquhart concession on 5 October 1922. The Council of People's Commissars, by a vote of 14–7 and 4 abstentions, added its rejection the following day. Precisely what transpired in the Politburo may never be known, but the decision on ratification, signed during Lenin's first illness, was one of the last major political decisions of his life. Lenin was already beginning to lose control, and the Urquhart concession posed basic questions that split the leadership of the Bolshevik party. The reason publicly given for rejection of the concession agreement was Britain's allegedly uncooperative attitude in the Turkish question. Urquhart at one point believed the Soviets wanted an invitation to the Lausanne conference on Turkey, and to obtain it they were prepared to negotiate a general economic agreement with Britain along the generous lines of the Urquhart concession. Later, Urquhart learned from his agent in Moscow that the Politburo had never considered the Eastern question in rejecting the concession agreement— that excuse was only adopted later as the best way to save Krasin's reputation and leave the door open to resumption of economic negotiations at a later date.[68]

The Politburo's rejection of Krasin's agreement with Urquhart stemmed from a variety of pressures, some reflecting competing foreign interests in Russia, some reflecting a power struggle among the Soviet leadership, some indicating philosophical differences among Bolshevik party leaders, and others reflecting personality conflicts within the Soviet government. Diplomatic reports reaching London indicated German and French maneuvers to sabotage any Anglo-Soviet agreement. Germany had already signed the Rapallo agreement with Russia, and France was rumored to be seeking its own commercial and military ties with the Soviet regime.[69]

If rejection of the Urquhart agreement was related to international political considerations, it was also clearly tied to the failure of the concessions policy as a whole and internal disputes concerning the future direction of the Soviet economy. Trotsky observed in November 1922 that the concessions policy had produced "big discussions, but small concessions." Western capitalists generally refused to take concessions on terms acceptable to the Soviets. Krasin, who negotiated the Urquhart agreement, was suspect in the eyes of his own government owing to his "western" background. Nikolai Bukharin, a candidate member of the Politburo, had been sent to Berlin to report on Krasin's negotiations with Urquhart. Burkharin characterized the deal as "an enslavement of the nationalized industry and an unheard-of insult to the Communist idea." His report touched off an uproar within the party hierarchy. The only point on which most accounts concur is that Krasin was in trouble. It is not clear whether Lenin favored or opposed approval of the Urquhart concession. Evidence culled from both the Soviet and the British side of the Urquhart affair leads to the plausible conclusion that Lenin did favor ratification but was forced to back down in order to preserve his own authority and maintain some semblance of party unity.[70]

Moscow's veto of the Urquhart concession did not end western efforts to gain access to Russian natural resources. Great Britain, the United States, France, and Belgium were all involved in the postwar scramble for control over resources, and the Russian oil prize appeared to be the crown jewel. Estimates of world oil reserves varied from source to source and from year to year, but everyone agreed that Russian reserves were among the largest in the world. Britain and the United States, the two largest consumers, recognized the importance of access to foreign oil sources. In 1918, Russia produced only 13 percent of the total world output. Given its reserves, investment opportunities in Russian oil seemed unlimited. Prerevolution British investment in Russian oil fields came to about $85 million, vastly outstripping that of the French (estimated between $25 million and $34 million), and the Belgians ($21 million). Two American firms, Standard of New York and Vacuum Standard, did some refining and marketing in Russia but did not participate in production.[71]

In the scramble for oil, Britain played the most vigorous role and appeared to come away the victor during the early postwar years. As the Russian and Ottoman empires collapsed, Britain sought to gain control over their oil resources. In the Middle East, the 24 April 1920 San Remo agreement may have placed as much as 42 percent of the world's oil reserves under British control. Lacking capital to develop oil in its own mandates, France signed over exploitation rights to Britain, agreed to construct an outlet pipeline across Syria, and consented to support Britain's attempts to obtain oil concessions in Russia. In return, Britain agreed to give France 25 percent of the Mesopotamian production. Most observers interpreted the San Remo agreement as a victory for Britain and a sell-out for France, prompting the comment that "the policy of France in the Near East since the War has been simply one long suicide." France, it seemed, had no oil policy at all, and critics began to ask "shall France decide to practice resolutely an oil policy, or will it remain a tributary and servant of the foreigner?"[72] For both Britain and France, a strong oil policy could only mean exploitation of someone else's resources. That path led inevitably to Russia.

Considering the stakes involved in the oil war of the early 1920s, the British government offered minimal support to British interests seeking Russian oil concessions. It was commonly assumed that firms such as Royal Dutch "invariably assured itself the support of the British government," but the evidence does not appear to support such a claim.[73] Russia's oil fields remained vulnerable to foreign exploitation during the four years of civil war following the Bolshevik takeover in Petrograd in November 1917. Russia seemed to be disintegrating. Mensheviks controlled much of the oil-rich Caucasus, and three break-away states, Armenia, Azerbaijan, and Georgia, set up independent republics and sought diplomatic recognition and Allied assistance against the Bolsheviks. For Allied help, they were prepared to offer extensive oil concessions.

Had the British desired to challenge Bolshevik authority, they could have done so by exploiting the situation in the Caucasus. There certainly was no lack of opportunities for British involvement in the area. On several occasions during 1921 and 1922, the Foreign

Office received requests from British-controlled oil companies such as Royal Dutch Shell, Anglo-Persian Oil Company, and smaller firms such as Gleboff Grosni Petroleum Company, asking for official backing in concession negotiations. Shell went so far as to claim that the Foreign Office's de facto recognition of the Azerbaijan government in January 1920 constituted an implied warranty that the British government would protect Shell's interests in the area, a claim characterized by one Foreign Office official "as immoral as it is absurd."[74]

Both the Foreign Office and the Board of Trade ruled out either diplomatic or military support for the Transcaucasian Republics. The Foreign Office refused to discuss the future status of the Transcaucasian states and "still less do they contemplate giving them 'a lead' against Russia if that implies any form of aggressive action." Sir Philip Lloyd-Greame assured Foreign Secretary Lord Curzon that the Board of Trade, too, "quite recognized that anything in the nature of aggressive action was out of the question."[75]

Britain's haphazard oil policy can be attributed to a combination of principle, incompetence, and jurisdictional disputes between the Foreign Office and the Petroleum Department of the Board of Trade. A critical Foreign Office memorandum on "Petroleum" was, according to a first secretary, "mislaid" for two months during negotiations with the Soviet government at Genoa and The Hague in 1922. Oil companies seeking Foreign Office assistance were often referred to the Board of Trade, with First Secretary Owen St. Clair O'Malley observing caustically that "I do not see why we [Foreign Office] should be held responsible in the City for policy in regard to British vested interests in Russia when we have in fact no say in the determination of that policy."[76]

The jurisdictional dispute, however, involved a principle. The Soviet government would grant new oil concessions only to large firms capable of exploiting an entire field, and supported its position on purely technical grounds of sound management of Russia's oil reserves. H. E. R. McDonell's Foreign Office memorandum on "Petroleum" gave credence to the Soviet stance, and at the same time dashed hopes for the restoration of oil properties to prewar investors, most of whom were relatively small holders. By December 1921, the Foreign Office had concluded that there was no chance the Soviets would restore oil properties to the former owners, and suggested to the Petroleum Department of the Board of Trade that former small foreign owners should henceforth be included as minority participants with new, large concessionaires such as Royal Dutch Shell. At the Petroleum Department, J. C. Clarke rejected the Foreign Office's approach. "For British interests to join the Soviet Government in wholly (in the case of Russian subjects) or partly (in the case of foreigners) expropriating the former owners appears unthinkable," wrote Clarke. "I do not see," he concluded, "how His Majesty's Government can be a party to any arrangement which deprives the former owners of their property without adequate compensation."[77]

The Board of Trade was thus unwilling to follow the lead of the Foreign Office in abandoning the interests of investors in Imperial Russia. But there were limits to the Foreign Office's support for "big oil." The Foreign Office provided a representative of Royal Dutch Shell with an introduction to Krasin, but withdrew its support when Shell refused to divulge to the Foreign Office details of an arrangement with Standard Oil for some Russian concessions. Shell's representatives were called to the Foreign Office and told that where the British government supported foreign operations of British firms, "they expected those interests more or less to lay their cards on the table." Shell was warned that "so long as we are in the dark about this [Shell's arrangements with Standard], it followed that active assistance from us to them would have to be suspended."[78]

Britain attempted to pursue an ambiguous Russian policy in 1921–22, recognizing definitively neither the Soviet government nor the Transcaucasian Republics, and supporting British oil interests in Russia only lukewarmly. The key to this policy appears to be the Genoa conference of 10 April–19 May 1922. Lloyd George refused to permit any extraneous issues to interfere with preparations for a conference that he regarded as critical for the economic reconstruction of Europe. Europe's economic reconstruction, he believed, hinged upon the economic rehabilitation of Russia, no matter which faction governed that country.

At the meeting of the Allied Supreme Council held at Cannes on 5–12 January 1922, Lloyd George won acceptance for his idea of a general European economic conference to which both outcast powers, Germany and Soviet Russia, would be invited as equals. The Cannes Resolutions stipulated, however, that all participating nations would have to accept certain basic principles. These stipulations obviously referred to none other than the Soviet government. The Allies conceded every nation's right to its own system of property, economy, and government. But no government could expect to obtain foreign capital without giving assurance that property and profits would be respected. Such security required that governments recognize public debts and obligations contracted by the state in the past or in the future, and restore or indemnify owners of property confiscated or sequestered by the state. This formula implied Allied recognition of the Soviet government's right to nationalize property, provided adequate compensation were given.

The Cannes Resolutions created a furor in Britain, spread disorder in Lloyd George's cabinet, and produced uneasiness in most European capitals. The uproar focused on the final clause of the Resolutions:

> If in order to secure the conditions necessary for the development of trade in Russia, the Russian Government demands official recognition, the Allied Powers will be prepared to accord such recognition only if the Russian Government accepts the foregoing stipulations.

Those stipulations included—in addition to those dealing with private property and recognition of debts—promises to halt subversive activities, propaganda, and hostile acts against foreign countries. Krasin told the United States consul general in London that on the basis of that clause of the Resolutions, Lloyd George had promised that diplomatic recognition of the Soviets would follow the Genoa conference.[79]

Krasin's interpretation differed from the understanding of other European leaders. Czechoslovakia's Foreign Minister Eduard Beneš, for example, regarded Soviet acceptance of the Cannes Resolutions as merely the first step in a lengthy process toward diplomatic recognition. The Allies might first proceed with economic agreements with the Russians. If those agreements proved successful, the Allies could then lay down additional political conditions for de jure recognition. Recognition could not be granted automatically after the Genoa conference—everything depended upon the concrete results reached at the meetings. Assistant Foreign Secretary John Duncan Gregory doubted that the Soviets would attend Genoa under such conditions. E. F. Wise, Britain's representative on the

Allied Supreme Council, harbored similar doubts, but Beneš, who had spoken with a Ukrainian Bolshevik leader named Kakovsky, assured Gregory that the Soviets would come to Genoa without assurance of automatic recognition.[80]

The Cannes Resolutions had been formulated by Lloyd George. He apparently proposed them without prior consultation with anyone in his government or Foreign Office. After the Cannes conference, Lloyd George's cabinet had second thoughts about the Resolutions. In fact, no one was quite certain what those Resolutions actually demanded and promised, or whether the British government should carry out their intent if the Soviets should comply with their conditions. If the Soviets accepted the Cannes conditions, was the British government bound to *grant* recognition, or was the government bound only to *consider* recognition?

To settle this question, Lloyd George appointed a special cabinet subcommittee, which reported on 28 January 1922 that the Cannes Resolutions "intended to convey that if the Russian Government accepts the stipulations, de jure recognition will be accorded." Rejecting the argument that nothing more than de facto recognition was implied, the report concluded that "the only apparent interpretation of this clause is that the official recognition contemplated is de jure recognition." This judgment, however, did not satisfy everyone, and "the Foreign Office representatives on the Sub-committee withhold their opinion on this question, which is one of political principle, pending its submission to the Secretary of State for Foreign Affairs." Assistant Foreign Secretary Gregory characterized the subcommittee's interpretation of the Cannes Resolutions as "to a certain extent ambiguous." The question of recognition now seemed to him a practical question rather than one of principle. "The question is whether it [recognition] is worth it. Economically it possibly is: politically it is doubtful. But the balance is on the whole in favour. Morally it is deplorable."[81]

The Foreign Office was confused. The rest of the cabinet was not only confused but refractory. Owing to Lloyd George's single-minded pursuit of a Russian settlement, the Genoa conference became the supreme test of the prime minister's political skills. He did not prepare his cabinet well for Genoa. Only three weeks before the conference opened, Austen Chamberlain warned him that "the Cabinet has not really discussed Genoa, and if there are any differences of opinion among our colleagues we should be in a very weak position." Trouble there was, because Winston Churchill, now colonial secretary, said he would resign from the government if Britain granted de jure recognition to the Soviets. Chamberlain was more moderate than Churchill, but he, too, felt it would be a "mistake" if Britain alone granted recognition in the face of almost certain refusal by France and the United States. He advised the prime minister to "concert" his action with France. Even if the Soviets should accept the Cannes stipulations, he observed, experience with them since the 1921 trade agreement "do not encourage us to place much faith in her word."[82]

Lloyd George next learned that Chancellor of the Exchequer Sir Robert Horne objected to his Russian policy. After receiving the warning from Chamberlain, the prime minister reminded Horne that "I told you I thought Winston would be a wrecker." Britain, he told Horne, was pledged to the Cannes Resolutions no matter what the cabinet might now desire. "You cannot put the Cannes conditions to the Russian delegates and then if they accept them still refuse recognition," wrote Lloyd George. The stipulations "are put forward in the Cannes project as conditions of recognition. We must act straightforwardly even with Revolutionaries," argued the prime minister. But Horne was not convinced. France, Belgium, Czechslovakia, and the entire Little Entente were most likely willing to go no further than de facto recognition. "It is I think possible," replied Horne, "to read the Cannes Resolution as to require Russia to give evidence of her good faith by performance." If, after a full discussion in cabinet, the prime minister still felt bound by the Cannes Resolutions to grant recognition if the Soviets accepted the stipulations, Horne would support his prime minister reluctantly. But he gave Lloyd George clear warning that the Coalition cabinet might break up on the issue.[83] Winston was not the only "wrecker."

Lloyd George mounted a counteroffensive to save both his Russian policy and the Coalition cabinet. He refused to back down from his position that "the conditions of recognition have been laid down at Cannes. They were never challenged by the Cabinet." He did admit to telling Poincaré at Cannes that the Genoa conference would still have to judge from the "demeanor" of the Soviet delegates whether the Russians really intended to carry out the stipulations. "This exposition of policy," asserted Lloyd George, "has never been challenged by the Cabinet." The cabinet, of course, had never discussed the Cannes Resolutions or the plans for Genoa.

To maintain his authority over the cabinet, Lloyd George launched a personal attack on Churchill, denounced French "dictatorship" in matters of foreign policy, and raised the specter of a Bolshevik revolution in Britain. He would not permit the British delegation to "tie themselves to the Chariot Wheels of France and go to Genoa to do what they are told by Poincaré." He was not suggesting that Britain should move alone, but "France must not be placed in the position of dictator" over Italy, Belgium, and the Little Entente. These countries could be convinced to support Lloyd George's position, and "unless the British delegates are fully authorized to cooperate with the majority of their Allies it is idle their going to Genoa." The prime minister could not emphasize too strongly how important it was that Genoa be a success. If the Genoa project for European cooperation and economic reconstruction failed, British unemployment would remain unacceptably high and "there will be such a revolt amongst the working classes that no government could withstand it."[84]

Lloyd George's apparent expectation of arriving at a settlement with the Soviets at Genoa was based on reasoning that can politely be termed naive at best. Keynes was not so charitable when he observed that "never, I think, at any Conference has the intellectual standard of the official policy sunk so low." Britain, Keynes asserted, simply demanded that the Soviets "unsay their doctrine," and offered nothing as quid pro quo because "Mr. Lloyd George's sleeves were empty, or sewn up by Sir Robert Horne" so that "there was no basis for a bargain."[85]

The prime minister did indeed intend to try to force the Soviets to "unsay their doctrine." He had received reports from Moscow describing attempts by Bolshevik "extremists" to gain the upper hand in the party. Lenin's health, Lloyd George believed, would determine the outcome. If the extremists succeeded, "there can be no question of recognition." But "if, on the other hand the party that is prepared to surrender its Bolshevism captures Soviet authority . . . if communism is prepared to surrender its principles," then recognition would be justified and "it would be folly not to help Russia to return to the community of civilized nations."[86]

Lloyd George gave his cabinet a clear choice. He told Chamberlain that "if Winston, who is obsessed by the defeat inflicted upon his military projects by the Bolshevik Armies, is determined that he will resign rather than assent to any recognition however complete the surrender of the communists and whatever the rest of Europe may decide, the Cabinet must choose between Winston and me." He suggested a cabinet meeting for the following Monday at 6:30 P.M. to decide the issue, and left no doubt as to the stakes involved. "That Cabinet," wrote Lloyd George, "must decide the fate of the Conference and incidently mine."[87]

Chamberlain now made another attempt to convince Lloyd George that the problem went far deeper than Winston's intransigence. He informed the prime minister that "since I wrote [21 March] I have looked at the Cannes Resolutions again and I see that they go further than I had supposed." Lloyd George, in other words, had slipped something past his own cabinet, and they were just now beginning to realize what they had agreed to. But Chamberlain had reread not only the Cannes Resolutions but also the record of the 16 December 1921 cabinet meeting at which his colleagues had given Lloyd George authority to discuss the economic rehabilitation and diplomatic recognition of Russia at Cannes. The record clearly indicates "that before diplomatic recognition of the Soviet Government was agreed to, the Cabinet should be consulted and that in the meantime Ministers were in no way committed." Chamberlain warned that "Winston may well claim, therefore, a free discussion in Cabinet before irrevocable steps are taken."[88]

Chamberlain was wrestling with both his loyalty to Lloyd George and his understanding of the realities of domestic and international politics. Two days later, on 25 March, he told the prime minister that "your policy of appeasement [of Soviet Russia] is clearly right," and he agreed that "we cannot put our representatives in the position of being the servants of French policy or giving Poincaré or his representatives the right of veto on your action." But realistically, Chamberlain believed implementation of Lloyd George's program was impossible. The Soviets would have to give "guarantees" (here he borrowed Poincaré's phrase regarding German reparations) because their record since the 1921 trade agreement proved that "something more than their mere word is now required." Soviet trade was the key to revival of Britain's economy, but that could be obtained without recognition. French and American interests, he noted, were already trading in Russia, and their governments had no agreements with the Soviets. British nationals could follow their example, and Chamberlain could find no support for de jure recognition among City financiers or manufacturers in the country at large. The Cannes Resolutions merely indicated the conditions under which recognition might be considered—if the Soviets accepted the stipulations— but did not pledge that recognition would be given. The prime minister would have to understand that the Conservative party (Chamberlain's party), the Belgians, the Italians, and other concerned parties all agreed with the position outlined by Chamberlain.[89]

Lloyd George temporarily patched up the cracks in his cabinet and went to Genoa determined to bring peace to Europe and Russian commerce to Britain. Each of the major powers represented distrusted the motives of the others. Secretary of State Charles Evans Hughes refused to send an official American delegation because it seemed to him that the economic conference was in fact a political conference from which no productive results could emerge. France attended only after assurances that reparations would not be discussed. French officials understood the conference as little more than a British device for exploiting Russian and East-Central European markets at the expense of a genuine long-term settlement of the Russian problem and the economic recovery of Europe.[90]

The organization of the Genoa conference reflected its ultimate result. The First Commission, with Lloyd George himself as Britain's delegate, was to deal with the important question, Russia. A Second Commission, with subcommittees on credit, exchange, and currency, handled the substantive financial problems hampering the revival of international trade. Because this was Lloyd George's conference, assessments of its accomplishments have centered on the skills and deficiencies of this one man. Former Italian Premier Francesco Nitti portrayed Lloyd George facing the narrow-minded French. The British prime minister, "by the breadth of his ideas, the clarity of his mind, the magnificent abundance of his resourcefulness, towered over the whole Conference." In Nitti's eyes, Lloyd George "showed himself so different and so much greater than every other personality in the Conference that even the most brilliant intelligences were reduced to the modest function of asteroids."[91]

Keynes, on the other hand, described Lloyd George at Genoa as being "more taken up than ever in the simultaneous absorption and creation of atmosphere and in the immediate personal and diplomatic problems; and more utterly oblivious of realistic constructive policy. He exhausted and degraded his experts in the drafting of endless subterfuges, and never sought their advice on the real merits of the case." He simply insisted on forcing the Soviets to acknowledge Russia's prerevolution debts while "offering no adequate *quid pro quo* which could induce a sane Bolshevik to agree." Keynes would have had Britain reopen trade with Soviet Russia and send to Russia "at the financial risk of our taxpayers" substantial quantities of material intended to promote Russian agricultural production and repair Russia's transportation system. "We should do it," he wrote, "with our eyes open, prepared to lose money." It might be expensive, but any advantage that might accrue would vastly outbalance the cost.[92]

Russia concluded the Rapallo agreement with Germany during the Genoa conference. This development alone signified defeat for Lloyd George's Russian policy. But the conference limped along after the Rapallo agreement (17 April) for another month. What was achieved by these negotiations between the capitalists and the Bolsheviks? At the time of the conference, the British were convinced that the Soviets had met many of their demands "in principle." Sir Edward Grigg, the prime minister's private secretary who accompanied Lloyd George to Genoa, claimed that "great progress was made; we got Russia up to a point at which she acknowledged her debts, we got Russia to a point at which she said where she could not restore private property she would compensate for it." He admitted that in practice "we did not succeed in doing very much at Genoa, but we got the thing remitted to the Hague, the Hague Commission is meeting to do the work; the work in that respect is going on." Assistant Foreign Secretary John Duncan Gregory claimed Chicherin had told the first plenary session that the Soviet delegation accepted the Cannes Resolutions "in principle, while reserving the right to present on their own part supplementary articles and amendments of existing articles."[93] In fact, what the Soviets accepted "in principle" they rejected with additional conditions, and by the time the conference ended they seemingly had withdrawn their original acceptance "in principle." It was all academic in any case, because France and the United States rejected the terms to which Lloyd George was willing to agree.

Negotiations with the Soviet representatives at Genoa centered on the questions of Russia's recognition of prewar and wartime debts and restoration or compensation of former owners of nationalized property. The Soviet delegates consistently rejected Allied proposals requiring them to repay old debts and restore property to former owners—the Germans made no such demands in the Rapallo agreement. On 24 April, the Allies informed the Soviets that their position that war debts should be written off completely was "incompatible with the Cannes conditions and wholly unacceptable."[94]

Hoping to salvage something from his conference, Lloyd George made what appeared to be a final offer to the Soviet delegates in his 2 May memorandum. Russia could begin importing vital necessities from the West "as soon as security in Russia has been re-established for former owners and debts are recognized." The memorandum then detailed, in five pages, conditions the Soviets would have to accept for repayment of old debts. The British prime minister tried to entice the Soviets with a promise of direct government assistance through credits for the export of British goods to the Soviet republics under the Trade Facilities Act. The government would request from Parliament an additional £25 million for this purpose.[95]

The Soviet delegates rejected Lloyd George's 2 May memorandum, but so did the French and Belgian delegates, who refused to sign it. They were particularly disturbed that the memorandum failed to insist on Soviet recognition of the property rights of French and Belgian nationals. Whereas Lloyd George would have settled for ninety-nine-year concessions as "compensation" for nationalized property, the French and Belgians wanted the property itself restored to foreign owners. The British prime minister now found himself besieged not only by intransigent foreigners, but also by his own Treasury and Foreign Office officials in London.

Austen Chamberlain cabled Lloyd George that his offer of £25 million in credits under the Trade Facilities Act was probably illegal, because the Soviet situation did not appear to meet the conditions specified in the act. In any case, the appropriated funds were already committed and "there is no Cabinet or Parliamentary authority for increasing the total. I have not consulted Cabinet but had message from Churchill this morning indicating opposition to any increase for Russia."[96] Foreign Office officials (privately) blasted Lloyd George's 2 May memorandum. First Secretary O'Malley noted that "the memorandum prepared for the Russians asks everything—or practically everything—and offers nothing in return. The Russians cannot possibly accept it without endangering the position of the present Russian government in the eyes of its supporters." He further observed that "this memorandum is not perfectly candid." The implied promises of credits under the Trade Facilities Act were "pure eyewash." Chamberlain renewed his plea in a 10 May cable pointing out that many in Britain sympathized with the French position on private property in Russia, and "no one would understand a quarrel with France for the sake of Russia."[97]

When Lloyd George convened the fourth meeting of the British Empire delegation on 10 May, he was prepared to split from the Allies and allow each creditor nation to negotiate with the Soviets for the restoration of its nation's private property. British property owners, he contended, "were more reasonable and would be inclined to make a bargain—it would be very hard that British subjects should be deprived of any chance of recovering their property because the Belgians insisted on standing out for the last penny."[98]

The official Soviet response to Lloyd George's 2 May memorandum arrived on 11 May, and further contributed to the disarray in the Allied camp. The Allies, claimed the Russians, had made "no precise proposals" for assistance to Russia. At Genoa, observed the Soviets, "the problems of the future, which interest everyone, have been subordinated to the interests of the past, which affect only certain groups of foreigners."[99] On this point the Russians were correct. Lacking capital to invest in Russia, France and Belgium were more interested in collecting past debts. But future profits foreseen by large British investors such as Royal Dutch Shell might easily outweigh uncollected prewar debts. This was especially true if prewar holdings of French and Belgian investors were now granted as concessions to British investors.

The collapse of the Genoa conference threatened to destroy what remained of a credible British foreign policy. Officials at the Foreign Office understood that if the prime minister's Russian rehabilitation program failed to materialize, countries bordering on the Soviet state would be "exposed to serious menace from a country driven to desperation by famine and pestilence." More serious yet would be the general diplomatic consequences of a disaster at Genoa, for "complete rupture will leave a disunited Europe face to face with a

Russo-German alliance as the only politically constructive result of Genoa."[100]

Lloyd George had to find some way to salvage something from his conference, and, paradoxically, it was the Soviet delegates who showed him the way. In their 11 May rejection of the prime minister's 2 May memorandum, the Soviets suggested the appointment of an expert Commission of Enquiry, minus the politicians, to look into the debt question at a subsequent conference. Sir Maurice Hankey told Chamberlain that Lloyd George at first rejected the suggestion of the Russians because it meant there would be no practical results from the Genoa conference, no solution to Britain's unemployment problem, and no European peace. "However," wrote Hankey, "his ingenious mind got to work, and he has been preparing a plan to turn this development of the situation to advantage." In less elegant language, Lloyd George intended to take the Soviet idea and propose it as his own. Gregory confirmed the plan the following day when he reported to London that the British delegation intended to propose a new commission which would meet at The Hague to consider the questions of Russian debts, credits, and property rights.[101]

By this time, Barthou, head of the French delegation, had received instructions from Poincaré to disassociate the French government from any further communications the conference might submit to the Soviet delegation. France would not attend the Hague conference (16–20 July). Gregory indicated French abstention from The Hague would be "inconvenient," but the British delegation felt the need to show a firm front against the French and the Belgians, for whom seats would be reserved in case they changed their mind.[102]

In a parting shot at Genoa delivered 17 May, Grigorii Chicherin forecast the failure of the Hague conference. The Soviets, he said, had intended at Genoa to work with the other powers for the reconstruction of Europe, despite their different economic systems. "But instead of that," observed Chicherin, "the other Powers preferred to divide the Conference into two parts, creditors and debtors, and wished to adopt the same system in the future [at The Hague]."[103] Nothing could be accomplished until the West dropped its ideological demand that Russia conform to capitalist standards, and treated Russia as an equal partner in European reconstruction rather than as a debtor. The Rapallo agreement stood as a stark example of what the Soviets had in mind.

Lloyd George's scheme for the Hague conference signified his belated recognition that the Soviet delegates had not accepted, and never would accept, the Cannes stipulations. The Soviets had not recognized past Russian debts "in principle." They had agreed to no principles at all, and had finally convinced Lloyd George that principles were irrelevant if a practical settlement with the Soviet government could be achieved on terms compatible with sound business practice. Gregory's message to the Foreign Office concerning the Hague conference noted that "in this connection members of the Russian delegation have constantly asserted that settlement can easily be reached in practice when agreement in principle is impossible." When he proposed the Hague conference to the British Empire delegation, Lloyd George conceded that "the basis of the policy now proposed was to endeavor to reach some practical agreement with Russia by means of a Commission which would avoid a continuation of a fruitless discussion on irreconcilable principles and seek by the examination of the actual claims to reach a business settlement."[104] Too Late, Lloyd George had recognized the futility of trying to force the Soviets to "unsay their doctrine."

By the end of 1922, the Allied entente was dead, and Lloyd George's Coalition cabinet was gone. The failure of the Genoa and Hague conferences hastened Lloyd George's downfall and strengthened France's resolve to go it alone with the Ruhr occupation. After the Russo-German agreement at Rapallo, Russia's return to the Western European economic system seemed more remote than ever. This proved unfortunate, for in retrospect, there was a certain validity to Lloyd George's belief that neither European reconstruction nor European peace could be achieved unless Russia were brought back into the European system.

Attempts at European financial and economic reconstruction between 1918 and 1923 had merely succeeded in politicizing financial and economic problems, thereby rendering them more difficult to resolve. Keynes regarded this as a catastrophic development—the politicians refused to listen to the experts. But Lloyd George's private secretary, Sir Edward Grigg, argued after the Genoa conference that economics could never be separated from politics. "You must attack the political questions, and try to get political sense established, in order that economics may have a chance," he told The 1920 Club. The experts, Grigg noted, had met before, at Brussels in 1920. "They met together, they passed resolutions, they told everybody exactly what they ought to do in order to get better." "What happened?" asked Grigg. "Nothing at all. The experts offered good advice, the governments took no heed." At Genoa, Lloyd George was determined to avoid the mistakes of Brussels. He was determined "to get the governments there, and to get the governments converted, and there is no other way of getting these sound principles of economics applied." Governments, claimed Grigg, had adopted the Genoa reports and had pledged to implement them. "I do not know," he conceded, "whether the governments will carry out these pledges, but at any rate it is a step forward."[105]

At the Brussels financial conference of 1920 and the Genoa conference of 1922, experts hammered out policies and suggested new institutions pointing to a genuinely international solution to the postwar financial and monetary crisis. Individual financiers were always coming forth with proposals for new international financial and commercial institutions designed to revive Europe's shattered economy. Keynes faulted the politicians for ignoring the experts' advice. But many experts rejected Keynes's advice, and the experts were by no means unanimous in the advice they offered the politicians. Could the experts have done better than the politicians? What would Europe's financial system have looked like had the programs of the experts been implemented?

8

An International Solution?

Intelligence is the divinity which reigns over all social and
economic phenomena . . . She will find solutions to all the
new and difficult problems appearing after the greatest war
humanity has ever experienced.
—Demètre I. Gheorghiu, Paris, November 1919

Schemes for an International Bank, like schemes for an
international police force, are too often a camouflage for
national irresponsibility.
—*Round Table*, December 1919

FOUR YEARS OF TOTAL WAR had shaken Europe's confidence in the
fundamental institutions and values of civilized society. No longer
was the nation-state so clearly the highest form of social organization, the gold standard the highest form of international monetary
order. The traditional pattern of creditor nations and debtor nations
lay in ruins. Could Britain, or any other nation, assume the burden
of "creditor of last resort" that went with the role of the world's
financial and monetary leader? Or would the prewar system be
replaced by new international financial and monetary institutions?
Would the war continue in the form of national economic rivalry, or
would a spirit of cooperation hasten the reconstruction of an international financial system?

The search for international solutions to Europe's postwar financial and monetary crisis produced meager results. Most schemes for
international financial and monetary cooperation were rejected as
crackpot ideas contrary to traditional notions of sound finance.
Creditor nations suspected most plans as attempts by nations with
shattered economies to evade responsibility for massive national and
international debts. With the failure of financial internationalism,
Europe fell back upon some shopworn notions of political and eco-

271

nomic nationalism, supplemented by a modified gold standard known as the gold-exchange standard.

The breakdown of the wartime Anglo-French-American financial entente dimmed hopes for international action against the postwar crisis during 1919. So long as the 1919–20 boom masked the gravity of the financial and monetary crisis, few experts and politicians understood the need for any international action aside from some temporary relief to prevent starvation in Eastern Europe. The Swedish economist Gustav Cassel was one of the first to recognize the crisis. In a 28 April 1919 letter to *The Economist*, he pointed to warning signals that could be ignored only at Europe's peril—declining trade, increasing unemployment, inflation and reduced purchasing power, and fluctuation of foreign exchange. The situation, Cassel warned, posed "a most formidable danger" for every country in the world, including those not seriously troubled at the moment. Lacking immediate steps to stabilize international monetary standards, "we shall run straight into the general collapse."[1] Within the next few months, the "general collapse" had begun.

By the autumn of 1919, other prominent economists had joined Cassel in calling for an international conference to lay the foundation for broad cooperation in Europe's financial and monetary reconstruction. At the request of the Netherlands' central banker, Gerard Vissering, several well-known economists from the United States, Britain, and France met on 13–14 October at Amsterdam to discuss Europe's urgent financial situation. Delegates from Sweden, Norway, Denmark, and Switzerland held a similar meeting on 2–3 November.

Out of these meetings came an "International Memorial" alerting the world's political leadership to the need for all-around solutions to the financial and monetary crisis. The Memorial called for an international conference to deal with creditor-debtor relationships (including German reparation payments), international credits and loans, and steps to balance national budgets. The Memorial suggested that owing to the inadequacy of normal banking channels to meet the postwar demand for credit, "a more comprehensive scheme is necessary." But unless the level of international indebtedness were somehow reduced, no comprehensive scheme could work. Germany and Austria, both invited to the conference, "must not be rendered bankrupt," warned the financiers. An adjustment of inter-

Allied debts must accompany any reduction in the debt of the Central Powers. The world's balance sheet had to be freed from some of the "fictitious items which now inflate it and lead to fear and despair on the part of some, and to recklessness on the part of others." The experts viewed "a deflation of the world's balance sheet" as the first step toward a cure.[2]

The framers of the International Memorial believed joint action would be effective only after vigorous steps by individual nations to set their own finances in order. Long-term credit was no substitute for national sacrifice. The financiers who drew up the Memorial followed an essentially Malthusian line of thought. Hardship and suffering represented the unfortunate facts of economic life. They believed that "it is only by the real economic conditions pressing severely, as they must, on the individual that equilibrium can be restored."[3]

Those countries most likely to be asked to make the greatest sacrifice for the common good tended to be least enthusiastic about an international conference. The Memorial appeared in American newspapers on 15 January 1920, on the 16th in Britain, and "some days later" in France, perhaps indicating some reticence among the French press. The six French delegates who participated in drawing up the Memorial had already attached reservations to the sections dealing with reduction of reparation obligations, new international loans taking precedence over other debt (including reparation payments), and the setting of a reasonable time for balancing national budgets. The paragraph advocating elimination of "fictitious items" from the world's balance sheet did not appear in the version of the Memorial published in the United States. Despite these hints of trouble, a glance at the list of signatories gave assurance that an international solution to the financial and monetary crisis was at hand. The version published in the United States bore the signatures of Andrew W. Mellon, Herbert Hoover, William Howard Taft, Elihu Root, J. P. Morgan, Jr., Frank Vanderlip, and Paul Warburg among the total of forty-four prominent Americans. Fifteen British leaders, including the chairman of each of London's major banks, signed the Memorial. If the financial leadership of the United States and Britain took the lead, the rest of the world would have no choice but to follow.[4]

Official reaction in Washington, London, and Paris, however, was negative. Secretary of the Treasury Carter Glass flatly rejected official American participation in any conference that might discuss additional United States loans and credits for Europe, and cancellation of all or part of Europe's obligations to the United States. Glass characterized these matters as "clearly not appropriate for consideration in such a conference as is contemplated by the memorial." Private channels would be only too willing to lend Europe additional credits as soon as the European states returned to sound fiscal policies.[5] Chancellor of the Exchequer Austen Chamberlain expressed his country's willingness to participate in an international financial conference, but only if the other participants understood that Britain was not prepared to grant further advances to other governments.[6] *The Economist*, disappointed that the United States would not participate in a conference which "ought to do some good," essentially agreed with Glass when it counseled that "ultimately every country must get its financial position right by paying its own way and checking its own financial debauchery."[7]

France held an ambiguous position as both a large debtor to the United States and the most powerful and determined creditor eligible for German reparation payments. At an international conference at which international indebtedness would be discussed—particularly one which Germany would attend and the United States would not—France stood to lose more than she could gain. The conference would have no trouble persuading Germany to accept a reduction in reparation obligations, but could never convince the United States to accept an adjustment of inter-Allied debt.

The French did not like the idea of victors and vanquished sitting around the same conference table as equals. Because the conference would be held under the auspices of the League of Nations, there was the possibility of League intervention in the internal financial affairs of sovereign nations. International loans might entail international controls on domestic finances. France feared a conference controlled by neutrals and other nations hardly affected by the war might attack the Versailles Treaty reparation clauses "under the pretext of facilitating the economic reconstruction of the world." In the French view, the League was becoming "a sort of financial consortium," thereby raising "the economic point of view over the political and moral point of view." The French believed "the ideas of Mr. Keynes" prevailed among the most ardent supporters of the proposed conference, and that alone was sufficient reason to stay away.[8]

The French Finance Ministry objected to discussion of practically every agenda item for the proposed Brussels financial conference. When Finance Minister François-Marsal received the proposed order of the day for the conference, he charged in an eight-page memorandum to the premier, Millerand, that the other participants had changed the agenda after France had agreed in principle to attend. When the League Council called for the conference on 13 February 1920, it was strictly a case of discussing the immediate world financial crisis and particularly the problems caused by exchange fluctuation. That was the conference France had agreed to attend.[9]

The agenda received from the League office in September, however, contained items concerning "commercial and economic questions" as well as "financial" matters that François-Marsal regarded as internal French business not subject to international discussion and control. In questions such as price differentials and export premiums, French interests differed profoundly from those of the British. And while conference recommendations regarding transit rights and foreign exchange controls might not be legally binding, France might have to "submit to moral constraint which could result to our detriment from discussion on this point at Brussels." The so-called "financial" portion of the conference might involve discussion of Germany's obligations under the Versailles Treaty. Even if that item were excluded from the agenda, it would be dangerous, warned the finance minister, to hold any discussions "around a table where neutrals and the Germans will be seated on a basis of equality with the Allies." The proposed consideration of "international loans" could easily touch the matter of repayment of prewar debts, which the French government considered a nonnegotiable issue. The agenda also mentioned financial questions of "exceptional gravity," such as the capital levy and compulsory loans. We do not want to take part in a conference, warned François-Marsal, if there is a risk of its voting for a policy of "class warfare and coercion."[10]

François-Marsal advised Millerand against French participation in the Brussels conference if the new agenda stood. France should demand that no questions relating to the Armistice or succeeding treaties be placed in discussion at Brussels. The finance minister proposed to Millerand a new agenda and some procedural stipulations, including the requirement of a unanimous vote for adoption of any resolution. He suggested to Léon Bourgeois, president of the League Council at the time, some additional procedural changes. He dropped his demand for unanimous votes, but asked for secret ballots and the provision that delegations might review and change their votes within twenty-four hours of the ballot.[11] These French-imposed limitations, combined with the absence of an official representative from the United States, virtually guaranteed that the Brussels conference would be little more than a discussion of competing financial theories among politically impotent experts.

Between 24 September and 8 October 1920, eighty-six representatives from thirty-nine countries governing three-fourths of the world's population met in Brussels to discuss and propose solutions to the world's financial and monetary crisis. Perhaps because most of the delegates represented the financial and intellectual establishment, the final resolutions adopted by the conference contained little that was startling or innovative. There were a few diplomats and politicians, fewer still representatives of labor. The Soviets were not represented at Brussels because they were not invited. The United States sent Ronald W. Boyden as its unofficial delegate. Strictly speaking *all* delegates were unofficial representatives of their respective countries—a point made clear at a procedural session held on the second day of the conference. That meeting decided that the delegates were to be regarded as experts and technicians whose votes represented only their personal opinions. The states that had appointed these delegates would in no way be bound to accept responsibility for implementing any resolutions adopted by the conference. Boyd's unofficial status was thus in fact no different from that of the other delegates, but Carter Glass's public refusal to send an official delegation had already created much dissatisfaction in Europe.[12]

Committees on Public Finance, Currency and Exchange, International Trade, and International Credit studied the issues and submitted reports and recommendations for the approval of the plenary conference. But before the conference opened, a committee of five experts met in Paris on 6 July to draw up a statement that set the tone of the proceedings. The document drafted by A. C. Pigou (Britain), Charles Gide (France), N. Panteleoni (Italy), Gustav

Cassel (Sweden), and G. Bruins (Netherlands) stressed Europe's need to resume production and work. To achieve that end, the experts recommended that governments balance their budgets, cease borrowing, consolidate floating debt, cut government spending by abolishing subsidies and restricting military expenditure, and raise interest rates to reflect the real scarcity of capital. New international credits should not be extended to states that failed to take these steps.[13]

The final resolutions adopted by the Brussels conference "emphasized those principles of economic and financial policy which were regarded at the time as most sound and constructive." The Committee on Public Finance stressed the need to make the public understand that government deficits were largely responsible for inflation, currency depreciation, and unstable foreign exchange. Budgets had to be balanced through spending cuts and higher taxes. While these fiscal resolutions were adopted unanimously, the French delegate on the Public Finance Committee, Joseph Avenol (the Finance Ministry's financial agent in London), had rejected them during Committee discussions. He charged the British delegation with attempting to impose its notions of sound fiscal policy on countries like France, which had no choice but to borrow more funds for national reconstruction.[14]

Resolutions on Currency and Exchange recommended that all countries establish central banks of issue. Central banks required freedom from political control so that they might operate under principles of "prudent finance." Governments must stop forcing central banks to issue additional currency, and permit interest rates set by central banks to once again regulate the money markets. "Futile and mischievous" foreign exchange controls must be removed. The Currency and Exchange Committee rejected proposals for innovative money and credit schemes with the argument that "neither an international currency nor an international unit of account would serve any useful purpose." There was only one way to restore depreciated and ruined currencies—a return to the gold standard at either the prewar parity or a new ratio that could be held comfortably. But the Committee warned that currency stabilization itself could not work until fundamental economic and financial stability had been restored throughout the world.[15]

The Committee on International Credits recommended an end to intergovernmental loans. International credits should be drawn only from real savings and should be granted to private interests rather than to governments. If some countries required temporary assistance of such magnitude as to require aid from foreign governments, it should be granted only to those nations which were friendly toward their neighbors, demonstrated a spirit of cooperation among their own people, and gave assurances that the nation was working hard and economizing. Under these terms, most observers believed, the Soviet government would not qualify for international assistance.[16] The only concrete plan for providing international credits for the promotion of trade adopted by the Brussels conference was a scheme proposed by C. E. Ter Meulen of the Netherlands. This project, which involved government guarantees, is discussed below.

What did the Brussels conference accomplish? Very little, in the sense of concrete financial and monetary reform. The editor of *Le monde économique* wrote that the conference resolutions "simply repeated, with the pomp adequate to the circumstances, what everyone has known for a long time"—that Europe's reconstruction required a return to the gold standard, sound finance, and balanced budgets. *The Round Table* believed the conference resolutions proved once again that financial stability could be achieved only "by governments and citizens recognizing their poverty and learning to live within their means." But the British economist Dennis Holme Robertson ridiculed the achievements of Brussels. A number of "wise and well-disposed men," several of whom had been "well trained in economic theory" had met in Brussels and recommended that "governments should forthwith reduce their expenditures and balance their budgets. Which was very good advice, and about as much use as recommending a drowning man to keep dry."[17]

Paradoxically, this conference of experts meeting unofficially in the absence of the diplomats and politicians turned out to be a diplomatic triumph for each of the Great Powers—Britain, France, the United States, and Germany. The mere fact that Germany received an invitation represented a diplomatic coup for the nation that only the year before had been forced to sign the Treaty of Versailles. The French delegation performed well and at least temporarily rehabilitated France's image as a responsible member of the European community. The failure of the Brussels conference strengthened America's diplomatic position, as it now became clear that European financial reconstruction could not succeed without the consent and active support of the United States government. But the biggest winner at Brussels was Britain.

Led by Cokayne from the Bank and Lord Chalmers from the Treasury, the British delegation convinced the Brussels conference to accept British notions of sound finance. The conference has been described as "the first European attempt, led by England, to impose a combined political-economic reconstruction plan on the United States."[18] This may be overstating the case, but Lord Chalmers himself reported to Chamberlain that the British government had every reason to be pleased with the results of the conference. He singled out the report of the Committee on Public Finance, whose "merit lies not in any novelty of the remedies it suggests," but in its affirmation of the principles of "sound finance." The Currency and Exchange Committee was to be commended for its "adherence to sound prescriptions when so many tempting and illusory remedies were put forward." The Committee's final report represented a "compromise" between the "Dear Money" delegates and the "Cheap Money" delegates. Overall, the conference produced, "for the enlightenment of public opinion and for the guidance of Governments, a conspectus of expert opinion on financial difficulties."[19]

By most accounts, the French delegation at Brussels reversed the commonly held notion of French financial irresponsibility and intransigence. According to *Le Matin*, the Allies now recognized France's sincerity in working toward "the restoration of our damage to the extent compatible with the capacity of Germany," whereas "prior to this conference, we were suspected of wishing to use our credit [against Germany] for political ends damaging to the reestablishment of economic peace in Europe."[20] E. F. Wise, formerly Britain's representative on the Supreme Economic Council and now an official in the Ministry of Food, received confirmation of the favorable impression left by the French from an informant connected with the League of Nations. Identified only as "Ted," the informant conceded that prior to the Brussels conference, "the general view amongst neutral financiers (largely shared in the City), was that France is the worst sinner financially. French policy was regarded as imperialistic, chauvinistic, and reactionary, and her financial policy a mere rake's progress." But as the conference broke up, "many delegates, the British among them, must have gone away with the impression that France is much maligned. Her representatives were moderate, enlightened, and conciliatory." Had France really moderated her position on reparations, inter-Allied debts, budget deficits, and currency inflation? Wise's informant thought not. Premier Millerand, he claimed, "could get no French financier or even politician to go to the Conference." France was thus represented by three officials from the Finance Ministry, Célier, Avenol, and Cheysson. "These three," explained the informant, "played their cards admirably, but they hardly represented French policy, still less French public opinion."[21]

As François-Marsal had feared, the Brussels conference did threaten French interests, and the French delegates were unable to defeat the will of the majority. The conference, for example, voted to establish under the League of Nations a new Economic and Financial Committee to complement the League's Committee on International Credits. The French delegates on the new Committee were certain to be outvoted by the other twenty members. François-Marsal believed it would be "extremely dangerous" to invest any French official with important functions on a committee which the French government did not control. Backed by Premier Leygues and Léon Bourgeois, the finance minister stipulated that French representatives on the League's Economic and Financial Committee should have little authority to act on their own and that the appointment of non-French delegates should be subject to a French veto.[22] Such stipulations, of course, would render the new Committee impotent.

If the Brussels conference failed to bring forth practical solutions to Europe's financial and monetary crisis, it was owing to a combination of factors—the incompetence of some of the delegates, a desire to protect special interests, popular disenchantment with any type of government intervention, and basic structural weaknesses in the capitalist system itself. Wise's British friend at the League, "Ted," captured all of these points in his perceptive account of the Brussels conference. The Dutch delegation, which included Vissering and Ter Meulen, was the most influential and best informed. The competence of some of the British delegates, however, remained dubious. Chalmers, who replaced R. H. Brand (chairman of Lloyd's Bank) as head of the Committee on Public Finance when

Brand came down with the flu, held a critical position at the confer- ence. Wise's correspondent wrote that "I heard from one of Lord Chalmer's staff that he did not know where the Ruhr was." All of the delegates, in fact, were "self-complacent and dreary old men" who only "made explicit and unmistakable what many of us have been suspecting for a long time, viz.—the complete intellectual bank- ruptcy of capitalism." The conference sought to discover a way back to the prewar economic system, but never considered "at what cost in human sacrifice can this pre-war system be restored?" There was never any thought of "an alternative system of co-operation and democratic organization of production and finance." When the financial "robber barons" spoke of "International Cooperation" they meant nothing more than a system allowing them to "meet together in a more friendly way to discuss their economic interests."[23]

At the Brussels conference, the world's financiers joined in "a gen- eral condemnation of every kind of government activity. The whole tone of the Conference was strongly anti-government, even anti- nationalist." The delegates "demanded that governments should get out of commerce and finance." On the other hand, reported Wise's informant, "the League of Nations has done well out of the Conference. Every scheme, nearly every resolution calls on the League of Nations to do something. I think they see in the League a way of dishing their own Governments. They hate their own Gov- ernments so much that they quite love us." This antigovernment, antinationalist attitude "gave a certain unreality to the debates and resolutions." The delegates "paid no regard to the strong forces of public opinion which compel governments to act—on the one side Nationalism, on the other side Socialism."[24]

Wise's unidentified observer at the League headquarters was one of the very few who understood the essence of Europe's interwar crisis. Of Europe's leadership between 1918 and 1945, only Musso- lini, Hitler, and Stalin understood the fundamental role played by both nationalism and socialism in modern political systems. Fascism, National Socialism, and Communism offered the only "alternative system" of economic organization. Postwar European stand-pat capitalism was indeed intellectually bankrupt.

Following Brussels, there was no major European financial con- ference until the Genoa conference during the spring of 1922. Dur- ing the interval, the League of Nations unsuccessfully attempted to implement the Ter Meulen plan for international credits approved at Brussels. Financial experts suggested many other schemes for the rehabilitation of the world's financial and monetary system. Most of the programs suggested involved the creation of new international financial institutions or new international paper monetary units. Proponents of a return to the prewar status quo inevitably opposed any proposal that might complicate the ultimate return to gold. The more innovative the plan, the more likely it was to be rejected.

An American, Frederick Mathews, made one of the earliest propositions for new international financial institutions. Educated in Paris, Mathews was visiting France in 1914 when the war broke out. He remained abroad and eventually received official assignments in the devastated regions of France. In a 1914 publication, *Taxation and the Distribution of Wealth*, Mathews proposed a central Allied bank patterned after the United States Federal Reserve Board. In 1919, he renewed his call for what he now termed an Inter-Ally Reserve Board again based on the Federal Reserve System. The Board would control a central reserve fund consisting of gold or negotiable instruments subscribed by each of the Allies. It would handle all inter-Allied credits and inter-Allied banking transactions.[25]

Woodrow Wilson's concept of a political League of Nations led to discussion, particularly among French politicians, of a complementary Financial League of Nations. The idea of a Financial League often appeared in conjunction with propositions for sharing the financial burden of the war equitably among the Allies. Under one such scheme proposed in the Chamber of Deputies by Jacques Stern in December 1918, a Financial League would issue a 5 percent international loan, payable in fifty years, guaranteed by tariff receipts, railway revenues, and other excise receipts collected by each Allied government. The French government never formally embraced Stern's proposal, but Klotz did suggest at the Paris Peace Conference that the Allies share the financial burden of the war.[26]

Proposals to create an international bank empowered to issue a new international currency—the "tempting and illusory remedies" to which Lord Chalmers referred—came from reputable economists. Bertrand Nogaro, professor of political economy at Caen in 1919, advanced a plan to increase the amount of disposable international currency by issuing a quantity of notes equivalent to the world stock of circulating gold, approximately 50 or 60 billion francs.

Debtor nations such as France, Belgium, Italy, and Serbia would use these notes to settle their international accounts. Provided the creditor nations would accept them, such notes would pass quickly to the United States and Britain. Nogaro conceded that creating currency in this manner contradicted the conventional wisdom that monetary circulation must rest on a metallic reserve. Why should Britain and the United States accept pieces of paper in return for real goods and services? What would they do with such currency? Nogaro observed that after the notes of the Bank of France had become legal tender for the liquidation of all internal debts under the *cours forcé*, they had become accepted with confidence in France. If international bank notes received status as legal tender in each of the contracting nations, they, too, would be accepted by the public.[27]

Responsible bankers as well as ivory-tower professors proposed new monetary schemes. During a European tour in November 1921, Frank A. Vanderlip, former president of the National City Bank in New York, outlined a new central bank which he called the Gold Reserve Bank for the United States of Europe. Nogaro, now a member of the faculty of law at the University of Paris, wrote approvingly of Vanderlip's project. The bank's initial capital of $1 billion (gold value) would be divided between a series of shares for American subscribers and a series for European subscribers. European shares were to be nonreimbursable, while American shares could be redeemed at any time at 120 percent of face value. With a gold reserve of 20 percent, the bank would be empowered to issue notes convertible to gold.[28]

Vanderlip's plan was designed to channel American capital into Europe and provide the United States an outlet for its excess gold. As a rediscount bank, the Gold Reserve Bank would furnish credit to European banks, and the credit would form a new international currency. The new money would help revive Europe's trade. Reasonable on its face, Vanderlip's scheme did have one flaw that supporters including Nogaro admitted—why would the new money retain its gold value and resist exchange fluctuation any better than the national currencies it was to supplement?[29]

Of the schemes for rehabilitating international trade, C. E. Ter Meulen's plan received the most widespread acceptance by the international financial community. For the financiers, the plan's chief merit was that it minimized the role of any international body

—trade exchanges were to take place between private importers and exporters—involved no government-to-government loans, and appeared to provide reliable guarantees for the credits granted. But despite its apparent advantages, the Ter Meulen plan approved by the Brussels conference never became operational.

Ter Meulen's plan constituted an alternative to a proposal submitted to the Brussels conference by the Belgian prime minister, Léon Delacroix. Delacroix proposed an International Institute of Issue empowered to issue "gold bonds" which were to be accepted by creditors. The Institute would grant such bonds to borrowing states against "reliable guarantees" including joint liability of the country's banks, specified tax revenues, customs revenues, agricultural yields, and mineral production. The Institute would verify the reliability of these guarantees, establish their gold value, and issue short-term bonds against them. The Institute would limit its issue to the actual requirements of international trade, and because the bonds would represent real values, they would create no inflationary pressure. After each use, the gold bonds would be returned to the Institute for reissue to new borrowers.[30]

Delacroix's proposal met opposition from financiers who wished to place responsibility for the issue of any new bonds in the hands of individual governments rather than with a new International Institute of Issue. Ter Meulen, an Amsterdam banker, offered a plan to overcome this objection the following day. His proposition called for the creation of an International Commission under League auspices. Governments wishing to participate in the project would inform the Commission what specific guarantees they were willing to provide as collateral against commercial credits that might be granted by the Commission. The Commission would examine these guarantees—tax receipts or other securities specifically pledged for this purpose—and fix the gold value of the credits it might be willing to authorize. Participating governments, rather than the Commission itself, could then issue bonds for the gold value approved by the Commission and guaranteed by the governments involved. Importers would then borrow from their own government bonds sufficient to cover their private transactions. The exporters would hold these bonds until they had been paid off.[31]

Ter Meulen's plan represented nothing more than a limited scheme to make available credit for the revival of international trade.

As described by Sir Drummond D. Fraser, the British administrator appointed by the League of Nations to implement it, the plan "does not claim to be the panacea for all the troubles that exist today."[32] It was the very modesty of the proposal that most appealed to its supporters. His plan precisely matched the conditions for an "international loan" set forth by Cassel at Brussels in his *Memorandum on the World's Monetary Problems*. Cassel had warned Europe to abandon its "fantastic ideas of huge world loans, sufficient to make up at once for all the damage caused by the war." Properly understood, an international loan could be nothing more than "a form for financing an export surplus from the lending world to the borrowing."[33] This is precisely what the Ter Meulen plan amounted to.

Two years after the Brussels conference had approved Ter Meulen's plan, this most modest of proposals remained a dead letter. An embarrassed League of Nations Economic and Financial Committee conceded in August 1922 that "some explanation is required of the fact that up to now, no use has been made of the plan by countries it was desiged to benefit." The League had taken steps to implement the plan. The Economic and Financial Committee redrafted the proposal into a detailed plan consisting of sixteen clauses. The League Council accepted the Committee's work on 14 December 1920, and entrusted the Committee with the execution of the program. In March 1921, the Committee set up an International Credits Department in London, and appointed the newly appointed "organizer," Sir Drummond Drummond Fraser, to coordinate the entire process. As a director of the Manchester and Liverpool District Bank, Fraser was expected to obtain the cooperation of the international banking community. For the next year, he worked to acquaint the various governments with the plan, worked out the details of its implementation, and sought the support of governments and financiers throughout the world.[34]

In Fraser, the League had found a respected banker committed to implementing the Ter Meulen plan. What the League really needed was a magician. Under the imprint of the League, Fraser published a pamphlet explaining the scheme. He had to demonstrate that the program was practical from a business point of view, that it would merely supplement and not replace normal commercial transactions, and that the state of the international economy was desperate enough to require special measures—but not so desperate as to require radical solutions that went farther than the Ter Meulen plan. Fraser hoped to reassure the business community that this was not some wild scheme to reconstruct the entire financial and monetary system. He promised to administer the program *"as a practical business man* [his italics]". Government intervention was to be limited to overcoming "abnormal obstacles" to business, to "strengthening the weak links in the chain of *normal commercial transactions* [his italics]." He would avoid so far as possible the construction of and reliance on "abnormal types of machinery."[35]

Fraser's efforts appeared to be paying off. The World Cotton Conference (Manchester and Liverpool, June 1921) and the International Chamber of Commerce (London, June 1921) endorsed the Ter Meulen plan. But the real test came in the United States, the world's storehouse of credit, and here the picture was cloudy. Benjamin Strong wrote Montagu Norman that he was "not at all hopeful" about the Ter Meulen scheme and "discouraged" about the success of export credit corporations being organized under the Edge Act. These programs were insufficient to meet Europe's requirements, and overlooked the fact that "the volume of business to be done is limited not by the amount of capital that can be raised, but by the quality of the business which is available to be done abroad." Political instability in Central and Eastern Europe deterred investment and credit. Of what value were government guarantees if the governments were going to be overthrown?[36]

Fraser took his case to the American Bankers' Association meeting in Los Angeles on 6 October 1921, delivered speeches to bankers and financiers in Los Angeles, San Francisco, and St. Louis, and held conversations with the comptroller of the currency and the governor of the Federal Reserve Board in Washington. At the close of his American tour, Fraser told the British ambassador in Washington that the Ter Meulen plan "was winning favor here." But Geddes was not so sure, and informed Foreign Secretary Lord Curzon that "the practical results of his visit will be difficult to determine for some time."[37] But Fraser and the British press believed American financiers would participate in the Ter Meulen program. *The Economist* noted that the American Bankers' Association had approved the scheme, and the League Economic and Financial Committee claimed that "the authoritatives [sic] of American finance were in particular persuaded of its merits. The Federal Reserve Board gave its complete approval to the plan, which it considered suitable to meet the needs of the various types of foreign trade financing."[38] Why, then, did the Ter Meulen plan fail to materialize?

Prospective borrowers and lenders found the Ter Meulen plan equally objectionable. For reasons of national pride and national security, borrowing nations were reluctant to surrender control over a portion of their national revenues and finances. Some borrowers found better terms elsewhere—Rumania and Bulgaria obtained credits in Switzerland, France, and Belgium. European borrowers continued to hope for more lenient terms from the United States. Lending nations, particularly the United States, viewed state-guaranteed credit as a clumsy mechanism involving unacceptable delay. In case of default, the process of recovery under the Ter Meulen plan was lengthy and complicated. Conventional lenders did not wish to tie up funds in relatively long-term credits under the Ter Meulen program. Because the plan was designed primarily to assist Eastern European countries with imports of raw materials needed to resume production, it held little interest for American, British, and French exporters of manufactured goods. Lenders, of course, could not guarantee approval of every application for credit. For a prospective borrower nation, the risk of an embarrassing rejection furnished a strong disincentive to seek credits.

For the United States, there was a disturbing connection between the proposed Ter Meulen credits and existing inter-Allied debt. According to Carl Parrini, the United States ambassador to Belgium, Brand Whitlock, claimed that the use of assets and revenues to secure Ter Meulen bonds would reduce the ability of borrowing governments to meet existing debts. Parrini concluded that "this meant that the Europeans were trying to evade settlement of war debts owed the United States."[39] Any American suspicion along these lines would have sufficed to kill the plan during the best of times, but the economic\crisis of 1920–21 rendered attempts to implement the scheme virtually hopeless. To some extent, accumulations of stocks and the easing of credit during the recession reduced the need for Ter Meulen credits.

Even though the Ter Meulen plan had not yet been implemented two years after its approval at the Brussels conference, the League's Economic and Financial Committee claimed that the knowledge that emergency credits might be available had helped restore economic confidence in Europe. Moreover, the plan's requirement of government revenues and public assets as security against credits had, according to the Committee, spurred reform of public finance in certain countries. The Committee reported to the League that it "has received reliable evidence proving that the Governments of these countries have had a direct incentive to put their finances in order."[40] The "evidence" proved no such thing to David Lloyd George, who believed it would require another general European financial conference—this one dominated by politicians rather than experts—to reconstruct Europe's economy. The British prime minister placed great hope in the Genoa conference of 10 April–19 May 1922.

Parrini has described the Genoa conference as an attempt by Britain and other European nations to control the reconstruction of Russia, relegate the United States to second place among the great economic powers, and solve their raw material and foreign exchange problems.[41] If these were the goals of the conference, then it must be classed as a failure, largely because neither the United States nor France wished to play the roles Lloyd George had cast for them. The American note declining the invitation to attend the conference in an official capacity appeared to place the burden on French intransigence. France had placed an "embargo" on any discussion of reparations. "It is not," observed the American response, "primarily an economic conference, as questions are excluded without a satisfactory determination of which the chief causes of economic disturbance must continue to operate. The Conference is of a political character, and the American people do not wish to become involved in European political questions."[42]

The British were setting up the French to take the blame should the Genoa conference fail as a result of American refusal to participate. Norman told Strong that he expected little from Genoa—"Poincaré will probably prevent that."[43] The British government intimated to Paris that the three-year moratorium on war debt payments might not be renewed when it expired at the end of April 1922. Americans believed the timing of this threat was "designed to show France the impossibility of excluding from the Genoa discussions the problems of reparations and inter-allied debts."[44] Strong-arm tactics against Poincaré did not work, and France held fast to its position.

Unofficial but informed American sources suggested that the State Department's rejection of the invitation to Genoa rested on something more than France's intransigence on reparations. On 18 February, Strong wrote Norman that he believed Washington favored participation, subject to certain reservations concerning the proposed agenda. The United States shared France's reluctance to sit at the same table with the Soviets. Just as France did not wish to discuss reparations, the United States did not wish to discuss inter-Allied debts. Strong also observed that the United States would not enter into any discussions that would probably lead to further American financial support for Europe so long as "certain European nations" refused to discuss their allegedly extravagant military expenditures. On 4 March Strong reiterated to Norman that the United States would probably refuse to participate in any international conference until other nations reduced their military spending, balanced their budgets, ceased the inflation of their currencies, and agreed to settle the reparation question on sound, practical lines.[45] These references could refer only to France.

French intransigence over the reparation question was only one of the factors influencing the new Harding administration's rejection of the invitation to Genoa. France's performance at the Washington Conference, which ended in February, had left a sour taste of French militarism among the top Republican leadership. Many Americans rejected Lloyd George's claim that Russian rehabilitation held the key to Europe's recovery just as they rejected France's claim to military and economic priority. By 1922, opinion in the United States believed Germany's economic restoration formed the keystone in the revitalization of Europe.[46] In this belief the Americans were joined by many prominent British financiers who did not share Lloyd George's enthusiasm for a *rapprochement* with the Russians at Genoa. Walter Leaf, chairman of London County Westminster and Parr's Bank, represented those in the City who doubted Russia's capacity to contribute much to European recovery. If Russia was to be the focus of the conference, then Leaf "would be sorry to stake much on any result that may come from the promised conference at Genoa." "It is to Central Europe, and notably to Germany," he believed, "that we must look for recovery." Until Germany recovered, "there seems to be little prospect of our return to normal prosperity," and "it would follow that our first policy should be to help

Germany on her legs again."[47] France could not accept this conclusion even if it meant her ioslation from both Britain and the United States.

Many have viewed the Genoa conference as the supreme test of Lloyd George's stature as one of Britain's greatest modern statesmen. Perhaps the prime minister himself claimed too much for the conference and raised popular expectations beyond a reasonable level. He portrayed Genoa not as an effort to stabilize exchanges or improve currencies, but rather as an opportunity to bring real peace to Europe. Perhaps Lloyd George did not fully realize, as did *The Economist*, that "a complete fiasco at Genoa would merely discredit the vital principle of international cooperation" and dash any hope for the revitalization of Europe. The conference was hastily thrown together, leaving the participating governments insufficient time to prepare adequately. *The Economist* speculated that Lloyd George's sagging political fortunes at home had prevailed over common sense. An unfortunate conjuncture of domestic political developments and "Mr. Lloyd George's chronic predilection for rush tactics" had driven the world into a conference before the time is ripe."[48]

Before the Genoa conference opened *The Economist* predicted trouble if Britain attempted to impose its solutions on the rest of Europe, and criticized Lloyd George for his tendency toward heavy-handed dealings with the Allies. The political intuition that served the prime minister so well in domestic politics had apparently "deserted him and allowed him to misinterpret international psychology." Lloyd George had not attended the conference at Brussels and Washington, or the assemblies of the League of Nations, where he might have learned the "true spirit of international cooperation." Britain's prime minister, wrote *The Economist*, "still clings to the auction-room atmosphere of the Supreme Council long after other nations have learned to appreciate the clearer air of Geneva and Washington." The Great Powers would have to avoid the appearance of laying down the law for other countries, and "until Mr. Lloyd George in particular rids himself of the idea of a diplomatic oligarchy of Allied statesmen settling the affairs of Europe, he will be unable to play the great part in Europe's reconstruction for which his great gifts and experience equip him."[49]

As an economic and financial conference, Genoa has passed into oblivion. Financial, economic, and transportation committees formulated resolutions which, according to one estimate, "aroused not a flicker of interest in the mind of any but those actually sitting on the commissions handling the technical problems." Sir Laming Worthington-Evans, the British war minister who assumed the chairmanship of the Genoa finance committee from Sir Robert Horne mid-way through the conference, told a plenary session that the financial code of Genoa would one day rival in importance the legal code of Justinian, "but the eminent financiers . . . freely gave it as their opinion in private that nothing of consequence was said or done in the Genoa discussions that had not been said or done elsewhere before."[50]

With the help of Keynes, the British delegation prepared important proposals on exchange stabilization and a return to the gold standard. In France, an interministerial committee charged with making preparations for the conference concentrated on issues that were more political than financial—Russian trade, Russian debts, Russian concessions to foreign investors. In these discussions, the Finance Ministry argued that the reconstruction of Eastern Europe and Russia must be a truly international enterprise, and ruled out any scheme for distributing zones of influence to particular western countries.[51] In a free-for-all for Russian resources, Britain would win the upper hand. This the French were determined to forestall.

In his program for action at Genoa, Keynes saw no stabilization solution "practicable now" except the "traditional" one of "a gold standard in as many countries as possible." He observed that most countries were more interested in raising the value of their currency than in stabilizing it at a particular level. This amounted to a "deliberate policy of altering" exchanges and ran counter to the pressing need for stabilization. Only Britain, Holland, Sweden, Switzerland, and Spain could reasonably hope to restore prewar parity soon. The others would have to be content with some other rate. "It would make but small difference to the financial prestige of France," argued Keynes, "whether the franc was stabilized at 40 or 50 to the gold sovereign." Countries whose currencies were weak had to be willing to devalue in order to stabilize at a level they could maintain. Ideally, the stabilization value chosen should be final and permanent, but as a "moderate concession to popular illusion," Keynes would contemplate an annual increase in the gold value of stabilized currencies of not more than 6 percent.[52]

Disregarding *The Economist*'s warning against proposing dubious expedients which the rest of Europe could never accept, the British Treasury prepared for Genoa a stabilization plan based on Keynes's suggestions. It called for an international agreement to establish a gold-exchange standard. Adherents would determine and fix the gold value of their monetary units—not necessarily at their prewar gold parity—and would maintain the chosen value under pain of suspension from full membership in the system.[53] Europe eventually adopted a gold-exchange standard, but France and Belgium resisted it at Genoa. They viewed the British plan as an attempt to force devaluation on the French and Belgian franc, while Britain and a few other favored nations pursued a deflationary program aimed at restoration of prewar gold parities. The franc would become a second-class currency against the American dollar and the British pound. Vissering, the president of the Netherlands Bank, supported the British position, suggesting that France and Belgium stabilize at about 40 to 50 percent of prewar parity and, at an "opportune" moment, replace their paper currencies with a new stabilized monetary unit at a rate of 2 or 2.5 paper francs to 1 gold franc. Vissering's proposition brought a fiery response from the Belgian delegate, who compared Vissering's suggestion with the "demonetizing measures of Philippe le Bel and the princes of the Middle Ages, measures which shook so severely popular confidence in the value of currency." He announced Belgium's determination to restore "by degrees" the Belgian paper franc to the value of a gold franc.[54]

To avoid more of these head-on clashes in public, Horne announced his intent to appoint a Committee of Experts to study the deflation-devaluation controversy and deliver its findings to the Currency Subcommittee of the Finance Committee. When the Soviet delegate asked for the appointment of a Soviet expert, Horne declined, assuring Rakowsky that the appointees would serve "as representatives of a universal science" rather than as representatives of their respective countries.[55] As chairman of these representatives of universal science, Horne appointed his colleague from the British Treasury, Sir Basil Blackett.

The Committee of Experts submitted a compromise proposal that the plenary session of the Genoa conference adopted. Restoration of prewar gold parities was desirable, but probably beyond the reach of many countries. Each nation was free to decide for itself whether to devalue or deflate, but the greatest contribution to European reconstruction would be made by those countries which chose to stabilize promptly at a new gold parity that could be maintained with reasonable certainty.[56] By thwarting a recommendation of mandatory devaluation, the anti-British forces had won a victory at Genoa. The British Foreign Office understood what this freedom of choice would mean. A minute to the Report of the Committee of Experts noted that "France and Italy have declared that devaluation is not to apply to them: in other words that they intend to perpetuate instability so far as the franc and the lira are concerned."[57]

Keynes expressed disappointment with the "old and stale declarations" emanating from Genoa and the nonbinding resolution on devaluation and stabilization. He sent Lloyd George's private secretary a copy of a just-completed article in which he called for a second Washington conference of central bankers and Treasury representatives to set up a gold standard.[58] The Genoa resolutions merely called for an international agreement to centralize and coordinate the demand for gold and economize its use should a gold standard be resurrected. The Bank of England was to call a meeting to set up such machinery, but, for one reason or another, Montagu Norman never found an appropriate moment to summon the conference. Other claims, such as inter-Allied debts, reparations, and the financial rehabilitation of central Europe, consumed the time and energy of Europe's central bankers.[59]

If the Genoa conference failed, it was, as Cassel observed, because the "official policy of Europe is at present moving in an absolutely fictitious world." Europe's financial and monetary policy was based on several illusions. There was the illusion that the intergovernmental debts from the war and postwar period could be or would be paid off, that financial equilibrium could be restored through increased taxation, and that the victors could recover economically while Germany was prevented deliberately from doing so. The Genoa conference, wrote Cassel, posted a "No Trespassing" sign on these illusions, and "thus the whole Conference was from the outset put on an altogether artificial basis." Without discussing the essential causes of the sickness, the conference was somehow to recommend a cure.[60]

Who was perpetuating these illusions? While the French pressed for reparation payments, the government of the United States demanded repayment of every penny of inter-Allied debt and refused additional credits to a war-torn Europe. The "intransigence" of the French was matched by the "intransigence" of Wilson, Glass, Houston, Harding, Hoover, Hughes, and Mellon. Melvyn P. Leffler has found the Wilson administration "initially sympathetic" and the Harding administration initially "not unsympathetic" to France's postwar financial requirements, but as the record set forth in the present work indicates, any such sympathy soon evaporated. Leffler attributes the fragility of France's position to America's conflicting desires to insure French security, promote European reconstruction through a revival of the German economy, and protect the interests of American industry and agriculture. A recalcitrant Congress thwarted the desire of the United States Treasury to extend a helping hand.[61] It is nevertheless difficult to escape the conclusion that the sympathy expressed by the United States Treasury was often nothing more than an attempt to humor the French, and that the intransigent Congress was a convenient screen for the Treasury's own reluctance to bend.

The British government thus found itself uncomfortably placed between two intransigents, one a creditor and the other a debtor. Because the British, too, owed the United States money, they tended to support the French position in theory. But as a practical people, the British understood that their material interests favored an eventual accommodation with the United States. Britain conceded that neither the French nor the Americans had taken a sensible position at Genoa. After the conference, the chancellor of the exchequer, Horne, told the British Bankers' Association that Genoa had failed because discussion of inter-Allied debts and reparations had been blocked. Without a settlement of the reparation question, exchanges could not be stabilized. Horne estimated that half the bill presented to Germany under the 1921 London Schedule of Payments represented debts that the Allies owed each other. "Therefore," Horne concluded, "when you begin to deal with the reparations bill you cannot get very far before you get right up against the problem of inter-Allied indebtedness."[62]

Lloyd George had indicated to French Minister for Liberated Regions Louis Loucheur at Chequers in December 1921 that he intended Genoa to be a general conference for the discussion of both reparations and inter-Allied debts. According to the British Foreign

Office, "it was apparently only after telegrams from Washington made it clear that the United States would have no part in such a conference that Mr. Lloyd George, a fortnight later, at the London meeting of December, 1921, evolved the idea of a general conference which (without the participation of America) was to reconstruct European trade, and so make possible the payment of reparations." Having retreated in the face of American opposition to discussion of inter-Allied debts, Lloyd George now encountered resistance from Paris, and "this idea, as we know, had to be yet further greatly modified some weeks later when M. Poincaré refused in February, 1922 to admit the discussion of reparations at Genoa, with the result that the conference finally degenerated simply into an attempt to come to some agreement with Russia."[63] Poincaré's intransigence on reparation discussions at Genoa was nothing more than a reaction to America's intransigence on the inter-Allied debts.

In Paris, comparisons were made between America's promotion of the Washington naval armaments limitation conference—which the United States government considered advantageous—and America's refusal to send official delegates to Genoa, "where a certain sacrifice of United States immediate financial interests might be required." Initially, the French were pleased to see the United States torpedo a conference that neither government wished to attend. But as it became clear that the conference would be held with or without American participation, more mature reflection led the French government to realize that "a conference of debtors in the absence of the chief creditor cannot achieve much." The French agreed to attend Genoa with "a malicious hope" that Europe would raise itself from financial and commercial chaos without American assistance.[64]

There was a logical connection between the successful Washington naval conference and the disastrous Genoa financial conference. In his opening remarks of 12 November 1921, Secretary of State Hughes strictly limited the scope of the conference to the question of naval armaments. This represented an attempt to squash moves by British and French officials, supported by segments of the American business community, to place financial questions on the conference agenda. During the Washington conference, Loucheur allegedly asked the Belgian government to sound out American officials on the possibility of calling an economic conference in Washington immediately following the naval discussions. French Premier

Briand had apparently picked up the idea in Washington that "remission of inter-allied debts was in the region of practical politics." Belgium's foreign minister thought Briand was mistaken, and Assistant Secretary for Foreign Affairs Sir William George Tyrrell thought Briand "must have been singularly misinformed" by Loucheur, whose business interests would benefit from improvement in French exchange if talks on the adjustment of inter-Allied debt could be started. France's activities at the Washington conference puzzeled Tyrrell. The French made what the British and Americans considered outrageous demands for a large navy, and "having thus produced the worst possible atmosphere for an economic conference the French approach the Belgian Government in order to induce the latter to bring the question up." Tyrrell advised that the matter of financial discussions "should be absolutely taboo until the disarmament and Pacific agreements have been finally negotiated and accepted."[65] If the French wanted financial discussions, they would first have to agree to reasonable military limitations.

Financial discussions, however, were not taboo during the Washington conference. On 12 December, the *Pall Mall Gazette* carried an interview with financier Sir Edward Mackay Edgar. Edgar dismissed the Washington naval conference as utopian and felt an international financial conference would be just as useless as the disarmament conference. For Britain, financial discussions were academic because Britain would pay its debts. But, he added, "while the air is full of ten-year naval holidays, it might not be a bad idea to have a ten-year debt holiday as well." Some officials at the Foreign Office found Edgar's public statement "almost incredible" at a "most unfortunate moment," but others viewed the Washington conference as an opportune moment for full-scale economic and financial discussions. On this question there seems to have been some disagreement between the Foreign Office and the Treasury.[66]

Prior to the Washington conference, Blackett had informed the Foreign Office that the chancellor of the exchequer was not prepared to furnish the British delegation with any Treasury memoranda on the Anglo-American debt. "The subject," he asserted, "is not regarded as being within the scope of the Conference, and the Chancellor of the Exchequer regards it as most undesirable that the British Delegation should enter into any discussion of it at Washington." Responding to Blackett, the Foreign Office implied it did wish to discuss Britain's debts at the Washington conference, but Assistant Foreign Secretary R. A. C. Sperling conceded that "of course I have no control over the nature of the subjects which the Prime Minister or Mr. Balfour may wish to discuss."[67] Typically, the Foreign Office backed off from direct involvement in financial affairs, even though an international financial settlement was the key to the pursuit of a rational foreign policy.

Throughout the Washington conference, Britain's Ambassador Geddes sought to quash persistent reports of Britain's desire to extend the talks to financial matters. He claimed that "no hint of any such desire had been received by the British Empire delegation, who are in no way equipped to deal with financial and economic problems and whose sole concern is to carry out the programme put before the Conference by the American government." But while making public disclaimers, Geddes was reporting to Lord Curzon that American industrial and financial leaders were beginning to recognize the importance of European economic reconstruction to their own prosperity. They now understood the importance of active American assistance. The American Manufacturers' Export Association had asked Secretary Hughes to place the matters of international indebtedness and exchange stabilization on the Washington agenda. Industrialist Charles M. Schwab, according to Geddes, had said he would "gladly see the great ammunition and shipbuilding plants of the Bethlehem Steel Corporation sink to the bottom of the sea" if that would help prospects for peace and international understanding.[68]

Geddes was convinced that if the Washington disarmament conference proved successful, commercial opinion in the eastern United States would favor the summoning of an international conference to deal with financial and economic problems. He cautioned Curzon that American foreign policy was still controlled by midwestern agrarian interests, whose support for assistance in Europe could be awakened only by a slackening in demand for farm produce. Geddes, nevertheless, claimed to have reliable information that the shift in American business opinion had already convinced President Harding to send an American fact-finding mission to study Europe's economic situation as soon as the Washington conference ended.[69]

Geddes's optimism proved to be unfounded. The United States refused to participate in any international conference at which inter-

Allied debts might be discussed, while France opposed discussion of reparations at any international conference. Without the full co-operation and participation of the United States and France, no international solution to Europe's postwar financial and monetary crisis was conceivable. That American and French policies contributed to the breakdown of the wartime financial entente is undeniable. But the financial and monetary resolutions approved at the Brussels and Genoa conferences demonstrate that the real problem was much more fundamental than French and American intransigence.

Had the wartime financial entente survived, it would have imposed the traditional and unimaginative prescriptions advanced by British, American, and French financial leaders, most of whom still inhabited a prewar dream world regulated by the gold standard. The basic problem was not anyone's intransigence, but rather the poverty of traditional financial and monetary theory in an international economy which no longer functioned under the old laws of economics. The myth of the self-regulating economy, governed only by restrictions on human appetite imposed by the finite supply of gold and rising interest rates, refused to die.

NOTES

BIBLIOGRAPHY

INDEX

Notes

Abbreviations

CAB	British Cabinet Office Records
DBFP	Great Britain, Foreign Office. *Documents on British Foreign Policy, 1919–1931*, 1st ser.
DSFEU	French Direction des services financières aux États-Unis
DWM	Dwight W. Morrow Papers, Amherst College Archives
F.B.I.	Federation of British Industries
FO	British Foreign Office Records
FRBNY	Federal Reserve Bank of New York, Strong Papers
HLRO	House of Lords Record Office, London
JOC: Doc. Parl.	Journal Officiel, Chambre des Députés, Documents parlementaires
MAE	French Foreign Ministry
N.U.M.	National Union of Manufacturers
Parl. Deb.	Great Britain, *Parliamentary Debates*, Commons
PRO	Public Record Office, London
T	British Treasury Papers
TWL	Thomas W. Lamont Papers, Baker Library, Harvard Graduate School of Business Administration

Introduction

1. Arno J. Mayer, *Political Origins of the New Diplomacy, 1917–1918* (New Haven: Yale University Press, 1959), and *The Politics and Diplomacy of Peacemaking, 1918–1919* (New York: Knopf, 1967).

2. Charles S. Maier, *Recasting Bourgeois Europe* (Princeton: Princeton University Press, 1975).

3. Keith L. Nelson, *Victors Divided: America and the Allies in Germany, 1918–1923* (Berkeley: University of California Press, 1975).

4. Denise Artaud, "Le gouvernement américain et la question des dettes de guerre au lendemain de l'armistice de Rethondes, 1919–1920," *Revue d'histoire moderne et contemporaine* 20 (1973), 201–229; Walter A. Mc-

Dougall, *France's Rhineland Diplomacy, 1914–1924* (Princeton: Princeton University Press, 1978); Hermann J. Rupieper, *The Cuno Government and Reparations, 1921–1923: Politics and Economics* (The Hague: Martinus Nijhoff, 1979).

5. Artaud, "Le gouvernement américain et la question des dettes."

6. Paul Abrahams, "American Bankers and the Economic Tactics of Peace: 1919," *Journal of American History* 56 (1969), 572–583; Benjamin Rhodes, "Reassessing 'Uncle Shylock': The United States and the French War Debt, 1917–1929," *Journal of American History* 55 (1969), 787–803; Paul Costigliola, "The Politics of Financial Stabilization: American Reconstruction Policy in Europe, 1924–1930," Ph.D. diss., Cornell University, 1973, and "Anglo-American Financial Rivalry in the 1920's," *Journal of Economic History* 37 (1977), 911–934; Michael J. Hogan, "The United States and the Problem of International Economic Control: American Attitudes Toward European Reconstruction, 1918–1920," *Pacific Historical Review* 44 (1975), 84–103, and *Informal Entente: The Private Structure of Cooperation in Anglo-American Economic Diplomacy, 1918–1928* (Columbia, Mo.: University of Missouri Press, 1977); Melvyn P. Leffler, *The Elusive Quest: America's Pursuit of European Stability and French Security, 1919–1933* (Chapel Hill: University of North Carolina Press, 1979).

7. Artaud, "Le gouvernement américain et la question des dettes."

8. Rhodes, "Reassessing 'Uncle Shylock,' " p. 803.

9. Abrahams, "American Bankers," p. 583.

10. Leffler, *The Elusive Quest*, pp. 24, 26, 32, 38, 79–80.

11. Costigliola, "Anglo-American Financial Rivalry," p. 911.

12. Hogan, *Informal Entente*, pp. 38–56.

13. David P. Calleo, "The Historiography of the Interwar Period: Reconsiderations," in *Balance of Power or Hegemony: The Interwar Monetary System*, ed. Benjamin M. Rowland (New York: New York University Press, 1976), p. 257.

14. Stephen A. Schuker, *The End of French Predominance in Europe: The Financial Crisis of 1924 and the Adoption of the Dawes Plan* (Chapel Hill: University of North Carolina Press, 1976).

15. Ibid., p. 13.

16. Ibid., p. 10.

17. Ibid., pp. 14, 44–46.

18. McDougall, *France's Rhineland Diplomacy*, pp. 4, 13, 375, 378.

19. Ibid., pp. 378–379.

20. Ibid., p. 6.

21. Abrahams, "American Bankers," p. 575.

22. Maier, *Recasting Bourgeois Europe*, pp. 589–590.

23. McDougall, *France's Rhineland Diplomacy*, p. 369.

24. Costigliola, "Anglo-American Financial Rivalry," p. 915.

25. Maier, *Recasting Bourgeois Europe*, p. 463.

26. Marc Trachtenberg, *Reparation in World Politics: France and Eu-*

ropean Economic Diplomacy, 1916–1923 (New York: Columbia University Press, 1980).

27. Calleo, "The Historiography of the Interwar Period," pp. 231, 257.

1. Financial Entente, 1914–1919

1. Derek H. Aldcroft, *From Versailles to Wall Street, 1918–1929* (Berkeley: University of California Press, 1977), p. 30. For other important accounts of Europe's postwar economic history see A. C. Pigou, *Aspects of British Economic History, 1918–1925* (London: Allen and Unwin, 1949); Alfred Sauvy, *Histoire économique de la France entre les deux guerres,* 4 vols. (Paris: Fayard, 1965–75); E. V. Morgan, *Studies in British Financial Policy, 1914–1925* (London: Macmillan, 1952).

2. Morgan, *Studies,* p. 122.

3. Raphael-Georges Lévy, "Finances de paix," *Revue des deux mondes* 49 (January 1919), 414. British war finance is discussed in A. W. Kirkaldy, *British Finance during and after the War, 1914–1921* (London: Pitman, 1921).

4. British taxation policy is covered in Bernard Mallet and C. Oswald George, *British Budgets* (London: Macmillan, 1929), 2d ser., 1913/14 to 1920/21; Ursala K. Hicks, *The Finance of the British Government, 1920–1936* (London: Oxford University Press, 1938); Morgan, *Studies,* pp. 89–94; Public Record Office (London), Treasury Papers, file T171/196 (hereafter cited as PRO T with file number).

5. French war finance policy is discussed in Edwin R. A. Seligman, "The Cost of the War and How It Was Met," *American Economic Review* 9 (December 1919), 739–770; L. Paul-Dubois, "L'effort fiscal de la France pendant la guerre," *Revue des deux mondes* 47 (October 1918), 671–696; J. Frédéric Bloch, "The Financial Effort of France During the War," *Annals of the American Academy of Political and Social Science* 75 (January 1918), 201–206. For details concerning *Bons de la défense nationale,* see René Delhoume, *L'inflation fiduciaire en France depuis la guerre, 1914–1922* (Poitiers: Société francaise d'imprimerie, 1922), pp. 89–90; Henri Pommier, *De la liquidation financière de la guerre* (Paris, 1920), p. 66; Germain Martin, *Les finances publiques de la France et al fortune privée, 1914–1925* (Paris: Payot, 1925), p. 150; James Harvey Rogers, *The Process of Inflation in France, 1914–1927* (New York: Columbia University Press, 1929), p. 73.

6. For a complete discussion of the 1916 Paris conference and Clémental's program see Marc Trachtenberg, " 'A New Economic Order': Etienne Clémentel and French Economic Diplomacy during the First World War," *French Historical Studies* 10 (Fall 1977), 315–341. A shorter version appears as chap. 1 in Trachtenberg's *Reparation in World Politics: France and European Economic Diplomacy, 1916–1923* (New York: Columbia University Press, 1980).

7. Trachtenberg, " 'A New Economic Order,' " p. 335.

8. "Note au sujet des dépenses de la France aux États-Unis pendant la guerre," November 1926, F30/772, Ministère des Finances, Paris (hereafter cited as F30/box number); "Historique sommaire des organization Franco-Américaines," n.d., F30/771.

9. For the history of the Argentine credits see "République Argentine. Engagements financières du Trésor Francais," 9 February 1921, F30/1426. As of December 1919, Britain owed $93.3 million, while France owed $23.2 million (gold parity).

10. Direction des services financières aux États-Unis (DSFEU), 2d report, May 1917; 3d report, June 1917, F30/723.

11. Strong to Norman, 22 November 1918, Federal Reserve Bank of New York, Papers of Benjamin Strong, S1116.1–1 (hereafter cited as FRBNY S followed by number); Norman to Strong, 11 December 1918, FRBNY S1116.1–2.

12. Maurice Casenave, "France Revives," *The Magazine of Wall Street* (6 March 1920), box 94, folder 19, Thomas W. Lamont Papers, Baker Library, Harvard Graduate School of Business Administration, Boston, Mass. (hereafter cited as TWL box/folder).

13. Strong Diary, 8 August 1919, FRBNY S1000.3–1.

14. Norman to Strong, 25 February 1922, FRBNY S1116.3–2.

15. Norman to Strong, 14 May 1921, FRBNY S1116.2–2.

16. Norman to Strong, 9 June, 13 July, 14 November 1921, FRBNY S1116.2–2.

17. DSFEU, 5th report, August 1917; 7th report, October 1917; 17th report, June–July 1918, F30/723.

18. Lucien L. Klotz, *De la guerre à la paix: souvenirs et documents* (Paris: Payot, 1924), pp. 117–118.

19. DSFEU, 27th report, December 1918; 28th report, January–February 1919, F30/723.

20. DSFEU, 28th report, January–February 1919, F30/723.

21. Strong Diary, 25 July 1919, FRBNY S1000.3–1.

22. DSFEU, 28th report, January–February 1919, F30/723.

23. "Note au sujet du compte de transferts de dollars à la Trésorerie britannique," 27 August 1920, F30/704.

24. DSFEU, 28th report, January–February 1919, F30/723.

25. Ibid.

26. Ibid., 31st report, February–March 1919.

27. Ibid.

28. Accounts of this "agreement" are found in the records of both the British and French Treasuries. For the French account see "Propositions de M. Chamberlain," 8 March 1919, F30/701. For the British account see PRO T176/1A, "Proposals Accepted by M. Klotz (March 1919)." The two accounts of the agreement are identical.

29. "Note au sujet du compte de transferts de dollars à la Trésorerie britannique," 27 August 1920, F30/704.

30. Chamberlain to Klotz, 13 March 1919, in "Financial Agreements

Relating to Allied War Debts," PRO T176/1A. This file contains Anglo-French wartime debt agreements, including the Calais agreement and the Avenol-Blackett agreement. The text of the Calais agreement has been reprinted in E. L. Woodward and Rohan Butler, eds., *Documents on British Foreign Policy, 1919–1939* (London: Her Majesty's Stationery Office, 1947ff.), 1st ser. (hereafter cited as DBFP), vol. 2, p. 781. As modified by the 1919 Blackett-Avenol agreement, the Calais agreement provided that "the French Government will not ask for the repayment of the gold handed over under the Calais Agreement until the moment arrives when the whole of the French debt to the British government is liquidated."

31. Avenol to Chamberlain, 14 March 1919, PRO T176/1A.

32. Dudley Ward (for Chamberlain) to Klotz, 14 March 1919, PRO T176/1A.

33. Montagu to Chamberlain, 28 March 1919, PRO T172/1025.

34. Chamberlain to Montagu, 31 March 1919, dictated telephone message and letter, PRO T172/1025.

35. Lord Derby memorandum, probably November or December 1919, House of Lords Record Office, Lloyd George Papers, ser. F, box 52, folder 3, no. 23 (hereafter cited as HLRO, Lloyd George Papers, F/box/folder/no.).

36. Finance Minister to Minister for Foreign Affairs, 16 October 1919; Finance Minister to President of the Council, 17 February 1920, in F30/1422; Mouvement général des fonds to Avenol, 16 April 1919, to French legation in Buenos Aires, 26 June 1919, and to French embassy in London, 10 July 1919, in F30/1424.

37. Geddes to Lloyd George, 12 May 1919, with enclosure of memorandum by the coal controller, 2 May 1919, in HLRO, Lloyd George Papers, F/17/5/33.

38. Ibid., and Geddes note of 2 May 1919; memoranda from the director of the Coal Mines Department, May 1920, HLRO, Lloyd George Papers, F/27/6/32.

39. Mouvement général des fonds to Avenol, 5 and 16 December 1919, F30/1424.

40. Mouvement général des fonds (for François-Marsal) to French Commissioner in New York, 11 February and 9 March 1920, F30/1424.

41. Ibid.; DSFEU, 31st report, February–March 1919, citing Rathbone-de Billy letter of 8 March 1919, F30/723.

42. Memorandum from George W. Whitney to Norman Davis, 10 April 1919, TWL 165/8; DSFEU, 31st report, F30/723.

43. Ibid.

44. "Scheme for the Rehabilitation of European Credit and for Financing Relief and Reconstruction," HLRO, Lloyd George Papers, F/60/1/13. The scheme apparently had the support of Chancellor of the Exchequer Austen Chamberlain.

45. Lloyd George to Wilson, 23 April 1919, HLRO, Lloyd George Papers, F/60/1/13.

46. Lamont to William Randolph Hearst, 19 October 1922, TWL

80/16; Wilson to Lloyd George, 3 May 1919, HLRO, Lloyd George Papers, F/60/1/14. Lloyd George's letter of April 23, Wilson's response of May 3, and the Keynes plan are reproduced in Ray Stannard Baker, *Woodrow Wilson and the World Settlement*, 3 vols. (Garden City and New York: Doubleday, 1923), III, 336–338, 344–346. For Lamont's "Suggestions for letter from the President to Mr. Lloyd George in acknowledgment of the British scheme of European financing" see TWL 165/12.

47. Lloyd George to Wilson, 26 June 1919, HLRO, Lloyd George Papers, F/60/1/16.

48. Rathbone to Davis, 28 April 1919; Strauss to Davis and Lamont, 28 April; Leffingwell to Davis, 28 April and 2 May, in TWL 165/12.

49. Whitney memorandum for Norman Davis, 10 April 1919, TWL 165/8.

50. Lamont to Leffingwell, 29 March 1919, TWL 165/8.

51. Ibid.

52. Strong to Leffingwell, 17 August 1919, FRBNY S1000.3–2.

53. "Draft Report on the Rehabilitation of Trade," Geddes memorandum to Lloyd George, 7 March 1919, HLRO, Lloyd George Papers, F/17/5/28.

54. Law to Sir Edward Carson, 25 October 1918, HLRO, Bonar Law Papers, 84/7/96. In 1942, Keynes wrote that the "lessons" of 1919 "for the next time" indicated that controls on raw material and bank credit, as well as high taxation, must be retained for at least two years after the war and then relaxed gradually as consumer goods become available. See his introduction to "Dear Money Papers," 7 January 1942, PRO T172/1384.

55. Derby to Lloyd George, 13 March 1919, HLRO, Lloyd George Papers, F/52/3/10; Derby to Curzon, 5 April 1919; Chamberlain to Curzon, 11 April 1919, PRO F172/1058.

56. Cabinet Finance Committee, 24 July 1919, PRO CAB27/71.

57. Strong to Norman, 5 February 1919, FRBNY S1116.1–1.

58. Lamont to R. H. Brand, 10 June 1919, TWL 165/10.

59. Norman to Strong, 25 February 1919, FRBNY S1116.3–2; Strong to Norman, 22 March 1919, FRBNY S1116.3–1.

60. "Interest Payments Upon Demand Obligations of the British Government Held by the United States Treasury, and the Question of Their Conversion into Long-Term Bonds: Instructions to British Treasury Representatives," War Cabinet Finance Committee memorandum, 23 September 1919, PRO CAB27/72.

61. Lloyd George to Bonar Law, 30 March 1919, HLRO, Bonar Law Papers, 101/3/38.

62. DSFEU, 28th Report, January–February 1919, F30/723.

2. Crisis in Economic Theory

1. Gustav Cassel, *Post-War Monetary Stabilization* (New York: Columbia University Press, 1928), p. 1.

tional Currency Experience, and Keynes, "The Stabilization of the European Exchanges: A Plan for Genoa," *Manchester Guardian Commercial*, Reconstruction Series, no. 1 (20 April 1922), 3–5.

36. Cassel, *Money and Foreign Exchange After 1914*, pp. 254–256; Hawtrey, *Currency and Credit*, p. 368; Keynes, "The Stabilization of the European Exchanges: A Plan for Genoa," p. 3.

37. Ibid.; Cassel, *Money and Foreign Exchange After 1914*, pp. 264ff.

38. Keynes, *Monetary Reform*, pp. 77–79.

39. Hardinge to Curzon 31 October 1922, PRO Foreign Office, FO371/8256.

40. Geddes to Curzon, 24 November 1922, PRO FO371/8256.

41. Cassel, *Money and Foreign Exchange After 1914*, pp. 150–153.

42. Decamps, *Les changes étrangèrs*, pp. 138, 144, 147; Nogaro, *Modern Monetary Systems*, pp. 158–161.

43. Frédéric François-Marsal, "Le problème monétaire," *Revue économique internationale* (1922), 15; Semaine de la monnaie, *La politique financière et monétaire de la France* (Paris: Alcan, 1922), pp. 485–489; Hawtrey, *Currency and Credit*, p. 389.

44. Martin, *Les finances publiques de la France*, pp. 413–416.

45. Joseph Caillaux, "Comments on Mr. Keynes's Proposals for Devaluation," *Manchester Guardian Commercial*, Reconstruction Series, no. 11 (7 December 1922), 661.

46. Delhoume, *L'inflation fiduciaire en France*, pp. 106–109.

47. François-Marsal, "Le problème monétaire," pp. 18–22.

48. Gaston Jèze, "The Fluctuation of the Franc," *Manchester Guardian Commercial*, Reconstruction Series, no. 1 (20 April 1922), 24; Edmond Villey, "Le problème monétaire. Deflation ou stabilisation," *Revue d'économie politique* 35 (1921), 755; Gerard Vissering, *Currency and Exchanges* (Brussels: League of Nations, 1920), p. 23.

49. Comments by François-Marsal, in Semaine de la monnaie, *La politique financière et monétaire de la France*, pp. 488, 493. He conceded that Germany, Austria, and Bolshevik Russia might have to devalue, but refused to place France in the same league with those countries.

50. Irving Fisher, "Devaluation Versus Deflation," *Manchester Guardian Commercial*, Reconstruction Series, no. 11 (7 December 1922), 664.

51. Lionel Robbins, *The Evolution of Modern Economic Theory and Other Papers on the History of Economic Thought* (London: Macmillan, 1970), p. 237.

52. J. M. Keynes, "The Stabilization of the European Exchanges—II," *Manchester Guardian Commercial*, Reconstruction Series, no. 11 (7 December 1922), 660–661.

3. Balancing the Budget

1. Georges Lachapelle, "Les finances britanniques après la guerre," *Revue de paris* 26 (1 November 1919), 205.

2. Sauvy, *Histoire économique*, p. 364.

3. Ibid., p. 366.

4. Hicks, *The Finance of British Government*, p. 3.

5. Some British Treasury officials such as Blackett agreed that France probably could not balance its budget without reparations. See Blackett's memorandum to the chancellor of the exchequer, "Inter-Governmental Debt," 12 July 1922, PRO T176/8.

6. Chamber of Deputies Budget Commission to François-Marsal, 24 December 1920, F30/2390; President of Senate Finance Commission to François-Marsal, 21 July 1920, F30/2389.

7. Stanley Baldwin, 5 March 1919, Great Britain, Parliamentary Debates (*Parl. Deb.*), 5th ser., vol. 113, p. 461.

8. Chamberlain, 30 April 1919, *Parl. Deb.*, 5th ser., vol. 115, p. 186.

9. *The Round Table*, 9 (December 1918–September 1919), 575, 578–579.

10. Niemeyer memorandum for the Chancellor, 11 March 1919, PRO T171/157.

11. Chamberlain to Stamfordham, 29 April 1919, PRO, T171/157.

12. Chamberlain, 30 April 1919, *Parl. Deb.*, 5th ser., vol. 115, pp. 187–188.

13. Mallet and George, *British Budgets*, 2d ser., p. 184.

14. E. Hilton Young, "The Financial Situation and the Way Out," *Contemporary Review* 115 (January–June 1919), 380; Walter Runciman, "Our Financial Plight," *Contemporary Review* 115, p. 602.

15. Chamberlain, 30 April 1919, *Parl. Deb.*, 5th ser., vol. 115, pp. 187–190.

16. Georges Lachapelle, "Les finances françaises après la guerre," *Revue de paris* 26 (1 July 1919), 209; Paul Louis, "La crise financière dans la monde," *Revue politique et littéraire* 57 (1919), 680–681; Germain Martin, "Notre situation financière," *Revue politique et littéraire* 57 (1919), 386.

17. Charles Gide, "French War Budgets for 1919–1920," *The Economic Journal* 29 (June 1919), 134–135; *L'économiste français*, 7 May 1919; Yves-Guyot, "La politique financière de M. Klotz," *Journal des économistes* 62 (June 1919), 290.

18. *L'économiste français*, 26 April and 10 May 1919.

19. Martin, "Notre situation financière," p. 385; Gide, "French War Budgets," p. 136.

20. *L'économiste français*, 7 June 1919.

21. Cited in *The Economist*, 7 June 1919; Martin, "Notre situation financière," p. 386.

22. Tardieu to Casenave, 24 October 1919, F30/701.

23. Derby to Lloyd George, 14 March 1919, HLRO, Lloyd George Papers, F/52/3/11.

24. See Younger memorandum to Bonar Law, 3 January 1918, HLRO, Bonar Law Papers, 82/8/2.

25. Bonar Law to Sir Robert Perks, 31 May 1919, HLRO, Bonar Law Papers, 101/3/94.

26. H. MacGeorge to Bonar Law, 31 May 1920; Bonar Law to Mac-George, 7 June 1920, HLRO, Bonar Law Papers, 99/1/26, 101/4/52. Kenneth O. Morgan has written that "further blows appeared to be looming from the hands of Chamberlain who seemed to be moving left as decisively as Balfour or Horne." The capital levy was not dead in 1920, and it was believed that "the government might outbid Labour by introducing its own capital levy. Some ministers, including Churchill and Addison, strongly favored such a levy." See Morgan, *Consensus and Disunity*, p. 240.

27. Younger to Bonar Law, 21 May 1920, HLRO, Bonar Law Papers, 99/1/15.

28. Ibid., H. MacGeorge to Bonar Law, 31 May 1920, HLRO, Bonar Law Papers, 99/1/26.

29. J. A. R. Marriott, "The 'Conscription of Wealth,' " *The Nineteenth Century and After* 83 (February 1918), 261; Francis Gribble, "Is Civilisation Committing Suicide?" *The Nineteenth Century and After* 85 (May 1919), 888.

30. League of Nations, International Financial Conference, 1920, *Proceedings of the International Financial Conference, Brussels, 1920*, vol. II, *Verbatim Record of the Debates* (Brussels, 1920), pp. 16–17; "The International Financial Conference at Brussels and its Lessons," *The Round Table* 11 (December 1920), 54–57.

31. In 1927, the minority report of the Parliamentary Committee on National Debt and Taxation (Colwyn Committee) still endorsed the capital levy as the only way to reduce seriously Britain's public debt. But the Report argued that the boom years 1919–1920 would have been the most favorable time to implement such a levy. See *Report of the Committee on National Debt and Taxation* (Cmd. 2800, 1927), pp. 411–413.

32. Hicks, *The Finance of British Government*, p. 231.

33. Cabinet Finance Committee, 6 November 1919, PRO CAB27/71.

34. Memorandum on "Use of War Assets to Meet Expenditures in 1920/21," undated, PRO T171/235.

35. Blackett memorandum to the Geddes Committee on economies in expenditure, "Liquidation of Post-War Liabilities," January 1922; Niemeyer memorandum, "Funding Pensions," 9 February 1922, PRO T171/202.

36. Hicks, *The Finance of British Government*, p. 235; note by Board of Customs and Excise on wine duties, 5 April 1920, PRO T171/183.

37. "Notes by the Board of Inland Revenue on Turnover and Sales Taxes Abroad," 1922, PRO T172/1229.

38. "Tax on Turnover," joint memorandum by Board of Inland Revenue and Board of Customs and Excise, 18 January 1918 and 18 January 1922, PRO T171/204.

39. Treasury data in PRO T171/196.

40. "Tax on Turnover," joint memorandum, 18 January 1918, PRO T171/204.

41. Hicks, *The Finance of British Government*, pp. 1, 4. Chamberlain's confidence in the strength of Britain's economy remained strong, and his April 1920 budget "contemplated the economic scene with confidence." See Morgan, *Consensus and Disunity*, p. 255.

42. Speeches by R. H. Brand and Lord Chalmers, 27 September 1920, *Proceedings of the International Financial Conference, Brussels, 1920*, II, *Verbatim Record*, pp. 18, 25.

43. Fisher-Hamilton memorandum to Chancellor of the Exchequer, 30 November 1918, PRO T171/162.

44. Memorandum from Board of Inland Revenue, 20 March 1920, PRO T171/177.

45. See statistics in Treasury memoranda, PRO T171/196.

46. N.U.M. deputation to Chamberlain, 13 February 1919, PRO T171/165.

47. Ibid.; F.B.I. deputation, 7 February 1919, PRO T171/165.

48. Fisher-Hamilton memorandum, "Repeal of the Excess Profits Duty," 15 November 1918, PRO T171/165.

49. Chamberlain to Bonar Law, 11 March 1920, describing meeting with delegation from F.B.I., HLRO, Bonar Law Papers, 98/8/8.

50. Maclay to Bonar Law, 28 April 1920, enclosing copy of note on EPD sent to Chamberlain, HLRO, Bonar Law Papers, 98/9/35, 98/9/36.

51. Deputation from Association of British Chambers of Commerce and F.B.I., 6 May 1920, PRO T171/177.

52. N.U.M. deputation, 19 May 1920, PRO T171/177.

53. F.B.I. deputation, 1 July 1920, PRO T171/177.

54. Blackett, "Note on Present Conditions in Finance and Industry," 2 July 1920, PRO T171/184.

55. Chamberlain's remarks to F.B.I. deputation, 1 July 1920, PRO T171/177.

56. Board of Inland Revenue note on replacing EPD revenues, 17 December 1920, PRO T171/182.

57. See for example McKenna's statement in *The Economist*, 28 January 1922, and Hawtrey's 16 June 1920 memorandum attacking McKenna's statements to London Joint City and Midland Bank shareholders, PRO T171/184.

58. Chamberlain memorandum to Cabinet, "Proposals for New Expenditure," 7 June 1920, PRO T171/184.

59. Exchange of letters between Chamberlain and Cecil, August 1920; Niemeyer memorandum, 31 July 1920, PRO T172/1262.

60. F.B.I. deputation, 10 February 1921, PRO T171/190.

61. On this point there was an exchange of views between Sir Alfred Mond (minister of health), and Blackett and Hawtrey. Hawtrey and Mond tended to agree on the "imprudence" of firms that had not saved to pay EPD; Blackett would "only partly concur." See Mond memorandum, 30 March

1922, and Hawtrey's response of 3 April, with Blackett's notation, PRO T171/202.

62. Hamilton (Inland Revenue) to Blackett, 6 July 1922, PRO T171/200; Cabinet Finance Committee, 6 December 1921, PRO CAB27/71.

63. Horne to Stamfordham, 22 April 1921, PRO T/171/196.

64. Board of Inland Revenue and Board of Customs and Excise, "Industry and the Weight of Taxation," 11 January 1922, PRO T171/203.

65. Ibid.

66. Ibid.

67. Montagu, memorandum to the Cabinet Finance Committee, 9 December 1921, PRO T171/202.

68. Ibid.

69. Blackett, "Budgeting for a Deficit," 24 March 1922, PRO T171/202,

70. Mond, memorandum 30 March 1922, PRO T171/202.

71. Blackett, memorandum 3 April 1922, PRO T171/202.

72. Sir Bernard Mallet and C. Oswald George, *British Budgets*, 3d ser., 1921/22 to 1932/33 (London, 1933), pp. 45–47, 53; Horne to Lloyd George, 27 April 1922, HLRO, Lloyd George Papers, F/27/6/61. Kenneth O. Morgan has criticized both Horne's budget of April 1921 and that of May 1922. Of the former, he writes that it was "quite inappropriate for the tasks with which it was confronted." Despite the recession, the budget still anticipated a large surplus. "Clearly," argued Morgan, "some new departure in policy was essential, lest the social cleavage introduced by unemployment on such a scale became unbridgeable." Of the latter budget, Morgan observed the "muddled calculations which left him with a surplus of £101m on the year, instead of a deficit." He implies Horne had become the captive of business and commercial interests. This view must be tempered somewhat by what follows here on Horne's insistence that the wealthy had more or less contracted for a share of the war debt burden. See Morgan, *Consensus and Disunity*, pp. 285, 296.

73. Horne to Lloyd George, 27 April 1922, HLRO, Lloyd George Papers, F/27/6/61.

74. Horne, "Notes for Speech on the Budget 1922–23," PRO T172/1235.

75. Ibid.

76. Ibid.

77. François-Marsal to Contrôleur des dépenses engagées, 11 January 1921, F30/2390; Lasteyrie to President of the Cour des comptes, November 1922, F30/2391.

78. See the exchange between Ogier and François-Marsal, October-December 1920; François-Marsal to President of the Council, 13 October 1920; François-Marsal to President of the Republic, 19 November 1920, F30/2389.

79. *L'économiste français*, 10 May 1919; *The Economist*, 4 January 1919.

80. Werner Wittich, "L'introduction du franc en Alsace et en Lorraine," *Revue d'économie politique* 37 (1923), 547. For the history of the German regime see Dan P. Silverman, *Reluctant Union: Alsace-Lorraine and Imperial*

Germany, 1871–1918 (University Park, Pa.: The Pennsylvania State University Press, 1972), particularly chap. 9, "Political Economy in the Reichsland: The Economic Subversion of Political Integration," pp. 165–189.

81. Wittich, "L'introduction du franc," p. 547.

82. François-Marsal to Labie, 26 November 1920, F30/2389.

83. Doumer to President of the Cour des comptes, 7 February 1921; Doumer to President of the Comité central des armateurs de France, 22 February 1921, F30/2390.

84. See the following material on the foodstuffs (*ravitaillement*) account: original report by the Contrôleur des dépenses engagées, 16 August 1919, and note added by the Inspector général des finances, 21 August, in F30/2386; François-Marsal letters to the under secretary of state for foodstuffs, 6 November and 29 December 1920, and letter from Contrôleur des dépenses engagées to the under secretary of state for food stuffs, 18 December 1920, in F30/2389; François-Marsal to the President of the Council, 28 June 1920, F30/2388.

85. Ibid.

86. Contrôleur des dépenses engagées, report on foodstuffs, 16 August 1919, F30/2386.

87. France, *Journal Officiel*, Chambre des Députés, Documents Parlementaires (hereafter cited as JOC: Doc. Parl.), 13 January 1920, no. 166, pp. 2–5, new tax legislation. See also Haig, *The Public Finances of Post-War France*, p. 61; *L'économiste français*, 31 January 1920; "Projets fiscaux d M. Klotz," *Journal des économistes* 65 (February 1920), 211–215.

88. JOC: Doc. Parl., 13 January 1920, no. 166, p. 5.

89. *L'économiste français*, 31 January 1920.

90. JOC: Doc. Parl., 13 January 1920, no. 168, pp. 59–60, explanation of budget.

91. Hawtrey to Chancellor of the Exchequer, 6 February 1920, PRO T171/235.

92. *The Economist*, 14 February 1920.

93. See the account in "Projets fiscaux de M. Klotz," *Journal des économistes* 65, pp. 215–216.

94. *The Economist*, 31 January 1920.

95. For an outline of his revised budget proposals see the 23 February 1920 letter of François-Marsal to the Chamber Budget Commission and the Senate Finance Commission, analyzed in *The Economist*, 28 February 1920. For an account of François-Marsal's fiscal principles see *The Economist*, 31 January 1920.

96. Jusserand to Ministère des Affaires Étrangeres, 27 and 28 April 1920 (copies), F30/702.

97. Haig, *The Public Finances of Post-War France*, pp. 62–70; *L'économiste français*, 31 July 1920.

98. Lucien L. Klotz, "La situation financière de la France," *Revue économique internationale* (1920–24), pp. 639–643; JOC: Doc. Parl., 31 July 1920, no. 1523, pp. 2254–2257, 1921 budget.

99. Ibid., p. 2261.

100. François-Marsal to President of the Council, 12 November 1920, F30/2389.

101. Ibid.

102. JOC: Doc. Parl., 31 July 1920, no. 1523, pp. 2261–2262.

103. *L'économiste français*, 12 February, 28 May 1921.

104. Klotz, "La situation financière de la France," pp. 642–643.

105. JOC: Doc. Parl., 8 July 1921, no. 3068, p. 2274, 1922 budget.

106. Ibid., pp. 2280–2282; Direction du budget et du contrôle financière to Finance Minister, 9 October 1920, report on turnover tax receipts.

107. JOC: Doc. Parl., 8 July 1921, no. 3068, p. 2276.

108. Frédéric François-Marsal, "La situation financière de la France," *L'expansion économique* 6 (8 October 1922), 6–7.

109. JOC: Doc. Parl., 31 March 1922, no. 4220, p. 497, 1923 budget. As in Doumer's 1922 budget, ordinary and extraordinary expenditures and receipts were combined in a general budget, while recoverable expenditures appeared separately.

110. Ibid., p. 524.

111. League of Nations, Economic and Financial Publications, no. 28, *Memorandum on Public Finance*, 1922 (Geneva, 1923), pp. 46–47.

112. Schuker, *The End of French Predominance*, pp. 21–23.

113. Lasteyrie to Adrien Dariac (president of the Chamber Budget Commission), 8 January 1923, F30/2392.

114. Ibid.

115. Ibid.

116. Schuker, *The End of French Predominance*, p. 47.

117. Report of Inspector of Finance de Peyster, 28 October 1920; François-Marsal to Labie, 26 November 1920, F30/2389.

118. Lasteyrie to President of the Council, 2 December 1922, F30/1427.

119. Ibid.

120. See the correspondence and telegrams between various Paris authorities and General Joseph Degoutte, Rhineland/Ruhr commander, March 1923, in F30/2392.

121. Lasteyrie to President of the Council, June 1923 (copy), F30/2392.

122. Ibid.

123. Ibid.

124. Ibid.

125. Lasteyrie to President of the Council, 9 and 13 November 1923, F30/2392. For other accounts of the Rhineland/Ruhr currency problem see McDougall, *France's Rhineland Diplomacy*, pp. 262–263, 323; Schuker, *The End of French Predominance*, p. 172.

126. France, Institut national de la statistique, Service d'études économiques et financières, Statistiques et études financières, Supplement no. 175, *Supplément rétrospectif 1900 à 1930* (Paris: Imprimerie Nationale, July 1963), pp. 960–961 (hereafter cited as *Supplément rétrospectif*).

127. Lasteyrie to President of the Council, 9 July 1923, F30/2392.

4. Managing the National Debt

1. Yves-Guyot, "L'illusion fiduciaire et la réalite économique," p. 17; Martin, *Les finances publiques de la France*, p. 142.

2. Schuker, *The End of French Predominance*, pp. 45–46.

3. See the following articles by Keynes: "The Stabilization of the European Exchanges—II," p. 661; "The Genoa Conference," Reconstruction Series, no. 3, *Manchester Guardian Commercial* (15 June 1922), 132–133; "Is a Settlement of the Reparation Question Possible Now?" Reconstruction Series, no. 8, *Manchester Guardian Commercial* (28 September 1922), 464.

4. Dulles, *The French Franc*, p. 12.

5. J. Ellis Barker, "Britain's True Wealth and the Unimportance of the War Debt," *The Nineteenth Century and After* 83 (May 1918), 926–929.

6. J. Ellis Barker, "The World's Debt to Italy and How to Pay It," *The Nineteenth Century and After* 83 (February 1918), 320–322.

7. Barker, "Britain's True Wealth," p. 933; Archibald Hurd, "The British Empire After the War," *Fortnightly Review* 100 (October 1916), 562–564; J. Saxon Mills, "The Empire and its Resources," *Fortnightly Review* 101 (May 1917), 884.

8. E. B. Osborn, "The Control of the Tropics," *The Nineteenth Century and After* 84 (July 1918), 33, 36–37.

9. Ibid., p. 33.

10. Arthur Girault, "Vie coloniale," *Revue d'économie politique* 37 (1923), 310–314; Joseph Chailley, "L'industrie française. Les matières premières et les colonies," *Revue économique internationale* (1921–I), 7–31.

11. Hanotaux, "Economic Metaphysics," pp. 67–69.

12. Jacques Arthuys, *Le problème de la monnaie* (Paris: Nouvelle librarie nationale, 1921), p. 179.

13. H. J. Jennings, "The World's War Bill," *Fortnightly Review* 101 (June 1917), 1059.

14. Gerard Vissering, *Currency and Exchanges*, p. 11.

15. Young, "The Financial Situation and the Way Out," pp. 378–379.

16. Maier, *Recasting Bourgeois Europe*, pp. 503, 511.

17. *Supplément rétrospectif*, p. 1008.

18. Morgan, *Studies*, pp. 122–123.

19. Ibid., pp. 138–141.

20. Ibid., p. 138.

21. Cokayne to Bonar Law, 16 October 1918, PRO T172/895.

22. Ibid.

23. Bradbury memorandum, "Reconstruction Finance," 21 February 1918, PRO T170/125.

24. Comptroller General to Chamberlain, 6 May 1920, enclosing scheme to consolidate and reduce debt submitted by J. L. Heath, National Debt Office, PRO T172/1092.

25. Norman to Strong, 23 May 1921, FRBNY S1116.2–2. The British Treasury had just begun its series of Conversion Loans.

26. Strong to Norman, 9 June 1922, FRBNY S1116.3–1.

27. Boyle, *Montagu Norman*, pp. 124–125; Sir Henry Clay, *Lord Norman* (London: Macmillan, 1957), p. 114; Susan Howson, *Domestic Monetary Management in Britain, 1919–1938* (Cambridge, Eng.: Cambridge University Press, 1975), p. 20.

28. Cokayne to Chamberlain, 12 February 1919; Bradbury memorandum to Chamberlain, 13 February 1919; Chamberlain to Cokayne, 15 February 1919, in PRO T172/1020. Howson, "The Origins of Dear Money," p. 95, also cites these documents.

29. Chamberlain's meeting with Committee of Clearing House Bankers, 15 May 1919, PRO T172/1080.

30. Chamberlain's meeting with Committee of Clearing House Bankers, 28 May 1919, PRO T172/1080.

31. *The Economist*, 3 January 1920.

32. Cokayne to Chamberlain, 10 July 1919, PRO T172/1059.

33. Boyle, *Montagu Norman*, pp. 140–141.

34. Goodenough to Chamberlain, 28 April and 4 May 1920; Chamberlain to Goodenough, 3 May 1920, PRO T172/1114.

35. Blackett memorandum, 26 July 1920, PRO T172/1146.

36. G. L. Bevan to Chamberlain, 5 July 1920, PRO T172/1146.

37. Blackett memorandum, 26 July 1920, PRO T172/1146.

38. Cited in Mallet and George, *British Budgets*, 2d ser., p. 235.

39. Herbert Samuel, "The Plight of the Taxpayer—and the Remedy," *Contemporary Review* 116 (December 1919), 603.

40. Ibid.

41. Ibid.

42. The full Select Committee report appears in Kirkaldy, *British Finance*, pp. 421–424.

43. Niemeyer Papers, "Premium Bonds, 1919–1928," PRO T/176/4; Norman to Strong, 6 November 1919, FRBNY S1116.1–2.

44. Morgan, *Studies*, p. 118.

45. Norman to Strong, 14 May 1921, FRBNY S1116.2–2.

46. Noel F. Hall, *The Exchange Equalization Account* (London: Macmillan, 1935), p. 13.

47. Schuker, *The End of French Predominance*, pp. 38–39.

48. Hall, *Exchange Equalization Account*, p. 13.

49. Hicks, *The Finance of the British Government*, p. 317.

50. *Report of the Committee on National Debt and Taxation* (Cmd. 2800, 1927), pp. 34–36, 364.

51. Ibid., pp. 50–51.

52. Horne's comments in Mallet and Oswald, *British Budgets*, 3d ser., pp. 30–31; Blackett memorandum, "Budgeting for a Deficit, 24 March 1922, PRO T172/1272.

53. League of Nations, International Financial Conference, Brussels, 1920, *Public Finance*, IV, pt. 2 (London, 1920), pp. 29, 31.

54. A. d'Aubigny, A. Célier, and others, *Problèmes financiers d'après-*

guerre (Paris: Alcan, 1922), p. 162; Pommier, *Liquidation financière*, p. 74.

55. Ibid., pp. 76–77.

56. *Supplément rétrospectif*, p. 1003; Rogers, *The Process of Inflation in France*, p. 342.

57. Martin, *Les finances publiques*, p. 143.

58. Pommier, *Liquidation financiére*, pp. 76–80; Gaston Jèze, *Les finances de guerre de la France*, 3 vols. (Paris, 1915–20), III, 42–49.

59. Pommier, *Liquidation financière*, pp. 91–93.

60. *L'économiste français*, 14 August 1920.

61. Ibid., 16 October 1920; Jacques Lagrenée, *Le problème monétaire en France après les guerres de 1870–1871 et 1914–1918* (Paris: Presses universitaires de France, 1923), pp. 163–165; Semaine de la monnaie, *La politique financière et monétaire*, pp. 549–551; Raphael-Georges Lévy, "La situation financière au lendemain de la paix," *L'expansion économique* 3 (November–December 1919), 32–34. French economists understood that the Bank advances constituted a type of compulsory loan made through the note circulation system.

62. Etienne Clémentel, *Inventaire de la situation financière de la France au début de la treizième législature* (Paris: Imprimerie Nationale, 1924), p. 52; Lagrenée, *Le problème monétaire*, p. 99.

63. Schuker, *The End of French Predominance*, p. 44.

64. Rogers, *The Process of Inflation in France*, pp. 37–41, 58, 60; circular from Mouvement général des fonds to Trésoriers-payers generaux, 25 September 1920, F30/2387. In fact, no significant Treasury deposits materialized until 1926, when they began to provide the means for repayment of Bank advances.

65. Doumer to Senator Gaudin de Villaine, 20 May 1921, F30/2390.

66. Rogers, *The Process of Inflation in France*, p. 73.

67. Georges Lachapelle, *La vérité sur notre situation financière* (Paris: Roustan, 1921), pp. 135–138; Martin, *La situation financière*, p. 842; Martin, *Les finances publiques*, p. 377.

68. In d'Aubigny, Célier, and others, *Problèmes financièrs*, p. 33.

69. "Note pour le ministre," 7 October 1922, F30/1427.

70. Yves-Guyot, "Le pire des emprunts," p. 137; Martin, *Les finances publiques*, pp. 171–172.

71. Yves-Guyot, "Baisse des prix et baisse des changes," *Journal des économistes* 66 (June 1920), 299–300.

72. Arthur Raffalovich, "Pour la déflation contre le défaillisme monétaire," *Journal des économistes* 69 (April 1921), 27.

73. Martin, *La situation financière*, pp. 838–839; Haig, *The Public Finances of Post-War France*, p. 239.

74. Rogers, *The Process of Inflation in France*, pp. 44–46.

75. *The Round Table* 9 (December 1918–September 1919), 116; Joseph Caillaux, "The Financial Situation of France—How to Remedy It," Reconstruction Series, no. 5, *Manchester Guardian Commercial* (27 July 1922), 277.

5. Inter-Allied Debt

1. Schuker, *The End of French Predominance*, p. 15; Sally Marks, "Reparations Reconsidered: A Reminder," *Central European History* 2 (December 1969), 363, 365; David Felix, "Reparations Reconsidered With a Vengeance," *Central European History* 4 (June 1971), 178.

2. Schuker, *The End of French Predominance*, p. 10.

3. Aldcroft, *From Versailles to Wall Street*, p. 93.

4. Strong Diary, conversation with Chamberlain, 19 September 1919, FRBNY S1000.3–1; War Cabinet Finance Committee, "Interest Payments Upon Demand Obligations . . . and the Question of Their Conversion into Long-Term Bonds: Instructions to British Treasury Representatives," 23 September 1919, PRO CAB27/72; Chamberlain note to the cabinet, 6 February 1920, PRO Foreign Office FO371/4563.

5. Blackett memorandum, 2 February 1920, PRO FO371/4563.

6. Minutes by Sperling, 11, 13 February 1920; Waterlow, 12 February; Waterlow and O'Malley, 17 February, PRO FO371/4563.

7. Geddes memorandum, 12 February 1920, PRO FO371/4563.

8. "Memorandum by Sir M. Ramsay on the financial outlook," 12 January 1918, PRO T172/774.

9. Sperling minute, 11 February 1920, PRO FO371/4563.

10. Draft of Sperling note to Lindsay, 4 March 1920, PRO FO371/4563.

11. Houston telegram to Chamberlain, sent through Lindsay, 5 March 1920, PRO FO371/4562.

12. "Inter-Allied Indebtedness and Attitude of the United States," 4 April 1922, PRO FO371/5662; Blackett memorandum to Niemeyer, 1922, which summarizes Blackett's memoranda of 6 February and 12 May 1920 dealing with Anglo-American debt negotiations, PRO T172/1288; Blackett memorandum of 12 May 1920, "Inter-Allied and Anglo-American Debts," with Chamberlain's comments attached, PRO FO371/4563.

13. Lloyd George to Wilson, 5 August 1920, HLRO, Lloyd George Papers, F/60/1/28. Early drafts date back to 28 June; Wilson to Lloyd George, 3 November 1920, HLRO, Lloyd George Papers, F/60/1/31. The Lloyd George–Wilson exchange is discussed in Michael F. Fry, *Illusions of Security: North Atlantic Diplomacy 1918–1922* (Toronto: University of Toronto Press, 1972), pp. 47–48.

14. Geddes telegram to Foreign Office, 18 June 1920, PRO FO371/4563.

15. Extract from minutes of 3 November 1920 cabinet meeting, PRO FO371–4563.

16. Curzon to Geddes, 5 November 1920, PRO FO371/4563.

17. Chamberlain memorandum to the cabinet and supplementary note, "Anglo-American Debt," 30 November 1920, PRO FO371/4563.

18. Ibid.

19. Seymour minute, 6 December 1920; Foreign Office cable to Geddes, 17 December 1920, PRO FO371/4563.

20. Lindsay memorandum on Anglo-American debt, with minute by Tyrell, 4 January 1921, PRO FO371/5661.

21. Ibid.

22. Draft Conclusions of 7 February 1921 cabinet meeting, PRO FO371/5661.

23. Geddes to Foreign Office, 3 May 1921, PRO FO371/5661.

24. Blackett to Crowe, 14 July 1921, PRO FO371/5662.

25. Norman to Strong, 1 and 17 December 1921, FRBNY S1116.2–2; Strong to Norman, 18 February 1922, FRBNY S1116.3–1.

26. D'Abernon to Curzon, 1 and 23 April 1921, including a copy of Simons's proposal, PRO, FO371/6026.

27. D'Abernon to Curzon, 1 April 1921, with Crowe's minute of 7 April, PRO FO371/6022. Simons's plan was in fact unacceptable to the British government.

28. Blackett memoranda, "German Reparation and Inter-Allied Debts, Plan for a Final Settlement," 6 December 1921, and "Relation Between Inter-Allied Indebtedness and German Reparations," 18 February 1922, PRO FO371/7475. Blackett gave his account of the 16 March 1922 Paris meeting of the Allied finance ministers to Ralph F. Wigram, a second secretary at the Foreign Office, who wrote a memorandum on his "Conversation with Sir Basil Blackett respecting Allied Finance Ministers' Meeting," PRO FO371/7475.

29. Blackett memorandum, "Relation Between Inter-Allied Indebtedness and German Reparations," 18 February 1922, PRO FO371/7475.

30. Robert K. Murray, *The Harding Era* (Minneapolis: University of Minnesota Press, 1969), pp. 360–364.

31. Lamont memorandum for the press, February 1922, TWL 80/15; Lamont memorandum circulated to prominent financiers, "The Allied Debt to the United States Government," November 1922, TWL 80/17; Leffingwell to Lamont, 16 November 1922, TWL 80/17; Leffingwell, article, "America's Interest in Europe," published by the Foreign Policy Association, July 1922. Lamont was a member of the executive committee of the national council of the Foreign Policy Association. Leffingwell became a partner in J. P. Morgan & Co. in June 1923. See TWL 103/10; Crosby, "The American War Loans and Justice," found in TWL 80/15. The date and title of the journal in which the article appeared are missing, but the piece was written between February and September 1922.

32. Blackett memorandum to Foreign Office, 22 May 1922, with 24 May Sperling minute and Seymour note, PRO FO371/7282.

33. Geddes to Foreign Office, 17 May 1922, with 19 May Seymour and Sperling minutes, PRO FO371/7282; Blackett memorandum of 6 June 1922, with Crowe's minutes of 6 and 7 June, PRO FO371/7382.

34. Blackett memorandum, 6 June 1922, PRO FO371/7282.

35. Lamont to Blackett, 8 June 1922, TWL 80/15.

36. Norman to Strong, 19 June 1922, FRBNY S1116.3–2.

37. Blackett to Lamont, 26 June 1922, TWL 96/12.

38. Luncheon conversation at 10 Downing Street, 5 July 1922, PRO FO371/7282.

39. Jacques Sordet, Office of Liquidation, to Bloc, 7 October 1919; Rathbone memorandum to Finance Ministry, 3 December 1919, both in F30/773.

40. Sordet to Mouvement général des fonds, 30 April 1920; Sordet to Marine merchande, 27 April 1920, F30/773; Casenave to Finance Ministry, 24 December 1919, F30/773.

41. For the definitive account of the "Franco-American balance" see "Note sur le compte 'Règlement Américain' " (undated, probably 1935), F30/784.

42. Rathbone to Célier, 20 November 1919; Rathbone to Finance Ministry, 25 November 1919; note by official of Mouvement général des fonds, in Célier's file, F30/773.

43. Office de Liquidation Franco-Américain, "Memorandum au sujet de la balance général Franco-Américaine," 4 May 1920; Klotz to Morel, 3 December 1919, both in F30/773; Klotz to President of the Council, 17 December 1919, F30/1422.

44. François-Marsal to Under Secretary of State to the President of the Council, 30 April 1920, F30/1424; Casenave to Office of Liquidation, 17, 18 April and 15 May 1920, F30/773.

45. de Vienne to Parmentier, 10 February 1921, F30/773.

46. Ibid.

47. Casenave to Finance Ministry and Office of Liquidation, 26 February, 6 March 1921, F30/773, F30/771.

48. Pergesol (director, Office of Liquidation) to President of the Council, 27 May 1921; Casenave to Office of Liquidation, 4 June 1921, F30/771.

49. Pergesol memorandum, "Compte de Liquidation Franco-Américain, Détails de l'accord Casenave-Mellon, juin 1921," 1 October 1921, F30/773; "Note sur le compte 'Réglement Américain' " (probably 1935), F30/784.

50. See Célier to Morel, 10 June; 5, 13, 22, 28 August 1919; Célier to Direction du Contrôle des Administrations Financières et de l'Ordonnancement, 3 January 1920, all in F30/1425; Doumer to Emmanuel Brousse (under secretary for finance, liquidation of stocks), 24 January 1921, F30/2390; Parmentier to Finance Minister, enclosing letter from Brousse and comments of de Vienne, 14 February 1921, F30/1426.

51. Parmentier to Finance Minister, 14 February 1921, F30/1426; Doumer to Brunet (Chamber of Deputies), 19 May 1921, F30/2390.

52. Parmentier to Finance Minister, 14 February 1921, F30/1426.

53. Mouvement général des fonds (for the finance minister) to French embassy, Washington, 1, 8 July and 6 August 1920, F30/1424; Chamberlain to Geddes, 21 July 1920, PRO FO371/4563; François-Marsal to French chargé d'affaires, Washington, 16 September 1920; François-Marsal to President of the Council, 16 September 1920, both in F30/1424; Chamberlain to Geddes, 23 September 1920, PRO FO371/4563; Geddes to Foreign Office, 29, 30 September, 1 October 1920, PRO FO371/4563; François-Marsal to Leygues, 20 October 1920, F30/1422.

54. Mouvement général des fonds to French commissariat in New York, 22 August 1919, F30/1424; Klotz to Avenol, 5 September 1919, F30/1425.

55. Klotz to Avenol, 5 September 1919, F30/1425.

56. Mouvement général des fonds (for Klotz) to French commissariat in New York, 22 August 1919, F30/1424.

57. Ibid.; Klotz to Avenol, 5 September 1919, F30/1425.

58. Mouvement général des fonds to Avenol, describing Casenave's cable from New York, 25 September 1919, F30/1424.

59. François-Marsal memorandum to President of the Council, 23 October 1920, F30/2389.

60. President of the Council to French chargé d'affaires, Washington, 15 November; Jusserand to President of the Council and Minister of Foreign Affairs, 24 December 1920, F30/785A.

61. "Renseignements sur les obligations remises en reconnaissance des avances de la Trésorerie Américain," 15 April 1921, F30/1426; Mouvement général des fonds to Casenave, 17 January 1921, F30/1424.

62. Geddes to Foreign Office, 28 February 1921; Hardinge to Curzon, 15 March 1921, PRO FO371/5687; Geddes to Foreign Office, 16, 31 March 1921, with minutes by Tyrrell and Seymour, PRO FO371/5692; Geddes to Foreign Office, 1 December 1921, PRO FO371/6981; Seymour minute of 2 December to Geddes's 1 December message, PRO FO371/5715.

63. Casenave to Office of Liquidation, 21 June, 1 July 1921, F30/771.

64. Mouvement général des fonds (for the minister) to French commissariat in New York, 18 June 1921, F30/1424; unsigned memorandum, 28 September 1921, in both F30/774 and F30/1426.

65. Finance Minister to President of the Council, 31 October 1921, F30/1423; memorandum from Finance Ministry to President of the Council, "Note Parmentier," 22 October 1921, F30/771. Parmentier's claim that France "owes nothing" was echoed in Doumer's note to Briand, 22 October 1921, F30/784.

66. Lasteyrie to President of the Council, 10 May 1922, citing Poincaré to Lasteyrie letter of 30 April, and enclosing Herrick's note, F30/2391.

67. Poincaré to Lasteyrie, 27 May 1922, F30/784.

68. St. Aulaire (for Avenol) to Ministère des Affairs Etrangères (MAE), 24 May 1922; Avenol to Finance Minister, describing talks with Blackett, 30 May 1922, F30/785A. Had the French government seriously desired the views of the British Treasury, French representatives at Genoa could have consulted Horne and Blackett. It appears that neither government wished to tip its hand to the other.

69. Ibid.

70. Ibid.

71. Poincaré to Parmentier, 7 June 1922, and a similar note to the Finance Minister, 8 June, F30/784.

72. Parmentier's instructions in Poincaré and Lasteyrie to Parmentier, 27 June 1922, F30/784.

73. Avenol to Finance Minister, 3 July 1922, F30/784.

74. St. Aulaire to President of the Council, 5 July 1922, F30/784. The Balfour note is published in Cmd. 1737 (1922). Britain's offer to wipe out debts if the United States would do the same was not new. Lloyd George had made such an offer to Millerand and François-Marsal at Lympne, 20 June 1920, and to Briand in London, 19–20 December 1921. See DBFP, 1st ser., vol. 8, pp. 314–316; DBFP, vol. 15, pp. 768–769, 782.

75. Bank of England cable to Federal Reserve Bank of New York, received 26 July 1922, FRBNY S1116.3–2; Blackett memorandum to chancellor of the exchequer, "Inter-Governmental Debt," 12 July 1922, PRO T176/8; Schuker, *The End of French Predominance*, pp. 245–246; Fry, *Illusions of Security*, pp. 195–198, who observes that the City also opposed the policy set by the Balfour Note. Morgan, *Consensus and Disunity*, p. 318, indicates that "Chamberlain and Horne both sought to placate the USA and asked that their dissent from the Balfour Note be formally recorded" in the 25 July 1922 cabinet meeting.

76. Blackett to Chancellor of the Exchequer, 3 July 1922; undated Niemeyer to Blackett memorandum (probably July 1922), PRO T176/8.

77. Poincaré to Hardinge, 1 September 1922, PRO FO371/8295; Poincaré to St. Aulaire, 3 September 1922, F30/784; Villiers minute, 11 September 1922, PRO FO371/8295.

78. Memorandum by the Foreign Office Central Department, "The Development of French Policy Since the August and December Conferences," 27 December 1922, PRO FO371/7491.

79. Parmentier to Finance Minister, 14 July 1922, F30/784.

80. Parmentier to Finance Minister, 1 August 1922; "Memorandum on the French Financial Situation," July 1922, both in F30/784.

81. Parmentier cable (sent by Chambrun) to MAE (copy), received 3 August 1922, F30/784.

82. Jusserand (for Parmentier) to MAE, received 28 July 1922 (copy), F30/784.

83. Parmentier to Lasteyrie, 1 August 1922, F30/784.

84. Jusserand (for Parmentier), to MAE, received 28 July 1922 (copy), F30/784.

85. Chambrun (for Parmentier) to MAE, received 3 August 1922 (copy), F30/784.

86. Poincaré to Parmentier, 6 August 1922, F30/784.

87. Chambrun (for Parmentier) to MAE, received 12 August 1922 (copy), F30/784.

88. *La Figaro*, 19 September; *l'Oeuvre*, 28 September 1922, in Press Reports file, F30/784.

89. Chambrun (for Parmentier) to MAE, received 12 August 1922 (copy), F30/784.

90. Ibid.; Lasteyrie to Parmentier, 15 August 1922, F30/784.

91. Chambrun (for Parmentier) to MAE, received 17 August 1922 (copy), F30/784.

92. Ibid.

93. Chambrun (for Parmentier) to MAE, received 18 August 1922 (copy), F30/784.

94. Lasteyrie to Parmentier, 18, 19 August 1922, F30/784.

95. Parmentier to Lasteyrie, 31 August; Lasteyrie to Poincaré, 2 September 1922, F30/784.

96. Ibid.

97. *Le Petit Bleu*, 16 September 1922, in Press Reports file, F30/784; Schuker, *The End of French Predominance*, p. 40.

98. Grenfell to Lamont, 9 October 1922, TWL 111/14.

99. Grenfell to Lamont, 16 October 1922, TWL 111/14.

100. Conservative party Central Office note concerning Baldwin's 1923 negotiations, released in 1931, forwarded by French ambassador in London to MAE, 22 January 1931 (copy), F30/783A.

101. Norman to Strong, 27 November 1922, FRBNY S1116.3–2.

102. Grenfell to Lamont, 9 October 1922; Lamont to Grenfell, 19 October 1922, TWL 111/14.

103. Lamont to Grenfell, 29 December 1922, TWL 111/15; Murray, *Harding Era*, p. 363; *The Economist*, 13 January 1923.

104. Murray, *Harding Era*, p. 363; Clay, *Lord Norman*, p. 176; *The Round Table* 13 (December 1922–September 1923), 284.

105. Strong to Norman, 22 February 1923, FRBNY S1116.4–1.

106. *New York Evening Post* editorial, 18 January 1923, in F30/783A.

107. Jean Boyer (financial attaché) to Finance Minister, 16 January 1923, enclosing copy of text of Baldwin's statement as released by British delegation in Washington, F30/783A.

108. Lamont to Grenfell, 26 January 1923, TWL 111/15.

109. Copy of "Address to the President of the United States to the Congress," 7 February 1923, in F30/783A.

110. Lamont to Morrow, 30 April 1921, Dwight W. Morrow Papers, Lamont file, Amherst College Archives, Amherst, Mass. (hereafter DWM); Rupieper, *The Cuno Government and Reparations*, demonstrates the early origins of French plans to occupy the Ruhr. McDougall's *France's Rhineland Diplomacy* traces the origin of the occupation in detail.

111. Cabinet Finance Committee, 31 July 1922, PRO CAB27/71.

112. Horne's memorandum on the German financial situation was discussed in the Cabinet Finance Committee meeting of 1 December 1921. See PRO CAB27/71. Rathenau was assassinated 24 June 1922.

113. Crowe's views are set forth in a memorandum by S. P. Waterlow, "German Reparations," 30 November 1921, PRO FO371/6039. See also the draft conclusions of the 16 December 1921 cabinet meeting, PRO FO371/6039.

114. Cabinet Finance Committee, 31 July 1922, PRO CAB27/71.

115. Ibid.

116. Bradbury to Horne, 14 June 1922, PRO FO371/7478.

117. "Minutes of the London Conference on Reparations," 7–14 August

1922, PRO FO371/7486, Maier, *Recasting Bourgeois Europe*, pp. 291–293, discusses the London conferences of August and December 1922.

118. Smuts telegram to Prime Minister, 13 December 1922, PRO FO371/7490.

119. Bradbury to Horne, 14 June 1922, PRO FO371/7478.

120. Crowe minute of 20 December to L. C. M. Troughton, "Memorandum on the Proposed Occupation of the Ruhr District," 10 December 1922, PRO FO31/7490. Troughton was economic adviser to the British Section of the Rhineland High Commission.

121. Brand's speech, sent to Miles Lampson, 28 December 1922, PRO FO371/7491.

122. Lampson minute, 19 December 1922, PRO FO371/7490.

123. Hardinge to Curzon, 14 December 1922, PRO FO371/7490.

124. Schuker, *The End of French Predominance*, pp. 57ff.

125. Poincaré to Lasteyrie, 21 January 1924, F30/783A; Schuker, *The End of French Predominance*, p. 83.

126. Mouÿ to Lasteyrie, 5 February, 14 November 1924; Lasteyrie to Poincaré, 20 February 1924, F30/783A.

127. Harold G. Moulton and Leo Pasvolsky, *World War Debt Settlements* (New York: Macmillan, 1926), pp. 39–41; Leffler, *The Elusive Quest*, pp. 130–138.

128. Leffler, *The Elusive Quest*, pp. 138–142; Roger Picard and Paul Hugon, *Le problème des dettes interalliées* (Paris: Plon, 1934), pp. 92–94, 105–107.

129. J. Saxon Mills, *The Genoa Conference* (New York: Dutton, 1922), pp. 122–124.

6. J. P. Morgan & Co.

1. Finance Minister to President of the Council, 29 May 1920, F30/1422.

2. Schuker, *The End of French Predominance*, pp. 10, 34, 45–46.

3. Ibid., p. 10.

4. J. Parker Willis and Jules I. Bogen, *Investment Banking* (New York: Harper, 1929), p. 31.

5. Ibid., pp. 375–377; John T. Madden and Marcus Nadler, *Foreign Securities* (New York: Ronald Press, 1929), pp. 53–55.

6. Morgan's wartime effort on behalf of the French government is treated in Chapter 1.

7. Willis and Bogen, *Investment Banking*, p. 42.

8. "Note sur le mode d'achat du matériel aux États-Unis pendant la guerre et la période post-armistice," 1 September 1921, F30/784; Lamont to the Marquess of Lothian (British ambassador), 12 September 1939, enclosing a "Historical Memorandum" on Morgan's role as French purchasing agent during the First World War, TWL 84/19.

9. Information on Harjes and Jay in TWL 112/16; for Stettinius see DWM, file "Morgan, Grenfell & Co., London, 1915–1924."

10. Simon memorandum, "Politique financière d'après-guerre aux États-Unis," 11 December 1918, F30/723.

11. Neuflize to President of Commission des Changes, 9 December 1918, F30/723.

12. DSFEU, 27th report, December 1918, F30/723.

13. Simon memorandum, 11 December 1918, F30/723.

14. Ibid.

15. Ibid.

16. Neuflize to Finance Minister, 8 July 1919, F30/701.

17. "Conversation avec. M. Harding, Gouverneur du Federal Reserve Board," undated, F30/701; Casenave to General Commissariat for Franco-American War Affairs, 27 October 1919, F30/701.

18. Baron Émile du Marais to President of the Republic, 2 November 1919, F30/701.

19. Klotz to President of the Council, 28 October 1919, F30/701.

20. Report of "Schneider Mission," 31 October 1919, F30/701.

21. DSFEU, 15th report, June/July 1918, F30/723.

22. Célier to Casenave, 12 June 1919, F30/1424.

23. Célier to Casenave, 23 August 1919, F30/1424; Parmentier to Finance Minister, 19 November 1921, F30/1426.

24. Célier to Casenave, 24 October 1919, F30/1424.

25. Neuflize report, 18 July 1919, forwarded to Célier, F30/701.

26. Baron du Marais to President of the Republic, 2 November 1919, F30/701.

27. Neuflize report, 18 July 1919, F30/701.

28. Baron du Marais to President of the Republic, 24 October 1919, F30/701.

29. Célier to Avenol, 16 December 1919, F30/1424.

30. Stettinius to Célier, 25 September 1919, F30/701.

31. Stettinius to Morgan, Harjes et Cie., 13 October 1919, F30/701.

32. Célier to Casenave, 12, 23 June 1919, F30/1424; Lamont to Leffingwell, "French Treasury Bills," 16 July 1919, TWL 94/19.

33. Célier to Casenave, 17 July 1919, F30/1919.

34. Klotz to J. P. Morgan & Co., 24 July 1919, F30/1422.

35. Vergé to Finance Ministry, 25 October 1919, F30/723.

36. "Bons du Trésor Français en Dollars," unsigned memorandum, 7 February 1921, F30/1426.

37. Célier (for Klotz) to Casenave, 14 November 1919, F30/1424.

38. Vergé to Célier, 29 January 1920, F30/726.

39. Célier (for Klotz) to Casenave, 17 January 1920, F30/1424; Célier (for Klotz) to Morgan, Harjes et Cie., 15 January 1920, F30/1422.

40. Klotz to Casenave, 29 January 1920, F30/1424; Vergé to Célier, 27 February 1920, F30/726.

41. Brown Brothers to Célier, 27 January 1920, F30/727.

42. Vergé to Célier, 27 February 1920, F30/726; J. P. Morgan & Co., to Morgan, Harjes et Cie., 2 February 1920, F30/727.

43. Célier to Casenave, 28 February 1920, F30/1424; Vergé to Célier, 29 March 1920, F30/726; Célier telegram to Casenave, 6 July 1920, F30/1424.

44. Vergé to Célier, 26 April 1920, F30/726; Sieyès to Célier, 18 May, 22 June, 18 August 1920, F30/726; "Bons du Trésor Français en Dollars," 7 February 1921, F30/1426.

45. Ibid.

46. Casenave to General Commissariat, 23 April 1920, F30/727.

47. An account of the speech is found in F30/702.

48. Morrow to Lamont, 9 September 1920, DWM, Lamont file; memorandum on twenty-five-year external gold loan, 13 September 1920, TWL 95/6.

49. Ibid.

50. François-Marsal to Parmentier, 28 August 1920, F30/1424.

51. Ibid.

52. Ibid.

53. François-Marsal to Parmentier, 2 September 1920, F30/1424.

54. "Détermination du prix de revient du remboursement de l'Anglo-French," 17 November 1920; "Produit effectif de la réalisation en monnaies étrangers des titres étrangers appartenant au Trésor pour les dix premiers mois de 1920," 18 November 1920; "Bons du Trésor Français en Dollars," 7 February 1921, all in F30/1426; Sieyès to Finance Ministry, 9 November 1920, F30/726. See also DWM, file "J. P. Morgan & Co.: French Loans 1920–1921," for Parmentier to J. P. Morgan & Co., 15 September 1920, and memorandum "French 90-Day Treasury Bills Outstanding in the United States."

55. Ibid.; Parmentier, "Note pour le ministre," 5 February 1921, F30/1426; Memorandum on twenty-five-year external gold loan, 13 September 1920, TWL 95/6.

56. Parmentier, "Note pour le ministre," 5 February 1921, F30/1426; François-Marsal to Casenave, 29 November 1920, F30/1424.

57. Harjes to Morrow, 25 September 1924, DWM, Harjes file.

58. J. P. Morgan & Co. to Morgan, Harjes et Cie., 18 November 1920, F30/702; Parmentier to Finance Minister, 17 November 1920, F30/772.

59. J. P. Morgan & Co. to Morgan, Harjes et Cie., 29 November 1920, F30/702; Casenave to Office of Liquidation, 11 December 1920, F30/772.

60. Casenave to Office of Liquidation, 22 December 1920, 11 January 1921, F30/728; J. P. Morgan & Co. to Morgan, Harjes et Cie., 4 February 1921, F30/728.

61. Morrow to Jean de Rinquesen, 1 December 1922, DWM, Jean de Rinquesen file.

62. Sieyès to Finance Ministry, 14 January 1921, F30/726.

63. Parmentier, "Note pour le ministre," 5 February 1921, F30/1426.

64. Ibid.

65. Ibid.

66. Ibid

67. J. P. Morgan & Co. to Morgan, Harjes et Cie., 3 February 1921, F30/1426; Casenave to Finance Ministry, 4 February 1921, F30/728.

68 J. P. Morgan & Co. to Morgan, Harjes et Cie., 14 February 1921, F30/728.

69. Ibid.

70. J. P. Morgan & Co. to Morgan, Harjes et Cie., 13 April 1921, F30/728.

71. Lamont to Harjes, 21 April 1921; J. P. Morgan & Co. to Morgan, Grenfell (cable), received 21 April 1921, both in TWL 95/7.

72. Ibid.; J. P. Morgan & Co. to Morgan, Harjes et Cie., 10 May 1921, TWL 95/7.

73. For details of the loan negotiations see the extensive cable file to and from J. P. Morgan & Co. during April and May 1921 in TWL 95/7. For the French side see Parmentier to Finance Minister, 13, 15, 23 May 1921, F30/1426.

74. Harjes to Lamont, 6 July 1921, TWL 112/17.

75. Doumer to J. P. Morgan & Co., 29 July 1921, F30/1423.

76. Parmentier to Pierre de Margerie, 31 May 1921, F30/1426.

77. Parmentier to Casenave, 4 October 1921, F30/1424; J. P. Morgan & Co. to Morgan, Harjes et Cie., 25 November 1922, F30/704.

78. N. Dean Jay to Harjes, 4 March 1922, F30/704.

79. Morrow to Lamont, 20 April 1921, DWM, Lamont file; Jay speech of 31 March 1922, copy in F30/704.

80. Lamont to Morrow, 5 May 1922, TWL 113/14.

81. N. Dean Jay to Harjes, 4 March 1922, F30/704.

7. Reconstructing International Trade

1. Minute by E. A. Crowe, 18 May 1922, on letter from Geddes to Foreign Office, 16 May, PRO FO371/8191.

2. R. H. Brand to Lamont, 7 June 1919, TWL 165/10.

3. Hoover, "Memorandum on the Economic Situation of Europe," 3 July 1919, TWL 165/10. The memorandum was submitted to the 10 July meeting of the Supreme Economic Council, and is reprinted in DBFP, vol. 5, pp. 26–31.

4. League of Nations, Papers of the International Financial Conference, Brussels, 1920, no. 1, *Memorial on International Finance and Currency with Relative Documents* (Brussels: League of Nations, 1920), for letter from Glass to Homer L. Ferguson (president, U.S. Chamber of Commerce), 28 January 1920, and extract from the Annual Report of the Secretary of the Treasury, 1919; Chamberlain to R. H. Brand, 11 February 1920, p. 25.

5. League of Nations, International Financial Conference, 1920, *Verbatim Record of the Debates*, Delacroix remarks, 1 October, p. 110; Célier remarks, 1 October, pp. 104–105.

6. Lamont to Davis and Wilson, 15 May 1919, TWL 165/13; Lamont and Davis to Leffingwell, 29 May 1919, TWL 165/9.

7. Lamont to Ivy L. Lee, 9 December 1919, TWL 94/18; Casenave to Office of Liquidation, 8 May 1920, F30/726.

8. Charles Sales (Hudson's Bay House) to E. H. Vilgrain (under secretary of state for foodstuffs), 17 November 1919, F30/727.

9. Vergé to Finance Ministry, 29 January 1920, F30/723; Casenave to Commissariat for Franco-American War Affairs, 20 December 1919, F30/727.

10. Casenave to Commissariat for Franco-American War Affairs, 20 September 1919, F30/701; Mouvement général des fonds to Casenave, 22 December 1919, F30/1424.

11. For French debt in South America see memorandum "République Argentine; Engagements financières du Trésor Français," 9 February 1921, F30/1426. Details of the Argentine debt can be pieced together from the following: Parmentier to Finance Minister, 10, 30 August 1920, 25 January 1923, in F30/1426; Finance Minister to President of the Council, 28 May, 27 December 1920, and Klotz to MAE, 16 October 1919, in F30/1422; Mouvement général des fonds to Avenol, 16 April 1919, and to French commissariat in New York, 4 September 1919, in F30/1424; Lasteyrie to President of the Council, 9 June 1922, F30/1423.

12. Klotz to MAE, 20 June, 7 August 1919, F30/1422. For an overview of the French debt to Spain see Célier to Direction du contrôle des administrations financières et de l'Ordonnancement, 8 December 1919, F30/1425, and Finance Minister to President of the Council, 5 February 1920, F30/1422.

13. Klotz to MAE, 7 August 1919, F30/1422.

14. Célier to Direction du contrôle, 8 December 1919, F30/1425.

15. Finance Minister to President of the Council, 5, 16 February 1920, F30/1422.

16. Finance Minister to President of the Council, 24 April 1920, F30/1422.

17. Finance Minister to President of the Council, 31 May 1920; Célier to Barrail, 4 June 1920, both in F30/1422.

18. Finance Minister to President of the Council, 1 September 1920, F30/1422.

19. Finance Minister to President of the Council, 10 November 1920, F30/1422; Célier to Finance Minister, 23 December 1920, F30/1426.

20. *The Economist*, 28 January 1922.

21. Pierre d'Autremont, "Les aspects de notre effort commercial," *Revue universelle* 2 (15 September 1920), 750–752, and "Pour notre relèvement commercial," *Revue universelle* 1 (15 April 1920), 239–242.

22. Estournelles de Constant to François-Marsal, 27 June 1920; François-Marsal to Constant, 12 August 1920, F30/2389.

23. *L'expansion économique* 5 (June–July 1921), 8–9.

24. Célier to Direction du contrôle, 29 July 1920, F30/1425; Parmentier to Finance Minister, 9 April 1921, F30/1426.

25. "Rapport sur la situation général aux Etats-Unis," 27 February 1922, written by A. Bexon for the Compagnie francaise pour l'Amerique du Nord, F30/697.

26. Célier to Direction du contrôle, 1 March, 25 June, 11 August 1920, F30/1425.

27. Fleurieu to MAE, 30 April 1920; Millerand to Finance Minister, 5 May 1920, both in F30/2388.

28. Director General of Customs to Finance Ministry, 3 April 1920; Célier to Finance Minister, 3 April 1920, both in F30/2387.

29. François-Marsal to President of the Council, 8 May 1920; Fleurieu to MAE, 30 April 1920, both in F30/2388.

30. J. H. Clapham, "Europe After the Great Wars, 1816 and 1920," *The Economic Journal* 30 (December 1920), 433.

31. Cabinet Financial Committee, 30 January 1920, PRO CAB27/71; Klotz to Clemenceau, 28 October 1919, F30/701.

32. For an example of Norman's concern with Central Europe see Norman to Strong, 1 December 1921, FRBNY S1116.2–2. Norman wrote that "I don't believe it would take a great deal of financial or political stupidity at the present moment to bring chaos into Austria similar to what we see in Russia; to break up Germany, and beginning in Portugal to spread revolution right through the Peninsula."

33. Aldcroft, *From Versailles to Wall Street*, pp. 111–112, for British statistics. Aldcroft also states that French exports had recovered to prewar levels by 1923, and by 1925 were almost one-quarter larger than in 1913. For French statistics see "Notes mensuelles sur le Commerce Extérieur de la France," 17th note, January–February 1921, F30/1511; Director General of Customs report to Finance Minister, 11 September 1920, F30/2387.

34. *The Economist*, 21 June 1919.

35. Ibid.

36. Supreme Council Conclusions of 23 February 1920, "Allied Policy in Russia," HLRO, Lloyd George Papers, F/202/3/1.

37. Louis Fischer, *The Soviets in World Affairs: A History of Relations Between the Soviet Union and the Rest of the World*, 2 vols. (London: J. Cape, 1930), I, 252.

38. See the following notes by E. F. Wise in HLRO, Lloyd George Papers: "Note on the Russian Position," 19 February 1920, F/202/3/2; "Negotiations for Re-Opening Trade with Soviet Russia," 18 April 1920, F/202/3/3; "Note on Economic Relations with Russia," 21 May 1920, F/202/3/5. Another Wise memorandum, "Economic Aspects of British Policy concerning Russia," 6 January 1920, is printed in DBFP, vol. 2, pp. 867–870. For the heavy influence of Wise's "expert" opinion on Britain's Russian trade policy see Richard H. Ullman, *Anglo-Soviet Relations, 1917–1921*, vol. 3, *The Anglo-Soviet Accord* (Princeton: Princeton University Press, 1972), pp. 11–19. Lloyd George and many at the Foreign Office (with the exception of Curzon) accepted Wise's assumptions about the size of the current Russian wheat harvest, the ability of the Soviet government to get

possession of it and ship it abroad, and the effect it would have on the food supply and political stability of Central Europe.

39. For biographical data on the Soviet trade delegation see Ullman, *The Anglo-Soviet Accord*, pp. 89–91. The invitation was issued following the 26 April resolution of the Allied Supreme Council at San Remo, authorizing trade talks between "representatives of the Allied governments" and "the Russian Trade Delegation."

40. Wise memorandum, 18 April 1920, HLRO, Lloyd George Papers, F/202/3/3; Note on the Soviet trade delegation, September 1920, F/203/1; Ullman, *The Anglo-Soviet Accord*, p. 92.

41. Wise memorandum, 19 February 1920, HLRO, Lloyd George Papers, F/202/3/2; memorandum, 21 May 1920, F/202/3/5.

42. Wise, "Note for the Prime Minister by the Russian Trade Committee," 27 May 1920, HLRO, Lloyd George Papers, F/202/3/6.

43. "Note by the Board of Trade on the principles which should guide British representatives who take part in any discussion with Russian (Soviet) delegates on resumption of trade with Russia," 26 May 1920, HLRO Lloyd George Papers, F/27/6/53.

44. Millerand note, delivered by Albert Gate House (French ambassador in London), 30 May 1920, HLRO, Lloyd George Papers, F/51/2/12. When France refused to participate in the talks, Britain decided not to issue an invitation to Italy. See Ullman, *The Anglo-Soviet Accord*, pp. 95–96.

45. Fisher, *The Soviets in World Affairs*, I, 282.

46. Hoare to Horne, 9 June 1920, HLRO, Lloyd George Papers, F/27/6/36.

47. Ibid.

48. Ibid.

49. John W. Davis (U.S. ambassador in London) to Curzon, 26 June 1920, HLRO, Lloyd George Papers, F/60/1/27.

50. Krasin statement, 29 June 1920, HLRO, Lloyd George Papers, F/202/3/18; Ullman, *The Anglo-Soviet Accord*, pp. 124–128. Krasin's statement may be found in DBFP, vol. 8, p. 385.

51. The British memorandum of 30 June 1920 is reprinted in Ullman, *The Anglo-Soviet Accord*, pp. 129–130. See pp. 399–400 for Chicherin's 7 July telegram accepting the "principles" of the 30 June memorandum.

52. Churchill memorandum, 25 August 1920, HLRO, Lloyd George Papers, F/203/1; Curzon memorandum, 2 September 1920, HLRO, Lloyd George Papers, F/203/1/3. These were followed by Churchill's 21 September memorandum, F/203/1/16, and Curzon's Cabinet Paper of 16 September, F/203/1/14.

53. Lloyd George, "Memorandum on the Proposal to Expel Messrs. Kameneff and Krassin," Lucerne, 2 September 1920, HLRO, Lloyd George Papers, F/203/1/3.

54. Wilson to Lloyd George, 3 November 1920, HLRO, Lloyd George Papers, F/60/1/31.

55. *Trade Agreement Between His Britannic Majesty's Government and*

the Government of the Russian Socialist Federal Soviet Republic, 16 March 1921 (Cmd. 1207, 1921). The text is reproduced in Ullman, *The Anglo-Soviet Accord*, pp. 474–478. Ullman covers the final stage of the negotiations, pp. 411ff.

56. Strong to Norman, 21 March 1921, FRBNY S1116.2–1; Norman to Strong, 2 May 1921, FRBNY S1116.2–2.

57. Edward Hallett Carr, *A History of Soviet Russia: The Bolshevik Revolution*, 1917–1923, 3 vols. (London: Macmillan, 1950–53), III, 287, 351–352.

58. Ibid. pp. 352–353.

59. Ibid., pp. 353–354; Fischer, *The Soviets in World Affairs*, I, 220. Fischer believed Sinclair actually exploited the lease, as, he says, Russia held the northern half of the island. Carr states that the Japanese occupied "the whole island."

60. Hodgson to Curzon, 2 June 1922, PRO FO371/8162.

61. Carr, *The Bolshevik Revolution*, III, 354; Fischer, *The Soviets in World Affairs*, I, 234; D'Abernon to Curzon, 11 October 1922, enclosing summary of Litvinov press interview in Berlin, PRO FO371/8163.

62. Carr, *The Bolshevik Revolution*, III, 431.

63. Ibid., pp. 431–432. Terms of the Urquhart contract are also found in papers on the Urquhart agreement, PRO FO371/8162.

64. Livinov press interview in D'Abernon to Curzon, 11 October 1922, PRO FO371/8163.

65. *Daily Telegraph* article, 11 September 1922, in PRO FO371/8162.

66. Leeper minutes, 9, 11 September 1922, PRO FO371/8162.

67. *Manchester Guardian*, interview with Urquhart, and article headlined, "A Real Anglo-Russian Trade Agreement," 13 September 1922, in PRO FO371/8162. The article outlines the terms of the agreement.

68. Litvinov press interview in D'Abernon to Curzon, 11 October 1922, PRO FO371/8163; Urquhart-Gregory conversation, as recorded by Gregory in memorandum, "The Urquhart Agreement, Russia and Turkey," 3 October 1922, PRO FO371/8162; S.I.S. report, I November 1922, "The Krassin-Urquhart Agreement;" Urquhart to Gregory, 17 November 1922, PRO FO371/8163.

69. D'Abernon to Curzon, 11 October 1922; Ernest C. Wilton (Riga) to Foreign Office, 22 October 1922, in PRO FO371/8163; William Peters (British Commercial Mission, Moscow) to Curzon, 10 October 1922; Urquhart to Philip Lloyd-Greame, 20 September 1922, in PRO FO371/8162.

70. From file PRO FO371/8162, see Urquhart to Lloyd-Greame, 20 September 1922; Peters to Curzon, 10 October 1922; *Morning Post*, 13 October 1922; Taube to Urquhart, undated. From file PRO FO371/8163, see S.I.S. report, 1 November 1922, "The Krassin-Urquhart Agreement"; Urquhart to Gregory, 17 November 1922.

71. Ludwell Denny, *We Fight for Oil* (New York: Knopf, 1928), p. 167; Louis Fischer, *Oil Imperialism: The International Struggle for Oil* (New York: International Publishers, 1926), p. 53; Louis Le Page, "L'impérialisme

du pétrole," *Revue universelle* 3 (15 October 1920), 182. For a table showing U.S. Geological Survey estimates of world oil reserves in 1920 see David White, "The Petroleum Resources of the World," *Annals of the American Academy of Political and Social Science* (May 1920), p. 123.

72. Le Page, "L'impérialisme du pétrole," p. 166.

73. Fisher, *Oil Imperialism*, p. 151.

74. J. D. Gregory to Foreign Office, 7 May 1922, with McDonell's minute of 10 May giving Foreign Office response to Shell's request; Oliphant to Gregory, 12 May 1922, PRO FO371/7729.

75. J. C. Clarke (Petroleum Department, Board of Trade) to O'Malley, 17 December 1921, enclosing letter of 16 December from H. E. Nichols, Anglo-Persian Oil Co.; Foreign Office to Petroleum Department, 24 December 1921, PRO FO371/6274; Clarke to Foreign Office, 4 January 1922, PRO FO371/7727.

76. McDonell memorandum, "Petroleum," 19 May 1922, with O'Malley minute of 20 July 1922, PRO FO371/8162; Gleboff Grosni Petroleum Co., Ltd., to Secretary of State for Foreign Affairs, 26 May 1922, PRO FO371/8162; O'Malley minute of 6 June 1922, appended to 26 May letter from Gleboff Grosni Petroleum Co., PRO FO371/8162.

77. Clarke memorandum attached to 13 September 1922 letter from Geoffrey Haly (Petroleum Department) to Sir John Dashwood (Foreign Office), PRO FO371/8162.

78. O'Malley memorandum, "Relations Between the Foreign Office and the Royal Dutch Shell Group," 4 May 1923, PRO FO371/9346; O'Malley minute giving account of meeting between Sir Robert Waley-Cohen (Shell) and Gregory (Foreign Office), 10 October 1922, PRO FO371/8162. For the text of Boyle's letter of introduction to Krasin, furnished by Esmond Ovey at Curzon's request, see Fischer, *Oil Imperialism*, p. 41.

79. Krasin's statement is cited in Carl P. Parrini, *Heir to Empire: United States Economic Diplomacy, 1916–1923* (Pittsburgh: University of Pittsburgh Press, 1969), p. 155. For the text of the Cannes Resolutions see DBFP, vol. 19, pp. 35–36.

80. Beneš to Lloyd George, 22 February 1922, with minute by J. D. Gregory, 25 February, PRO FO371/7421.

81. Discussion of Cannes Resolutions, with Gregory minute of 1 February 1922, PRO FO371/8190.

82. Chamberlain to Lloyd George, 21 March 1922, HLRO, Lloyd George Papers, F/7/5/20. For the cabinet crisis over the issue of recognition see also Morgan, *Consensus and Disunity*, pp. 308–311, and Peter Rowland, *David Lloyd George: A Biography* (New York: Macmillan, 1975), pp. 569–570.

83. Lloyd George to Horne, 22 March 1922; Horne to Lloyd George, 23 March; Horne to Lloyd George, 24 March, in HLRO, Lloyd George Papers, F/27/6/57, 58, 59.

84. Lloyd George to Chamberlain, 22 March 1922, HLRO, Lloyd George Papers, F/7/5/21.

85. J. M. Keynes, "The Genoa Conference," Reconstruction Series, no. 3, *Manchester Guardian Commercial* (15 June 1922), 132.

86. Lloyd George to Chamberlain, 22 March 1922, HLRO, Lloyd George Papers, F/7/5/21.

87. Ibid. In the 28 March cabinet meeting, Lloyd George "carried a much modified form of recognition," limited to an exchange of chargés d'affaires in London and Moscow, and this only if it proved consistent with the consensus at Genoa. See Morgan, *Consensus and Disunity*, p. 310.

88. Chamberlain to Lloyd George, 23 March 1922, HLRO, Lloyd George Papers, F/7/5/22.

89. Chamberlain to Lloyd George, 25 March 1922, HLRO, Lloyd George Papers, F/7/5/24.

90. Memorandum by Sir S. Chapman on meeting with Jacques Seydoux (French Foreign Ministry, Commercial Relations Department) and Joseph Avenol (French financial delegate in London), 10 March 1922, PRO FO371/7422.

91. Francesco Nitti, "The Genoa Conference," Reconstruction Series, no. 3, *Manchester Guardian Commercial* (15 June 1922), 134.

92. Keynes, "The Genoa Conference," p. 132–133.

93. Grigg speech of 15 June 1922 to The 1920 Club, HLRO, Lloyd George Papers, F/150; Gregory to Foreign Office, 13 May 1922, Pro FO371/8190.

94. Meeting of the Committee of Experts on Russian Questions, 22 April, HLRO, Lloyd George Papers, F/150; DBFP, vol. 19, pp. 491–493. Records of the meetings of the First Commission are found in HLRO, Lloyd George Papers, F/150.

95. "Memorandum to the Russian Delegation," 2 May 1922, HLRO, Lloyd George Papers, F/150. For the French offer see "Draft Memorandum to the Russian Delegation," 29 April 1922, PRO FO371/8189. See also DBFP, vol. 19, pp. 692–702.

96. Foreign Office to Genoa Delegation, received 2 May 1922, HLRO Lloyd George Papers, F/150.

97. Curzon (for Chamberlain) to Delegation, 9 May 1922, HLRO, Lloyd George Papers, F/150, and PRO FO371/8190; O'Malley minute, 8 May 1922, PRO FO371/8189, also reproduced in DBFP, vol. 19, pp. 702–703. Curzon agreed with O'Malley's assessment. See also Chamberlain to Prime Minister, 10 May 1922, PRO FO371/8190.

98. "Draft Minutes of the Fourth Conference of the British Empire Delegation," 10 May 1922, PRO FO371/8190; also in DBFP, vol. 19, pp. 789–794. For Shell negotiations with the Russians see Parrini, *Heir to Empire*, pp. 158ff.

99. Russian response to 2 May memorandum, delivered 11 May, HLRO Lloyd George Papers, F/150. It also appears in Parliamentary Command Papers, Cmd. 1667 (1922).

100. Gregory to Foreign Office, 12 May 1922, PRO FO371/8190.

101. Hankey to Chamberlain, 11 May 1922, PRO FO371/8191.

102. Gregory to Foreign Office, 2 cables, 12 May 1922, PRO FO371/8190.

103. Fourth Meeting of the Sub-Commission of the First Commission, 17 May 1922, DBFP, vol. 19, p. 955.

104. Gregory to Foreign Office, 12 May 1922, PRO FO371/8190; Draft Minutes of the Sixth Conference of the British Empire Delegation, 13 May, Sir Laming Worthington-Evans speaking for the Prime Minister, DBFP, vol. 19, p. 871.

105. Grigg speech to The 1920 Club, 15 June 1922, HLRO, Lloyd George Papers, F/150.

8. An International Solution?

1. Cassel's letter to *The Economist*, 17 May 1919.

2. Gerard Vissering, *International Economic and Financial Problems* (London: Macmillan, 1920), p. 88. See pp. 92–98 for text of Memorial.

3. Ibid.

4. Ibid.

5. Glass to Homer L. Ferguson, 28 January 1920, in League of Nations, Papers of the International Financial Conference, Brussels, *Memorial on International Finance and Currency*, pp. 37–43.

6. Chamberlain to Brand, 11 February 1920, in *Memorial on International Finance and Currency*, pp. 21–25.

7. *The Economist*, 31 January 1920.

8. L. Dumont-Wilden, "La conférence financière de Bruxelles et la Société des Nations," *Revue politique et littéraire* 58 (16 October 1920), 629–631.

9. François-Marsal to President of the Council, 9 September 1920; "projet de resolution" for the cabinet, drawn up by the Finance Ministry, September 1920, both in F30/2389.

10. Ibid.

11. François-Marsal to President of the Council, 14 September 1920; François-Marsal to Léon Bourgeois, 14 September 1920, F30/2389.

12. Deane E. Traynor, *International Monetary and Financial Conferences in the Interwar Period* (Washington: Catholic University of America Press, 1949), p. 51.

13. League of Nations, International Financial Conference, Brussels, *Monetary Problems: Introduction and Joint Statement of Economic Experts* (London, 1920), Paper nos. 1, 2, and 3.

14. Traynor, *International Monetary and Financial Conferences*, pp. 56–57, 65; League of Nations, International Financial Conference, Brussels, *Verbatim Record of the Debates*, p. 30, Avenol's remarks, 27 September meeting of the Public Finance committee.

15. Traynor, *International Monetary and Financial Conferences*, pp. 57–59; H. A. Siepmann, "The International Financial Conference at Brussels," *The Economic Journal* 30 (December 1920), 448–449; Arthur Raffalo-

vich, "La conférence financière internationale de Bruxelles, 24 septembre–8 octobre, 1920," *Journal des économistes* 67 (November 1920), 361–362.

16. Traynor, *International Monetary and Financial Conferences*, pp. 60–63; Raffalovich, "La conférence financiere," pp. 362–368.

17. *Le monde économique*, 16 August 1920; "The International Financial Conference at Brussels and Its Lessons," *The Round Table* 11 (December 1920–September 1921), 60; Robertson, *Money*, p. 103.

18. Carl P. Parrini, *Heir to Empire: United States Economic Diplomacy, 1916–1923* (Pittsburgh: University of Pittsburgh Press, 1969), p. 142.

19. Chalmers report to Chamberlain, 8 October 1920, PRO T172/1108.

20. Hardinge to Curzon, 17 January 1921, enclosing 16 January article from *Le Martin*, PRO FO371/6981.

21. "Ted" to Wise, 20 October 1920, HLRO, Lloyd George Papers, F/175/13.

22. François-Marsal to Leygues, 30 October 1920, F30/2389.

23. "Ted" to Wise, 20 October 1920, HLRO, Lloyd George Papers, F/175/13.

24. Ibid.

25. Frédéric Mathews, "Une politique du change," *Journal des économistes* 63 (July 1919), 53–66, and "Une politique du change et sa réception," *Journal des économistes* 64 (October 1919), 23–27.

26. Jèze, *Les finances de guerre*, pp. 91–105. For Stern's proposal see JOC: *Débats parlementaires*, 28 December 1918, pp. 3679ff.

27. Nogaro's plan is discussed in Yves-Guyot, "L'illusion fiduciaire et la réalité économique," pp. 9–13.

28. Vanderlip's plan is discussed in Bertrand Nogaro, "Une banque d'émission internationale: Le projet Vanderlip," *Revue économique internationale* (1922–I), 147–156.

29. Ibid.

30. League of Nations, International Financial Conference, Brussels, *Verbatim Record of the Debates*, Delacroix remarks, 1 October 1920, p. 112.

31. Ibid., Ter Meulen's remarks, 2 October 1920, pp. 117–119.

32. Pamphlet authored by Sir Drummond Drummond Fraser, *International Credits* (London, 1921), p. 8.

33. Cassel, *Memorandum on the World's Monetary Problems*, p. 74.

34. League of Nations, *Report Presented to the Third Assembly from the Economic and Financial Organization*, 24 August 1922 (Geneva, 1922), p. 8.

35. Fraser, *International Credits*, p. 8.

36. Strong to Norman, 21 March 1921, FRBNY S1116.2–1.

37. Geddes to Curzon, 28 October 1921, PRO FO371/5715; "Report to the Financial Committee from the Organizer of International Credits," in League of Nations, Provisional Economic and Financial Committee, *Reports Presented by the Committee in September 1921* (Geneva, 1921), pp. 22–24.

38. *The Economist*, 2 April 1922; League of Nations, *Report Presented to the Third Assembly*, p. 8.

39. Parrini, *Heir to Empire*, p. 147.

40. League of Nations, *Report Presented to the Third Assembly*, p. 9.

41. Parrini, *Heir to Empire*, p. 153.

42. Department of State, *Papers Relating to the Foreign Relations of the United States, 1922* (Washington: Govt. Printing Office, 1923), I, 384–394.

43. Norman to Strong, 23 February 1922, FRBNY S1116.3–2.

44. H. G. Chilton to Curzon, 7 April 1922, citing American press opinion, PRO FO371/7426.

45. Strong to Norman, 18 February, 4 March 1922, FRBNY S1116.3–1.

46. Leffler, *The Elusive Quest*, p. 36.

47. Leaf's statement in *The Economist*, 4 February 1922.

48. *The Economist*, 1 April 1922.

49. Ibid.

50. H. Wilson Harris, "Why Genoa Failed," *Contemporary Review* 121 (January–June 1922), 681–682.

51. Lasteyrie to President of the Council, 9 March 1922, F30/1427.

52. Keynes, "The Stabilisation of the European Exchanges: A Plan for Genoa," pp. 3–5.

53. "Draft Proposals for an International Gold Standard," Treasury memorandum to Foreign Office, 10 April 1922, PRO FO371/7427.

54. International Economic Conference, Genoa, "Note on Currency," by G. Vissering, 24 April, and "Observations on M. Vissering's Note," by C. Lepreux, PRO FO371/7432.

55. Currency subcommittee, 2d meeting, 13 April 1922, PRO FO371/7426.

56. J.-B. Legros, "Chronique de l'inflation," *Journal des économistes* 72 (April–June 1922), 166–167.

57. Minute of 20 April 1922, signed "JR," PRO FO371/7427.

58. Copy of Keynes's article, sent to Sir Edward Grigg, in HLRO, Lloyd George Papers, F/204/1/10.

59. Clay, *Lord Norman*, pp. 138–139.

60. Cassel, "The Economic and Financial Decisions of the Genoa Conference," pp. 139–140.

61. Leffler, *The Elusive Quest*, pp. 26, 32, 38.

62. Extract from Horne's 10 May speech, from *The Times*, 11 May 1922, PRO FO371/7432.

63. R. F. Wigram minute of 10 November 1922, on Loucheur's 8 November speech in the Chamber of Deputies, PRO FO371/7486.

64. Milne Cheetham to Curzon, 11 March 1922, PRO FO371/7422.

65. Geddes to Foreign Office, 16 December 1921, with Tyrrell minute of 17 December; Grahame to Foreign Office, 21 December 1921, PRO FO371/5662.

66. *Gazette* interview and Foreign Office minute, PRO FO371/5625.

67. Blackett to Sperling, 19 October 1921; Sperling to Blackett, 21 October 1921, PRO FO371/5662.

68. Geddes's communiqué of 14 December 1921; Geddes to Curzon, 30 November 1921, PRO FO371/5625.

69. Geddes to Curzon, 30 November 1921, PRO FO371/5625.

Bibliography

Primary archival sources utilized for this work are listed below. Printed documents, memoires, articles, and monographs are cited fully in the notes at first reference. Most references to printed material are found in the Introduction and Chapters 1 and 2.

France

Ministère des Finances (series F30), Ministère de l'Économie et Ministère du Budget, Service des Archives Économiques et Financières, Paris.

Great Britain

Official Archives, Public Record Office, London:

Cabinet Office
 CAB27: Cabinet Committees
Foreign Office
 FO371: Foreign Office General Correspondence, Political
Treasury
 T160: Finance Files (Banking)
 T170: Sir John Bradbury Papers
 T171: Chancellor of the Exchequer's Office, Budget and Finance Bill Papers
 T172: Chancellor of the Exchequer's Office, Miscellaneous Papers
 T176: Sir Otto Niemeyer Papers
 T185: Committee on Currency and Exchanges after the War, Hearings

Personal Papers, House of Lords Record Office, London:

David Lloyd George Papers
Andrew Bonar Law Papers

United States

Benjamin Strong Papers, Federal Reserve Bank of New York, New York
Thomas W. Lamont Papers, Baker Library, Harvard Graduate School of Business Administration, Boston, Mass.
Dwight W. Morrow Papers, Amherst College Archives, Amherst, Mass.

Index

Alsace-Lorraine: reintegration costs, 72, 94–95, 135
Anglo-American financial entente, 38–39
Anglo-French loan (1915), 30–31, 168–169, 215, 217, 237
Anglo-Soviet trade agreement, 243, 244, 245, 248, 250, 251
Argentina: war credits to Allies, 18, 29–30; French credits, 234
Armenia, 256
Avenol, Joseph, 26, 27, 178, 280; policy paper on war debts, 175–177
Azerbaijan, 256, 257

Baker, Newton D., 155, 166
Baldwin, Stanley, 161; war debt settlement, 186–187, 188, 189
Balfour note, 178–179, 183
Bankers, British: reject credit controls, 47–48
Bank of England: Bank rate, 48, 50. *See also* Cunliffe; Cokayne; Norman
Bank of France: sterling purchases, 25; London gold deposit, 26–29; advances to Treasury, 50–52, 134–137
Barthou, Louis, 158
Beneš, Eduard, 259, 260
Benson, Robert H., 47
Bérenger, Henry, 197
Billy, Edouard de, 21, 24, 32, 33
Blackett, Basil P.: Avenol-Blackett agreement, 26; Anglo-French loan, 30, 31; dear money policy, 48; spreading pensions, 78; French budgeting practices, 78; defends Treasury policy, 85–86; deficit budgeting, 90, 91; capital levy and compulsory loan, 126, 127; floating

debt, 132; funding U.S. war debt, 148, 154, 159, 160, 175–176, 178; funding talks with Rathbone, 150; reparations and inter-Allied debt, 155–156; Parmentier mission, 175–176; Balfour note, 179; Genoa conference, 292; Washington conference, 296
Bloc, Frédéric, 162
Bonar Law, Andrew: wartime controls, 37; capital levy, 73–75; war debt funding agreement, 189
Boyden, Ronald W., 276
Boyer, Jean, 196
Bradbury, Sir John, 122, 124; French credits, 37; reparations and war debts, 192; Ruhr occupation, 193
Brand, Robert Henry: capital shortage, 76; Ruhr occupation, 194; Britain's credit requirements, 230; Brussels conference, 280
Briand, Aristide, 9, 106, 174, 296
Brussels financial conference (1920), 270, 275–281
Budget, British: (1919–1920), 67–70, 72; (1920–1921), 75, 81, 128; (1922–1923), 91–93
Budget, French: (1919), 98; (1920), 98–99, 100, 101–102; (1921), 102–104; (1922), 104–105; (1923), 106–107, 108
Budgets: deficits, 10, 63, 69, 70, 89–91; procedures and structures, 63, 64, 65, 67; estimates, 64; debt service, 66, 70
Bukharin, Nikolai, 255
Burton, Theodore, 157, 182, 183, 184

Caillaux, Joseph, 60, 196

Cannes resolutions, 258, 259–261, 263
"Capacity to pay," 146–147
Capitalism: crisis in theory, 11; crisis in theory and structure, 280, 281, 298
Capital levy: Klotz, 71, 73; François-Marsal, 73; Bonar Law, 73–75; British industry and banking, 75; survival of civilization, 76
Capital shortage, 76–77
Casenave, Maurice, 72, 163, 165, 173, 205, 213, 214, 218
Cassell, Gustav, 40, 54; quantity theory, 42; purchasing power parity, 54–55; gold standard, 55, 57; U.S. monetary policy, 56; stabilization, 57; French reparation demands, 59; predicts postwar crisis, 272; Genoa conference, 293
Caucasus, 256. See also Armenia; Azerbaijan; Georgia
Cecil, Lord Robert, 87
Célier, Alexandre: Three Cities loan, 207; J. P. Morgan & Co., 208, 209; French treasury bill sales in U.S., 210, 211, 212, 213; foreign credits, 232; Spanish debt, 237; Brussels conference, 280
Chalmers, Lord Robert: U.S. funding mission, 152, 153, 154; Brussels conference, 279, 280, 281, 282
Chamberlain, Austen: debt to U.S. Treasury, 22, 147, 150, 152; postwar assistance to France, 25–29, 37; breaks financial ties to France, 29, 31; credit controls, 48; budget (1919–1920), 67–70, 72; EPD, 68–69, 72, 83, 84; budget (1920–1921), 81; criticizes business, 83, 84, 87; taxable capacity, 87; assumes chancellorship, 123; domestic funding operation, 124–125, 126, 127; conversion loans, 131; Russian gold, 169; Soviet recognition, trade, and property settlement, 263–264, 266, 267
Cheysson, Pierre, 280
Chicherin, Grigorii, 265, 268
Churchill, Winston: anti-Bolshevism, 242, 246, 248, 263; Soviet recognition, 261
Clarke, J. C., 258
Clemenceau, Georges, 1, 10, 28, 32, 94, 95, 99, 113

Clémentel, Etienne: Paris conference (1916), 17; J. P. Morgan & Co., 218
Cokayne, Brien: currency note cancellation, 45; credit controls, 48; Bank's control over money markets, 50; floating debt, 122, 123, 124, 125; Brussels conference, 279
Colwyn committee, 131, 132
Conversion loans, British, 88, 92, 129, 131, 132
Corporatism, 3, 238
Crosby, Oscar T., 157, 158
Crowe, Sir Eyre: Anglo-French relations, 155, 190–191; funding U.S. debt, 159; Ruhr occupation, 193
Cunliffe, Baron Walter: anti-French statements, 19; French gold, 28; currency note cancellation, 45–47
Currency: "pegging," 15; British circulation, 15, 42, 45–47; French circulation, 15, 42, 50–52
Curzon of Kedleston, George Nathaniel, Marquess: U.S. debt, 151; reparations, 190; Russian trade mission, 249

D'Abernon, Edgar Vincent, Viscount, 155
Dawes, Charles G., 202
Dawes Plan, 1, 6, 8, 112, 196
Davis, Norman H., 24, 34, 35, 153, 206, 207, 232
Davison, Henry P., 213, 214
Dear money, 45, 48
Death duties, 68, 72
Debt, public: magnitude and structure, 14; distribution, 120–121; high cost of, 130, 133; statistical comparison of, 133; social conflict over, 142, 143–144
Debt service, see Budgets
Décamps, Jules: exchange rivalry, 56; gold exchange standard, 59; Bank advances, 134
Deficit budgeting, see Budgets
Deflation, 10, 50–52, 141, 142
Delacroix, Léon, 284
Depreciation, monetary, 53, 54, 58, 59, 60
Derby, Lord, 29
Deschanel, Paul, 99
Devaluation, 57–58, 59, 60–61

Dixon, Sir Herbert, 85
Double décime, 108
Doumer, Paul: shipping subsidy, 96; budget (1922) ,104–105; national defense bonds, 140; U.S. debt, 174; J. P. Morgan & Co., 225–226

Edgar, Sir Edward Mackay, 296
Edge Act, 238, 239
Excess Profits Duty (EPD), 68–69, 72, 75, 80–81; reduced (1919–1920), 68, 72, 75; increased (1920–1921), 75, 81; unsatisfactory characteristics of, 81–82; business opposition, 83, 84; termination (1921), 83, 87; defaulted payments, 88

Federal Reserve Board, 233
Federation of British Industries (F.B.I.), 83, 84
Finance Ministry, French: organization and morale, 66; operational problems, 93–94; interministerial conflicts, 94; contradictory policies of, 130, 136–137; debt to U.S. Treasury, 172, 173
Fisher, Irving: quantity theory, 42; devaluation, 61
Fisher, N. F. Warren, 83
Floating debt, 15; British policy, 121–132; French policy, 134–143
Flux, A. W., 89
Food subsidy, French, 96–97
Forced loan: Britain, 125–126; France, 136
Fordney-McCumber tariff, 239
Foreign Office, British: inter-Allied debt, 148–149, 152, 158, 175, 176; Parmentier mission, 185; Russian oil, 256–258
Foster, Sir Harry, 84
Franc: depreciation, 54, 58, 60; Ruhr occupation currency, 108–111
Franco-American balance, 161–166
François-Marsal convention, 51–52, 137–138, 139–141
François-Marsal, Frédéric: Anglo-French loan, 29, 31, 214–215, 216; gold exchange standard, 59; devaluation, 59, 60; interministerial conflict, 94; Saar, 95–96; food subsidy, 97; foreign loans (1920, 1921), 99–100, 216, 218;

budget (1920), 100, 101–102; budget (1921), 102–103; reparations and budget, 105–106; Casenave-Mellon negotiations, 164; war debts and reparations, 172, 173; treasury bills, 212; Spanish credits, 236, 237; economic warfare, 240, 241; Brussels conference, 275, 276, 280
Fraser, Sir Drummond D.: Ter Meulen plan, 285, 286
Friedman, Milton, 138
Funding operation, domestic debt: Britain, 122–127, 129; France, 140, 141, 142

Geddes, Sir Auckland, 58; wartime controls, 30, 36; debt cancellation, 149; funding U.S. debt, 151, 152, 153, 154, 158; reports French intentions, 172–173; Ter Meulen plan, 286; Washington conference, 287
Genoa conference (1922), 1; exchange stabilization, 57, 58, 291–293; inter-Allied debts, 158; Russia, 258, 259, 265–268; organization of, 264; assessment of, 265, 267–268, 269–270, 294–295; financial goals, 288; U.S. absence, 288, 289, 295
Georgia (Caucasus), 256
Gide, Charles, 51
Gignoux, Claude Joseph, 51
Glass, Carter: assistance to France, 24–25; inter-Allied debt, 31; "Keynes Plan," 34; assistance to Europe, 231; international financial conference, 274
Gold: French deposit in London, 17, 26–29; Russian, 168–169
Gold exchange standard, 8, 56–58, 272
Gold standard, 4, 41, 51, 52–56
Goodenough, Frederick, 126
Goschen, W. H. N., 123
Grain Corporation, 232, 233
Gregory, John Duncan, 259, 260, 265, 268, 269
Grenfell, Edward C., 186, 187
Grigg, Sir Edward, 265, 269–270

Hague conference (1922), 265, 268, 269
Hamilton, H. P., 83, 88
Hammer, Armand, 252

Hankey, Sir Maurice, 158, 268
Harding administration: war debts, 4, 153–154, 156
Harding, Warren G.: war debts, 171, 172; WWDFC, 188, 189
Harding, Warren P. G., 203, 205
Hardinge of Penhurst, Lord, 58
Harjes, Herman, 202, 216, 217, 228
Harvey, George, 160
Hawtrey, Ralph George: dear money, 48; French deflation, 51; economize gold, 55; gold standard, 57; stabilization, 57; devaluation, 59; Treasury taxation policy, 86–87; EPD arrears, 87–88; deficit budgeting, 91; French budget (1920), 99
Herrick, Myron T., 174, 175, 177
Hoare, Sir Samuel: Soviet trade negotiations, 246–247
Holden, Sir Edward, 38; currency notes, 45–47; funding operation, 123
Hoover, Herbert: corporatism, 5; WWDFC, 157, 182; war debts, 173; criticized by Lamont, 189; International Memorial, 273; "Memorandum on the Economic Situation of Europe" (1919), 231
Horne, Sir Robert: EDP payments, 88; tax cuts, 88, 91, 92; sinking fund, 91, 92; pensions, 92; war debt service burdens, 92–93; funding operations, 132; WWDFC, 186, 187; reparations moratorium, 190; Anglo-Soviet trade agreement, 243; Soviet recognition, 261, 262; Genoa conference, 292, 294
Houston, David F.: opinion of French finance, 101; debt cancellation, 150, 166; French debt, 172
Hughes, Charles Evans, 9; WWDFC, 157, 160, 182, 184; inter-Allied debts, 173; British funding settlement, 189; Genoa conference, 264; Washington conference, 295
Hythe conference (1920), 171

Imperialism: and debt problem, 114–116
Inchcape, Lord, 123
International Memorial, 272–273

Jay, N. Dean, 202, 226, 227, 228

Jusserand, Jules, 101, 172

Kamenev, Lev B., 245, 248
Kennedy, John F., 67
Keynes, John Maynard, 9, 51; Anglo-American banking entente, 38; quantity theory, 42–43; dear money, 48; McKenna's inflation theory, 49; stabilization, 49, 54, 57, 61, 291–292; U.S. monetary policy, 56; managed currency, 56; gold standard, 56, 57; gold exchange standard, 57; devaluation, 57–58; Genoa conference, 57, 291–292, 293; French politics, 58; economists and politicians, 114; floating debt, 131; British settlement with WWDFC, 189; German reconstruction, 241; Britain's Russian policy, 262, 264–265, 269, 270
"Keynes Plan," 33–35
Klotz, Louis-Lucien: British credits, 21, 24; relations with Ausetn Chamberlain, 26–29; war debt redistribution schemes, 32; budget (1919), 70–71, 98; capital levy, 71; budget (1920), 98–99, 102; "sincere budget," 104; Bank advances, 135–136; Rathbone agreement, 162; Parker-Morel accord, 164; Anglo-French common front, 170–171; French securities in U.S., 206, 211; Spanish credits, 234, 235; German trade, 241, 242
Krassin, Leonid: Anglo-Soviet trade agreement, 243, 244, 245, 248; Urquhart concession, 252, 254, 255; Royal Dutch Shell, 258; Soviet recognition, 259
Kuhn, Loeb & Co.: Three Cities loan, 207; advance to French Finance Ministry, 208; City of Paris loan, 224

Lamont, Thomas W.: "Keynes Plan," 34; Paris Peace conference, 34–36; war debts, 35–36, 157, 159, 173; Anglo-American entente, 38; French finance and foreign policy, 58, 227; British war debt settlement, 187; criticizes Hoover, 189; French loans, 215, 222; U.S. credits for Europe, 230–232
Lampson, Miles W., 194

Lasteyrie, Charles de, 58; Finance Ministry operational problems, 93–94; budget (1923), 106; Ruhr occupation, 107–112; *double décime*, 108; Parmentier misison, 175, 177–178, 183, 184, 185; war debt funding, 196; Argentine credits, 234

Leaf, Sir Walter: currency note cancellation and credit controls, 47; funding operation, 123

Leeper, Reginald W. A., 253–254

Leffingwell, Russell C., 25, 36; "Keynes Plan," 35; debt cancellation, 153, 157, 158; French securities, 206; French franc, 207; J. P. Morgan & Co., 208

Lenin, V. I., 1; foreign concessions, 251, 253, 254; Urquhart concession, 252, 254, 255

Lever, Sir Hardman, 21, 24, 25

Leygues, Georges, 104

Lindsay, R. C., 150, 153

Litvinov, Maxim, 253

Lloyd George, David, 1, 9, 10, 92; "Keynes Plan," 33–34; French credits, 37–38; Anglo-American entente, 39; war debts, 178; war debt funding agreement, 186–187; reparations and war debts, 191; Russian reconstruction and trade, 241, 243, 244, 247, 249; Soviet trade negotiations, 246, 249; Genoa conference, 258–268, 294, 295; Soviet recognition, 260–264; Hague conference, 268, 269; failure of Russian policy, 269; Genoa tactics criticized, 290

Lloyd-Greame, Sir Philip, 257

London Schedule of Payments, 145–146, 224

Lottery bonds, 127–128, 205–206

Loucheur, Louis, 225

McAdoo, William, 31

McDonell, H. E. R.: petroleum memorandum, 257

McKenna, Reginald: dear money, 48; inflation theory, 49; taxable capacity, 86; loan (1915), 130; British war debt funding settlement, 189

Marais, Émile du, Baron, 206, 209

Martin, Germain, 142, 143

Mason, D. M., 53

Mathews, Frederick, 282

Mellon, Andrew W.: war debts, 154, 156, 173: WWDFC negotiations, 157, 180, 181, 182, 183; British war debt settlement, 189; International Memorial, 273

Mellon-Casenave agreement (1921), 161, 163, 164–166

Miliutin, V. P., 245

Millerand, Alexandre, 99; Spanish debt, 236, 237; protectionism, 240; Soviet negotiations, 246

Mond, Alfred M.: deficit budgeting, 90–91

Montagu, Edwin S.: Bank of France, 28; deficit budgeting, 89–90, 91

Morel, Paul: negotiations with U.S., 163, 164, 167, 168

Morgan, J. P., Jr.: Bankers' Committee, 107; Legion of Honor, 199; privacy of customers' accounts, 228

Morgan & Co., J. P., 6; wartime financial agent, 18; war contract commissions, 202; French Treasury bills, 210–214, 216, 217, 219, 226; French loan negotiations, 216, 222–225

Morrow, Dwight W.: French loan (1920), 215, 217, 219; French finance, 227

Mouÿ, Pierre de, 196

National defense bonds, 15, 16–17, 120, 139–140

National Union of Manufacturers, 83, 84

Neuflize, Jacques de, Baron, 203, 204, 205, 208

Niemeyer, Sir Otto: dear money, 48; taxation, 68; pensions, 78, 79; deficit budgeting, 91; lottery bonds, 128; debt cancellation, 179

Nitti, Francesco, 264

Nogaro, Bertrand: quantity theory, 43–44; gold exchange standard, 59; international currency, 282–283

Norman, Montagu, 44; Anglo-American cooperation, 19, 38; British war debt, 20; attitude toward France, 20, 34; Bank rate, 50; Bank-Treasury cooperation, 50; central bank cooperation, 50; gold exchange standard and devalua-

Norman, Montagu—*cont.*
tion at Genoa conference, 57; interest
rates, 76; funding operation and Conversion Loan, 123, 129, 131; forced
loan, 125–126; lottery bonds, 128;
Bank supremacy, 129; reparations and
inter-Allied debt, 154–155; debt to
U.S. Treasury, 159–160; WWDFC,
186, 187, 188, 189; Austrian reconstruction, 241; anti-Bolshevism, 242;
Anglo-Soviet trade agreement, 251
Nurkse, Ragnar, 54, 56

Ogier, Émile, 94
Oil: Russian, 255, 256, 257; British policy
in Near East, 256; British policy in
Russia, 256–258
O'Malley, Owen St. Clair, 257, 266

Paris Peace conference, 1, 10, 12, 19, 115;
inter-Allied debts, 31–36
Parker, Edwin B., 163, 164, 165, 167
Parker-Morel accord (1919), 161, 163–
164
Parmentier, Jean: Parmentier mission,
160, 161, 180–185; surplus war stock,
168; "Note Parmentier," 174; competence questioned, 186; French dollar
requirements (1920–1921), 218, 226;
criticizes J. P. Morgan & Co., 220, 221;
U.S. credit operations, 222, 224, 225,
226; Argentine credits, 234
Poincaré, Raymond, 1, 106; Ruhr occupation, 107–110; U.S. war debt, 175,
177, 195–196; Parmentier mission,
177–178, 182, 183; Balfour Note, 179–
180; reparations, 192; Genoa conference, 295
Purchasing power parity, 43, 54–55. *See
also* Cassell

Quantity theory, 41–44

Rapallo agreement (1922), 1, 265, 266,
269
Rathbone, Albert: postwar assistance to
France, 22, 24; war debt cancellation,
32, 34–35; "Keynes Plan," 34; funding
talks with Blackett, 150, 171; settlement of French accounts, 162, 163

Rathenau, Walter, 190
Reading (Rufus Daniel Isaacs), Baron,
24, 25
Redfield, William C., 232
Reparations: and inter-Allied debt, 2,
154–156; and French reconstruction,
6; French policy, 10, 11; and French
deficit, 70, 71, 103, 106; London
Schedule of Payments, 145–146; capacity to pay, 146–147; moratorium, 190–
191; reduction, 191–192
Ribot, Alexandre, 18, 140
Rist, Charles, 51
Robbins, Lord (Lionel), 61
Root, Elihu, 273
Rothschild, Edouard de, Baron, 28
Royal Dutch Shell, 256, 257, 258, 267
Ruhr occupation, 1, 2, 5, 107–112, 190,
195; British opinion, 193–194; impact
on French credit, 222
Russia: British trade negotiations, 244,
245, 248, 250, 251; foreign concession
policy, 251, 255; Soviet recognition,
251, 259–261, 263–264; Urquhart
concession, 252–255; oil concessions,
255, 256, 257; Genoa conference, 265–
268
Rylands, W. P., 84

Saar, 95–96, 109
Saint-Aulaire, Auguste Félix de, Count,
175, 178
Samuel, Herbert, 127
San Remo agreement (1920), 256
Sarraut, Albert, 116
Seydoux, Jacques, 196
Seymour, Horace James, 158, 159
Sièyes, Jean de, 174, 219–220
Simon, Joseph, 24, 32, 203, 204, 210
Simons, Walter, 155
Smoot, Reed, 157, 182
Smuts, Jan Christiaan, 193
Snyder, Carl, 44
Soviet Union, *see* Russia
Spain: French war credits, 234–237
Sperling, R. A. C., 148, 149, 297
Stettinius, Edward R., 203, 209, 210,
211, 222
Straus, Albert, 35
Stresemann, Gustav, 9

Strong, Benjamin: Anglo-American cooperation, 19, 38; French finance, 20; assistance to France, 36; quantity theory, 44; British war debt, 123, 188; reparations and inter-Allied debt, 154–155, 157; Anglo-Soviet trade agreement, 250–251

Supreme Economic Council, 17, 243, 244

Switzerland: French trade agreement, 239–240

Taft, William Howard, 160, 273

Tardieu, André, 18, 25, 29, 71

Taxation: tax structure, 16, 72, 80; EPD, 68–69, 80–88; turnover tax, 79; tax psychology, 80; taxable capacity, 86–87; burden on industry, 88–89; debate in British cabinet, 89–91; French policy, 98, 100, 101, 102, 105, 108

Ter Meulen, C. E., 278, 284; Ter Meulen plan, 282, 283–287

Three Cities loan, 207, 208

Transcaucasian Republics, 256, 258

Treasury bills, French: sale in U.S., 210–214, 216, 217, 219, 226

Treasury, British: Anglo-Saxon superiority, 19; relations with France, 21; debt to U.S. Treasury, 22, 147, 150, 151, 159; dear money policy, 48–50; domestic funding operation, 122–123; contradictory policies of, 129–130; debts owed by Allies, 149. *See also* Blackett; Chamberlain

Treasury Department, U.S.: war debts, 3, 4, 6, 19, 20–21; wartime advances to Britain and France, 17, 22, 23, 24. *See also* Davis; Glass; Houston; Leffingwell; McAdoo

Treasury, French, *see* Finance Ministry, French

Trotsky, Leon, 255

Tyrrell, Sir William George, 152, 296

Urquhart, Leslie: Russian concession, 252–255

Vanderlip, Frank, 273, 283

Vergé, Emmanuel, 211, 213, 214

Vienne, Mathieu de, 165

Vissering, Gerard: opinion of French finance, 20; devaluation, 60; war debt securities, 117–118; economists' conference (1919), 272; Brussells conference, 280; Genoa conference, 292

Wadsworth, Eliot, 159, 166

Warburg, Paul, 273

War debt funding agreements: Britain, 188; France, 197

War Finance Corporation (WFC), 232

War Surplus stock: Britain, 69, 77, 78; France, 102, 103, 166–168

Washington conference (1922), 1; financial discussions, 174; and Genoa conference, 295–297

Webb Act, 239

Whitney, George W., 35

Wilson, Sir Henry, 248

Wilson, Woodrow, 1, 3, 9, 10, 15; war debts, 3, 4; "Keynes Plan," 33–34; British war debt, 151; Russian gold, 169; Anglo-Soviet trade negotiations, 249–250

Wise, E. F.: Soviet trade, 244, 245, 246; Genoa conference, 259

World War Debt Funding Commission (WWDFC), 5, 154, 156–157, 174, 175; Parmentier mission, 180–185; Balfour Note, 183; British mission, 187–188

Younger, Sir George, 75